Abraham V.W. Jackson

An Avesta Grammar in Comparison with Sanskrit

Abraham V.W. Jackson

An Avesta Grammar in Comparison with Sanskrit

ISBN/EAN: 9783337428655

Printed in Europe, USA, Canada, Australia, Japan

Cover: Foto ©Andreas Hilbeck / pixelio.de

More available books at **www.hansebooks.com**

AN

AVESTA GRAMMAR

IN COMPARISON WITH SANSKRIT

BY

A. V. WILLIAMS JACKSON

OF COLUMBIA COLLEGE, NEW YORK CITY

———

PART I

PHONOLOGY, INFLECTION, WORD-FORMATION

WITH AN INTRODUCTION ON THE AVESTA

———————

STUTTGART

W. KOHLHAMMER

1892

Inscribed

to

Professor K. F. Geldner

with gratitude and regard.

PREFACE.

The present Grammar is a work of no pretensions; it is offered as a small contribution toward advancing the Avesta cause. It is written in part fulfilment of a design formed when I first began to study the Avesta and became deeply interested in the true value and importance of that monument of antiquity.

The end for which the book is intended would perhaps have been better accomplished, however, if the work had been a mere grammatical sketch. This was my first design; and it may at another time be carried out. But as the work grew under my hands, it seemed desirable to enlarge it somewhat further, and to embody additional material which for reference might be serviceable to the general philologist, not to the specialist alone. The linguist may thus find in it useful matter and fresh illustrations, especially in the new readings from Geldner's edition of the Avesta texts.

No attempt, on the other hand, has been made to secure absolute completeness. Numerous minor points have been purposely omitted. These may perhaps later be taken up in a more extended work including also the Old Persian by the side of the Avesta and the Sanskrit. Little of im-

portance, however, it is believed, has been overlooked.
A fairly symmetrical development has been aimed at, although at times certain less familiar points have received
fuller illustration than those that are well-known. This was
intentional. They are chiefly matters that had not as yet
been sufficiently emphasized elsewhere, or points which are
peculiarly individual to the Avesta. They will easily be
recognized.

The method of treatment is based throughout on the
Sanskrit grammar; a knowledge of Sanskrit is presupposed.
At every step, therefore, references have been made to
Whitney's *Sanskrit Grammar* 2 ed. 1889; and it is a
pleasure here to express thanks to the author of that work
for the abundant suggestions received from it.

In the Grammar it might have been easier and more
practical in many respects to use the Avesta type itself
instead of employing a transcription. On the whole, however, it seemed best under the circumstances to transliterate.
For general reference at present this method appears more
convenient, and is useful in showing grammatical formations. The original type, it is expected, will be employed,
as hinted above, in a little book *Avesta for Beginners,*
planned for a date not far distant.

In regard to the t r a n s c r i p t i o n here adopted, my
views have already been given in *The Avestan Alphabet
and its Transcription,* Stuttgart, 1890. The phonetic and
palaeographic character of each of the Avestan letters is
there discussed. Reasons are likewise presented for transliterating Av. ı, ı by the 'turned' *ə, з,* so familiar in phonetic works. The composite *w̄ (āə)* for *ʷ* (ı ʷ) is also

there explained (p. 13). The choice of the old Germanic characters *h̯, ɟ, þ, ḏ* for the spirants *ƀ, ʮ, ð, ᴚ*, and for the nasal *ʋ* (1), as well as the method of transliterating *ᴍ* (1+ᴍ) by *h̯ (h + v)* is defended (pp. 14, 21). The 'tag' (ᵢ) appearing in the letters *t̯, ʋ̯, n̯, h̯, a̯* is an attempt at systematically representing the 'derivation stroke' *ʮ ʟ ʃ* by which many of the letters palaeographically are formed. Thus, *ʀ t̯, ɯ ʋ̯, ʊ ƀ̯, ʊ ð̯ ʊɾ, ᴩ ʀ̯, ᴜ ʮ* etc. — the dotted line denoting the 'derivation stroke'. See *Av. Alphabet* pp. 16—17. The same 'tag' appears in the transcription of *ɯ* (ʟ + ᴜ) by *š̯ (ᴄ + š)*. See *Av. Alphabet* p. 20. In the case of *ɾʊ š̯* (beside *š̯*), the 'subscript' tag is merely turned in the opposite direction so as to correspond with the hooked part (ɂ) of the letter. The threefold differentiation *š̯, š̯, š̯* for *ᴜ, ɯ, ɾʊ*, is not necessary, however, except in transliterating a text for purely scientific purposes. In practise, *š̯* may everywhere be written. A 'substitute alphabet' to be used in popular articles is offered in the same monograph p. 28. I wish again to repeat my thanks to the authorities there quoted (*Av. Alphabet* p. 7) who so kindly aided me with advice and suggestions in regard to the transcription adopted.

In reference to the transliteration of Sanskrit, the familiar system (cf. Whitney, *Skt. Gram.* § 5) is followed; but be it observed that for comparison with the Avesta it seems preferable to transcribe the palatal sibilant by *ś* (Whitney *ç*), the palatal nasal by *ń* (Whitney *ñ*), the guttural nasal by *ʋ* (Whitney *ṅ*).

A word may now be added in regard to my manifold indebtedness in the present book. The general grammatical works from the early contribution of Haug (*Essays*, 1862), through Hovelacque (*Grammaire*, 1868) down to the present date have been on my table. Justi's *Hand-buch der Zendsprache* (1864) was of course consulted continually. Constant reference has been made also to Bartholomae's *Altiranische Dialekte* (1883) and to his other admirable grammatical contributions. Spiegel's *Vergl. Gram. der altêran. Sprachen* (1882) was often opened, and will be specially acknowledged with others under the Syntax (Part II). C. de Harlez' *Manuel de l'Avesta* (1882), Darmesteter's *Études Iraniennes* (1883), W. Geiger's *Handbuch der Awestasprache* (1879) furnished more than one good suggestion, for which I am much indebted.

Acknowledgment is also due to some special contributions on grammatical subjects. In the Phonology, selections were made from the rich material collected by Hübschmann in *Kuhn's Zeitschrift* xxiv. p. 323 seq. (1878). My indebtedness to that well-known standard work Brugmann's *Grundriss der vergl. Gram.* (= *Elements of Compar. Grammar of the Indg. Languages*, English translation by Wright, Conway, Rouse, 1886 seq.) may be noticed from the citations below. Under Declension, frequent reference was made to Horn's *Nominalflexion im Avesta* (1885) and Lanman's *Noun-Inflection in the Veda* (1880). Under Verbal Inflection, in addition to Bartholomae's contributions below cited, acknowledgments are due to other authors to be mentioned in connection with Syntax (Part II). Caland's *Pronomina im Avesta* (1891) unfortunately came too late for the Inflections, but is cited under the Syntax of the Pronouns. I also regret that the work of Kavasji Edalji Kanga,

A Practical Gram. of the Av. Language (1891) was not received in time. My indebtedness to Whitney's *Skt. Gram.* is noticed above. For grammatical training in Sanskrit, moreover, I shall always thank my teachers in America and Germany—Professors Perry, Hopkins, and Pischel.

To my honored instructor and friend, Professor K. F. Geldner of Berlin, I owe, as I have owed, a lasting debt of gratitude. The book was begun when I was a student under his guidance; since I returned to America it has progressed with the aid of his constant encouragement, suggestion, and advice. He has been kind enough, moreover, not only to read the manuscript, as it was sent to Stuttgart, but also to look through the proof-sheets before they came back to me in America. The work I may call a trifling expression of the inspiration he gave me as a student. Let what is good in it count as his; the faults are my own.

It is a pleasure to add my cordial thanks to the publisher, Herrn W. Kohlhammer, for the characteristic interest which, with his usual enterprise, he has taken in the work. Special praise is due to his compositor, Herrn A. Säuberlich, whose accuracy is in general so unfailing that I fear I must say that the misprints which may have escaped notice are probably due to original slips of the author's pen, and not to inaccuracies on the part of the type-setter—a thing which cannot always be said. I should like also to express to Messrs. Ginn & Co., of Boston and New York, my appreciation of their willing co-operation in advancing the Iranian as well as other branches of the Oriental field in America.

The present part of the Grammar (Part I) is confined
to the Introduction, Phonology, and Morphology. The
prefatory sketch of the Avesta and the Religion of Zoroaster may perhaps prove not without use. The second
volume (Part II), a sketch of the Syntax, with a chapter
also on Metre, is already half in print, and is shortly to
appear. The numbering of sections in the second part
will be continued from the present part; the two may
therefore be bound together as a single volume if preferred.

With these words and with the suggestion to the
student to observe the Hints for using the Grammar, given
below, and to consult the Index, the book is offered to
the favor of Oriental scholars. Any corrections, suggestions, or criticisms, which may be sent to me, will
be cordially appreciated and gladly acknowledged.

A. V. Williams Jackson

October 1891.   Columbia College

NEW YORK CITY.

INTRODUCTION.

Avesta: The Sacred Books of the Parsis.[1]

The Avesta as a Sacred Book.

§ 1. The Avesta, or Zend-Avesta, as it is more familiarly, though less accurately called, is the name under which, as a designation, we comprise the bible and prayer-book of the Zoroastrian religion. The Avesta forms to day the Sacred Books of the Parsis or Fire-Worshippers, as they are often termed, a small community living now in India, or still scattered here and there in Persia. The original home of these worshippers and of their holy scriptures was ancient Iran, and the faith they profess was that founded centuries ago by Zoroaster (Zarathushtra), one of the great religious teachers of the East.

§ 2. The Avesta is, therefore, an important work, preserving as it does, the doctrines of this ancient belief and the customs of the earliest days of Persia. It represents the oldest faith of Iran, as the Vedas do of India. The oldest parts date back to a period of time nearly as remote as the Rig-Veda, though its youngest parts are much later. The religion which the Avesta presents was once one of the greatest; it has, moreover, left ineffaceable traces upon the history of the world. Flourishing more than a thousand years before the Christian era, it became the religion of the great Achæmenian kings, Cyrus, Darius, and Xerxes, but its power was weakened by the conquest of Alexander, and many of its sacred books were lost. It revived again during the first centuries of our own era, but was finally broken by the Mohammedans in their victorious invasion. Most of the Zoroastrian worshippers were then compelled through persecution to accept the religion of the Koran; many, however, fled to India for refuge, and took with them what was left of their sacred writ-

---

[1] This sketch, with additions and some alterations, is reprinted from my article AVESTA, simultaneously appearing in the *International Cyclopaedia;* for which courtesy I am indebted to the kindness of the Editor, my friend, Professor H. T. Peck, and that of the Publishers, Messrs. Dodd, Mead & Co., New York.

ings. A few of the faithful remained behind in Persia, and, though persecuted, they continued to practise their religion. It is these two scanty
peoples, perhaps 80,000 souls in India, and 10,000 in Persia, that have
preserved to us the Avesta in the form in which we now have it.

§ 3. The designation *Avesta*, for the scriptures, is adopted from
the term *Avistāk*, regularly employed in the Pahlavi of the Sassassian time.
But it is quite uncertain what the exact meaning and derivation of this
word may be. Possibly Phl. *Avistāk*, like the Skt. *Veda*, may signify
'wisdom, knowledge, the book of knowledge'. Perhaps, however, it means
rather 'the original text, the scripture, the law'. The designation 'Zend-
Avesta', though introduced by Anquetil du Perron, as described below, is
not an accurate title. It arose by mistake from the inversion of the oft-
recurring Pahlavi phrase, *Avistāk va Zand* 'Avesta and Zend', or 'the Law
and Commentary'. The term *Zand* in Pahlavi (cf. Av. *āzaiŋti-*), as the Parsi
priests now rightly comprehend it, properly denotes 'understanding, explanation', and refers to the later version and commentary of the Avesta texts,
the paraphrase which is written in the Pahlavi language. The proper designation for the scriptures, therefore, is *Avesta;* the term *Zend* (see below)
should be understood as the Pahlavi version and commentary.

Allusions to the Avesta; its Discovery and History of Research.

§ 4. Of the religion, manners, and customs of ancient Persia, which
the Avesta preserves to us, we had but meagre knowledge until about a
century ago. What we did know up to that time was gathered from the
more or less scattered and unsatisfactory references of the classic Greek
and Latin, from some allusions in Oriental writers, or from the later Persian epic literature. To direct sources, however, we could not then turn.
Allusions to the religion of the Magi, the faith of the Avesta, are indeed
to be found in the Bible. The wise men from the East who came to
worship our Saviour, the babe in Bethlehem, were Magi. Centuries before
that date, however, it was Cyrus, a follower of the faith of Zoroaster,
whom God called his anointed and his shepherd (Isaiah 45.1,13; 44.28;
2 Chron. 36.22,23; Ezra 1.1—11) and who gave orders that the Jews
be returned to Jerusalem from captivity in Babylon. Darius, moreover
(Ezra 5.13—17; 6.1—16), the worshipper of Ormazd, favored the rebuild-
ing of the temple at Jerusalem as decreed by Cyrus. Allusions to the
ancient faith of the Persians are perhaps contained in Ezek. 8.16; Is. 45.7,12.
See also Apocryphal New Test., The Infancy, 3.1—10.

§ 5. The classical references of Greek and Roman writers to the
teachings of Zoroaster, which we can now study in the Avesta itself, may
be said to begin with the account of the Persians given by Herodotus

(B. C. 450) iu his History 1.131—141. To this account may be added references and allusions, though often preserved only in fragments, by various other writers, including Plutarch 'On Isis and Osiris', and Pliny, down to Agathias (A. D. 500).

§ 6. After the Mohammedan conquest of Persia, we have an allusion by the Arabic writer, Masūdī (A. D. 940), who tells of the *Avesta* of Zeradusht (Zoroaster), and its commentary called *Zend*, together with a *Pazend* explanation. The *Abasta* (Avesta) is also mentioned several times by Al-Birūnī (about A. D. 1000). The later Mohammedan writer, Shahrastani (A. D. 1150), sketches in outline the creed of the Magi of his day. An interesting reference is found in the Syriac-Arabic Lexicon of *Bar-Bahlūl* (A. D. 963) to an *Avastāk,* a book of Zardusht (Zoroaster), as composed in seven tongues, Syriac, Persian, Aramæan, Segestanian, Marvian, Greek, and Hebrew. In an earlier Syriac MS. Commentary on the New Testament (A. D. 852) by 'Ishō'dād, Bishop of Hadatha, near Mosul, mention is made of the Abhāstā as having been written by Zardusht in twelve different languages. These latter allusions, though late, are all important, as showing the continuity, during ages, of the tradition of such a work as the Avesta, which contains the teachings of Zoroaster, the prophet of Iran. All these allusions, however, it must be remembered, are by foreigners. No direct Iranian sources had been accessible.

§ 7. From this time, moreover, till about the 17th century we find there was little inquiry into the sacred books of the Persians. One of the first series of investigations into the Greek and Roman sources seems then to have been undertaken by a European, Barnabé Brisson, *De Persarum Principatu* (Paris 1590). The Italian, English, and French travelers in the Orient next added some information as to the religion and customs of the Persians. Among them may be mentioned the works of Pietro della Valle (1620), Henry Lord (1630), Mandelso (1658), Tavernier (1678), Chardin (1721), Du Chinon. Most important, however, was the work of the distinguished Oxford scholar, Thomas Hyde (1700). It was written in Latin, and entitled *Historia Religionis veterum Persarum*. Hyde resorted chiefly to the later Parsi sources; the original texts he could not use, although an Avesta MS. of the Yasna seems to have been brought to Canterbury as early as 1633. Hyde earnestly appealed to scholars, however, to procure MSS. of the sacred books of the Parsis, and aroused much interest in the subject. In 1723 a copy of the Vendidād Sādah was procured by an Englishman, George Boucher, from the Parsis in Surat and was deposited as a curiosity in the Bodleian Library at Oxford.

§ 8. No one, however, could read these texts of the Avesta. To a young Frenchman, Anquetil du Perron, belongs the honor of first deciphering them. The history of his labors is interesting and instructive. Happening, in 1754, to see some tracings made from the Oxford MS., and sent to Paris as a specimen, du Perron at once conceived the spirited idea of going to Persia, or India, and obtaining from the priests themselves the knowledge of their sacred books. Though fired with zeal and enthusiasm, he had no means to carry out his plan. He seized the idea of enlisting as a soldier in the troops that were to start for India, and in November, 1754, behind the martial drum and fife this youthful scholar marched out of Paris. The French Government, however, recognizing at once his noble purpose, gave him his discharge from the army and presented him his passage to India. After countless difficulties he reached Surat, and there after innumerable discouragements, and in spite of almost insurmountable obstacles, he succeeded in winning the confidence and favor of the priests, with whom he was able to communicate after he had learned the modern Persian. He gradually induced the priests to impart to him the language of their sacred works, to let him take some of the manuscripts, and even to initiate him into some of the rites and ceremonies of their religion. He stayed among the people for seven years, and then in 1761, he started for his home in Europe. He stopped at Oxford before going directly to Paris, and compared his MSS. with the one in the Bodleian Library, in order to be assured that he had not been imposed upon. The next ten years were devoted to work upon his MSS. and upon a translation, and in 1771, seventeen years from the time he had first marched out of Paris, he gave forth to the world the results of his untiring labors. This was the first translation of the Avesta, or, as he called it, Zend-Avesta (*Ouvrage de Zoroastre*, 3 vols., Paris 1771), a picture of the religion and manners contained in the sacred book of the Zoroastrians.

§ 9. The ardent enthusiasm which hailed this discovery and opening to the world of a literature, religion, and philosophy of ancient times was unfortunately soon dampened. Some scholars, like Kant, were disappointed in not finding the philosophical or religious ideas they had hoped to find; while others missed the high literary value they had looked for. They little considered how inaccurate, of necessity, such a first translation must be. Though Anquetil du Perron had indeed learned the language from the priests, still, people did not know that the priestly tradition itself had lost much during the ages of persecution or oblivion into which the religion had fallen. They did not sufficiently take into account that Anquetil was learning one foreign tongue, the Avesta, through another, the modern Persian; nor did they know how little accurate and scientific training du Perron had had. A discussion as to the authenticity

of the work arose. It was suggested that the so-called Zend-Avesta was
not the genuine work of Zoroaster, but was a forgery. Foremost among
the detractors, it is to be regretted, was the distinguished Orientalist, Sir
William Jones. He claimed, in a letter published in French (1771), that
Anquetil had been duped, ·that the Parsis had palmed off upon him a
conglomeration of worthless fabrications and absurdities. In England, Sir
William Jones was supported by Richardson and Sir John Chardin; in
Germany, by Meiners. In France the genuineness of the book was universally accepted, and in one famous German scholar, Kleuker, it found
an ardent supporter. He translated Anquetil's work into German (1776,
Riga), for the use of his countrymen, especially the theologians, and he
supported the genuineness of those scriptures by classical allusions to the
Magi. For nearly fifty years, however, the battle as to authenticity, still
raged. Anquetil's translation, as acquired from the priests, was supposed
to be a true standard to judge the Avesta by, and from which to draw
arguments; little or no work, unfortunately, was· done on the texts themselves. The opinion, however, that the books were a forgery was gradually
beginning to grow somewhat less.

§ 10. It was the advance in the study of Sanskrit that finally won
the victory for the advocates of the authenticity of the Sacred Books.
About 1825, more than fifty years after the appearance of du Perron's
translation, the Avesta texts themselves began to be studied by Sanskrit
scholars. The close affinity between the two languages had already been
noticed by different scholars; but in 1826, the more exact relation between
the Sanskrit and the Avesta was shown by the Danish philologian, Rask,
who had travelled in Persia and India, and who had brought back with
him to the Copenhagen library many valuable MSS. of the Avesta and of
the Pahlavi books. Rask, in a little work on the age and authenticity of
the Zend-Language (1826), proved the antiquity of the language, showed
it to be distinct from Sanskrit, though closely allied to it, and made some
investigation into the alphabet of the texts. About the same time the
Avesta was taken up by the French Sanskrit scholar, Eugène Burnouf.
Knowing the relation between Sanskrit and Avestan, and taking up the
reading of the texts scientifically, he at once found, through his knowledge
of Sanskrit, philological inaccuracies in Anquetil's translation. Anquetil,
he saw, must often have misinterpreted his teachers; the tradition itself
must often necessarily have been defective. Instead of this untrustworthy
French rendering, Burnouf turned to an older Skt. translation of a part
of the Avesta. This was made in the 15th century by the Parsi Naryo-
sangh, and was based on the Pahlavi version. By means of this Skt.
rendering, and by applying his philologial learning, he was able to restore

sense to many passages where Anquetil had often made nonsense, and he was thus able to throw a flood of light upon many an obscure point. The employment of Skt., instead of depending upon the priestly traditions and interpretations, was a new step; it introduced a new method. The new discovery and gain of vantage ground practically settled the discussion as to authenticity. The testimony, moreover, of the ancient Persian inscriptions deciphered about this time by Grotefend (1802), Burnouf, Lassen, and by Sir Henry Rawlinson, showed still more, by their contents and language so closely allied to the Avesta, that this work must be genuine. The question was settled. The foundation laid by Burnouf was built upon by such scholars as Bopp, Haug, Windischmann, Westergaard, Roth, Spiegel —the two latter happily still living—and to day by Bartholomae, Darmesteter, de Harlez, Hübschmann, Justi, Mills, and especially Geldner, including some hardly less known names, Parsis among them. These scholars, using partly the Sanskrit key for the interpretation and meaning of words, and partly the Parsi tradition contained in the Pahlavi translation, have now been able to give us a clear idea of the Avesta and its contents as far as the books have come down to us, and we are enabled to see the true importance of these ancient scriptures. Upon minor points of interpretation, of course, there are and there always will be individual differences of opinion. We are now prepared to take up the general division and contents of the Avesta, and to speak of its Pahlavi version.

Contents, Arrangement, Extent, and Character.

§ 11. The Avesta, as we now have it, is but a remnant of a once great literature. It has come down in a more or less fragmentary condition; not even a single manuscript contains all the texts that we now have; whatever we possess has been collected together from various codices. All that survives is commonly classed under the following divisions or books:

1. *Yasna,* including the *Gâthâs*
2. *Vispered*
3. *Yashts*
4. Minor texts, as *Nyâishes, Gâhs* etc.
5. *Vendîdâd*
6. Fragments, from *Hâdhôkht Nask* etc.

§ 12. In the first five divisions two groups are recognized. The first group (i) comprises the Vendidad, Vispered, and Yasna; these as used in the service of worship are traditionally classed together for liturgical purposes and form the Avesta proper. In the manuscripts, moreover, these three books themselves appear in two different forms, according as they are accompanied, or not, by a Pahlavi version. If the books are kept separate as three divisions, each part is usually accompanied by a rendering in Pahlavi. On the contrary, however, these three books are not usually recited each as a separate whole, but with the chapters of one book mingled with another for liturgical purposes, on this account the MSS. often present them in their intermingled form, portions of one inserted with the other, and arranged exactly in the order in which they are to be used in the service. In this latter case the Pahlavi translation is omitted, and the collection is called the Vendidâd Sâdah or 'Vendidâd pure' i. e. text without commentary. (ii) The second group comprising the minor prayers and the Yashts which the MSS. often include with these, is called the *Khordah Avesta* or 'small Avesta'. Of the greater part of the latter there is no Pahlavi rendering. The contents and character of the several divisions, including the fragments, may now be taken up more in detail.

§ 13. (1) The *Yasna*, 'sacrifice, worship', is the chief liturgical work of the sacred canon. It consists principally of ascriptions of praise and prayer, and in it are inserted the *Gâthâs*, or 'hymns', verses from the sermons of Zoroaster, which are the oldest and most sacred part of the Avesta. The Yasna (Skt. *yajñâ*) comprises 72 chapters, called *Hâ, Haiti*. These are the texts recited by the priests at the ritual ceremony of the Yasna *(Izashne)*. The book falls into three nearly equal divisions. (a) The first part (chap. 1—27) begins with an invocation of the god, Ormazd, and the other divinities of the religion; it gives texts for the consecration of the holy water, *zaothra*, and the *baresma*, or bundle of sacred twigs, for the preparation and dedication of the Haoma, *haoma*, the juice of a certain plant — the Indian Soma — which was drunk by the priests as a sacred rite, and for the offering of blessed cakes, as well as meat-offering, which likewise were partaken of by the priests. Interspersed through this portion, however, are a few chapters that deal only indirectly with the ritual; these are Ys. 12, the later Zoroastrian creed, and Ys. 19—21, catechetical portions. — (b) Then follow the Gâthâs lit. 'songs', 'psalms' (chap. 28—53), metrical selections or verses containing the teachings, exhortations, and revelations of Zoroaster. The prophet exhorts men to eschew evil and choose the good, the kingdom of light rather than that of darkness. These Gâthâs are written in meter, and their language is more archaic and somewhat different from that used elsewhere in the Avesta. The Gâthâs, strictly speaking, are five in number; they are arranged according to meters, and are named after the opening words, Ahunavaiti, Ushtavaiti etc. The Gâthâs comprise 17 hymns (Ys. 28—34; 43—46; 47—50; 51, 53), and,

like the Psalms, they must later have been chanted during the service. They
seem originally to have been the texts or metrical headings from which
Zoroaster, like the later Buddha, preached. In their midst (chap. 35—42)
is inserted the so-called Yasna of the Seven Chapters *(Yasna Haptanghāiti)*.
This is written in prose, and consists of a number of prayers and ascriptions
of praise to Ahura Mazda, or Ormazd, to the archangels, the souls of the
righteous, the fire, the waters, and the earth. Though next in antiquity
to the Gāthās, and in archaic language, the Haptanghaiti represents a
somewhat later and more developed form of the religion, than that which
in the Gāthas proper was just beginning. Under the Gāthās also are included three or four specially sacred verses or formulas. These are the
Ahuna Vairya or Honovar (Ys. 27.13), Ashem Vohu (Ys. 27.14), Airyama
Ishyo (Ys. 54.1) and also the Yenghe Hātām (Ys. 4.26), so called from
their first words, like the Pater Noster, Gloria Patri, etc., to which in a
measure they answer.—(c) The third part (chap. 52, 55—72) or the 'latter
Yasna' *(aparō yasnō)* consists chiefly of praises and offerings of thanks-
giving to different divinities.

§ 14. (2) The *Vīspered* (Av. *vīspĕ ratavo*) consists of additions to
portions of the Yasna which it resembles in language and in form. It
comprises 24 chapters (called *Karde*), and it is about a seventh as long
as the Yasna. In the ritual the chapters of the Vispered are inserted
among those of the Yasna. It contains invocations and offerings of homage to 'all the lords' *(vīspĕ ratavō)*. Hence the name Vispered.

§ 15. (3) The *Yashts* (Av. *yešti* 'worship by praise') consist of
21 hymns of praise and adorations of the divinities or angels, *Yazatas
(Izads)*, of the religion. The chief Yashts are those in praise of Ardvi-
Sura, the goddess of waters (Yt. 5), the star Tishtrya (Yt. 8), the angel
Mithra, or divinity of truth (Yt. 10), the Fravashis, or departed souls of
the righteous (Yt. 13), the genius of victory, Verethraghna (Yt. 14), and
of the Kingly Glory (Yt. 19). The Yashts are written mainly in meter,
they have poetic merit, and contain much mythological and historical matter
that may be illustrated by Firdausi's later Persian epic, the Shāh Namah.

§ 16. (4) The minor texts, *Nyāishes, Gāhs, Sīrōzahs, Afrīngāns*,
consist of brief prayers, praises, or blessings to be recited daily or on
special occasions.

§ 17. (5) The *Vendidād*, or 'law against the daevas, or demons'
(vīdaēvō dātu), is a priestly code in 22 chapters (called *Fargard*), corresponding to the Pentateuch in our Bible. Its parts vary greatly in time
and in style of composition. Much of it must be late. The first chapter
(Farg. 1) is a sort of an Avestan Genesis, a dualistic account of creation.

Chap. 2 sketches the legend of Yima, the golden age, and the coming of a destructive winter, an Iranian flood. Chap. 3 teaches, among other things, the blessings of agriculture; Chap. 4 contains legal matter — breaches of contract, assaults, punishments; Chap. 5—12 relate mainly to the impurity from the dead; Chap. 13—15 deal chiefly with the treatment of the dog; Chap. 16—17, and partly 18, are devoted to purification from several sorts of uncleanness. In Chap. 19 is found the temptation of Zoroaster, and the revelation; Chap. 20—22 are chiefly of medical character. In the ritual, the chapters of the Vendidad are inserted among the Gâthâs.

§ 18. (6) Besides the above books there are a number of f r a g-
m e n t s, one or two among them f r o m the *Hadhôkht Nask.* There are also quotations or passages from missing Nasks, likewise glosses and glossaries. Here belong pieces from the *Nîrangistân*, *Aogemadaêca*, *Zand-Pahlavi Glossary*, and some other fragments. These are all written in the Avesta language, and are parts of a once great literature. Under the Zoroastrian religious literature, moreover, though not written in Avesta, must also be included the works in Pahlavi, many of which are translations from the Avesta, or contain old matter from the original scriptures.

§ 19. From the above contents, it will be seen that our present Avesta is rather a Prayer-Book than a Bible. The Vendidâd, Vispered, and Yasna were gathered together by the priests for liturgical purposes. It was the duty of the priests to recite the whole of these sacred writings every day, in order to preserve their own purity, and be able to perform the rites of purification, or give remission of sins to others. The solemn recital of the Vendidâd, Vispered, and Yasna at the sacrifice might be compared with our church worship. The selections from the Vendidâd would correspond to the Pentateuch when read; the preparation, consecration, and presentation of the holy water, the Haoma-juice, and the meat-offering, described in the Yasna and Vispered would answer to our communion service; the metrical parts of the Yasna would be hymns; the intoning of the Gâthâs would somewhat resemble the lesson and the Gospel, or even the sermon. In the Khordah Avesta, the great Yashts might perhaps be comparable to some of the more epic parts of our Bible; but as they are devoted each to some divinity and preserve much of the old mythology, they really have hardly a parallel, even in the apocryphal books.

§ 20. Such, in brief outline, is the contents of the books known to-day as the Avesta; but, as implied above, this is but a remnant of a literature once vastly greater in e x t e n t. This we can judge both from internal and from historical-evidence. The character of the work itself in its present form, sufficiently shows that it is a compilation from various

sources. This is further supported by the authority of history, if the Parsi
tradition, going back to the time of the Sassanidæ, be trustworthy. Pliny
(*Hist. Nat.* 30.1,2) tells of 2,000,000 verses composed by Zoroaster. The
Arab historian, Tabari, describes the writings of Zoroaster as committed
to 12,000 cowhides (parchments); other Arabic references by Masudi, and
Syriac allusions to an Avesta, which must have been extensive, have been
noted above § 6. The Parsi tradition on the subject is contained in the
Rivâyats, and in a Pahlavi book, the Dinkard. The Dinkard (Bk. 3)
describes two complete copies of the Avesta. These each comprised
21 Nasks, or Nosks (books). The one deposited in the archives at Perse-
polis, as the Arda Viraf says, perished in the flames when Alexander burned
the palace in his invasion of Iran. The other copy, it is implied, was in
some way destroyed by the Greeks. From that time the scriptures, like
the religion under the Græco-Parthian sway, lived on, partly in scattered
writings and partly in the memories of the priests, for nearly 500 years.

§ 21. The first attempt again to c o l l e c t these writings seems to
have been begun under the reign of the last Arsacidæ, just preceding the
Sassanian dynasty. Pahlavi tradition preserved in a proclamation of King
Khusro Anoshirvân (6th cent. A. D.), says it was under King Valkhash, probably Vologoses I., the contemporary of Nero, that the collection was
begun of the sacred writings as far as they had escaped the ravages of
Alexander, or were preserved by oral tradition. Valkhash was among the
last of the Arsacidæ. The Sassanian dynasty (A. D. 226) next came to
the throne. This house were genuine Zoroastrians and warm upholders of
the faith, and they brought back the old religion and raised it to a height
it had hardly attained even in its palmiest days. The first Sassanian mon-
archs, Artakhshir Pâpakân (Ardeshir Bâbagân, A. D. 226—240) and his son
Shahpuhar I. (A. D. 240—270), eagerly continued the gathering of the
religious writings, and the Avesta again became the sacred book of Iran.
Under Shahpuhar II. (A. D. 309—380) the final revision of the Avesta texts
was made by Atur-pât Mâraspend, and then the king proclaimed these as
canonical, and fixed the number of Nasks or books.

§ 22. Of these Nasks, 21 were counted, and a description of them,
as noted, is found in the Rivâyats, and in the Dinkard; each received a
name corresponding to one of the twenty-one words in the Ahuna-Vairya
(Honovar), the most sacred prayer of the Parsis. Each of these Nasks
contained both Avesta and Zend, i. e. original scripture and commentary.
This tradition is too important to be idly rejected. Its contents give an
idea of what may have been the original extent and scope of the Avesta.
The subjects said to have been treated in the 21 Nasks may practically
be described in brief, as follows: Nask 1 (twenty-two sections), on virtue

and piety; 2 (likewise twenty-two sections), religious observance; 3 (twenty-one sections), the Mazdayasnian religion and its teachings; 4 (thirty-two sections), this world and the next, the resurrection and the judgment; 5 (thirty-five sections), astronomy; 6 (twenty-two sections), ritual performances and the merit accruing; 7 (fifty sections before Alexander, thirteen then remaining), chiefly political and social in its nature; 8 (sixty sections before Alexander, twelve after remaining), legal; 9 (sixty sections before Alexander, fifteen later preserved), religion and its practical relations to man; 10 (sixty sections before Alexander, only ten afterwards surviving), king Gushtâsp and his reign, Zoroaster's influence; 11 (twenty-two sections originally, six preserved after Alexander), religion and its practical relations to man; 12 (twenty-two sections), physical truths and spiritual regeneration; 13 (sixty sections), virtuous actions, and a sketch of Zoroaster's infancy; 14 (seventeen sections), on Ormazd and the Archangels; 15 (fifty-four sections), justice in business and in weights and measures, the path of righteousness; 16 (sixty-five sections), on next-of-kin marriage, a tenet of the faith; 17 (sixty-four sections), future punishments, astrology; 18 (fifty-two sections), justice in exercising authority, on the resurrection, and on the annihilation of evil; 19, the Videvdâd, or Vendidâd (twenty-two sections, still remaining), on pollution and its purification; 20 (thirty sections), on goodness; 21 (thirty-three sections), praise of Ormazd and the Archangels.

§ 23. During the five centuries after the ravages of Alexander much, doubtless, had been lost, much forgotten. The Parsi tradition itself acknowledges this when it says above, for example, that the seventh Nask consisted originally of 50 sections, but only 13 remained 'after the accursed Iskander (Alexander)'. So says the Dinkard and so the Rivâyats. Like statements of loss are made of the eighth, ninth, tenth, eleventh Nasks. The loss in the five centuries from the invasion of Alexander, however, till the time of the Sassanian dynasty, was but small in comparison with the decay that overtook the scriptures from the Sassanian times till our day. The Mohammedan invasion in the seventh century of our era, and the inroad made by the Koran proved far more destructive. The persecuted people lost or neglected many portions of their sacred scriptures. Of the twenty-one Nasks that were recognized in Sassanian times as surviving from the original Avesta, only one single Nask, the nineteenth — the Vendidâd — has come down to us in its full form. Even this shows evidence of having been patched up and pieced together. We can furthermore probably identify parts of our present Yasna and Vispered with the Staot Yasht (staota yesnya) or Yasht (yesnya), as it is also called. The two fragments Yt. 21 and 22 (as printed in Westergaard's edition) and Yt. 11, in its first form, are recognized in the MSS. as taken from the 20th, or Hâdhokht Nask. The Nirangistân, a Pahlavi work, contains extensive Avestan quotations, which are believed to have been taken from the Husparam, or 17th Nask. Numerous quotations in Pahlavi works contain translations from old Avestan passages. The Pahlavi work, Shâyast-lâ-Shâyast, quotes briefly from no less than thirteen of the lost Nasks; the Bundahish and other Pahlavi works give translations of selections, the original Avesta text of which is lost. Grouping together all the Avesta texts, we may roughly calculate that about two-thirds of the total scriptures have disappeared since Sassanian times.

§ 24. The present form of the Avesta belongs to the Sassanian period. Internal evidence shows that it is made up of parts most varied in age and character. This bears witness to the statement that during that period the texts, as far as they had survived the ravages of Alexander, and defied the corrupting influence of time, were gathered together, compiled, and edited. According to the record of Khusro Anoshirvân (A. D. 531—579), referred to above, King Valkhash, the first compiler of the Avesta, ordered that all the writings which might have survived should be searched for, and that all the priests who preserved the traditions orally should contribute their share toward restoring the original Avesta. The texts as collected were re-edited under successive Sassanian rulers, until, under Shahpuhar II. (A. D. 309—379) the final redaction was made by his prime minister, Atur-pât Mâraspend. It is manifest that the editors used the old texts as far as possible; sometimes they patched up defective parts by inserting other texts; occasionally they may have added or composed passages to join these, or to complete some missing portion. The character of the texts, when critically studied, shows that some such method must have been adopted.

§ 25. Parts of the Avesta, therefore, may differ considerably from each other in regard to a g e. In determining this the text criticism by means of m e t r i c a l r e s t o r a t i o n is most instructive. Almost all the oldest portions of the texts are found to be metrical; the later, or inserted portions, are as a rule, but not always, written in prose. The g r a m m a t i c a l t e s t also is useful; the youngest portions generally show a decay of clear grammatical knowledge. The metrical Gâthâs in this respect are wonderfully pure. They are, of course, in their form the oldest portion of the text, dating from Zoroaster himself. The longer Yashts and metrical portions of the Yasna contain much that is very old and derived doubtless from the ancient faith of Iran; but in their form and in general composition, they are probably some centuries later than the Gâthâs. The Vendidâd is in this regard most incongruous. Some parts of it are doubtless of great antiquity, though corrupted in form; other parts, like younger portions also of the Yashts, may be quite late. The same is true of formulaic passages throughout the whole of the Avesta, and some of the ceremonial or ritual selections in the Vispered and Nyāishes, etc. Roughly speaking, the chronological order of the texts would be somewhat as follows:

   i. Gāthās (Ys. 28—53) and the sacred formulas Ys. 27.13,14, Ys. 54, including also

   ii. Yasna Haptanghāiti (Ys. 35—42) and some other compositions, like Ys. 12, 58, 4.26, in the Gāthā dialect.

   iii. The metrical Yasna and Yashts, as Ys. 9, 10, 11, 57, 62, 65; Yt. 5, 8, 9, 10, 13, 14, 15, 17, 19; portions of Vd. 2, 3, 4, 5, 18, 19, and scattered verses in the Vispered, Nyāishes, Afringāns, etc.

   iv. The remaining prose portions of the Avesta.

In the latter case it is generally, but not always, easy to discover by the style and language, where old material failed and the hand of the redactor came in with stupid or prosaic additions.

§ 26. Considerable portions, therefore, of our present Avesta, especially the Gāthās, we may regard as coming directly from Zoroaster himself; still, additions from time to time must have been made to the sacred canon from his day on till the invasion of Alexander. The so-called copy of the Zoroastrian Bible which it is claimed was destroyed by that invader, doubtless contained much that was not directly from the founder of the faith, but was composed by his disciples and later followers. The Parsis, however, generally regard the whole work as coming directly from Zoroaster; this is a claim that the Avesta itself hardly makes. The Gāthās, however, undoubtedly came directly from the prophet; the Avesta itself always speaks of them as 'holy' and especially calls them the 'five Gāthās of Zoroaster'. We may fairly regard many other portions of the Avesta as direct elaborations of the great teacher's doctrines, just as the Evangelists have elaborated for us portions of the teachings of our Lord.

§ 27. In regard to the locality in which we are to seek the source of the Avesta and the cradle of the religion, opinions have been divided. Some scholars would place it in the West, in Media; the majority, however, prefer to look to the East of Iran, to Bactria. Both views probably have right on their side, for perhaps we shall not be amiss in regarding the Avesta as coming partly from the East, and partly from the West. The scene of most of it doubtless does belong in the East; it was there that Zoroaster preached; but the sacred literature that grew up about the Gāthās made its way, along with the religion to the West, toward Media and Persia. Undoubtedly some texts, therefore, may well have been composed also in Media. The question is connected also with that of Zoroaster's home which may originally have been in the West. On the native place of Zoroaster, see Jackson in *Amer. Or. Society's Journal*, May 1891 pp. 222 seq. The language itself of the texts, as used in the church, became a religious language, precisely as did Latin, and therefore was not confined to any place or time. We may regard the Avesta as having been worked upon from Zoroaster's day down to the time of the Sassanian redaction.

Religion of the Avesta.

§ 28. The religion contained in the Avesta is best called Zoroastrianism, a name that gives due honor to its founder and which is thus parallel with Christianity, Buddhism, Mohammedanism. Other designations are sometimes employed. It has often been termed Mazdaism, from its supreme god; or again Magism, from the Magi priests; sometimes we hear it styled Fire-Worship, or even Dualism, from certain of its characteristic features. The designation Parsiism, from the name of its modern followers, is occasionally applied.

§ 29. Beyond our own Bible, the sacred books perhaps of hardly any religion contain so clear a grasp of the ideas of right and wrong, or present so pure, so exalted a view of the coming of a Saviour, a resurrection and judgment, the future rewards and punishments for the immortal soul, and of the life eternal, as does the Avesta, the book of the scriptures of ancient Iran.

§ 30. In Zoroastrianism, however, as in other religions, we recognize a development. In the older stage of the Gâthâs, we have the faith in its purity as taught by Zoroaster (Zarathushtra) himself, more than a thousand years perhaps before our Lord. But later, and even before the invasion of Alexander had weakened the power of the religion, we find changes creeping in. There was a tendency, for example, to restore many of the elements of the primitive faith of Iran, which Zoroaster had thrown into the background. Traces of the different stages are plainly to be recognized in the Avesta.

§ 31. The most striking feature of Zoroaster's faith, as taught in the Gâthâs, is the doctrine of Dualism. There are two principles, the good and the evil, which pervade the world. All nature is divided between them. These principles are primeval. Good and evil have existed from the beginning of the world. Ahura Mazda, the Lord of Wisdom (the later Persian Ormazd) is Zoroaster's god; Angra Mainyu, or the Spiritual Enemy (the later Persian Ahriman) is the devil. The evil spirit is also called Druj 'Deceit, Satan'. The good spirit and the evil are in eternal conflict. The good, Zoroaster teaches, however, will ultimately triumph. Man, a free agent, will bring the victory by choosing right and increasing the power of good. Evil shall be banished from the world. This will be the coming of the 'kingdom' or 'the good kingdom' — *vohu ḫṣapra*—as it is called. To the right choice Zoroaster exhorts his people. The question whence Zoroaster derived his idea of dualism, and how far he was a reformer, will not here be entered into.

§ 32. According to the prophet's teaching, Ahura Mazda, the god of good, is not without the aid of m i n i s t e r i n g a n g e l s. These are called A m e s h a S p e n t a s, 'Immortal Holy Ones', the later Persian Amshaspands. They correspond in a measure to our idea of Archangels. They are six in number and constitute, with Ahura Mazda, the heavenly host. Their names are personifications of abstractions or virtues, Righteousness, Goodness, or the like. The seven-fold group, or celestial council, is as follows.

Ahura Mazda
aided by
Vohu Manah
Asha Vahishta
Khshathra Vairya
Spenta Armaiti
Haurvatãt
Ameretãt
also
Sraosha.

These abstractions or personifications may be noticed more in detail.

§ 33. V o h u M a n a h (lit. 'good mind', Plutarch εὔνοια) is the personification of Ahura Mazda's good spirit working in man and uniting him with God. In the later development of the religion, this divinity was specialized into the good mind or kindliness that is shown toward c a t t l e. He thus became the guardian genius of the flocks.

§ 34. A s h a V a h i s h t a (lit. 'best righteousness, Plutarch ἀλήθεια) is the next divinity in the celestial group and is the personification of r i g h t (Skt. *ṛtá*), the divine order that pervades the world. In the heavenly court Asha stands almost in the relation of prime minister to Ormazd. To live 'according to Asha' (Right, or the Law of Righteousness e. g. Ys. 31.2) is a frequent phrase in the Avesta. The attribute *Ashavan* is the regular designation of 'the righteous', as opposed to *Dregvant* 'the wicked', or one that belongs to Satan or the Druj. In later times Asha Vahishta came to preside as guardian genius over the f i r e, a symbol of perfect purity.

§ 35. Khshathra Vairya or Vohu Khsbathra (lit. 'the wished-for kingdom, the good kingdom', Plutarch εὐνομία) is the personification of Ahura Mazda's good rule, might, majesty, dominion, and power, the Kingdom which Zoroaster hopes to see come on earth. The establishment of this kingdom is to be the annihilation of evil. In later times, Khshathra Vairya, as a divinity, came to preside over metals. The symbolic connection may have been suggested by the fact that the coming of the Kingdom (khshathra) was presumed to be accompanied by a flood of molten metal, the fire that should punish and purge the wicked, and which should purify the world. The metals thus became emblematic of Khshathra.

§ 36. Spenta Armaiti (lit. 'holy harmony, humility', Plutarch σοφία) is the harmony, peace, and concord that should rule among men. She is represented as a female divinity; the earth is in her special charge. She plays an important part at the resurrection. The earth is to give up its dead.

§ 37. Haurvatāt (Plutarch πλοῦτος) literally means 'wholeness, completeness, the saving health, the perfection', toward which all should strive, in short 'Salvation', with which word it is etymologically cognate. This divinity is always mentioned in connection with Ameretāt. In the later religion, Haurvatāt came to preside as guardian angel over the health-giving waters.

§ 38. Ameretāt literally means 'immortality', and is always joined with Haurvatāt. In later Zoroastrianism, Ameretāt presides over the trees. The pair of Haurvatāt and Ameretāt together seem to symbolize the waters of health and the tree of life.

§ 39. To the number of the celestial council also is to be added the divinity Sraosha (lit. 'obedience'). This genius completes the mystic number seven when Ahura Mazda is excepted from the list (cf. also Ys. 57.12). Sraosha is the angel of religious obedience, the priest god, the personification of the divine service that protects man from evil.

§ 40. Beside the above divinities in the Gāthās, mention is also made of Geush Tashan, the creator of the cow, and Geush Urvan, the personified soul of the kine. We sometimes also find Spenta Mainyu, the Holy Spirit of Ormazd, the will of God, represented practically as a distinct personage. Lastly, the Fire, Atar, is personified in the Gāthās as one of God's ministering servants, and is a sacred emblem of the faith.

§ 41. Such is the heavenly hierarchy, and such the faith of Ormazd in which Zarathushtra exhorts the people to believe. The faithful are called Ashavans 'righteous', or later more often Mazdayasnians i. e. 'wor-shippers of Mazda'. This is the true religion in contradistinction to the false. The false religion is the worship of the Daevas 'demons' (Av. *daêva* opposed to Skt. *dêva* 'god'). The Daeva-worshippers are misguided and live in error. They are the wicked Dregvants (lit. 'belonging to the Druj, Satan'), 'the children of the wicked one' (St. Matt. xiii. 38—43). The two religions themselves are a part of the dualism.

§ 42. In juxtaposition to Ahura Mazda, Zoroaster sets the fiend Druj 'Deceit, Satan' or Angra Mainyu (Ys. 45.2). The spirit of evil in co-existent with Ormazd (Ys. 30.3), but is less clearly pictured in the Gâthâs. In later times, to carry out the symmetry of dualism, Angra Mainyu is accompanied by a number of Arch-Fiends, in opposition to the Archangels of Ormazd. The number of the infernal group is not sharply defined, but the chief members are

> Angra Mainyu
> aided by
> Aka Manah
> Indra
> Saurva
> Taro-maiti
> Tauru
> Zairica
> also
> Aeshma.

Each is the opponent of a heavenly rival. Aka Manah or 'Evil Mind' is the antagonist of Vohu Manah; Taro-maiti, the demon of 'Presumption', is the opponent of Armaiti or humility; Aeshma, 'Fury, Wrath', the foe of Sraosha or holy obedience. The antagonism in the case of the others is less marked, and the connection somewhat more mechanical.

§ 43. In the final struggle between the two bands, the powers of light and the powers of darkness, the good eventually shall triumph. That was an ethical idea which Zoroaster inculcated. But the warfare that rages in the world between the two empires and between the true religion and the false, the belief in Mazda and the Daeva-worship, pervades also the soul of man and leaves the way uncertain. Yet on his choice the ultimate triumph of right or of wrong depends. Each evil deed which man commits, increases the power of evil (e. g. Ys. 31.15); each good deed he does, brings nearer the kingdom of good. As Ahura Mazda's creature, man should choose the right. Zoroaster's mission, as shown in the Gâthâs (e. g. Ys. 31.2 et al.), is to guide man's choice. A summary of the prophet's moral and ethical teachings may best be given in the triad, so familiar later, 'good thoughts, good words, good deeds'. This forms the pith of the whole teaching. Purity alike of body and soul, and the choice of the good Mazda-religion rather than the wicked Daeva-worship, are inculcated. Zoroaster enjoins also the care of useful animals, especially the cow, and commends the good deeds of husbandry. He is the teacher of a higher and nobler civilization, as may be judged from the Avesta creed Ys. 12.1 seq.

§ 44. Man's actions, according to Zoroaster, are all recorded in Ormazd's sight as in a life-book (e. g. Ys. 31.13,14, Ys. 32.6). By his own actions man shall be judged, and rewarded or punished. The doctrine of a future life, the coming of the Kingdom, the end of the world, forms a striking feature in the teachings of the Avesta. This is the tone that Zoroaster himself constantly strikes in the Gāthās. This very doctrine, and a belief also in a resurrection of the body characterises the entire Persian faith. The resurrection is to be followed by a general judgment when evil shall be destroyed from the world. This general division and new dispensation is called the Vidāiti ($vi + \sqrt{da}$ 'dis-pose').

§ 45. The views in regard to a future life, though incomplete in the Gāthās, are carried out in the Younger Avesta, and are fully given in the Pahlavi books. That the belief in a resurrection and a life here-after was common among the Persians, some centuries before our Saviour, we have evidence in the early Greek writers, such as Theopompus, Herodotus, etc. The belief in an immediate judgment of the soul after death, the weighing in the balance, the leading of the soul across the Cinvat Bridge and through the mansions of paradise to bliss, or through the grades of hell to torment, or again in special cases to an intermediate state to await the final judgment—are all to be recognized in the Zoroastrian books and have their prototypes in the Gāthās.

§ 46. In the Yasna of the Seven Chapters, though not much later than the Gāthās, we find in some respects a slight descent from the lofty level on which the religion had been placed by its founder. There is a tendency to revive ancient ideas and forms from the old worship, in which nature had played a prominent part. The elements, earth, air, fire, and water, receive adoration; the Fravashis, or guardian angels of the righteous, are worshipped and praised together with Ahura Mazda and the Amesha Spentas. The deity Haoma, the divinity of the plant which produced the intoxicating Soma drink, again finds place in the religious rites.

§ 47. In the Younger Avesta, especially in the Yashts, we find still further restorations or innovations. The gods of the ancient mytho-

logy, like Mithra, Verethraghna, once more appear in honor by the side
of the supreme deity; the divinities of the stars, moon, and sun have
their share of pious worship. In the later parts of the Yasua, the sacrifice is developed into a somewhat elaborate ritual. The Zoroaster presented
in certain portions of the Vendidad, moreover, is evidently no longer a living,
moving personage as in the Gāthās; he has become a shadowy figure, around
whom time has thrown the aureola of the saint. These passages differ widely
from the old hymns; they show unmistakeable signs of lateness. They
present a religion codified in the hands of the priests; superstitious beliefs
and practices have found their way into the faith; intricate purifications
in particular are enjoined to remove or to avoid the impurity arising from
contact with the dead. The spirit of the Gāthās is gone. It is only here
and there that passages in late texts are old and have the genuine Zoroastrian ring. They must not be overlooked. In general, a distinction
must be drawn between what is old and what is young. We must recall,
as above (§ 27), that the Avesta was probably worked upon from Zoroaster's own day down to the time of the Sassanian redaction.

The Pahlavi Version of the Avesta.

§ 48. To the period of the Sassanian editing of the texts belongs
the Pahlavi translation and interpretation of the Avesta. At the date
when the texts were compiled and edited (§ 21), the general knowledge
of the Avesta and the understanding of the sacred texts was far from
perfect. The preparation of a translation or version became necessary.
Accordingly, the great body of the texts was rendered into Pahlavi, the
language used in Persia at the time of the Arsacidæ and Sassanidæ. The
Pahlavi version and interpretation of the entire Yasna, Vispered, and
Vendidad, with some portions of the other texts, has been preserved.
We have not as yet a thorough enough understanding of this version, as
the Pahlavi question is still a vexed one; but as our knowledge of this
translation increases, we see more and more its importance. Owing to a
somewhat imperfect knowledge of the Avesta texts at the time when the
version was made, and owing to the unskilfull and peculiar manner in
which the Pahlavi translation is made, this version abounds in numerous errors
and inaccuracies. Its renderings, however, are often of the greatest value
in interpreting allusions, particularly also in giving hints for the meanings of
obscure words, and in such matters it is many times our best and only guide.
When more fully understood and properly used in connection with the 'comparative method', referring to the Sanskrit in interpreting the sacred texts,
the 'traditional method' or native explanation is destined to win great results.
The 'traditional' and the 'comparative' methods must go hand in hand.

Manuscripts of the Avesta.

§ 49. The manuscripts of the Avesta are quite numerous. Some of our specimens were copied down over five hundred years ago. They are written on parchment. The oldest was copied about the middle of the 13th century. From that date onward we have a considerable number of codices still extant. They come to us from India and from Yezd and Kirman in Persia. A number of the manuscripts are deposited in the libraries at Copenhagen, Oxford, London, Paris, Munich. The Parsi priests, especially the Dasturs, Dr. Jamaspji Minocheherji and also Peshotanji Behramji, have shown princely generosity in aiding Western scholars in editing texts by putting valuable MSS. in their possession. , It is thus that the new edition of the Avesta texts by Professor Geldner of Berlin, is able to be presented in so critical a manner. No codex is complete in containing all the texts (§ 11). The different MSS. themselves, moreover, show certain variations in reading; but these chiefly affect the form and construction of single words, rather than entire passages and the sense. As a rule, the older the MS. is, the better is its grammar; and the later, the more faulty. Notable exceptions, however, must be made, especially in favor of some later MSS. from Persia.

Importance of the Avesta.

§ 50. The importance of the Avesta, as stated above (§ 2), lies not alone in the field of p h i l o l o g y, e t h n o l o g y and e a r l y l i t e r a-t u r e, but especially also is it of importance from the standpoint of comparative r e l i g i o n. Resemblances to Christianity in its teachings become significant when we consider the close contact between the Jews and the Persians during the Babylonian captivity. These are beginning more and more to attract the attention of students of the Bible.

Language of the Avesta.
Grammatical Summary.

§ 51. The language in which the Avesta is written belongs to the I r a n i a n branch of the Indo-Germanic tongues. With the Ancient Persian of the inscriptions it makes up the Old Iranian division. The later Iranian languages, New Persian, Kurdish, Afghan, Ossetish, Baluchi, Ghalcha, and some minor modern dialects, complete the younger division. The intervening Pahlavi and Pāzand, or Parsi, do not quite complete the link between the divisions. The extent of its relationship with the Armenian is not yet defined with sufficient exactness. On the positive kinship between the language of the Avesta and Sanskrit, see below § 55.

§ 52. The language in which the Avesta is written may best be termed *Avesta* or *Avestan*. The designation *Avesta* for the language, as well as the book, is in keeping with the Pahlavi *Avistāk*, which is used both of the tongue and of the scriptures. The term *Avestan*, both for the language and as an adjective, is preferred by some scholars, in order to distinguish the speech from the work itself. This is sometimes found very convenient. The term *Zend* for the language, as noted above (§ 3), is a misnomer. The designation Old Bactrian, occasionally used for the tongue, has little to recommend it.

§ 53. The a l p h a b e t in which the Avesta is written is far younger than the language it presents. The characters are derived from the Sassanian Pahlavi, which was used to write down the oral tradition when the texts were collected and edited under the dynasty of the Sassanidæ. The writing is read from right to left. What the original Avestan script was we do not know.

§ 54. Two dialects may be recognized in the Avesta: one the 'G ā t h ā d i a l e c t' or the language of the oldest parts, the Gāthās, or metrical sermons of Zoroaster; the other 'Y o u n g e r A v e s t a' or the 'classical dialect'. This latter is the language of the great body of the Avesta. The Gāthā dialect is more archaic, standing in the relation of the Vedic to the classical Sanskrit, or the Homeric Greek to the Attic. Possibly the Gāthā language may owe some of its peculiarities noticed below, also to an original difference of locality. The Gāthā dialect was the speech of Zoroaster and his followers. Its grammatical structure is remarkably pure. The younger Avesta, but only in its late compositions, owing to linguistic decay, shows many corruptions and confusions in its inflections. All that is old or is written in meter, however, is correct and accurate. Inaccuracies that have there crept in, we must generally attribute to the carelessness of the scribes. In its forms, as a rule, the Avesta is extremely antique; it stands in general on the same plane as the Vedic Sanskrit, and occasionally, though not often, it even shows more ancient forms.

§ 55. The language of the A v e s t a is most closely allied to the S a n s k r i t, though individually quite distinct from the latter. Together they may be classed as making up an Indo-Iranian group. Almost any Sanskrit word may be changed at once into its Avestan equivalent, or vice versa, merely by applying certain phonetic laws. As example may be taken the metrical stanza Yt. 10.6 in the Avesta:

> *təm amavaṇtəm yazatəm*
> *sūrəm dāmōhu səviśtəm*
> *miþrəm yazāi zaoþrābyō—*

'Mithra that strong mighty angel, most beneficent to all creatures, I will
worship with libations'—becomes when rendered word for word in Sanskrit:

> *tam ámavantam yajatám*
> *súram dhámasu sávistham*
> *mitrám yajāi hótrābhyah.*

§ 56. In its p h o n o l o g y the Avesta agrees with the Sanskrit in
its vowels in general, but the Avesta shows a greater variety in using *e*- and
o-sounds instead of *a*. Final vowels, except *ō*, are shortened as a rule.
The Skt. diphthong *e* appears in Av. as *aē, ōi, ē* (final). Thus Av. *vat-
nōipe* 'they two are seen' = Skt. *vēn-e-te*. Skt. *ō* appears as Av. *ao, āu,
ō (final), thus Av. *aojō* 'strength' = Skt. *ōjō, ōjas;* Av. *hratuš* 'of wisdom'
= Skt. *krátōs*. A striking peculiarity in Av., moreover, is the introduction
of epenthetic vowels and help sounds, giving rise to improper diphthongs,
Av. *bavaiti* 'he becomes' = Skt. *bhávati;* Av. *haurva-* 'whole' = Skt.
sárva-; Av. *vaḫdra-* 'word' = Skt. *váktra-;* Av. *hvarᵉ-* 'sun' = Skt. *svàr.*
The Skt. voiceless stops *k, t, p* generally become spirants *ḫ, ḫ, f* in Av.
before consonants. Thus, Av. *ḫšaḫra-* 'rule, kingdom' = Skt. *kšatrá-;*
Av. *fra* 'forth' = Skt. *pra.* The original voiced aspirates *gh, dh, bh*, become in Av. simply voiced stops *g, d, b.* They are so preserved in the
old Gāthā dialect; the younger dialect commonly resolves them again before consonants and between vowels into voiced spirants. Thus, GAv.
adā, YAv. *aδa* 'then' = Skt. *ádha.* Similarly spirantized in YAv. the
voiced stops YAv. * uγra-*, GAv. *ugra-* 'mighty' = Skt. *ugrá-.* The sibilant
s, when initial in Skt., becomes Av. *h*, as in Greek. Thus, Av. *hapta*
'seven' = Skt. *saptá.* When internal, Skt. *s* may also appear as *nh*.
Thus, Av. *vanhana-* 'vesture' = Skt. *vásana-.* Final *-as* of Skt. appears
regularly as *-ō.* Thus Av. *aspō* 'horse' = Skt. *ásvas.*

§ 57. The Gāthā dialect regularly lengthens all final vowels. It
frequently inserts the anaptyctic vowels: GAv. *fᵉrā*, YAv. *frā* = Skt. *pra.*
Original *ns* appears in GAv. as *ṇg.* Thus GAv. *daēvᵉṇg* (acc. pl.), YAv.
daēvqn 'demons' = Skt. *dēván;* GAv. *mᵉṇghāi* 'I shall think' = Skt. *maṁsāi.*

§ 58. In i n f l e c t i o n the Avesta shows nearly the richness of the
Vedic Sanskrit. There are three genders, masculine, neuter, feminine;
likewise three numbers, singular, dual, plural. The dual is not extensively
used. There are eight well-developed cases of the n o u n and the a d-
j e c t i v e; the normal endings are: Singular. Nom. *-s;* Acc. *-ᵃm;* Instr. *-ā;*
Dat. *-ē;* Abl. *-aṭ;* Gen. *-ō (-as);* Loc. *-i;* Voc. —. Dual. Nom., Acc., Voc.
-ā; Instr., Dat., Abl. *-byā;* Gen. *-ᴕ;* Loc. *-ō, -yō.* Plural. Nom., Voc. *-ō*
(-as), -ā; Acc. *-ō (-as, -ns), -ā;* Instr. *-biš;* Dat. *-byō (-byas);* Gen. *-ąm;*
Loc. *-su, -hu, -šva.* The classes of declension agree exactly with the

Sanskrit; the method of forming comparison of adjectives likewise
corresponds. The numerals answer to Skt. forms, except Av. *aēva-*
'one', opposed to Skt. *ēka-*, Av. *baēvar-* '10,000', but Skt. *ayúta*. The
Av. pronouns closely resemble the Skt., but show also individual peculiarities. Noteworthy is the remote demonstrative Av. *ava, hāu* 'that,
yonder', contrasted with Skt. *amú, asāu*. The verbal system in Av.
and in Skt. are in general identical. The roots are chiefly monosyllabic
and are subject to the same modifications as in Skt. In voice, mode,
and tense, and in their conjugation-system the two languages quite agree.
The endings show equal antiquity with the Sanskrit. The primary active
endings in Av. are: Sing. 1, *-mi*, 2, *-hi*, 3, *-ti;* Dual. 1, *-vahi*, 3, *-tō, -ṭō;*
Plur. 1, *-mahi*, 2, *-ṭa*, 3, *-ṇti*. The other endings also are parallel with
the Sanskrit.

§ 59. The Av. possesses like facility with the Sanskrit in forming
words by means of prefixes, and by adding suffixes of primary and secondary derivation. The same classes of compounds may be recognized
in both tongues. The rules of external Sandhi, or joining together of
words in a sentence, so universal in Skt., are almost wanting in Avesta.
The Avesta separates each word by a dot. The vowels are fully expressed as in Greek etc., by individual letters. No diacritical points or
accents are written in the texts. The meters in which the Gāthās are
composed have analogies in the Veda. Almost all the metrical parts of
the younger Avesta are in eight-syllable lines. The syntax, however,
differs from the Sanskrit in certain points, and shows some marked in-
dividualities, especially in the later portions.

Specimens of the Avesta Text.

I. From the Gathas.

Yasna 45.1—2.

Zoroaster preaches upon The Two Spirits.

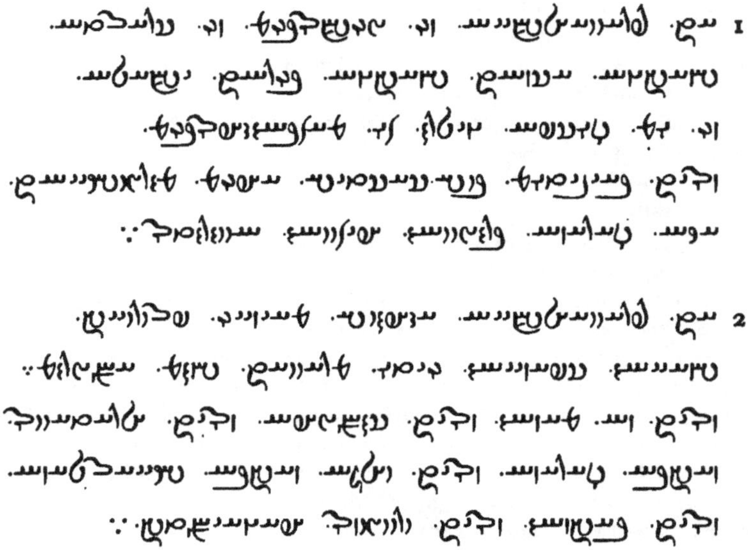

Ys. 45.1 translated.

Now shall I preach, and do you give ear and hear,
Ye who hither press from near and from afar,
Therefore lay ye all these things to heart as clear
Nor let the wicked teacher your second life destroy—
The perverted sinner your tongues with his false faith.

Transliteration of the same.

(See opposite page.)

1 *aṭ fravaḫṣyā nū gūṣōdūm nū sraotā*
yaēcā asnāṭ yaēcā dūrāṭ iṣaþā
nū īm vīspā ciþrə̄ zī mazdǣvhōdūm
nōiṭ daibitīm duš.sastiš ahūm mərą̄ṣyāṭ
akā varanā drəgvā̊ hizvā̊ āvərətō.

2 *aṭ fravaḫṣyā avhə̄uš mainyū pouruyē*
yayā̊ spanyā̊ ūiti mravaṭ yə̄m angrəm
nōiṭ nā manā̊ nōiṭ sə̄nghā nōiṭ ḫratavō
naēdā varanā nōiṭ uḫdā naēdā šyaoþanā
nōiṭ daēnā̊ nōiṭ urvąnō hacainṭē.

———

Ys. 45.2 translated.

Now shall I preach of the world's Two primal Spirits
The Holier One of which did thus address the Evil:
'Neither do our minds, our teachings, nor our concepts,
Nor our beliefs, nor words, nor do our deeds in sooth,
Nor yet our consciences, nor souls agree in aught.'

II. From the Younger Avesta.

a. Yasna 9.5 (metrical).
The Golden Age of Yima.

[Avestan script text]

5 *yimahe xšaþre aurvahe*
   nōiṯ aotəm ǣuha nōiṯ garəmain
   nōiṯ zaurva ǣuha nōiṯ marəpyuš
   nōiṯ araskō daēvō.dātō;
   pança.dasa fracarōiþe
   pita puþrasca raoδaēšva [katarascit]
   yavata xšayōiṯ hvąþwō
   yimō vīvavuhatō puþrō.

In the reign of princely Yima
There was neither cold, nor heat
Old age was not, death there was not,
Nor disease, the work of Demons,
But the son walked with the father
Fifteen years old each in figure;
Long as Vivanghvat's son, Yima
The good shepherd, ruled as sovereign.

b. Vendidad 6.44—45 (prose).
Disposal of the Dead.

44

[. m u ā ʒ a	. m q n i t i a v t s a	. m q n a p ʒ a g	.ᴊr a t ā d]
ašāum	astvaitinąm	gaēþanąm	dātarᵊ
O holy One	material`	of beings	O Creator

[. a r u h a	. a m ā r a b	. m ū n a l	. m q n a t s i r i	. m q r a n	. a v k]
ahura	barāma	tanūmi	iristanąm	narąm	kva
O Ahura	shall-we-bear	body	dead (gen.)	of men	where

45

[. ō r u h a	. ʃ o a r m	. ʃ a ā	. a m ā p a d i n	. a v k	. a dz a m]
ahurō	mraoʈ	āaʈ	nidaþāma	kva	mazda
Ahura	spake	Then	deposit	where	Mazda

[. a c a v ʒ u t ā g	. i t i a p	. a c a v ʒ ʒ a t ʒ i z ᴊr a b	. ☉ dz a m]
gātušvaca	paiti	barezištaēšvaca	mazdā̊
and-on-beds	upon	the heights	Mazda

[. m ᴊ t ʒ i d i ā b	. m i d	. ʃ i ō d a y	. a r t ʒ u þ a r a z	. a m a t i p s]
bāidištəm	dim	yaðōiʈ	zaraþuštra	spitama
always	it	where	Zarathushtra	O Spitama

[. ā v	. ō y a v	. ō r a h . ʒ f ᴊr ᴊk	. ā v	. ō n ū s	. n q n a z a v a]
vā	vayō	kᴊrᴊfš.hᵥarō	vā	sūnō	avazanąn
or	birds	corpse-eating	either	dogs	may-see

[. ō r a h . ʒ f ᴊr ᴊk]
kᴊrᴊfš.hᵥarō
corpse-eating.

TRANSCRIPTION OF AVESTAN ALPHABET.

(Compared with Justi, *Handbuch der Zendsprache*).[1]

A. Vowels.

Short	✘ *a*	╷ *i*	╵ *u*	╷╵ *ə*	⍵ *e*	➳ *o*
	a	*i*	*u*	*(e)*	*(ĕ)*	*o*
Long	✘ *ā*	╷ *ī*	╵ *ū*	╷╵ *ō*	⍵ *ē*	➳ *ō*	⍩ *ō̄*	× *ą*
	ā	*ī*	*u*	*(ĕ)*	*ē*	*ō*	*(āo)*	*(ā)*

B. Consonants.

Guttural	╻ *k*	ઉ *ḫ*	℮ *g*	ι *ǰ*		
	k	*(kh)*	*g*	*(gh)*		
Palatal	⌐ *c*	—	ц *j*	—		
	c		*j*			
Dental	℘ *t*	♭ *þ*	♩ *d*	ц *d*	℮ *ṭ*	
	t	*(th)*	*d*	*(dh)*	*(ṭ)*	
Labial	⍵ *p*	∂ *f*	⌐ *b*	⍺ *w*		
	p	*f*	*b*	*w*		
Nasal	╷ *v*	℧ *ŋ*	╷ *n*	⍳ *ṇ*	♭ *m*	
	(ṅ)	*(ṅ)*	*n*	*(ñ)*	*m*	

Semivowel and
Liquid	℧ (,,) *y* (*i̭*)[2]		╵ *r*	⍭ (,,) *v* (*ṷ*)[2]	
	y		*r*	*v*	
Sibilant	℧ *s*	⍵ *š*	⍵ *š́*[3]	℧ *š̀*[3]	∫ *z*	⍵ *ž*
	(s)	*(s)*	*(sh)*	*(sk)*	*z*	*(zh)*
Aspiration	⍵ *h*	ц *ḥ*				
	h	*(q)*				
Ligature	⍭ *hv*					
	(q)					

---

[1] Forms in parentheses ( ) show where Justi has been deviated from.

[2] The signs *i̭*, *ṷ* need only be employed for purely scientific purposes; the letters *y*, *v* for both initial and internal ℧ ,,, ⍭ ,, answer fully for practical purposes.

[3] The differentiation *š́*, *š̀*, *š* need only be made in scientific articles. The single sign *š* is ordinarily quite sufficient for the three ⍵, ℧, ℧.

SUGGESTIONS.

The following hints may be helpful to the student in using the Grammar. The chief points on which stress should be laid, and which it will be sufficient for the beginner to acquire, are:

1. In the Preface, the remarks on Transcription, pp. vi—vii.

2. In the Introduction, the sketch of the language of the Avesta, pp. xxx—xxxiii.

3. Throughout the Grammar, the large print alone need be studied. Every thing marked 'GAv.' (Gāthā Avesta), and all that is in small type, may be practically disregarded.

4. Under. Phonology, only the sections (§§) referred to in the Résumé pp. 60—61.

5. Under the Declension of Nouns and Adjectives, the following sections should suffice: §§ 236, 243, 251, 262, 279, 291, 300, 322, 339, 362, 363.

6. Under Numerals, note merely the Cardinals § 366.

7. Under Pronouns, compare the Av. and Skt. forms in the case of §§ 386, 390, 399, 409, 417, 422, 432. No attempt need be made to commit the paradigms to memory.

8. Under Verbs, the following sections relating to the Present-System are important: §§ 448, 466, 469, 470, 478—481, 483—488. The remaining conjugations, and the Perfect, Aorist, Future, etc., may be learned as needed.

9. The rest of the book may be overlooked by the beginner.

10. In consulting the Grammar, the I n d e x will be found of service for reference.

A FEW OF THE BOOKS
MOST NECESSARY FOR THE BEGINNER.

The following list contains a few books that the beginner will find most useful. The list is very brief; the student as he advances will see how rapidly it may be enlarged.

a. Texts.

GELDNER — *Avesta, or the Sacred Books of the Parsis.* — Stuttgart 1885 seq.
> The new standard edition.

WESTERGAARD — *Zendavesta, or the Religious Books of the Zoroastrians.* — Copenhagen.
> Hard to procure, but useful until Geldner's edition is complete.

W. GEIGER — *Aogemadaēca, ein Pārsentract in Pāzend, Altbaktrisch und Sanskrit.* —Erlangen 1878.
> Useful for the brief Av. fragment it contains.

SPIEGEL — *Die altpersischen Keilinschriften,* im Grundtexte mit Übersetzung, Grammatik und Glossar. 2. Aufl. — Leipzig 1881.
> Good for comparative purposes.

b. Dictionary.

JUSTI — *Handbuch der Zendsprache,* Altbaktrisches Wörterbuch. — Leipzig 1864.
> The only dictionary at present, and indispensable for reference. Possible to obtain second-hand.

c. Translation.

DARMESTETER AND MILLS — *The Zend-Avesta* translated, in the *Sacred Books of the East,* ed. by F. Max Müller, vols. iv, xxiii, xxxi. — Oxford 1883-7.
> This translation is complete. Translations of separate portions are to be found in the works mentioned under (d) and (e).

d. Grammar and Exegesis,
including also Translations of selected portions.

(Books specially mentioned above in Preface, are not repeated here.)

BARTHOLOMAE—*Arische Forschungen* i-iii.—Halle 1882-7.
Grammatical and metrical investigations, with translations of selected Passages.

GELDNER — *Ueber die Metrik des jüngeren Avesta.* — Tübingen 1877.
A useful treatise on Metre. Also contains translations.

— *Studien zum Avesta.*—Strassburg 1882.
Grammatical contributions, and numerous translations.

— *Drei Yasht aus dem Zendavesta* übersetzt und erklärt.—Stuttgart 1884.
Translation of Yt. 14, 17, 19, with Commentary.

SPIEGEL — *Commentar über das Avesta.* Bd. i-ii.—Wien 1864-8.
Useful for occasional reference.

e. Literature, Religion, Antiquities.

DARAB PESHOTAN SANJANA—*Civilisation of the Eastern Iranians.* Vols. i-ii; being a translation from the German of W. Geiger's *Ostiranische Kultur im Alterthum.*—London 1885-6.
Useful for reference.

GELDNER—*Zend-Avesta, Zoroaster,* articles in the *Encyclopaedia Britannica.* Ninth edition.—1888.
By all means to be consulted.

HAUG AND WEST—*Essays* on the Sacred Language, Writings, and Religion of the Parsis. 3 ed.—London 1884.
Contains much useful information.

FIROZ JAMASPJI—Casartelli's *Mazdayasnian Religion under the Sassanids.*—Bombay 1889.
Treats fully of the later development of Zoroastrianism.

RAGOZIN —*Media, Babylon and Persia.* (Story of Nations' Series.)—New York 1888.

A good and readable book.

WINDISCHMANN —*Zoroastrische Studien,* herausgegeben von Fr. Spiegel.—Berlin 1863.

Contains much good material.

Beside the above works the student will find abundant and valuable contributions on the Avesta and kindred Iranian subjects in the philological journals and periodicals of the last few years. Reference need only be made to the names Bartholomae, Bang, Bezzenberger, Caland, Casartelli, Darmesteter, de Harlez, Geiger, Geldner, Horn, Hübschmann, Fr. Müller, Mills, Pischel, Spiegel, Wilhelm, and some others, in the following:

> *Bezzenberger's Beiträge;*
> *Kuhn's Zeitschrift;*
> *Zeitschrift der deutschen morgenländischen Gesellschaft;*
> *Brugmann und Streitberg's Indogermanische Forschungen;*
> *Le Muséon;*
> *American Oriental Society's Proceedings;*
> *American Journal of Philology;*
> *Babylonian and Oriental Record.*

TABLE OF CONTENTS

OF

PART I.

(The Numbers refer to the Sections §§.)

GRAMMAR.
PHONOLOGY.
ALPHABET AND PRONUNCIATION.

ABBREVIATIONS.

adj. = adjective

advl. = adverbial

etc. = *et cetera*

et al. = *et alia*

fr. = from

indecl. = indeclinable

infin. = infinitive

nom. propr. = *nomen proprium*

num. = numeral

orig. = original, originally

opp., opp. to = opposed to

pret. = preterite

ptcpl. = participle

str. = strong

subst. = substantive

v. l. = *varia lectio*

var. = variant

wk. = weak.

Afr. = Afringan

Av.[1] = Avesta

GAv.[2] = Gatha Avesta

Ind. Iran. = Indo-Iranian

Indg. = Indogermanic

MS. = manuscript

MSS. = manuscripts

Ny. = Nyaish

Phl. = Pahlavi

Sir. = Sirozah

Skt. = Sanskrit

Vd. = Vendidad

Vsp. = Vispered

Wg. = Westergaard

YAv.[3] = Younger Avesta

Ys. = Yasna

Yt. = Yasht

ZPhl. Gloss. = Zand-Pahlavi Glossary.

The other abbreviations require no remark.

Observe.

1. A v. (Avesta) prefixed to a word indicates that the word or form in question is either found in both GAv. and YAv. or has nothing peculiar about it which would prevent its occurence in both.

2. G A v. (Gâthâ Avesta) is prefixed (1) when the word, or form, or construction is peculiar to the Gâthâ dialect and is not found in YAv.; (2) to contrast a Gâthâ form with a younger form (YAv.) which may stand beside it; (3) to emphasize the fact that the form in question is found even in the Gâthâs, e. g. *stavas* § 143.

Under G A v. are comprised the usual 17 hymns and the sacred formulas (Introd. p. xxiii, § 25), the Yasna Haptanghâiti, and those portions, such as Ys. 12, that are written in the Gâthâ dialect even including some possible later imitations, e. g. Ys. 58, 4.26.

3. Y A v. (Younger Avesta) comprises everything that is n o t written in the dialect of the Gâthâs.   For its usage see preceding note.

4. The sign (•) is placed before a form to denote that the first part of the word is omitted.

5. In the paradigms under Inflection, the f o r m s i n p a r e n -
t h e s e s ( ) do not actually occur, but are made up after the form in small print which stands beside them.   See § 236 foot-note.   Thus

Loc. *(yasnaēšu) vīraēšu.*

GRAMMAR.

PHONOLOGY.

Alphabet.

§ 1. The Avesta is written in the following characters

A. Vowels.

Short	*a*	*i*	*u*	*ə*	*e*	*o*
Long	*ā*	*ī*	*ū*	*ə̄*	*ē*	*ō*	*ā̊*	*q*

B. Consonants.

Guttural . . .	*k*	*χ*	*g*	*ǰ*
Palatal . . .	*c*	—	*j*	—
Dental	*t*	*ϑ*	*d*	*ḍ*	*t̤*
Labial	*p*	*f*	*b*	*w*
Nasal	*ŋ*	*ŋ́*	*n*	*ṇ*	*m*
Semivowels and Liquid . . .	*u̯, (")y*	*r*	*ẏ, (")v*
Sibilant . . .	*s*	*š*	*ś*	*š́*	*z*	*ž*
Aspiration . .	*h*	*ḫ*
Ligature . . .	*hv*

§ 2 The writing runs from right to left. The vowels are fully expressed by individual letters as in Greek

Note. The epenthetic and anaptyctic vowels (§§ 70, 72) will be expressed in transcription, in the Grammar only, by a small vowel slightly raised: e. g. Av. *aᵘruǰa-* 'white' = Skt. *aruṣá-*; Av. *antarᵉ* 'within' = Skt. *antár*.

1

etc.; there are no diacritical points; nor are any accents written in the Avesta texts.

§ 3. In the manuscripts numerous l i g a t u r e s occur; these except ᴎᴜ *št* are generally resolved in printing. Observe that ᴘ *h* is different from ᴍᴏ *hv*. Many MSS. have a sign ᴥ *m̄* interchanging with ᴒ *hm*.

§ 4. In Avesta, all w o r d s except some enclitics are w r i t t e n s e p a r a t e l y and each is followed by a point (.); the compounds even are mostly written separately in the MSS.; but in printed texts these are written together, a point (.) being used to divide the members.

§ 5. The p u n c t u a t i o n in the MSS. is meagre, mostly arbitrary and quite irregular; the following symbols borrowed from the MSS. have been adopted to correspond to our signs, namely ⁚ for colon or semicolon; ⁚⁚ a full stop; ⁰⁰ a larger break; ⁰⁰ ⁰⁰ the end of a chapter; • symbol of abbreviation.

Pronunciation.

§ 6. **Vowels.** ᴗ *a*, ᴗ *ā*, ᴗ *i*, ᴗ *ī*, and ᴗ *u*, ᴗ *ū* are pronounced as ordinarily in Sanskrit, but *a, ā* perhaps duller. —ᴗ *ə* is most probably obscure like the short indefinite vowel familiar in English, 'gard*e*ner', 'meas*u*ring', 'hist*o*ry', 'sach*e*m'; it often corresponds to the vulgar 'chim*e*ney', 'rheuma-tis*u*m'. In the combination ᴥ *ərə*, cf. Skt. *ṛ*, much like English 'pretty' (when pronounced 'p*e*r*e*tty'), e. g. ᴒᴗᴥ *pərəsaṭ* 'he asked', cf. Mod. Persian *pursīdan* 'to ask'; Av. *mərəja-* 'bird', Skt. *mṛga-*, Mod. Pers. *murj*. See above, 'Introduction, on Transcription. —ᴗ *ə̄* is the corresponding long vowel to ᴗ *ə*. —ᴗ *e* and ᴗ *ē*, both narrow, about as English 'let, veil', French 'été'. —ᴗ *o* and ᴗ *ō* probably somewhat muffled. —ᴗ *ā̊*, as English 'extra*o*rdinary, f*au*lt, f*aw*ing', i. e. approaching '-aw' in 'saw'. — ᴋ *ą*, nasalized *a*, or *ā*, French 'sans', likely rather dull.

§ 7. **Diphthongs.** ᴗᴗ *āi* and ᴊᴗ *āu* are pronounced as in Sanskrit. — ᴧ *ōi* as a Gk. ωι. — ᴦ *aē*, ᴗᴗ *ao* and ᴊ *ʒu* as a union of the two elements *a i* etc. — ᴋᴊ *ʒe* as forming two distinct sounds.

§ 8. **Tenues** ʒ *k*, ᴦ *t*, ᴗ *p*, and **Mediae** ᴦ *g*, ᴊ *d*, ᴊ *b*, as ordinarily. — ᴩ *c*, ᴋ *j*, as in Sanskrit, English 'church, judge'.

§ 9. **Spirants.** ᴦ *ḥ*, as *ch* in Scotch 'loch', Mod. Gk. χ. — ᴊ *j*, a roughened *g*, guttural buzz, cf. (often) Germ. 'Tage', Mod. Gk. γ. — ᴗ *ḫ*, as English 'thin', surd. — ᴊ *d*, as English 'then', sonant. — ᴩ *ṭ*, apparently a spirant, § 81. — ᴗ *f*, as in English. — ᴗ *w*, corresponding sonant, Germ. *w*, Mod. Gk. β (cf. Eng. *v*). — ᴗ *s*, sharp as in 'sister'. — ʃ *z*, corresponding sonant, English 'zeal'. — ᴗ *š*, as English *sh* in 'dash'. — ᴗ *ž*, corresponding sonant, English 'pleasure, azure'. — ᴦᴗ *š*, a more palatal *sh*, generally before *y*. — ᴗ *š*, apparently a variety *sh*, differing little from ᴗ *š*; etymologically it most often equals original *rt*.

§ 10. **Nasals.** ᴊ *v*, guttural = Skt. *v*. — ᴊ *ŋ*, a modification of the preceding, -mouillé; the two (ᴊ *v* and ᴊ *ŋ*) respectively perhaps as in Eng. 'longing'. — ᴊ *n*, as Eng. 'nun'. — ᴩ *ṇ* (modified from *an*), a variety of *ṅ*. — ᴦ *m*, as ordinarily.

§ 11. **Semivowels and Liquid.** ᴦᴗ *y* (initial), probably spirant as Eng. 'youth'; — ᴗ *y* (internal), probably semivowel, *i̯*, English 'many a man'. — ᴊ *v* (initial), probably spirant as Eng. 'vanish'; — ᴗ *v* (internal), probably semivowel, *u̯*, cf. Eng. 'lower, flour'. — ᴗ *r* is a liquid vigorously pronounced. Observe *l* is wanting.

Note. On ᴗ in *srvaḍbya*, see Vocabulary after ᴊ *u*.

§ 12. **Aspiration.** 𐬵 *h*, as ordinarily.—𐬒 *ḥ*, a modification of *h* before *y*, possibly stronger.

§ 13. **Ligature.** 𐬓 h^v, perhaps more vigorous than 𐬵𐬬 *hv*, and possibly already shading towards the later Pers. $\underline{h}^v$.

Sounds.

SYSTEM OF VOWELS.

§ 14. **General Remark.** The Avesta presents a greater variety than the Sanskrit in its vowel-system, especially through the frequent presence of *e*- and *o*-sounds instead of *a*.

Simple Vowels.

A. Agreement in Quality between Avesta and Sanskrit Vowels.

Av. 𐬀, 𐬌, 𐬎, — 𐬁, 𐬍, 𐬏.
a, *i*, *u*, — *ā*, *ī*, *ū*.

i. Agreement in both Quality and Quantity.

§ 15. The Av. vowels *a, ā, i, ī, u, ū*, agree in general with the corresponding vowels in Sanskrit.

(1) Av. *a* = Skt. *a*;—Av. *ā* = Skt. *ā*.

Av. *asti* 'is' = Skt. *ásti*; Av. *mātarō* 'mothers' = Skt. *mātáras*; Av. *vātāiš* 'with winds' = Skt. *vā́tāis*.

(2) Av. *i* = Skt. *i*;—Av. *ī* = Skt. *ī*.

Av. *cistiš* 'wisdom' = Skt. *cíttis*; Av. *hiṇcaⁱti* 'he sprinkles' = Skt. *siñcáti*; Av. *jīvyąm* 'living, fresh' (acc. f.) = Skt. *jīvyā́m*.

(3) Av. *u* = Skt. *u*;—Av. *ū* = Skt. *ū*.

Av. *uta* 'also' = Skt. *utá*; Av. *dāᵘru* 'wood' = Skt. *dā́ru*;—Av. *būrōiš* 'of richness' = Skt. *bhū́rēs*; Av. *būmīm* 'earth' = Skt. *bhū́mim*.

ii. **Agreement in quality; difference in quantity.**

§ 16. As to the relation between long and short quantity, the Avesta and the Sanskrit do not always coincide with each other. This is probably due in part to shifting of accent, partly to deficiencies or inaccuracy in Avesta writing, partly to dialectic peculiarities.

§ 17. (1) Av. *a* = Skt. *ā*.

GAv. *nanā* 'differently' = Skt. *nǎnā;* GAv. *mavaᵗē* 'to one like me' = Skt. *mǎvatē;* YAv. •*kasaṭ* 'looked' = Skt. *kǎṣaṭ;* YAv. *bajina* 'dishes' = Skt. *bhājana-;* YAv. *dvarɔm* 'door' = Skt. *dvǎram;* YAv. *urvaranqm* 'of trees' = Skt. *urvǎrāṇām.*

§ 18. (2) Av. *ā* = Skt. *a*.

Av. *varᵊzānāi* 'for the community' = Skt. *vṛjǎnāya;* Av. *yatārō* 'which of two' = Skt. *yatarás;* Av. *āþrava* (nom. sg.) 'priest' = Skt. *átharvā.*

Note 1. The manner of writing the same word or form in the Av. itself, sometimes varies between *a* and *ā*. — Av. *hāmō* beside *hamō* 'same' = Skt. *samás;* Av. *ayu-* beside *āyu* 'age' = Skt. *āyu-;* Av. *hutāštɔm, hutaštɔm* 'well-formed' = Skt. *sútaṣṭam;* Av. *yazamaᵗde* 'we worship' beside (rarer) *barāmaᵗde* 'we carry' (Yt. 11.7) = Skt. *yájāmahē, bhárāmahē;* Av. *uštanɔm* beside *uštānɔm* 'vital power'; YAv. *adwānɔm* (but GAv. *advānɔm*) 'way' = Skt. *ádhvānam;* GAv. *ayārᵊ* beside YAv. *ayarᵊ* 'days'. — Especially does the preposition *ā,* Av. *ā (a),* vary: Av. *avazaᵗti* 'he rides to' = Skt. *ā-vahati;* GAv. *akā-* beside *ākā-* 'judgment'.

Note 2. A part of the differences between *a* and *ā* in Av. and Skt., as well as the variation in the Av. itself, may be explained, as said (§ 16), by vowel-gradation: e. g. Av. -*mna-*, -*mana-*, ptcpl. pres. mid. = Skt. -*māna-*. The treatment of the old vowel-gradation must be sought in the comparative grammar, cf. Brugmann, *Grundriss der vergl. Gram.* § 307. Examples in Avesta are

Lower-grade	Higher-grade
apqm 'of waters'	*āpō* 'waters'
(1) *da-dᵊ-maᵗde* 'we give', (2) *daþra-* 'gift' *haᵘrva-fš-u-* 'with full flocks'	*dātar-* 'giver' *pasu* 'flock, sheep'
(1) *fra-bd-a-* 'fore-foot', (2) *padō* (acc. pl.) *caþru-gaoša-* 'four-eared'	*pāda* (acc. du.) *caþwar-aspa-, caþwārō.*

See also under guṇa and vṛddhi § 60.

Note 3. On the relation, Av. *hātqm* 'of beings' = Skt. *satā́m;* or
GAv. *drəgvāitē* 'for the wicked', cf. YAv. *drvataḟ,* see Bartholomae, in *B.B.*
x. 278 seq.; *K.Z.* xxix. p. 543 = *Flexionslehre* p. 124.

§ 19. Similarly (§ 18 Note 1) in Av. itself, internal
a often takes the place of *ā*, when *ca* etc. is suffixed or
the word otherwise grows by increment:

(a) Av. *katārō* 'which' but *katarascit;* Av. *dahā́ka* 'dragon' but
dahā́kāca; Av. *ābyō* 'with these' but *aⁱwyasca* (initial *ā*); GAv. *dᵊmā́-*
nᵊm 'house' (acc.) but (gen.) *dᵊmānahyā;* Av. *bipaⁱtiʒtānᵊm* 'biped'
(acc.) but *bipaⁱtiʒtānayā̊* Yt. 13.41.—(b) Likewise a lightening of *ā*
to *a* in ablative *-āt* occurs before enclitic *haca:* Av. *yimat haca*
'from Yima'; *apaxtarat haca naēmā́t* 'from northern region'; *huɪ-*
hqm.bᵊrᵊtat haca h̨aētā́t 'from well-collected possessions'.

§ 20. (3) Av. *ī, ū* = Skt. *i, u.*

Very often, Av. *ī* and *ū* are found where the Skt. has
i, u. The long vowel *ī*, occurs most frequently in the
vicinity of *v;* the long vowel *ū*, chiefly when followed by
epenthetic *i* § 70.

Av. *sīʃōit* 'might direct, teach', cf. Skt. *śiṣyā́t* ($\sqrt{śās}$-, *śiṣ*-); Av.
vīspᵊm 'all' = Skt. *viśvam;* Av. *vītastīm* 'a span length' = Skt.
vitastim.—Av. *sūnō* 'of a dog' = Skt. *śúnas;* Av. *yūʃmat, yūʃmā́kᵊm*
'from, of you' = Skt. *yuṣmát, yuṣmā́kam;* Av. *srūtō* 'heard' = Skt.
śrutás; Av. *ᵒdrūta-* 'run' = Skt. *drutá-;* Av. *stūtō* 'of praise' = Skt.
stutás.—Av. *āhūiriʃ* (but gen. *āhurōiʃ*) 'Ahurian' = Skt. *āsuris;* Av.
āzūⁱtiʃ (but gen. *āzutōiʃ*) 'oblation' = Skt. *āhutis;* Av. *stūⁱtiʃ* 'praise'
= Skt. *stutis;* Av. *stūⁱdi* 'praise thou' = Skt. *stuhí;* Av. *yūⁱdyeⁱti*
'he fights' = Skt. *yúdhyati.*

§ 21. (4) Av. *i, u* = Skt. *ī, ū.*

Sometimes Av. *i* and *u* are found where the Skt.
shows *ī, ū.*

Av. *izyeⁱti* 'he seeks', cf. Skt. *īhate;* Av. *aⁱnikᵊm* 'face' = Skt.
ánīkam; Av. *isānᵊm* 'having power' = Skt. *īśānam;* Av. *hunavō*
'sons' = Skt. *sūnávas;* Av. *tanunqm* 'of bodies' = Skt. *tanū́nām.*

Note 1. In general as to *i, ī* and *u, ū*, the MSS. themselves often
vacillate between the long and the short in the same passage, or in the
same word at different places: — e. g. at times Av. *srīra-* written instead
of *srīra-* 'fair'; Av. *miʒti* and *ᵔmiʒti* 'with moisture'; Av. *vispᵊm* for *vīspᵊm*

'all'; Av. *miždɔm* and *mīždɔnt* 'reward'.—Av. *dura-* written for *dūra-* 'far'; Av. *drūjō* and *drujō* 'of the Druj'; Av. *yūḫta-* and *yuḫta-* 'yoked'.

§ 22. GAv. shows everywhere an overwhelming preference for long vowels, especially for ǀ *ō*.

GAv. *azɔm* 'I', YAv. *azɔm* = Skt. *ahám;* GAv. *apɔma-* 'last', YAv. *apɔma-* = Skt. *apamá-;* GAv. *jɔmyāǀ* 'might come', YAv. *jamyāǀ* = Skt. *gamyāt;*—GAv. *-cīǀ, īǀ,* particles, YAv. *-cīǀ, īǀ* = Skt. *cid, -id;* GAv. *dɔjīǀ-* 'victorious', YAv. *jīǀ-;* GAv. *ratūǀ* 'chief, Ratu' (nom. sg.) beside *ratuǀ.*

Note. Similarly, GAv. *-bīǀ* (pada-ending) compared with YAv. *-bīǀ* or *-bīǀ,* Skt. *-bhis;* but GAv. *cīǀ* etc. No rule for lengthening is laid down.

Principal Rules for Quantity of Vowels.

§ 23. (1) In Avesta, original *i* and *u* are regularly lengthened before final *m*.

Av. *paⁱtīm* 'lord' (acc.) = Skt. *pátim;* Av. *dāhīm* 'creation' = Skt. *dhāsim;*—Av. *tāyūm* 'thief' = Skt. *tāyúm;* Av. *pitūm* 'food' = Skt. *pitúm.*

Note. Likewise *i* arising from reduction of *ya,* § 63 is lengthened; but the *u,* arising from reduction of *va,* appears mostly short before *m :—* Av. *maⁱdīm* 'middle' (acc.) = Skt. *mádhyam;* but often Av. *priǀum* beside *priǀūm* (from **priǀ-va-m*) 'third'.

§ 24. (2) Monosyllables ending in a vowel show regularly the long vowel.

Av. *zī* 'for' = Skt. *hi;* Av. *nī* 'down' = Skt. *ni;* Av. *nū* 'now' = Skt. *nú, (nû);* Av. *frā* 'forth' = Skt. *prá.*

Note. The enclitic *-ca,* as united with the preceding word, does not regularly fall under this law.

§ 25. (3) Polysyllables in YAv. shorten as a rule all final vowels except *ō.*

YAv. *haēna* 'army' (nom. sg. fem.) = Skt. *sénā;* YAv. *pita* 'father' = Skt. *pitá;* YAv. *para* 'before' = Skt. *párā.* —YAv. *āfriti* 'blessing' (instr. f.), cf. Skt. *dhītī* 'with devotion'; YAv. *nāⁱri* 'woman' = Skt. *nārī.* —YAv. *sūre* 'O mighty one' (fem.) = Skt. *sūrē;* YAv.

baraite 'he carries' = Skt. *bháratē.*—YAv. *dahyu* 'two nations', cf. Skt. *dásyū;* YAv. *dva ər²zu* 'two fingers' = Skt. *dvá ŗjú.*

Note. Exceptions occur: YAv. *pāyū* 'two protectors' = Skt. *pāyú;* YAv. *maᶦnyū* beside *maᶦnyu* 'two spirits', cf. Skt. *manyū;* YAv. *asrū* 'tears'; etc.

§ 26. (4) In GAv. all final vowels are long without exception.

(a) GAv. *ahurā* 'O Ahura, Lord' = YAv. *ahura,* Skt. *ásura;* GAv. *utā* 'also' = YAv. *uta,* Skt. *utá;* GAv. *kuþrā* 'whither' = YAv. *kuþra,*, Skt. *kútra.*— GAv. *ahī* 'thou art' = YAv. *ahi,* Skt. *ási.* — GAv. *yaēšū* 'among whom' = Skt. *yéṣu.*—(b) Even the anaptyctic vowel (§ 72), with trifling exceptions, is lengthened: GAv. *ǣvhar³* 'they have been' = YAv. *ǣvhar³,* cf. Skt. *āsúr;* GAv. *vadar³* 'weapon' = YAv. *vadar³,* Skt. *vádhar;* GAv. *aṇtar³* (but also *aṇtar³*) 'within' = YAv. *aṇtar³,* Skt. *antár.*

Note. Before *-cā* 'que' in GAv. a vowel is sometimes found lengthened, sometimes again shortened: — e. g. GAv. *yehyācā* 'and of which'; *vacahīcā* 'and in word';—*aṣicā* 'and Ashi' (fem. *i*); *vohucā manavhā* beside *vohū manavhā* 'with the Good Mind'.—Similar fluctuations are to be observed in YAv. also.

B. Differences in Quality between Avesta and Sanskrit Vowels.

Av. ı, ı̣, ɯ, ℧, ⸾, ⸽,—ⱳ, ℵ.

ə, ə̃, e, ē, o, ō,—ǣ, ą.

§ 27. The above vowels are found under special conditions as representatives of Skt. *a* and *ā.*

§ 28. **Summary.** The Av. ı *e* answers oftenest to Skt. *a* before *n* or *m,* also occasionally before *v.* It is commonly the anaptyctic vowel.—The corresponding long is ı ə̃ very frequent in GAv., more rare in YAv.—The

letter ʀ *e* is commonly a shading from *a* after *y*.—The
corresponding long is ʀ *ē*.—Avesta ❧ *o* and ❧ *ō* stand sometimes for *a* under influence of a labial, *u, v*.—Av. ﹏ *ō* is
either Skt. *ās*, or it answers to Skt. *ā* before *n* plus stop-
sound.—Av. ⲕ *ą* is nasalization of *a, ā* before *m, n;* it often
answers to Skt. *a* with anusvāra.

<h3 style="text-align:center">Av. ᵻ ᵊ.</h3>

§ 29. Av. *ə* often corresponds to Skt. *a* before *n* or
m—regularly so before the latter when final; occasionally
also before *v*.

Av. *viŋdən* 'they found' = Skt. *ávindan;* Av.
həŋtəm 'being' = Skt. *sántam;* Av. *upəməm* (beside
upaməm) 'highest' = Skt. *upamám;*—GAv. *evistī* 'by
ignorance', cf. Skt. *ávittī;* Av. *mainyəvīm* 'spiritual'
beside Av. *mainyavō;* Av. *səvišta-* 'most mighty, beneficent' (beside *savō*) = Skt. *śáviṣṭha-;* Av. *hvaṇhəvīm*
'blessed life' Ys. 53.1 (acc. from *hvaṇhavya-*).

Note. The MSS. sometimes vary between *ə* and *a :* e. g. Av. *barəŋtō*
beside *barəŋtō* 'carrying'; *jasaŋtu* beside *jasəŋtu* 'let them come'; *vazaŋti*
beside *vazəŋti* 'they drive'; etc.

§ 30. The *ə* (§ 29) arising from *a* before *m* or *n*,
is often palatalized to *i* when either *y, c, j* or *ž*, immediately precedes.

Av. *yim* 'whom' = Skt. *yám;* Av. *vācim* 'voice'
beside *vācəm* = Skt. *vácam;* Av. *drujim* beside *drujəm* 'Deceit, Fiend' = Skt. *drúham;* Av. *būjim* beside *būjəm* 'absolution'; Av. *bajina* 'dishes' = Skt.
bhājana-; Av. *dražimnō* 'holding' beside Av. *dra-
žəmnō*.

§ 31. In GAv., *ə* appears sometimes to be written
(as a kind of dissimilation) for *u* or *i*, when in the following syllable an *u (v)* or *i* stands. The epenthetic vowel
is written beside it, according to rule § 70. Thus is to

be explained GAv. *drəgvaṇt-* 'wicked' (= **drugvaṇt-* to Av. *druj-*); GAv. *bəzvaṇt-* 'advantageous' (= **buzvaṇt-* to Skt. √*bhuj-*); GAv. *uṣəᵘru-* 'zeal' (?) see Ys. 34.7, cf. *uṣuruyē* Ys. 32.16; GAv. *huṣəⁱti-* 'well-being'; GAv. *ṣnəⁱti-* Ys. 30.11; GAv. *āskəⁱti-* Ys. 44.17.

Note. This interchange of *ə* with *u* and *i* may be added as a further suggestion in regard to the intermediate character of Av. ι *ə*, before suggested.

Av. ι *ə̄*.

§ 32.   Av. *ə̄* is the corresponding long vowel to *ə*; it is especially common in GAv.—answering to YAv. *ə*, *a* and sometimes to YAv. *ō*, *ạ*.

GAv. *azə̄m* 'I' = YAv. *azəm*, Skt. *ahám*; GAv. *yə̄m* 'whom' (beside GAv. *yim*) = YAv. *yim*, Skt. *yám*; GAv. *ə̄mavaṇtəm* 'strong' = YAv. *amavaṇtəm*, Skt. *ámavantam*; GAv. *ə̄hmā* 'of us' Ys. 43.10 beside YAv. *ahmā*, cf. Skt. *asmākam*;—GAv. *yə̄* 'who' = YAv. *yō*, Skt. *yás*; GAv. *nə̄* 'us' = YAv. *nō*, Skt. *nas*.—Sometimes, GAv. *starə̄m* 'of stars' = YAv. *strạm*; GAv. *hə̄m* 'with, together' = YAv. *hạm*, Skt. *sám*.—Also GAv. *hvarə̄* 'sun' = YAv. *hvarə*, Skt. *svàr*; GAv. *vadarə̄* 'weapon' = YAv. *vadarə*, Skt. *vádhar*.

Note. On GYAv. *ə̄* in *aməṣ̌ə̄ spəṇtə̄*, and GAv. *ə̄ng* (final), *ə̄ngh* (internal) from original *ans*, see §§ 128, 129.

§ 33.   In YAv., *ə̄* (not common) is used apparently often without fixed rule, perhaps being borrowed from GAv.; it occurs most often for *an*, *ah* before *b*, also for *ā*.

YGAv. *spə̄ništa-* 'holiest'; YGAv. *aməṣ̌ə̄ spəṇtə̄* 'Immortal Holy Ones'; YAv. *yazatə̄* beside *yazata* 'divinities'; YAv. *draomə̄byō* 'from assaults'; YAv. *avə̄biš* 'with helps'; YAv. *raocə̄byō* 'to light'; YAv. *haēnə̄byō* (!) abl. 'from enemies' Yt. 10.93;—as contraction YAv. *frə̄rᵊnaoṭ* (i. e. *fra-ərᵊnaoṭ*) 'he offered'.

Av. 𐬈 *e*.

§ 34. Av. *e* generally answers to Skt. *a, ā,* after *y,* if *i, ī, e, ē* or *y* follows in the next syllable.

YAv. *raocaye*^{i}*ti* 'lights up' = Skt. *rōcáyati;* GAv. *ẖšayehī* 'thou rulest' = Skt. *kṣáyasi;*—YAv. *ayeni,* GAv. *ayenī* 'I shall go' = Skt. *áyāni;*—YAv. *yesne,* GAv. *yesnē* 'in worship' = Skt. *yajñé;*—YAv. *yeŋhå* 'of whom' (f.) = Skt. *yásyās;* GAv. *yehyā* 'of whom' (m.) = Skt. *yásya.*

Note. Observe, however, that *y* does not always thus change *a* to *e:* e. g. *māzdayasniš* 'Mazdayasnian'; *yave* 'for ever'; *yahmi, yahmī, yahmya* 'in which'. Sometimes the MSS. vary.

§ 35. YAv. *e* answers to Skt. *ē* only when final. See §§ 54 α, 25.

YAv. *avaŋhe* 'for help' = Skt. *ávasē;* YAv. *yaza*^{i}*te* 'he worships' = Skt. *yájatē.*

Note 1. On Av. *e* for *ya* in reductions, see § 67.

Note 2. In the MSS. final *e* often interchanges with *i.*

Av. 𐬉 *ē*.

§ 36. Av. *ē,* the corresponding long to *e,* stands:— (1) in the combination Av. *aē* = Skt. *ē;* (2) at the end of monosyllables § 24; (3) everywhere when final in GAv. § 26.

(1) GYAv. *daēva-* 'demon'.—(2) GYAv. *mē* 'me', *hē* 'him'.—(3) GAv. *yaza*^{i}*tē* 'he worships' (opp. to YAv. *yaza*^{i}*te*); GAv. *ārma*^{i}*tē* 'O Armaiti' (opp. to YAv. *sūre* 'O mighty one' fem.).

Note. See Geldner, in *K.Z.* xxvii. p. 259.

Av. 𐬊 *o*.

§ 37. Av. *o* occurs chiefly in the combination Av. *ao* = Skt. *ō,* see § 57.

§ 38. Av. *o* rarely corresponds to Skt. *a* when followed by *u.* Labialization.

Av. *vohu* 'good' = Skt. *vásu*; Av. *mošu* 'quickly'
= Skt. *makšú*; Av. *vohunąm* 'of good things' = Skt.
vásūnām.

Av. ꝛ *ō.*

§ 39. Av. *ō* often corresponds to Skt. *a*, *ā* when
followed by a labial vowel *u*, *ū*, *ō*; rarely before *r* plus
consonant.

Av. *dāmōhu* (beside *dāmahva*) 'among creatures'
= Skt. *dhámasu*; GAv. *gūšōdūm* 'may ye hear', beside GAv. *gūšahvā* 'hear thou'; GAv. *vərᵊzyōtū* 'let him
do', beside Av. *vərᵊzyaṇtō.*—Av. *astō.vīdōtuš* 'Bone-
divider', beside *vīdātaoṭ*= Skt. -*dhātus.*— GAv. *bahšō-
hvā* 'share thou' = Skt. *bhákšasva*; Av. *aojōṅhvaṇtəm*,
beside *aojaṅhvaṇtəm* 'mighty' = Skt. *ójasvantam*; Av.
hšapōhva 'in nights, at night' = Skt. **kšápasu*; so
locatives Av. *yavōhva* 'in granaries' variant *yavahva*;
garᵊmōhva 'jaws', *karᵊšvōhu* 'regions', *ravōhu* 'freedom' (*an*-stems).—GAv. *uzᵊmōhī* 'we may respect',
influence of labial *m.*—YAv. *þwōrᵊštāra* (dual) 'de-
ciders', beside YAv. *þwarštahe*; GAv. *cōrᵊṭ* 'he made'
= Skt. *ákar* (for *ákart*); GAv. *frōrᵊti-*, beside YAv.
frərᵊti- 'forth-coming'.

Note. Observe GAv. *vōtōyōtū* 'let him make known' = Skt. *vātáyatu;*
GAv. *ahtōyōi* 'for sickness' (for -*ayōi*),—the first *ō* being due to the influence of the following *ō.*

§ 40. On Av. *ō* = Skt. *as*, see § 120.

§ 41. On Av. *ō* in compounds, see under Composition.

§ 42. Av. *ō* (final) sometimes answers to Skt. *āu*

Av. *garō* 'on a mountain' = Skt. *girāú;* Av. *dva yaska acištō*
'the two worst sicknesses'.

Av. ꝭ *ǣ.*

Av. *ǣ* = Skt. *ās.*

§ 43. (1) On Av. *ǣ* answering to Skt. *ās*, see § 121 seq.

Av. *ā̊* = Skt. *ā.*

§ 44. (2) Av. *ā̊* also corresponds to Skt. *ā* before *nt.*
Av. *mazā̊ntəm* 'great' = Skt. *mahā́ntam;* Av. *pā̊ntō*
'guarding', pres. ptcpl. nom. pl. = Skt. *pā́ntas.*

Note. Similarly, Av. *vīrō.nyā̊ncim* 'striking men down' = Skt. *nyàñcam.*

Av. *ą̇ ą.*

§ 45. (1) Av. *ą* presents a nasalization of *a, ā* before
Av. *m* or *n.*

Av. *hąm* 'with, together' = Skt. *sám;* Av. *mąm*
'me' = Skt. *mā́m;*—Av. *ayąn* 'they may go' = Skt.
áyan; Av. *daēvąn* 'demons' = Skt. *dēvā́n;* Av. *ᵘrvąnō*
'souls' beside Av. *ᵘrvānəm* (acc. sg.).

Note 1. In the MSS., *ā* often stands as variant beside *ą:* e. g. Av. *dąmi, dāmi* 'creature', et al.

Note 2. D e f e c t i v e   w r i t i n g :— instances often occur in endings where the final nasal after *ą* is omitted:—e. g. *imą haomą* 'these haoma-offerings' = Skt. *imā́n sómān;* Av. *yą* 'quos' = Skt. *yā́n.*

Note 3. P l e o n a s t i c   w r i t i n g :—a pleonastic *n* is sometimes intro-duced after *ą* before *m:* e. g. *dąnmahi* 'we shall give' Ys. 68.1 (variant) cf. Skt. *dā́ma;* Av. *hvąnmahī* variant *hvąmahī* 'we put foward'; Av. *fryąnmahi* variant *fryąmahī* 'we bless'.

§ 46. (2) Av. *ą* is often a union of *a (ā)* w i t h nasal be-fore Av. sibilants (cf. Skt. anusvāra); also before Av. spirants.
Av. *apąš* 'backward' = Skt. *ápāv;* Av. *hąs* 'being'
(haṇt-) = Skt. *sán;* GAv. *mąstā* 'he thought' = Skt.
ámąsta; Av. *ąsayā̊* 'of two parties' = Skt. *ąsayōs;*
Av. *ązō* 'distress' = Skt. *ąhas;* Av. *bązaⁱti* 'he sup-ports' = Skt. *bąhaté.*—Av. *mąþrəm* 'word, spell' =
Skt. *mántram;* Av. *·dąþrəm* 'tooth'; Av. *ąḫnā̊* 'reins'.

Original *r* (*r*-sonant).
Av. *ərə, (arə)* = Skt. *r̥.*

§ 47. The Skt. *r̥* is represented in Av. by *ərə* or
often *arə.*

Av. *kerᵊnaoⁱti* 'he makes' = Skt. *kṛṇóti*; Av. *marᵊ-*
ḃyuš 'death' = Skt. *mṛtyús*; Av. *hakᵊrᵊṭ* 'at once' =
Skt. *sakṛt*.— Av. *anarᵊtāiš* 'with the untrue' = Skt.
ánṛtāis; Av. *varᵊšᵊm* 'wood' = Skt. *vṛkṣám*; Av.
arštiš 'spear' = Skt. *ṛṣṭis*.

Note. The MSS. vary, often writing *arᵊ* for *ᵊrᵊ*. The new edition
of the Avesta has restored many instances of *ᵊrᵊ*: e. g. *frastᵊrᵊta-* (where
Westergaard *frastarᵊta-*).

§ 48. Av. *ar, ᵊr* (also *arᵊ, ᵊrᵊ, aⁱr, aᵘr*) often = (orig. *ṛ*)
Skt. *ir, ur*;—sometimes = (orig. *ṝ*) Skt. *īr, ūr*. See Brugmann, *Grundriss der vergl. Gram.* I. § 288 seq., 306 seq.

Av. *zaranyehe* 'of golden' = Skt. *híraṇyasya*; Av.
gaⁱriš 'mountain' = Skt. *giris*; Av. *ǣṅharᵊ*, (GAv.
ǣṅharᵊ) 'they have been' = Skt. *āsúr*; Av. *taᵘrva-*
yeⁱti 'he overcomes' = Skt. √*turv-, tūrv-*; Av. *darᵊ-*
jᵊm 'long' = Skt. *dīrghám*. — So sometimes Av. *ᵊrᵊ, ra*
= Skt. *ra, ṛ*:—Av. *ᵊrᵊzatᵊm* 'silver' = Skt. *rajatám*;
Av. *ratu-* 'chief, point of time', cf. Skt. *ṛtú-*.

§ 49. Av. *ᵊrq* may represent original *ṛ + n*.

GAv. *nᵊrq̃š* (acc. pl.) 'men', cf. *nṛ́š cyāutnṓ* RigVeda 10.50.4;
GAv. *mātᵊrq̃šcā* (acc. pl.) 'mothers', cf. Skt. *mātṝn* RV. 10.35.2.

Concurrence of vowels.
Contraction and Resolution.

§ 50. **General Remark.** In Avesta, the rule for the
union of two vowels within a word or in composition, corresponds in general to the Sanskrit. (1) Two similar vowels
coalesce into their corresponding long (sometimes short).
(2) Two dissimilar vowels, when the first is *a* unite in
giving guṇa § 60. (3) Before dissimilar vowels, the
i- or *u*-vowel (simple or in diphthongs), passes over into
the corresponding semi-vowel. (4) In Avesta compounds,
however, hiatus is often allowed to remain.

§ 51. The following are instances of c o n t r a c t i o n
of similar vowels.

Av. *a, ā + a, ā = ā:* Av. *parōzɔŋti* 'they drive away' = *para + aẕ•;*
i, ī + i, ī = ī: Av. *nīre* 'I let go down' = *ni + īre;*
u, ū + u, ū = ū: Av. *hūḥtāiš* 'by good words' *(hu + u•)* = Skt. *sūktāis.*
a + q = q: Av. *nɔmyqsuš* 'with pliant branches' = *nɔmya qsuš* § 46.

Note 1. Instead of the long vowel in contractions, the short vowel
is often written: e. g. Av. *frapayemi* 'I shall attain to' *(= fra + ap•);*
Av. *paᵢtiᵢɔm* 'atoned' *(= paᵢti + i•);* Av. *anuḥtᵢe* 'speak after' *(= anu
+ uḥti-).*

Note 2. Hiatus sometimes remains in compounds: Av. *ava-aᵢnaoᵢti*
'he attains'; GAv. *ciprā-avavhɔm* Ys. 34.4, beside YAv. *cipravavhqm* Ny. 3.10
'manifestly aiding'; Av. *ḥᵢviwi-iᵢuš* 'having darting arrows'.

Note 3. Metrically, contractions of like vowels are often to be resolved in reading. See Geldner, *Metrik*, p. 13 seq.

§ 52. Av. *i*- and *u*-vowels, simple or in diphthongs,
before dissimilar vowels, pass over into *y* or *v.*

(a) Av. *vyānō* 'pursued' *(√vī-)* = Skt. *vyānás;* Av. *ḥᵢayehi* 'thou
rulest' *(√ḥᵢi-);* Av. *vīdōyūm* 'anti-demoniac' *(daēva-*, on *ōi = aē* § 56);
nᵢityaojanō 'thus speaking' beside *uᵢti aɔjanō; paᵢtyūpɔm* 'up stream'
(paᵢti + ūp•); *nmānaya* (loc. *•aē + á* postpos.) 'in a house' beside
nmānē. — (b) *tanvō* 'of body' *(tanu-as);* *hāvana* 'haoma-mortars'
(√hu); *hvaspɔm* 'well-horsed' *(hu + aspɔm);* *anaɣraēᵢva* 'among
the infinite' (loc. *-ᵢu + a).* — (c) With lengthening after the semivowel: Av. *aᵢwyāmanqm* 'of the over-mighty' *(aᵢwi + am•);* *aᵢwyā-
vavha* 'with protection' *(avavh-);* *aᵢpyūḥda* 'interrupted in speaking
mispronounced' *(uḥda-).*

Note 1. In compounds the hiatus often remains: e. g. Av. *tiẕi-arštīm*
'sharp-speared'; Av. *āsu-aspɔm* 'swift horsed' = Skt. *āśvàśvam.*

Note 2. Metrically, the resulting semi-vowel *y, v* is often to be restored as vowel or read *iy, uv.*

Diphthongs.

§ 53. **General Remark.** The Avesta vowel-combinations
(diphthongs with triphthongs) are of four-fold origin, and
may conveniently be divided and designated as follows:

i. P r o p e r diphthongs, corresponding to Sanskrit *guṇa*
(more rarely *vṛddhi*) in its two-fold sense: (1) vowel-

strengthening, (2) the result of contraction of two dissimilar vowels. See § 60 seq.

ii. Reduction-diphthongs, resulting from reduction by contraction of two syllables. See § 64 seq. Metrically often dissyllabic.

iii. Improper diphthongs (and triphthongs) arising from epenthesis. See § 70 seq.

iv. Protraction-diphthong *āa*, a peculiar extension of *a* or *ā* into *āa* in ablative singular before *-ca* 'que'; likewise in *āaṱ* 'then' (abl. as adv.), GAv. *bāaṱ* 'verily' Ys. 35.5. Cf. Av. *daēvāaṱca* 'and from the Demon' (*daēva-*); *apāaṱca* beside *apaṱ* 'from water', etc.

Proper Diphthongs.

Av. ꬐, ꭗ — ꭗ, ꭗ — ꭗ, ꭗ

aē, ōi — ao, ȝu — āi, āu.

§ 54. The above are real diphthongs when they correspond to the Skt. diphthongs. The relation between the Av. and the Skt. diphthongs is concisely this:

α. Skt. *ē* is represented in Av.

(1) chiefly by *aē*, (2) less often by *ōi*, (3) again by *ē*, only when final, but there regularly.

β. Skt. *ō* is represented in Av.

(1) chiefly by *ao*, (2) more rarely by *ȝu*, (3) again by *ō*, only when final, but there regularly.

γ. Skt. *āi* and *āu* are represented in Av. by *āi* and *āu*.

Note. In some instances Skt. *āu* (final) seems to be represented in Av. by *ō*, § 42.

Av. *aē* = Skt. *ē*.

§ 55. The diphthong Av. *aē* (very common) answers to Skt. *ē* (old *ai*), initial or internal; likewise as ending in first member of a compound, or again before enclitic *-ca* 'que'

Av. *aētaṭ* 'this' = Skt. *ētát;* GAv. *vaēdā,* YAv. *vaēda* 'knows' = Skt. *vêda.* — Av. *fraēšyeⁱti* 'he drives forth' *(fra + iš-)* = Skt. *prêsyati.* — Av. *dūraēdars* 'far-seeing' (loc. *dūⁱrē)* = Skt. *dūrē.dŕś-;* Av. *rapaēštā-rəm* 'warrior in chariot' = Skt. *rathēṣṭhā́m* (loc. *ráthē).*

Note 1. Observe that in gen. *ašaheca* 'and of righteousness', the *e* is reduction-vowel (= *ya*), therefore of course no *aē* appears.

Note 2. On reduction-diphthong *aē,* see § 64.

Av. *ōi* = Skt. *ē.*

§ 56. Av. *ōi,* as real diphthong, also answers to Skt. *ē* (old *ai).* It interchanges often with Av. *aē,* being of like etymological value; but *ōi* occurs perhaps oftenest in monosyllables and in declensional endings generally. It is especially frequent in GAv.

GAv. *vōistā* 'thou knowest' = Skt. *vêttha;* YAv. *sōire* 'they lie' = Skt. *śêrē;* Av. *ẖšōiṗni* (fem.) 'shining, princely', beside Av. *ẖšaētō* (masc.); Av. *maⁱdyōi.paⁱti-štāna-* 'to middle (loc.) of foot', beside Av. *dūraē.srūta-* 'far (loc.) renowned'. — GYAv. *yōi* 'who' (beside *yaē-ca)* = Skt. *yê;* GYAv. *kōi* 'who' (interrog.) = Skt. *kê.* — YAv. *ažōiš* 'of Dragon' = Skt. *áhēs;* GAv. *būrōiš* 'of richness' = Skt. *bhū́rēs;* GYAv. *barōiṭ* 'he might carry' = Skt. *bháret;* Av. *paⁱri.vaēnōiṗe* 'they two are seen' = Skt. *vênēthē.* — GAv. *gavōi* 'for the cow', YAv. *gave* = Skt. *gávē;* GAv. *zastōibyā* 'with both hands' = YAv. *zastaēⁱbya;* GAv. *ẖšaṗrōi* 'in the kingdom', YAv. *ẖšaṗre* = Skt. *kṣatrê.*

Av. *ao* = Skt. *ō.*

§ 57. Av. *ao* as real diphthong answers to Skt. *ō* (old *au),* initial and internal.

Av. *aojō* 'strength' = Skt. *ójas;* Av. *raodənti* 'they grow' = Skt. *róhanti;* Av. *tāyaoš* 'of a thief' = Skt.

2

tāyós. — Av. *fraohtō* 'pronounced' *(fra + u̯)* = Skt. *prōktás.*

Note. On reduction-diphthong *ao,* see § 64.

Av. *ə̄u* = Skt. *ō.*

§ 58. The diphthong Av. *ə̄u* (as strengthening of *u*), also sometimes answers to Skt. *ō,* internal. It occurs in the genitive of *u*-stems, and in a very few words. Observe the pair *ə̄u* and *ao* as *ōi* and *aē.*

Av. *ḥratə̄uš* 'of wisdom' = Skt. *krátōs;* Av. *vaṇhə̄uš* 'of the good' = Skt. *vásōs;* Av. *ma͡inyə̄uš* 'of spirit' = Skt. *manyós.*—Also in *də̄uš.sravā̊* 'things of ill-repute', cf. *haosravaṇha; də̄uš.manahya-* 'evil-minded', cf. *haomanaṇha-;* GAv. *gə̄ušāiš* 'with ears' = Skt. *ghóṣāis.*

Av. *āi* = Skt. *āi;*—Av. *āu* = Skt. *āu.*

§ 59. Av. *āi, āu* when they are r e a l diphthongs (i. e. not epenthetic or reduction) correspond to Skt. *āi, āu.*

Av. *mąprāiš* 'with words' = Skt. *mántrāis;* Av. *gāuš* (nom.) 'cow' = Skt. *gáus.*

i. Vowel-Strengthening — *a*-Vowel Contraction.

§ 60. **Guṇa and Vṛddhi.** The terms *guṇa* and *vṛddhi* are conveniently borrowed from the Sanskrit Grammar for the Avesta. In Avesta, as in Sanskrit, guṇa- and vṛddhi-vowels in the fullest sense have a d o u b l e origin: (1) vowel-strengthening in vowel-gradation;[1] (2) c o n t r a c t i o n of t w o d i s s i m i l a r vowels whether in composition or in inflection.

---

[1] Brugmann, *Grundriss der vergl. Gram.* § 307 seq.

Guṇa in Avesta, owing to the greater richness in the vowel system, has a greater variety than in Sanskrit.— The vṛddhi-increment, however, is comparatively rare, and is not so regularly carried out as in Sanskrit; nor are the instances always certain (cf. § 18 Note 1); but vṛddhi is not to be denied to the Avesta.

Synopsis of Guṇa and Vṛddhi modelled after the Sanskrit.

	Avesta.		
Simple Vowel . *a, ā*	*i, ī*	*u, ū*	*ər*
Guṇa . . . . . . —	*aē (ay), ōi (öy), -ē*	*ao (av), ău, -ŏ*	*arə (ar)*
Vṛddhi . . . . : *ā*	*āi (āy)*	*āu (āv)*	*ārə (ār)*

(The forms in parentheses appear before vowels. On the interchange of *aē, ōi*, see § 56).

Strengthening: *a*-vowel.

Vṛddhi: Av. *āhurōiš* 'of the Ahurian' *(ahura-)* cf. Skt. *ásurēs*; GAv. *vācī, avācī* 'is spoken' (aor. pass.) = Skt. *ávāci*; Av. *dāhyumā̃* (var. *dāhyumā̃*) 'belonging to the region' *(dahyu-)*; Av. *hācayene* 'I may cause to follow' *(√hac-)*; Av. *tācayeⁱṇti* 'they cause to run' *(√tac-)*; Av. *rāmayeⁱti* 'he makes content' = Skt. *rāmáyati*.—Cf. also the patronymics in Yt. 13.97 seq.

Strengthening: *i*-vowel.

Guṇa:—Av. *daēsayən* 'they showed' *(√dis-)*, *daēdōišt* 'he showed' (intens. *√dis-*); *saēte* 'he lies down', *sōire* 'they lie down'*(√sī-)*; *ḫšayehe*'thou rulest'*(√ḫši-)*; *vīdōyūm* 'anti-demoniac' (acc. fr. *vīdaēva-*, fr. *√div-*). —Vṛddhi:—Av. *dāiš* 'thou sawest' (aor. *√dī-*); *staomāyō* 'praises' (fr. *staomi-*); *þrāyō* 'three' (fr. *þri-*, but cf. § 18 Note 1), *nāismī* Ys. 12.1.

Contraction:

Av. *upaēta-* 'approached' *(upa + √i-)*; YAv. *ḫšaþre*, GAv. *ḫšaþrōi* 'in the kingdom' *(ḫšaþra-)*; Av. *upōisayən* 'they might seek' *(upa+√is-)*;—*upāiti* 'he approaches'

Strengthening: *u*-voweL

Guṇa: — Av. *haomɔm* 'haoma' (√*hu-*); *zaotārɔm* title of priest, cf. Skt. Hotar (√*zu-*); *staomi* 'I praise', *stavanō* 'praising' (√*stu-*); *vavhave, vavhɔuš* 'for, of the good' *(vavhu-)*; *daiɳhavō* 'countries' *(daiɳhu-)*; *dɔuš.sravɔ̄* 'having evil repute' *(duš).*—Vṛddhi:—Av. *srāvayōiš* 'shouldst recite' (√*sru-*); GAv. *srāvī* 'he was heard' (√*sru-*); *vavhāu* 'in good' *(vavhu-)*; *daiɳhāvō* 'countries' *(daiɳhu-)*; *ujra.bāzāuš* 'strong-armed' *(bāzu-)*; *fraṣāupayeiti* 'he propels' Yt. 8.33.

Contraction:

Av. *fraohtō* 'pronounced' *(fra + uhta-)* = Skt. *prōktás*; so also Av. *vaocat* (redupl. aor.) 'he spoke' = Skt. *vôcat*, cf. Av. *vaokuṣe* = Skt. *ūcuṣe* pf. act. ptcpl. √*vak/c*, weak form *uk/c*.

Strengthening: *r*-voweL

From Av. *vɔrɔþrajna-* 'victory', *vārɔþrajni-* 'victorious'; so Av. *kɔrɔnɔm* 'I cut', *karɔtɔm* 'knife' (acc.), *karanɔm* 'limit, dividing line' (acc.), *kārayeiti* 'he cuts'. But see § 47 Note.

Note. (a) The Avesta sometimes has guṇa where the Skt. has a long vowel: Av. *staorɔm* 'bullock' = Skt. *sthūrám*; Av. *gaozaiti* 'he hides' = Skt. *gūhati.*—(b) Conversely, the Av. sometimes has a long vowel where the Skt. shows guṇa: Av. *yūhtar-* 'yoker' = Skt. *yōktár-*; GAv. *ʷrūpayeiɳti* 'they cause pain' = Skt. *rōpáyanti*; GAv. *ʷrūdōyatā* 'he made lament' = Skt. *rōdáyata.*—(c) The Av. has sporadically guṇa where the Skt. has vṛddhi: Av. *haomanavhɔm* 'well-minded' = Skt. *sáumanasám*; Av. *ɟyaoþna-* 'deed' = Skt. *cyáutná-*; Av. *haēnyō* 'belonging to the army' = Skt. *sáinyás.*—(d) Sporadically, Av. vṛddhi, where Skt. guṇa: Av. *gāvya-nqm* beside *gaoya-* 'belonging to the cow' (§ 18) = Skt. *gavyá-.*—(e) Observe Av. *dɔuš.sravah-* 'ill-famed'; *dɔuš.manahya-* 'evil-minded' opp. to Skt. *duḥṣqsa.*

ii. Changes in *y*- or *v*-Syllables.

§ 61. **General Remark.** The syllables containing internal *ɯ y* and *ɯ v* often suffer reduction and abbreviation. This is partly old and due to the vowel character of *y (i)* and *v (u)*; in part it is young and is to be explained from the character of the writing—the close graphic resemblance of · *i* to ·· *y (ii)* and ι *u* to ıı *v (uu)* often producing awkward accumulations of signs which are avoided.

(a) Vocalization of *y* and *v*.

§ 62. In the combinations original internal *vy, vn, vr, yv*, the first element is g e n e r a l l y v o c a l i z e d to *u, i*. When *a* immediately precedes this *u*, the two are contracted according to § 60 into *aô*. For *ao* an *āu* is frequently found in GAv.

(1) Orig. *vy* = Av. *uy;—yv* = Av. *iv*.

Av. *vaŋhuyā̊* 'of the good' (fem.) = Skt. *vásvyās;* GAv. *poᵘruyō* 'first' = Skt. *pūrvyás;* Av. *maršuyā̊* 'of the belly' (stem *maršvī̆-*); Av. *snáuya-* 'made of sinew', cf. Skt. *snávan-.* — Av. *maᵢnivā̊* 'of the two Spirits' (for *maᵢnyvā̊* § 68, b).

(2) Orig. *avy* = Av. *aoi;—avn* = Av. *aon (āun);—*
        avr = Av. *aor*.

Av. *haoyąm* 'the left' = Skt. *savyám;* Av. *gaoyaoᵢ-tīš* 'cow-pastures' = Skt. *gávyūtīs.—*Av. *vaonarᵉ* 'they have won', cf. Skt. *vavné;* Av. *raonąm* 'of valleys' *(ravan-);* Av. *ašaonō* 'of the righteous' *(ašavan-),* cf. Skt. *maghónas.*—GAv. *vāunuš* 'having striven', ptcpl. pf. √*van-;* GAv. *ašāunē* 'to the righteous' = Skt. *r̥távnē* (cf. Note 1); Av. *apaᵘrun-* wk. stem of *āpravan-* 'priest' = Skt. *átharvan-.—*Av. *fraoᵢrisaᵢti* 'he comes forward' (for orig. *fra-vris-aᵢti*), cf. *fraoᵘrvaēsayeni;* Av. *fraorᵉnta* 'they confessed', cf. Skt. *ávr̥ṇīta;* Av. *fraorᵉt* (i. e. **pravr̥t*) 'prone, ready'.

Note 1. Often in YAv., *aȷ̄aun-* is found in the formulaic connection *aȷ̄aunąm frava∫ayō*. The original difference is to be explained thus: *āu* = orig. *āv*, and *ao* = orig. *av;* cf. Av. *aȷ̄āvan* = Skt. *ŗtāvan-*.

Note 2. In YAv., *paoiryō* is written for GAv. *pouruyō* 'first' above.

Note 3. A like vocalization of Av. *v* = Av. *w* (orig. *bh*) § 87 may take place:—e. g. Av. *vōiȷnāuyō* (for •*nāvyō*, •*wyō*, •*byō*) 'from plagues'; Av. *adaoyō* (for *adawyō*) 'undeceived' = Skt. *ádābhyas;* Av. *nuruyō aȷ̄avaoyō* (for •*vyō*, •*wyō*, •*byō*) 'to righteous men' Yt. 10.55; Av. *rasmaoyō* (for •*vyō*, •*wyō*, •*byō*) 'to the ranks'. Perhaps Av. *aoi*, beside *avi* (for Av. *aiwi*) = Skt. *abhí*.

(b) Reduction and Abbreviation.

α. Reductions.

§ 63. The syllables *ya* and *va* before *m* or *n*, especially when final, are generally r e d u c e d to *i (ī)*, or *u (ū)* respectively—a kind of samprasāraṇa.

Old *ya* = Av. *i (ī); va* = Av. *u (ū)*—before *m, n.*

Av. *zaranim* 'golden' (acc.) = Skt. *híraṇ-ya-m;* Av. *uḫšin* 'they increased' (for **uḫš-ya-n*); Av. *mainimna* 'thinking' (fem.) = Skt. *mán-ya-mānā;* Av. *paipimnō* 'possessing' = Skt. *pát-ya-mānas;* Av. *iriþiṇti* 'they die' (for *iriþ-ya-ṇti*).—GAv. *asrūždūm* 'ye were heard of' Ys. 32.3 = Skt. *áśrōḍh-va-m;* Av. *daēūm* 'demon' = Skt. *dē-vá-m;* Av. *þrišum* 'third' (for *þriš-va-m*); Av. *mourum* 'Merv' (for **mar-va-m*);— Av. *təmavhuṇtəm* 'dark' = Skt. *támasvant-;* Av. *hvarʾnavhuṇtəm* 'glorious' beside *hvarʾnavuhaṇtʳ* for *hvarʾnavh-va-ṇtəm*.

Note 1. In the acc. sg. of *-va-*stems, *ŭm* instead of *ūm* is mostly written.

Note 2. Av. *-aȷ̄va-* commonly becomes *-ōyu-* before *m* (cf. §§ 60, 52 a): Av. *vidōyūm* 'anti-demoniac' acc. to *vīdaȷ̄va-* (but also Av. *daȷ̄ūm*); Av. *harō-yŭm* 'Haraeva', cf. Anc. Pers. *haraiva-;* Av. *hōyŭm* 'scaevum', if stem *haȷ̄va-*.

Note 3. Instead of *i* (= *ya*), an *ȷ* appears in Av. *madȷma-* 'midmost' = Skt. *madh-ya-má-*.

§ 64. On the same principle as § 63, the syllables *aya* and *ava*, r e d u c e d before *m* or *n*, give rise to diphthongs, *aē* and *ao* (*āu* §§ 62, 195).

Old *aya* = Av. *aē; ava* = Av. *ao* (also *āu* § 195)—
before *m, n*.

Av. *aēm* 'this' (nom.) = Skt. *ayám;* Av. *vīdāraēm*
'I upheld' = Skt. *-dhārayam;* Av. *cikaēn* 'they atoned'
(i. e. **cikayan*) cf. Av. *cikayaṭ.*—Av. *yaom* 'grain' =
Skt. *yávam;* Av. *maⁱnyaom* 'spiritual', acc. to *maⁱ-
nyava-;* Av. *mraom* 'I spake' = Skt. *ábravam.*—Av.
nāumō also *naomō* 'ninth' = Skt. *navamás;* Av. *kər²-
nāun* (var. *kər²naon*) 'they made' = Skt. *kṛṇávan;* Av.
bāun also *baon* 'they were' = Skt. *ábhavan.*

Note. Similarly, Av. *raēⁱ-ca* Ys. 68.11 cf. instr. *raya* 'splendor'.

§ 65. The syllables internal *āya, āva* likewise reduced
§ 64, give rise to the diphthongs *āi, āu*.

Orig. *āya, āva* = Av. *āi, āu*—before *m, n*.

Av. *dasa.gāim* 'space of ten steps' = Skt. *ᵒgāyam;*
Av. *avāin* 'they came down' = Skt. *aváyan;* Av. *nasāum*
'corpse' (i. e. *nasāvam*).

Note. Metrically the reduced syllables *aēm, aom, āum, aēn, āin*
(§§ 63, 64) are dissyllabic.

§ 66. Final *aye* is reduced to Av. *ᵒe*,—metrically
dissyllabic.

Av. *apa.gatᵒe* 'for going away' = Skt. *gátayē;*
Av. *paⁱtištātᵒe* (beside *paⁱtištātayaē-ca*) 'to withstand'
= Skt. *sthítayē;* Av. *ārmatᵒe* 'to Piety'; Av. *zaṇtu.patᵒe*
'for the lord of a town'.

§ 67. Final *ya* in polysyllables appears in YAv. as *e*
(GAv. shows *yā*).

YAv. *kahe* 'of which' (GAv. *kahyā*) = Skt. *kásya;*
YAv. *gayehe* 'of life' (GAv. *gayehyā*) = Skt. *gáyasya;*
YAv. *aṣahe* 'of Righteousness' (GAv. *aṣahyā*) = Skt.
ṛtásya; YAv. *aⁱre* (for *uⁱrya*, nom. pl.) 'the Aryans';
YAv. *fravrase* (for *ᵒsya*, nom. sg.) 'Franrasyan' cf.
acc. *ᵒsyānəm;* YAv. *maⁱre* (for *ᵒrya*, nom. sg. fem.)

'deadly', cf. gen. *maⁱryayā̊*; YAv. *bāzuwe* 'with both
arms' (§ 85 a, end), beside YAv. *bāzubya*.

Note. Isolated is i n t e r n a l *e (= ya)* in *vahehiŝ* 'better' (fem. pl.)
cf. § 137 = Skt. *vásyasīs.*

β. Abbreviated Writing.

Av. ᴖ *y (i̯) = iy;* ᴖ *v (u̯) = uv.*

§ 68. To avoid awkward combinations of letters, the
original syllables *iy* (graphically Av. ᴖᴖ *iii*) and *uv* (graph.
Av. ᴖᴖ *uuu*) are respectively abbreviated in writing ᴖ *y*
(graph. *ii*) and ᴖ *v* (graph. *uu*). See § 61. Metrically, to
such *y* or *v* the syllabic value *iy* or *uv* is generally to
be restored.

(a) Av. ᴖ for ᴖᴖ.

(1) In composition:—Av. *paⁱtyaṇtu* 'let them come
to' = Skt. *prátiyantu;* Av. *þryaḥštīš* 'three twigs'
(for *þri-yaḥštīš*) cf. *paṇca-yaḥštīš.*—(2) Internal:—Av.
fryō 'friend' (graphically *friiō* for *friiiō*) = Skt. *priyás;*
Av. *yasnyō* 'worshipful' = Skt. *yajñiyas.*—(3) Initial:
—Av. *yeyą̇n* (written *iieiiąn* for orig. **iyáyān*); GAv.
yadacā 'and here' Ys. 35.2 (written *iiadā* for Av. *iiiadā*).

(b) Av. ᴖ for ᴖᴖ.

(1) In composition:—Av. *hvacaṇhəm* 'having good
words' = Skt. *suvácasam;* Av. *hvidātā̊* 'well-built
(houses)' Yt. 17.8 (i. e. *hu-vidāta-* cf. Ys. 57.21); Av.
vohvarᵊz- 'doing good' (i. e. *vohu + v°*).—(2) Internal:
—Av. *yvānəm* 'juvenem' = Skt. *yúvānam;* Av. *drvahe*
'firm' (gen.) = Skt. *dhruvásya;*—Av. *hva-* 'suus' (metrically *huva-*) cf. Skt. *svà-.* See Geldner, *Metrik*, p. 20 seq.

Note 1. Similarly when *v* (ᴖ) stands for *w (= bh)* § 87: Av. ᴖᴖᴖ
uuaēibya for *uuuaēibya* for *uwaēibya* cf. GAv. *ubōibyā* 'with both' = Skt.
ubhốbhyām.

Note 2. Instances of Av. *v* (ᴖ) equal Skt. *īv, iv* may be found: Av.
jvaṇti 'they live' = Skt. *jīvanti;* Av. *cvaṭ* 'quantum' = Skt. *kīvat;* Av. *vīdidvå*

'looking around' ($\sqrt{di}$) = Skt. *dīdivān;* perhaps Av. *jajnva* 'having smitten' cf. Skt. *jaghnivān.*

Note 3. Internal *ay, av* are sometimes found written as an e x t e n - s i o n of *y, v* (i. e. *iy, uv*): Av. *nāvaya-* 'navigable, flowing' = Skt. *nāvyà;* Av. *aspaya-* (cf. acc. *aspaêm* § 64) 'belonging to a horse' = Skt. *āśvya-;* Av. *hava-* (cf. gen. f. *haoya*) 'suus' = Skt. *svà-;* Av. *kava* variant for *kva* 'where' = Skt. *kvà.*

iii. Epenthesis, Prothesis, and Anaptyxis.

Cf. Brugmann, *Grundriss der vergl. Grammatik* § 637 seq.; § 623 seq.

§ 69. Two of these viz. Epenthesis, Prothesis (and certain cases of Anaptyxis like *surunvata*)—may be considered fundamentally the same, as each consists in the introduction of an anticipatory parasitic sound. For convenience, however, in the following, Epenthesis and Prothesis will be distinguished thus: (1) Epenthesis—an anticipatory vowel attached i n t e r - n a l l y to a vowel; (2) Prothesis—an anticipatory vowel attached i n i t i a l l y before a consonant.

§ 70. **Epenthesis** is one of the characteristic sound-phenomena of the Avesta. It consists in the insertion of a light a n t i c i p a t o r y *i* or *u*, when in the following syl-lable respectively an *i, ī, e, ē, y,* or an *u, v* stands.—Epen-thesis of *i* takes place before *r, n, ṇt, t, þ, þr, d, p, b, w,* also before *ṇh* (= orig. *sy*).—Epenthesis of *u* takes place only before *r*.

Note. The epenthetic vowel attaches itself parasitically to diphthongs as well as to the simple vowels including *a*-privative. In the MSS., the law of epenthesis is not always consistently carried out; many times it is omitted: e. g. *manyus̄* beside *mainyus̄* 'of the Spirit'.

Epenthetic i.

Av. *bavaiti* 'he becomes' = Skt. *bhávati;* Av. *aēiti* (GAv. *aēitī*) 'he goes' = Skt. *éti;* Av. *inaoiti* 'he forces, drives' = Skt. *inóti;* Av. *aipi* 'unto, in' = Skt. *ápi;* Av. *barainti* 'they carry' = Skt. *bháranti;* Av. *ainikəm* 'face' = Skt. *ánīkam;* Av. *būiri* 'fullness' = Skt. *bhúri;* Av. *airištəm* 'unhurt' = Skt. *áriṣṭam.* —GAv.

rāᵢtī 'with offering' = Skt. *rātī;* GAv. *aᵢbī* (YAv. *aᵢwi*)
'unto, to' = Skt. *abhí;* YAv. *maᵢdīm* 'middle' (acc. sg.)
= Skt. *mádhyam;*—Av. *baᵢryeᵢṇte* 'they are brought' =
Skt. *bhriyantē;* Av. *nivōᵢryeᵢte* 'is confined' (√*var-*);
Av. *niᵘruᵢdyāṭ* 'should flow' (√*rud-*). — Av. *aᵢryō*
'Aryan' = Skt. *aryás;* Av. *naᵢryąm* 'manly' (acc. fem.)
= Skt. *náryām;* Av. *maᵢnyuš* 'Spirit' = Skt. *manyús.*—
With vanishing of the *y* which caused the epenthesis,
*aᵢŋhā * gen. sg. fem. of *aēm* 'this' = Skt. *ásyās.*

Epenthetic u.

Av. *aᵘrvaṇtō* 'swift steeds' = Skt. *árvantas;* Av.
aᵘruna- 'wild, fiery', cf. Skt. *aruṇá-;* Av. *aᵘrušō* 'bright,
white' = Skt. *arušás;* Av. *paᵘrvata* 'two mountains' =
Skt. *párvatāu;* Av. *taᵘrunəm* 'young' = Skt. *táruṇam;*
Av. *haᵘrvąm* 'whole' = Skt. *sárvām;* Av. *poᵘru-* (also
paoᵘru-) 'many', for *paru-.*

Note 1. Epenthetic *i* is even attached to the anaptyctic vowel (§ 72):
Av. *hąm.varᵊitīm* 'courage' Vsp. 7.3; GAv. *mᵊrᵊ ŋgᵊidyāi* 'to destroy' Ys. 46.11;
fraorᵊitīm 'confession' Ys. 13.8.

Note 2. Epenthetic *u* is found also before *v* for *w* (§ 87): *gᵊⁿrva-
yeite* 'he seizes' (√*garw-* = Skt. √*grabh-*).

§ 71. **Prothesis.** As intermediate between Epenthesis
and Anaptyxis, we may distinguish Prothesis, which consists in the similar introduction of an anticipatory *i* or *u*
initially before a consonant. It takes place regularly
before *r* followed by *i* or *u (v)*. An instance is found
also before *þ*.

Av. *ⁱrinaḥti* 'he lets go, drives' = Skt. *riṇákti;*
Av. *ⁱrišyeⁱti* 'is hurt' = Skt. *rišyati;* GAv. *ᵘrūpayeⁱṇtī*
'they cause pain' = Skt. *rōpáyanti;* Av. *ᵘrune* 'for the
soul', *ᵘrvan-* 'soul' (i. e. for *ruvan* § 68 = Mod. Pers.
ruvān).—Before *þ*, Av. *ⁱþyejō* 'destruction' = Skt. *tyájas.*

§ 72. **Anaptyxis.** An irrational vowel (Anaptyxis),
which does not count in the metre, is often developed

in Avesta b e t w e e n two consonants, especially if one be
r, and r e g u l a r l y a f t e r final *r.* The anaptyctic vowel is
generally *ə (ᵈ),* more rarely *a, i* or *ō.* In GAv., anaptyxis
is still more common than in YAv.

Av. *vaḥᵊdra-* 'word' = Skt. *vaktrá-* Av. *nafᵊdraṭ*
'offspring' (abl. from *naptar-*); Av. *zᵊmō* 'of earth';
GAv. *dadᵊmahī* 'we give' = Skt. *dadmási;* Av. *ga-*
rᵊmō 'hot' = Skt. *gharmás;* GAv. *fᵊrā* 'forth', YAv.
frā § 24 = Skt. *prá;* GAv. *aēšᵊmō* 'Fury' = YAv. *aēšmō;*
GAv. *raēḥᵊnavhō* 'of share' = Skt. *rékṇasas.*— GAv.
dᵊbāvayaṭ 'he deceived'.—YAv. *aṇtarᵊ* 'within', GAv.
aṇtarᵊ = Skt. *antár;* YAv. *hvarᵊ* 'sun', GAv. *hvarᵊ*
= Skt. *svàr.*—GAv. *šyaopᵊna-* 'deed', YAv. *šyaopna-*
= Skt. *cyāutnà-;* GAv. *marᵃka-* 'death', YAv. *mahrka-*
= Skt. *markà-.*—GAv. *yezⁱvī* 'young' = Skt. *yahvī́;*
YAv. *nisⁱrinaoⁱti* 'he delivers over'.—YAv. *māᵛⁱya*
'to me' = GAv. *maⁱbyā;* YAv. *hāvₒya-* 'left' = Skt.
savyá-; GAv. *dužazᵒbǣ* 'maledictus'. — YAv. *sᵘrun-*
vata (instr.) 'worthy of being heard'.

Note. Anaptyxis occurs sometimes between the members of a compound: e. g. GAv. *duᵊ.ḥṣapra-* 'evil-ruling'; GAv. *həmᵊ.fraštā* 'he questioned
with'; YAv. *usᵊ.hištaṭ* 'he stood up'.—More rarely in the few instances of
sandhi: YAv. *hᵛaᵊpaⁱþyǣsᵊ tanvō* 'of his own body'; YAv. *yasᵊ tē* 'who to thee'.

SYSTEM OF CONSONANTS.

§ 73. **General Remark.** Viewing the Av. and the Skt.
system of consonants side by side, it may be noted: (1) The
Av. p a l a t a l series is incomplete — the Av. possesses
only *c* and *j.* (2) The Skt. c e r e b r a l series is entirely
w a n t i n g in the Avesta. (3) The Av. has n o a s p i r a t e s,
their place being in part taken by the corresponding
spirants. (4) The n a s a l s are only in part identical. (5) The

Av. is richer than the Skt. in sibilants, especially through the presence of the sonant sibilants *z* and *ž*.

§ 74. **Surd and Sonant (Voiceless and Voiced).** For the distinction between surd and sonant (voiceless and voiced), we may refer to the Sanskrit. The law, moreover, that in internal combination, surd (voiceless) consonants stand before surd consonants, and sonant (voiced) before sonants, has in general the same extent as in Sanskrit.[1] Observe that *n* and in part *m* are at times treated as surd.[2]

§ 75. Sandhi between words (§ 4) is wanting in Avesta, except in case of some enclitics and compounds.

Tenues — Surd Spirants.

Av. ꞩ, ꭒ, ꭒ and ꞃ — *b̦*, *b̦*, *ɟ* — *c̦*.
k, *t*, *p* and *c* — *ḫ̦*, *p̦*, *f* — *ț*.

Av. *k*, *t*, *p* and *c*.

§ 76. The Av. tenues *k*, *t*, *p* and *c* agree mostly with the corresponding tenues in the Sanskrit.

Av. *katārō* 'which of two' = Skt. *katarás*; Av. *tāpayeiti* 'makes hot' = Skt. *tāpáyati*; Av. *patⁱnti* 'they fly' = Skt. *pátanti*.—Av. *caraⁱti* 'he moves' = Skt. *cárati*; Av. *cakana* 'has been pleased' = Skt. *cākana*.

Note. In the distinction between guttural and palatal *k/c*, the Av. and the Skt. do not always agree: Av. *paskāț* 'from behind, behind' = Skt. *paścāt*, cf. Av. *pasca*; Av. *cicipwā* 'through the wise one' = Skt. *cikitvā*; Av. *fraș̌ō.carⁱtar-* 'converter' = Skt. *•kartar-*, cf. Av. *fraș̌ō.kⁱrⁱti-*; Av. *vaokuș̌e* dat. sg. pf. ptcpl. √*vak/c* = Skt. *ūcuș̌e*.

Av. *ḫ̦*, *p̦*, *f*.

§ 77. The surd spirants *ḫ̦*, *p̦*, *f* in Av. are of two-fold origin: — (1) they are the representatives

---

[1] Cf. Whitney, *Sanskrit Grammar*, § 156 seq.; Stenzler, *Elementarbuch der Sanskritsprache*, § 44 seq.
[2] See Sievers, *Grundzüge der Phonetik*, pp. 114, 133.

of the old surd aspirates *kh, th, ph;* or (2) they have
arisen from the tenues *k, t, p* regularly changed
before most consonants in Av. to corresponding *ḫ, ƀ, f.*
Observe that *ƒ* has in general the treatment of a spirant § 81.

(1) Av. *ḫ, ƀ, f* = Skt. *kh, th, ph.*

Av. *ḫ☼* 'fountains' = Skt. *khás;* Av. *ḫarəm* 'ass'
= Skt. *kháram;* Av. *haḫa* 'friend' = Skt. *sákhā.*—
Av. *haptaƀəm* 'seventh' = Skt. *saptátham;* Av. *gāƀ☼*
'hymns' = Skt. *gáthās;* Av. *arᵊƀa-* 'part, portion' =
Skt. *ártha-.*—Av. *saf☼vhō* 'hoofs' = Skt. *śaphásas;*
Av. *kafəm* 'foam, slime' = Skt. *kapham.*

(2) Av. *ḫ, ƀ, f* = Skt. *k, t, p.*

Av. *ḫratuš* 'wisdom' = Skt. *krátus;* Av. *ⁱrinaḫti*
'he lets go, drives' = Skt. *riṇákti;* Av. *taoḫma* 'seed'
= Skt. *tókma;* Av. *ḫšaƀrəm* 'rule, kingdom' = Skt.
kṣatrám.—YAv. *šyaoƀnāiš,* GAv. *šyaoƀᵃnāiš* 'by deeds'
= Skt. *cyáutnāis;* Av. *haⁱƀyō* 'true' = Skt. *satyás.*—Av.
drafšō 'spear, banner'=Skt. *drapsás;* Av. *ʰafnəm* 'sleep'
= Skt. *svápnam;* YAv. *frā,* GAv. *fᵊrā* 'forth, before' =
Skt. *prá;* Av. *fraoḫtō* 'pronounced' = Skt. *próktás.*

Note 1. In Av., we sometimes find *ḫ* prefixed to *š,* initial or internal, apparently without etymological value: e.g. *ā-ḫšnuš* 'up to knee', cf. Skt. *abhi-jñu.* See Bartholomae, *A.F.* iii. 19 seq., and § 188 below.

Note 2. In Av., *ƀ* sometimes takes the place of *s* (Skt. *s*): e.g. Av. *ƀamnōvhaṇt-* 'healing' from √*ƀam-* = Skt. √*śam-* 'to heal', cf. also Av. *sāma-;* Av. *aⁱwiƀyō* 'over-sleeping' (nom. pl.) with √*sī-* = Skt. √*sī-* 'lie, sleep'; Av. *aⁱwiƀūrō* 'very mighty', beside Av. *sūrō* 'mighty' = Skt. *śúras;* Av. *anaƀaḫtqm* (fem.) 'whose time of delivery is not come', beside *frasaḫtahe* (masc.) 'whose time is come, dead' √*sac-.*

Note 3. Original *th* (Iranian *ƀ*) becomes *d* after *ḫ* and *f:* e.g. GYAv. *uḫda-* 'spoken, word' = Skt. *ukthá-;* Av. *ƀrafᵊda-* 'satisfied' = Indo-Iran. *⁎tramptha-;* Av. *anaⁱwi.druḫdō* 'not to be deceived' Yt. 10.5. See Bartholomae, *K.Z.* xxix. 483, 502 = *Flexionslehre* pp. 63, 82.

Note 4. On Av. *f* apparently for earlier *pv,* see § 95.

§ 78. (a) Exception. The change of *k, t, p*, to *ḥ, p̄, f*, before consonants § 77, does not take place when a sibilant or a written nasal (not *ą*) immediately precedes; nor under these circumstances, are *ḥ, p̄, f*, as answering to older aspirate § 77, allowed. In all such cases, simple *k, t, p* are employed.

Av. *uštrəm* 'camel' *(-štr-)* as opposed to *kupra* 'where' *(-pr-)* = Skt. *úštram, kútra;* Av. *ḥrafstrāiš* 'with noxious creatures'; Av. *pištrəm* 'bruising, wound'; Av. *zaṇtvō* 'in this *(ahmi)* tribe' *(-ṇtv-* § 94) as opposed to *haoząpwa (-ąpw-)*.—Av. *staorəm* 'bullock' = Skt. *sthūrám (-th-);* Av. *sparaṭ* 'he darted' = Skt. *ásphurat,* § 48; Av. *skarayaṇt-* 'springing, turning' (in nom. propr.) cf. Skt. *skhalayati;* perhaps Av. *skarᵊna-* 'turning, active' = Skt. *skhalana-*.—Av. *paṇtānəm* 'path' (beside Av. *pap̄ō* acc. pl.) = Skt. *pánthānam, pathás.*

§ 79. (b) Exception. (1) Similarly *pt* remains unchanged; but (2) not original *ptr* which becomes (with assimilation) *fᵊdr* as original *ktr* becomes *ḥdr,* in both GAv. and YAv.

(1) Av. *hapta* 'ἑπτά' = Skt. *saptá;* Av. *supti-* 'shoulder' = Skt. *súpti-*.—But (2) Av. *nafᵊdrō apąm* 'of offspring of waters', cf. Skt. *náptrē;* Av. *rafᵊdrəm* 'aid' cf. Av. *rap-əṇtəm, rap-akō;* Av. *apāḥdre* 'in north', beside *apāḥtara-;* Av. *ᵊyaoḥdra-* 'girdle' = Skt. *yóktra-.*

Note. Some further exceptions occur: Av. *dāitya-* 'lawful', *pritya-* 'third', *bitya-* 'second', see § 92 Note 1. Observe especially *ātrəm* 'fire', and *trᵊfyāṭ* 'may steal' for *tarᵊfyāṭ, tᵊrᵊfyāṭ* see variants—an abbreviated writing.

§ 80. On *p̄w* for original *tv*, see § 94.

Av. ç ʃ.

§ 81. There can be little doubt that Av. *ʃ* has in general a spirant value. It seems to occupy a position

intermediate between *t*, *d* and *þ*, *đ*. It is both surd and
sonant (voiceless and voiced); to find a distinction palaeo-
graphically when it- appears as surd or as sonant is n o t
warranted by the MSS. It occurs chiefly as f i n a l for *t*,
except when *s* or *š* precede; in that case *t* appears § 192.
As i n i t i a l, surd and sonant, it is found in a few words,
ţkaēšəm 'faith, faithful'; *ţbaēšō* 'hatred, harm' = Skt. *dvéṣas*,
cf. § 96. As i n t e r n a l it occurs in a few wǫrds, compound or in the MSS. treated as compound, and therefore
handled as if it were final.

Av. *ašāţ* 'from Right' = Skt. *ṛtát*; Av. *bavaţ* 'he
became' = Skt. *ábhavat*; Av. *yavaţ* 'how much' =
Skt. *yávat*; Av. *hakərəţ* 'once' = Skt. *sakṛt.*—GAv.
haēcaţ.aspa- nom. propr.; YAv. *aᵘrvaţ.aspa-* 'swift-
horsed'; Av. *brvaţbyąm* 'both brows'; Av. *•taţkušiš*
'running' (MSS. *•taţ kušiš*); Av. *aţca* 'atque'.—GYAv.
ţkaēšəm 'faith, faithful'; YAv. *ţbaēšō* 'hatred, harm',
cf. GAv. *dvaēšavhā* = Skt. *dvéṣas*.

Note 1. Sometimes, *ţ* appears as variant of *d* before *k:* e. g. *adkəm*
'robe' (variant *aţkəm*) = Skt. *átkam*.

Note 2. In *taţ.āpəm* 'with running water' (adj.), Yt. 13.43, *ţ* stands
for final *c*, cf. Av. *taci aᵖpya* 'in running water' (loc.), Vd. 6.26.

Mediae   — Sonant Spirants.

Av. ℮, ꝑ, ﻠ and ɤ —   ᶅ, ℓ, ꭚ.

g, *d*, *b* and *j* —   *ȷ*, *d*, *w*.

§ 82. The m e d i a e *g*, *d*, *b*, in Av. have a t w o - f o l d
value:—(1) they represent o l d m e d i a e, agreeing with the
Skt. *g*, *d*, *b;* or (2) they are the representatives of the
o l d s o n a n t a s p i r a t e s, *gh*, *dh*, *bh*; that is to say,
originally in Av. the sonant aspirates lost their aspiration
and fell together with the mediae. In GAv., the m e d i a e

thus arising are regularly preserved unchanged
throughout. But see § 82 (a).

The following scheme shows the standpoint of the
Gāthās in comparison with the Sanskrit.

Skt.	$g\ gh$	$d\ dh$	$b\ bh$
	V	V	V
Original- and GAv.	g	d	b

(1) GAv. (old) g, d, b = Skt. g, d, b.

GAv. *ugrэng* 'mighty' (acc. pl.) = Skt. *ugrán;*—
GAv. *yadā* 'when' = Skt. *yadá;* GAv. *vīdvэ* 'knowing' = Skt. *vidván.*

(2) GAv. g, d, b = Skt. gh, dh, bh.

GAv. *darэgэm* 'long' = Skt. *dīrghám;*—GAv. *adā*
'then' = Skt. *ádha;* GAv. *advānэm* 'way' = Skt. *ádhvānam;*—GAv. *ubōibyā* 'both', cf. Skt. *ubhábhyām;* GAv.
aibī 'unto' = Skt. *abhi.*

§ 82a. Observe in connection with this rule § 82 that
the sonant spirants appear before *ž:* cf. § 180. GAv. *aojžā*
't' ı spakest'; *diwžaidyāi.*—See § 89 Bartholomae's Law.

Note. On the sonant spirants—in GAv. *rafэdra-* 'aid'; *uɣda-* 'spoken,
word'—arising from old tenues or aspirate tenues, cf. § 77 Note 3.

§ 83. (1) In YAv. these mediae g, d, b—of double
origin § 82—are preserved unchanged when initial; or
again when internal, if immediately preceded by a nasal
consonant or by a sibilant. (2) Under all other circumstances in YAv. these mediae—whether representing old mediae or old sonant aspirates—are regularly
changed to the corresponding sonant spirant *(j, d, w).*
Exceptions to the rule are not many. The secondary relation of GAv. to YAv. may thus be tabulated (cf. § 82):

GAv.	g	d	b
	∧	∧	∧
YAv.	$g\ j$	$d\ d$	$b\ w$

(1) YAv. *g, d, b* (GAv. *g, d, b*) = Skt. *g, d, b*.

YAv. *gąm* 'cow' (GAv. *gąm*) = Skt. *gām*; YAv. *grīvā-* 'neck' = Skt. *grīvā-*; YAv. *anguštaēⁱbya* 'toes of both feet', cf. Skt. *avgusthābhyām.*—YAv. *dūrāṭ* 'from afar' (GAv. *dūrāṭ*) = Skt. *dūrāt*; YAv. *viṇdāⁱti* 'may find, receive' = Skt. *vindāti*; YAv. *hazdyāṭ* 'might sit' opt. pf. = Skt. *sasadyāt, sēdyāt.*—YAv. *bar^əzište* 'on the highest' (cf. GAv. *bar^əzištəm*) = Skt. *bárhiṣṭhē.*

(2) YAv. *g, d, b* (GAv. *g, d, b*) = Skt. *gh, dh, bh*.

YAv. *gaošəm* 'ear' (cf. GAv. *g͘šaiš*)=Skt. *ghóṣam*; YAv. *zangəm* 'foot' = Skt. *jávghām.*—YAv. *dārayaṭ* 'he held fast' (GAv. *dārayaṭ*) = Skt. *dhāráyat*; YAv. *drvahe* 'firm' (gen.) = Skt. *dhruvásya*; YAv. *baṇdəm* 'bond, sickness'=Skt. *bandhám*; YAv. *dazdi* 'give thou' = Skt. *daddhí.*—YAv. *būmīm* 'earth' (GAv. *būmīm*) = Skt. *bhūmim*; YAv. *brāta* 'brother' (GAv. *b^arātā*) = Skt. *bhrātā*; YAv. *zəmbayadwəm* 'crush ye' = Skt. *jambháyadhvam*.

(3) YAv. *ʒ, d, w* (GAv. *g, d, b*) = Skt. *g, d, b*.

YAv. *uʒrəm* 'mighty' (GAv. *ugra-*) = Skt. *ugrám*; YAv. *baʒəm* 'portion, lot' (GAv. *baga-*)= Skt. *bhágam*; YAv. *mər^əjō* 'bird' = Skt. *mṛgás.*—YAv. *vīdvͣ* 'knowing' (GAv. *vīdvͣ*) = Skt. *vidván*; YAv. *paⁱdyavuha* 'set foot' = Skt. *pádyasva*.

(4) YAv. *ʒ, d, w* (GAv. *g, d, b*) = Skt. *gh, dh, bh*.

YAv. *dar^əʒəm* 'long' (GAv. *dar^əgͣm*)=Skt. *dīrghám*; YAv. *maēʒəm* 'cloud' = Skt. *méghám*; YAv. *jaʒnvͣ* 'having smitten' = Skt. *jaghniván.*—YAv. *ada* 'then' (GAv. *adā*)= Skt. *ádha*; YAv. *adwanəm* 'way' (GAv. *advānəm*) = Skt. *ádhvānam*; YAv. *ar^ədəm* 'side, half' = Skt. *árdham.*—YAv. *aⁱwi* 'unto' (GAv. *aⁱbī*) = Skt. *abhí*; YAv. *gar^əwəm* 'foetus' = Skt. *gárbham*; YAv. *awrəm* 'cloud' = Skt. *abhrám*.

§ 84. Exception 1. Initial *j*, not *g*, is found before *n:* YAv. *jºnå,*
jnå 'women' (GAv. *gºnå*) = Skt. *gnås;* YAv. *jºnqm* 'to smite' inf. to
√*jan-* = Skt. √*han-*.

§ 85. Exception 2. Exceptions to the law for internal change
are also found.

(a) Commonly in the endings *•bi̥ʃ, •byō, •bya:*

    YAv. *tanubyō* 'to bodies' = Skt. *tanûbhyas;* YAv. *āfrivanaɛbi̥ʃ*
'with blessings', cf. Skt. *samānɛ-bhis,* etc. But YAv. *aⁱwyas-ca* 'and
with these' (fem. abl.) beside *ābyō* Yt. 10.82 = Skt. *ābhyás;* YAv.
bāzuwe 'with both arms' § 67 cf. Skt. *bāhúbhyām;* YAv. *hinûⁱwyō*
'from fetters' Yt. 13.100 beside YAv. *gātubyō.*

(b) The combination internal *dr* remains generally unchanged:

    YAv. *h̥ʃudrḁ̄ʈ* 'from seed' = Skt. *kʃudrā́t;* YAv. *udrɔm* 'otter' =
Skt. *udrám;* GYAv. *arɔdra-* 'pious';' GYAv. *sādra-* 'misfortune'; YAv.
dadrāna- 'being held' √*dar-* = Skt. √*dhar-*.

(c) In some other instances internal *d* remains in YAv. unchanged:

    YAv. *vadarº* 'weapon', GAv. *vadarⁿ* = Skt. *vádhar;* YAv. *yaza-
maⁱde* 'we worship' = Skt. *yájāmahɛ,* etc.; YAv. *varºdapɔm* 'growth',
beside *varºdaya* 'make thou grow' = Skt. *vardháya.*

§ 86. Instead of internal *d* in YAv., *þ* is sometimes
written; especially before *u, w*.

    YAv. *vīþuʃi, vīþuʃīm* 'having knowledge' = Skt.
vidúʃī, vidúʃīm, GAv. *vīduʃē;* YAv. *caraþwe* 'ye go'
Yt. 13.34 = Skt. *cáradhvē;* YAv. *daþuʃō* 'of creator'
= GAv. *daduʃō;* YAv. *ɔrºþwa-* 'uplifted' as variant to
ɔrºdwa-. So YAv. *daþaⁱti* 'he gives' = Skt. *dádati*
RV. 2.35.10; YAv. *zgaþaⁱti* 'vanishes' beside YAv.
zgadaⁱti; GAv. *vaēþā* Ys. 5.6 'he knows', beside GAv.
vaēdā = Skt. *vɛda.*

§ 87. Instead of internal YAv. *w*, we sometimes find
YAv. *v* written.

    YAv. *avarōⁱʈ* 'should bring out' = Skt. *ā-bharēt;*
YAv. *h̥ʃmāvºya* 'to you', beside GAv. *h̥ʃmaⁱbyā,* YAv.
yuʃmaoyō = Skt. *yuʂmábhyam;* YAv. *māvºya* 'to me',
GAv. *maⁱbyā;* YAv. *gɔurvayeⁱte* 'he seizes' (for **gɔr-
wayeⁱti* § 70 Note 2) = Skt. *grbháyati;* YAv. *vaēⁱbya*

'with both' (for *uvaë̄ibya* § 68 for *uwaë̄ibya*), cf. Skt. *ubhåbhyām,* GAv. *ubōibya;* YAv. *frabavara* 'he brought forth' = Skt. *babhāra.* Perhaps YAv. *a̮iwi > avi > aoi* 'unto' = Skt. *abhi.*

Note. On Av. *pw* for *tv, dw* for *dhv,* etc., see §§ 94, 96.

Av. ६ *j.*

§ 88. From the fact that the original sonant aspirates fell together with the mediae in Avesta, § 82, and also from the two-fold nature of Skt. *j* and *h*—see Brugmann, *Grundriss der vergl. Gram.* §§ 452, 480, 451,—is to be explained the following relation between the Avesta and the Sanskrit.

$$\text{Av. } j < \overset{\text{Skt.}}{\underset{h}{\overset{j}{}}} > \text{Av. } z$$
$$\text{Skt.}$$

(1) Av. *j* = Skt. *j.*

YAv. *jvantəm,* GAv. *jvaṇtō* 'living' = Skt. *jίvan-tam,* etc. (§ 68 Note 2); YAv. *jaɣnvā̊* 'having smitten' = Skt. *jaghnivån;*—YAv. *jyā̊* 'bowstrings' = Skt. *jyås;* GAv. *jyātəuš* 'of life', cf. Skt. *jῑvåtōs;* also GYAv. *aojištō* 'strongest' = Skt. *ójisṭhas;* GYAv. *i̮pyejō* 'destruction' = Skt. *tyåjas.*

(2) Av. *j* = Skt. *h.*

YAv. *jaṇtārəm* 'smiter' = Skt. *hantåram;* YAv. *ja̮iṇti* 'he smites' = Skt. *hånti;* YAv. *arəja̮iti* 'is worth' = Skt. *árhati;* GYAv. *drujəm* 'Deceit, Fiend' = Skt. *drúham.*

Note 1. According to § 83, the media *j* when initial should in YAv. pass over into its corresponding sonant s p i r a n t, this spirant has in our alphabet fallen together with the sonant sibilant *ź.* Hence the relation §§ 177, 178 below YAv. *ź* = Skt. *j;*—YAv. *ź* = Skt. *h.*

Note 2. Owing to the etymological relation *g/j,* we sometimes find Av. *j* = Skt. *g:*— e. g. GYAv. *haṇjamana-* 'assembly' = Skt. *saġámana-;*

GYAv. *jasôiţ* 'he might come' = Skt. *gáchēt;* Av. √*jad-* 'to beseech', cf. Skt. √*gad-*.

Note 3. Av. *j* also sometimes answers to Skt. *gh:*—e. g. Av. *drāj-iŝtəm* 'longest' = Skt. *drāghiṣ͂ham;* Av. *drājô* 'length, duration', cf. Skt. *drāghmán-*.

Bartholomae's Law.

See Bartholomae, *A. F.* i. p. 3 seq.; *A. F.* iii. p. 22 Note.

§ 89. The combination, original a s p i r a t e m e d i a e $+ t$ or $+ s$, had already in the Indo-Iranian period become m e d i a $+ dh$ or $+ zh$; the consonant group thus arising is then treated according to the special laws of the language, Indic or Iranic. In GAv. the law is carried through without exception (but see § 82 a, and Note). In YAv., however, the law shows a number of exceptions § 90.—Examples of the law from GAv. are:

GAv. *aogˮdā* 'he spake' to √*aug₁h* $+$ ending *ta*, cf. Gk. εὔχομαι, Skt. *ôhatē;* GAv. *cagˮdō* 'they two grant' to √*k₁ag₁h* $+ -tas.$—GYAv. *vərˢsda-* 'grown great, mighty', to √*vardh* $+ -ta-,$ cf. Skt. *vṛddhá-;* GAv. *dazdē* 'he makes', to √*dhā-*, pres. stem *dadh* $+ -tē;$ GYAv. *mazdāh-*, nom. *mazdā̊* 'wisdom, Mazda', to orig. √*mandh* $+ -tas$ $=$ Skt. *-mēdhás-.*—GAv. *gərˢïdā* 'he complained', to √*garg₁h* $+ -ta,$ cf. Skt. *gárhatē.*—With orig. *s*, GAv. *aojŝā* 'thou spakest', to √*aug₁h* $+ -sa,$ 2nd. sg. pret. mid.;—GAv. *diwŝaidyāi* 'to deceive', to orig. √*dabh* $+ -sa-,$ infin. desiderative, cf. YAv. *diwŝaţ* 'from deceit', a substantive from desid. stem, cf. Skt. *dípsati.*

§ 90. In YAv., as compared with GAv., this law holds good only in part; as for the rest, the old tenues *t*, or surd sibilant *s*, is restored and assimilation then takes place. Thus:—

YAv. *aoẖta* 'he spake', to √*aug₁h* $+$ ending *ta*, beside GAv. *aogˮdā;* YAv. *druẖtō* 'deceived', to √*draug₁h* $+ -ta-,$ = Skt. *drugdhás.* —YAv. *dastē* 'he makes', to √*dhā-*, pres. stem *dadh* $+ tē,$ beside GAv. *dazdē;* YAv. *mastīm* 'wisdom' to orig. √*mandh* $+ -ti-,$ beside GAv. *humazdra-*, YAv. *mazdra-.*—YAv. *dapta* 'deceived' nom. f. past ptcpl. to orig. √*dabh*, cf. Skt. *dabdhá-.*—With orig. *s*, YAv. *vaŝata* 'he carried' (*s* restored § 165), 3rd. sg. mid. *sa-* aor. to √*vag₁h*, beside YAv. *vaŝaţ* 'he carried'.

Semivowels.

Av. ꝶ *y* (initial), ꞌꞌ *y* (internal); Ꝿ *v* (initial), ꞌꞌ *v* (internal).

§ 91. General Remark. The semivowels ꝶ *y* and Ꝿ *v* were probably spirants; internal ꞌꞌ*y* and ꞌꞌ *v* were apparently sometimes spirant, sometimes vocalic (see § 92 Note 1).

Note. In a few instances ꞌꞌ *y* and ꞌꞌ *v* stand as initial, when representing *iy*, *uv:* GAv. ꝶꞌꞌ *iyadacā* 'and here' Ys. 35.2 (pron. stem *i*); YAv. ꞌꞌꝶꞌꞌ *uvaēibya* 'with both', Skt. *ubhābhyām*—see §§ 87, 68.

Av. *y* = Skt. *y*.

§ 92. Av. *y* (initial and internal) corresponds to Skt. *y:*

Av. *yasnəm* 'worship' = Skt. *yajñám;* Av. *tāyuš* 'thief' = Skt. *tāyús;* GAv. *ahurahyā* 'of Ahura' = Skt. *ásurasya.*

Note 1. (a) A possible test as to when ꞌꞌ *y* is spirant or semivowel, may perhaps be found in the treatment of a preceding *t*, e. g. *haiþya* 'true' (*y* spirant) but *dāitya*- 'lawful' (*y* semivowel *dāit-i-a-*). (b) Moreover the metre shows that *y* is often to be read with vowel value *iy* § 68: GAv. *fryō* 'friend' (read *fr-iy-ō*) = Skt. *priyás;* YAv. *bitya*- 'second' (read *bit-iy-a-*) = Skt. *dvitīya-.*—In Yt. 13.99 initial ꝶ must be read *iy* in *yaēša* 'he has sought' = Skt. *iyēṣa.*

Note 2. On Av. *y* = Skt. *v*, in *tanuyē* etc., see § 190.

Av. *v* = Skt. *v*.

§ 93. Av. *v* (initial and internal) corresponds to Skt. *v:*

Av. *vastrəm* 'vesture' = Skt. *vástram;* Av. *vātō* 'wind' = Skt. *vātas;*—Av. *tūtava* 'he has power' = Skt. *tūtāva;* Av. *hvaspō* 'with good horses' = Skt. *sváśvas.*

Note 1. Metrically ꞌꞌ *v* is often to be read as a vowel. Thus: Av. *gaēþāhva* 'among beings' Ys. 9.17 (loc. °*āhu* + *a* postpos.); °*cipraēšva* 'among seeds'; GAv. *tvəm* 'thou' (read *tuəm*) = Skt. *tvám (tuám);* YAv. *kva* 'where' (read *kua*) = Skt. *kvà (kúa).*

Note 2. On Av. *v* for *w*, see § 87.

Note 3. On Av. *v* for Skt. *uv* see § 68.

Original *v* in Combination with Consonants.
Av. representative of Skt. *tv*.

§ 94. The combination original *tv* (1) g e n e r a l l y becomes Av. *þw;* (2) it remains unchanged when a sibilant

precedes or when v preserves its vocalic character u.—
When samprasāraṇa with following a takes place, t remains
unaltered.

(1) GYAv. *ḫraþwā, ḫraþwō* 'by, of wisdom' = Skt.
krátvā, krátvas; YAv. *þwąm* 'thee' = Skt. *tvám;* Av.
maþwa- 'to be thought, thought', for **mantva-;—*
(2) Av. *varštva-* 'to be done, act'; Av. *ratvō* 'O
Master', *gātvō* 'from the seat' (prob. *rat-u-ō, gāt-u-ō*);
GAv. *tvȝm* 'thou' *(tuȝm)*.—YAv. *tūm* 'thou' = Skt. *tvám*.

Original *þv.*

§. 95. The combination original *þv* apparently seems to become *f*
in Av.:—e. g. Ys. 57.29 *áfȝṇte* 'they are overtaken', for earlier **áþvaṇte*
(cl. 8); Av. *áfȝṇtȝm* 'aquosum' for· older **áþvaṇtam;* Av. *huřřvafa* 'slumber-
ing' nom. sg. from orig. **suṣvapvan(t)-.*

Original *dv, dhv.*

§ 96. The combination original *dv, dhv* becomes
(1) when initial, GAv. *dv, dᵃb;* in YAv. *þb, b (dv);—*
(2) when internal, GAv. *dv;* in YAv. *dv, dw (dv).*

(1) Initial.

GAv. *dvaēšavhā* 'through hatred' (YAv. *þbaēšavha*)
= Skt. *dvéšasā;* GAv. *dᵃibišȝṇtī* 'they hate' (cf. YAv.
þbaēšayāþ) = Skt. *dvišánti;* GAv. *dᵃibitīm* 'second'
(YAv. *bitīm*)=Skt. *dvitíyam.*—YAv. *þbaēšavha* 'through
hatred' = Skt. *dvéšasā;* YAv. *þbaēšayāþ* 'may harm
through hatred' = Skt. *dvēšáyāt;* YAv. *bitīm* 'second'
= Skt. *dvitíyam.*—YAv. *dva* 'two' = Skt. *dvá;* Av.
dvarȝm 'door' = Skt. *dváram;* Av. *dvąsaⁱti* 'rushes,
springs' = Skt. *dhvąsati.*

(2) Internal.

GAv. *advaēšō* 'without harm' = Skt. *advēšás;* GAv.
vīdvā̊ 'knowing', YAv. *vīdvā̊* = Skt. *vidván;*—GAv.
advānȝm 'path', YAv. *adwanȝm* = Skt. *ádhvānam.*

—Av. *didvaēṣa* 'I have hated' = Skt. *didvēṣa;* YAv. *vīdvaēštvō* 'foe to harm'.

Note. In YAv. *viṭbaẕfaшhɔm* 'foe to malice' and *vīdvaẕštvō* 'foe to harm', the *ṭb, dv* is treated apparently as initial,—prefix *vi.*

Av. representative of Skt. *śv.*

§ 97. The combination *śv* (Skt.) appears in Av. as *sp.*

Av. *vīspɔm* 'all' = Skt. *viśvam;* Av. *aspō* 'horse' = Skt. *áśvas;* Av. *spaētɔm* 'white' = Skt. *śvētám.*

§ 98. On Av. representative of *sv* (Skt.), see § 130.

Av. representative of Skt. *hv.*

§ 99. The combination Skt. *hv* appears in Av. as *zb.*

Av. *zbayemi* 'I invoke' = Skt. *hváyāmi;* GAv. *dužazᵒbⱥ* 'male-dictus' cf. Skt. $\sqrt{hvā}$-.

Liquid.

Av. ᐱ *r.*

§ 100. The Av. liquid is *r;* it corresponds to Skt. *r* and *l,* the letter *l* being wanting in Av.

Av. *r* = Skt. *r (ij.*

Av. *rapɔm* 'wagon' = Skt. *rátham;* Av. *narɔm* 'man' = Skt. *náram;* Av. *srīrō* 'beautiful' = Skt. *śrī-rás, śrīlás.*—Av. *hukɔrɔpta-* 'well-formed' = Skt. *-klptá-;* GAv. *hrapaⁱtī* 'arranges', cf. Skt. *kálpatē.*

Note 1. In Av., *hr* appears instead of simple *r* when immediately followed by *k* or *p:*—YAv. *vɔhrkō* 'wolf' = Skt. *vŕkas;* GYAv. *kɔhrpɔm* 'corpus' = Skt. *kŕpam;* YAv. *mahrkō* 'death' = Skt. *markás,* cf. GAv. *marᵃkaẕ-cⱥ* 'morti-que'; YAv. *kahrkana-* nomen propr., cf. Skt. *kŕkaṇa-.* See Bartholomae, *A.F.* ii.39; Brugmann, *Grundriss der vergl. Gram.* § 260.

Note 2. On *urv-* (i. e. *ᵘrv-* for *vr-*), see § 191.

Note 3. On *r* in vowel combinations *ar, aⁱr, aᵘr, ɔrᵉ,* see § 48.

Nasals.

Av. ı, ᴇ, ı, ᴊ, ᴌ.

n, n̨, v, v̨, m.

§ 101. **General Remark.** Of the nasals in Av., ᴌ *m* corresponds in general to Skt. *m.*—To the Skt. *n* there correspond in Av., ı *n* and ᴇ *n̨*,—the latter, a modification of ı *n*, stands before stopped consonants.—The letter ı *v* is evidently guttural in Av. *pavtavhəm* 'fifth' from **pavktasva.* Otherwise ı *v* stands in the combination *vh, vuh* derived from orig. *s*-syllable § 108.—The character ᴊ *v̨* is palaeo-graphically, from the manuscripts, a modification of ı *v*; it occurs for *v* in connection with *h* when it is preceded by an *i*- or *e*-sound § 118 Note.

§ 102. Av. *n* occurs initial, internal (except before stopped-sounds), and final.

> Av. *nāma* 'name' = Skt. *nāma;*—Av. *tanuš* 'body' = Skt. *tanūs;* —Av. *anyō* 'another' = Skt. *anyás;* Av. *vavanva* 'victorious' = Skt. *vavanvān;*—Av. *varšnōiš* 'of a male' = Skt. *vŕṣṇās;*—Av. *barən* 'they carried' = Skt. *ábharan.*

§ 103. Av. *n̨* occurs before *k, g, c, j, t, d* and *-byō* (for *-dbyō*), *bya:*

> Av. *zan̨ga-* 'upper part of foot' = Skt. *jáṅghā-;*—Av. *pan̨ca* 'five' = Skt. *páñca;*—Av. *ran̨jaiti* 'bestirs, hurries' = Skt. *ráṅhati;*—Av. *an̨tarə* 'inter' = Skt. *antár;* Av. *baran̨ti* 'they carry' = Skt. *bháranti;* Av. *bərəzan̨bya* 'for the two great ones'.

Note. For *-n̨g* see under Sibilants § 128.

§ 104. On Av. ı *v*, ᴊ *v̨*, see above General Remark.

§ 105. Av. *m* occurs initial, internal, final.

> Av. *madəməm* 'midmost' = Skt. *madhyamám;* Av. *aməm* 'strength' = Skt. *ámam;* Av. *mraom* 'I spake' = Skt. *ábravam.*

Note 1. The *m* in Av. √*mru-* (opp. Skt. √*bra-*) is probably the more original.

Note 2. On initial *m* = Skt. *sm*, see § 140.

Sibilants.

Av. ϑ, ϑ, ϑ, ϑ—*ʃ*, ϑ.
s, *š*, *ṣ̌*, *ṣ̌*—*z*, *ž*.

§ 106. **General Remark.** Of the sibilants, *s, š, ṣ̌, ṣ̌* are surd; and *z, ž* are sonant. In Avesta, *s* corresponds to both Skt. *s* and to *ś*.—Av. *ṣ̌* answers in general to Skt. *ṣ*. The letter Av. *š* is chiefly final after *i, u* and consonants, also in some ligatures. Av. *ṣ̌* is not so common, chiefly before *y*.

Note. Av. *š, ṣ̌, ṣ̌* are palaeographically closely related. In most MSS., *š* and *ṣ̌* interchange with each other. In the younger Indian MSS., *š* is the predominant character; the Persian MSS. often (though by no means throughout) show a preference for *ṣ̌* when the sound answers to orig. *rt*. In the four oldest MSS., with Pahlavi translation, *ṣ̌* is the principal character,—*š* standing as final or in ligatures. This rule is there preserved almost without exception.—In the old Mss. ϑ *ṣ̌* has a double value—(1) as a ligature for *š* + *k*, *hiška* 'dry', et al.; or (2) it is a modification of *š*, *ṣ̌* before *y*, § 162. Younger MSS. write in the (1) first case *šk*; in the (2) second case they have a special ligature.—See Geldner, *Drei Yasht* p. viii seqq.

Av. *s*.

§ 107. **General Remark.** Av. *s* is of three-fold origin:—

1. = original *s*,
2. = older palatal *ś* (Skt. *ś*),
3. = developed.

---

1. Original *s*.

§ 108. **General Remark.** Original *s* (1) under certain conditions remains *s* in Avesta (2) but generally otherwise becomes *h* (*vh*).

i. Original *s* remains *s*.

§ 109. Original *s* remains *s* in Avesta before initial *k, c, t, p, n*, or internal before the same letters when it is preceded by *a, ą, ā*.

Av. *skəmbəm* 'scaffold' = Skt. *skambhám;* Av. *yās*
-kərᵊt- 'making efforts', cf. Skt. *a-yás-;* Av. *skəndəm*
'broken', *sciṇdayeⁱti* 'breaks asunder', cf. Lat. *scindere.*
—Av. *staotārəm* 'praiser' = Skt. *stōtáram;* Av. *vaste*
'he clothes' = Skt. *váste;* Av. *āste* 'he sits' = Skt.
áste; GAv. *mạstā* 'he thought' = Skt. *amạsta;* Av.
dạstvạm 'cunning, skill', cf. Skt. *dạsas-;* GAv. *spərᵊ-*
dānī 'I will strive' = Skt. *spárdhāni;* Av. *manaspaoⁱrya-*
'having the mind pre-eminent'.—Av. *snayaēta* 'should
wash' = Skt. *snáyēta;* Av. *āsnatārəm* 'priest who washes
the utensils', cf. Skt. *a-snātáram* 'dreading water'.

ii. Original *s* becomes *h*.

§ 110. Original *s* becomes *h* in Av., regularly when
initial before vowels.

Av. *hapta* 'ἑπτά' = Skt. *saptá,* Lat. *septem;* Av.
haca 'with, from' = Skt. *sácā;* Av. *haoməm* 'Haoma'
= Skt. *sómam;* Av. *hō* 'he' = Skt. *sás;* Av. *hūhtəm*
'good word' = Skt. *sūktám;* Av. *hakərᵊṭ* 'at one time'
= Skt. *sakŕt.*

as.

§ 111. The combination old *as* becomes in Avesta
(1) *ah-*, (2) *aṽh-, aṽ-*, (3) *-ō* (final).

Old *as-* = (1) Av. *ah-*.

§ 112. α. Old *as-* = Av. *ah-* — regularly before *i, ī.*

YAv. *ahi* 'thou art', GAv. *ahī* = Skt. *ási;* GAv.
nəmahī 'in homage' = Skt. *námasi.*

§ 113. β. Old *as-* = Av. *ah-* — before *i, ī,* when the
a becomes *e,* § 34.

> Av. *dārayehi* 'thou holdest fast' = Skt. *dhāráyasi;* Av. *jaⁱdyehi*
> 'thou askest'; Av. *sadayehi* 'thou appearest' = Skt. *chadáyasi;* Av.
> *aojyehī̆* 'more strong' (acc. pl. fem.) = Skt. *ójyasīs.*

§ 114. γ. Old *as-* = Av. *ah-*, generally before *u, ū*
and their strengthenings.

Av. *ązahu* 'in distress' = Skt. *ąhasu;* Av. *ahurəm* 'Ahura, Lord' = Skt. *ásuram;* Av. *ahūm* 'life' = Skt. *ásum.*

§ 115. δ. Old *as-* = Av. *ah-*, the *a* before *u, v* then passing over into *o, ō*.

> Av. *vohu* 'good' = Skt. *vásu;* GAv. *baḫ{j}ōhvā* 'distribute' = Skt. *bhákṣasva.*

§ 116. ε. Old *as-* = Av. *ah-* rarely before *e*, cf. perhaps § 35 Note 2.

> Av. *raodahe* 'thou growest' = Skt. *rṓdhasi;* Av. *pāᵐhahe* 'thou mayest protect' (aor. subj.) Yt. 8.1 = Skt. *pāsasi.*

Old *as-* = (2) Av. *avh-*.

§ 117. α. Old *as-* = Av. *avh-*, regularly before *a, ā, ə, ǝ̄, ō, ōi, ą*.

> Av. *vavhanəm* 'vesture' = Skt. *vásanam;* GAv. *nəmavhā* 'with homage' = Skt. *námasā.*—Av. *vavhǝuš* 'of good' = Skt. *vásōs.*—Av. *avavhō* 'of help' = Skt. *ávasō.*—GAv. *rāᵐhavhōi* 'thou mayest offer' (aor. subj.) = Skt. *rāsase;* Av. *uṣavhąm* 'of dawns' = Skt. *uṣásām.*

> Note. An exception is Av. *dahākō* 'Dragon', *dahakāca.*

§ 118. β. Old *as-* = Av. *avh-*, generally before *e, ē, aē-ca*, but cf. § 116.

YAv. *avavhe, avavhaē-ca*, GAv. *avavhē* 'for help' = Skt. *ávase;* GAv. *nəmavhē* 'for homage' = Skt. *námase.*

> Note. Here Av. *vh-* may appear instead of *vh-* when epenthetic *i* precedes it, or when *a* is shaded to *e* after *y* § 34:—YAv. *avaⁱvhe* 'for help' beside *avavhe* = Skt. *ávase;* GAv. *didaⁱvhē* 'I was made wise' (redupl. aor.).—YAv. *yevhe* 'of which' = Skt. *yásya;* GAv. *srāvayevhē* 'to make heard'; GAv. *rāṣ̌ayevhē* 'to harm'—cf. the Skt. infinitives in *-ase.*

§ 119. γ. Old *as-* = Av. *avh-*, seldom before *u:*

> Av. *vavhuš* 'good' = Skt. *vásus;* Av. *avhuš* (beside *ahūm*) 'life' = Skt. *ásus.*

Old -*as* = (3) Av. -*ō*.

§ 120. Old -*as* final = Av. -*ō*,—(GAv. often has -*ʒ* § 32).

Av. *puþrō* 'son' = Skt. *putrás*; Av. *išavō* 'arrows' = Skt. *íṣavas*; Av. *dārayō* 'didst hold fast' = Skt. *dhāráyas.*—Cf. GAv. *yʒ* 'who' (YAv. *yō*) = Skt. *yás*; GAv. *vʒ* 'of ye' (YAv. *vō*) = Skt. *vas*; GAv. *mazʒ* 'great' (gen.) = Skt. *mahás.*

Note. Observe that *as* is retained before enclitic *ca* 'que', etc. Av. *išavasca* 'and arrows' = Skt. *íṣavaš-ca;* Av. *išavasciṭ* 'even the arrows' = Skt. *ísavaš-cit;* Av. *yasca* 'and who' = Skt. *yáš-ca.*—Av. *nəmasᵊ tē* 'homage to thee' = Skt. *námas tē;* Av. *yastaṭ* 'qui id' = Skt *yás tát.*

ās.

§ 121. The combination old *ās* becomes in Avesta (1) *āh-*, (2) *ā̄ṇh-*, (3) -*ā̄* (final).

Old *ās-* = (1) Av. *āh-*.

§ 122. Old *ās-* = Av. *āh-* regularly before *i, ī, u, ū*.

Av. *bavāhi* 'mayest thou be' = Skt. *bhávāsi*; Av. *pāhi* 'thou protectest' = Skt. *pāhi.*—Av. *dāhīm* 'creation' = Skt. *dhāsím*; GAv. *rāhī* 'I offer' (aor.) = Skt. *rāsi.*—Av. *āhurōiš* 'of the Ahurian', cf. Skt. *ásurēs*; GAv. *āhū* loc. pl. fem. of *aēm* 'this' = Skt. *āsú.*

Old *ās-* = (2) Av. *ā̄ṇh-*.

§ 123. Old *ās-* = Av. *ā̄ṇh-*,—before *a, ā, ə, e, ē, ō, ōi, ą.*

Av. *ā̄ṇha* 'has been' = Skt. *ása*; Av. *þrā̄ṇhayeⁱte* 'he terrifies' = Skt. *trāsáyatē*; Av. *nā̄ṇhābya* 'with both nostrils' = Skt. *nāsābhyām*;—Av. *mā̄ṇhəm* 'moon' = Skt. *mā́sam*;—GAv. *rā̄ṇhē* 'I offer' = Skt. *rāsē*;—Av. *ā̄ṇhō* 'of mouth' = Skt. *āsás*;—Av. *dā̄ṇhōiṭ* 'creation' (abl.), cf. Skt. *dhāsi-*;—Av. *ā̄ṇhąm* 'of these' (fem.) = Skt. *āsā́m.*

Old -*ās* = (3) Av. -*ə̄*.

§ 124. Old -*ās* final = Av. -*ə̄*—regularly.

Av. *buyə̄* 'mightest be' = Skt. *bhūyās;* Av. *haēnayə̄* 'of an army' = Skt. *sēnāyās;* Av. *də̄* 'thou madest' = Skt. *ádhās*.

Note. Before enclitics (*ca* etc.), orig. -*ās* appears as -*ə̄s*:—Av. *gā- θə̄sca* 'and the Gathas' = Skt. *gā́thāsca;* Av. *urvarə̄sca* 'and trees' = Skt. *urvárāsca;* Av. *haēnayə̄sca* 'and of the army' = Skt. *sēnāyāsca;*—GAv. *də̄scā* 'and madest', *də̄s-tū* 'thou madest' = Skt. *ádāsca,* etc.

Original *ns*.

§ 125. The combination old internal -*ans*- before vowels becomes:—(1) in YAv. -*avh*-, -*əvh*-, -*q̇h*-;—(2) in GAv. -*ə̄ngh*-, -*š̌h*-.

Old -*ans*- = (1) YAv. -*avh*-, -*əvh*-, -*q̇h*-.

§ 126. α. Old -*ans*- internal = YAv. -*avh*-, -*əvh*- before *ā, a, ə, ōi*.

YAv. *savhāni* 'I shall proclaim' = Skt. *śasāni;* YAv. *davhavha* 'with cunning, skill' (Ny. 1.16) = Skt. *dasasā.* —YAv. *vəvhən* 'they will struggle' (Yt. 13.154) = Skt. *vasan.*—YAv. *savhōiš* 'shouldst proclaim' = Skt. *śasēs.* —Similarly YAv. *javhəntu* 'shall injure' (Vd. 2.22), cf. Skt. *hisantu.*

§ 127. β. Old -*ans*- = YAv. -*q̇h*-, before *i, y*.

YAv. *dq̇hištəm* 'most cunning, skilled' = Skt. *da- sistam;* YAv. *zq̇hyamnanqm* 'of those who will be born' (√*zan*- = Skt. √*jan*-).

Old -*ans*- = (2) GAv. -*ə̄ngh*-, -*š̌h*-.

§ 128. Old -*ans*- internal = (α) GAv. -*ə̄ngh*- (ᵥᶜᵏᵉᵢ) before vowels;—and = (β) GAv. -*š̌h*- before *m*.

(a) GAv. *sə̄nghānī* 'I shall proclaim' = Skt. *śasāni;* GAv. *və̄nghat̯, və̄nghən* 'shall strive' (aor.) = Skt. *vasat;*

GAv. *sэ̄ṅghō* 'proclamation, proclaimer' = Skt. *śṃsas*.
—GAv. *mэ̄ṅghī* (also *mэ̄ṅhī*) 'I thought' = Skt. *mṃ́si*.
—GAv. *fśэ̄ṅghyō, fśэ̄ṅghīm* 'thrifty' = orig. **psansyas*.
—(b) *mэ̄hmaᶦdī* 'we thought' (*s*-aor. from √*man*-).

§ 129. The combination old final *-ans* = (1) YAv.
-ąn, or *-ą* (*-ąs-ca*), *-э̄* (*-э̄s-ca*);—(2) GAv. *-э̄ṅg*, *-ą*.

YAv. *daēvąn*, GAv. *daēvэ̄ṅg* 'Demons' = Skt. *dēvā́n*.
—GAv. *spэ̄ṇtэ̄ṅg amэ̄śэ̄ṅg* Ys. 39.3 = YAv. *amэ̄śэ̄ spэ̄ṇtэ̄*
= YAv. *amэ̄śэ̄s-ca spэ̄ṇtэ̄* = GAv. *amэ̄śą spэ̄ṇtą* = YAv.
amэ̄śąs-ca spэ̄ṇtą (acc. pl.) = Skt. *amŕtān*.— YAv.
aēsmąn, aēsmąs-ca 'wood', cf. Skt. *áśvān, áśvāśca;*
YAv. *varᵉsэ̄s-ca* 'hair'.

Note. In some of the above examples, it might be suggested that
YAv. *э̄* is perhaps due to Gatha influence.

Original *sv.*

§ 130. The combination orig. *sv* becomes in Avesta
ᴍᴍ *hv* or ᴍ *h*.—Sometimes, *sv* when internal, becomes *vuh*
(also written *vh*).

(1) Orig. *sv*- initial = Av. *hv*-, *h*-.

GYAv. *hva*-, also *ha*- 'suus' = Skt. *svá*-; GYAv. *hvarᵉ* 'sun' =
Skt. *svàr;* YAv. *hvaspō* 'having good horses' = Skt. *svā́śvas*.—YAv.
hvaharəm 'sister' = Skt. *svásāram;* GYAv. *harᵉnā̄* 'splendors', cf.
Skt. *svàrṇara-;* YAv. *hῑsaṭ* 'he sweated', fr. Av. √*hvid*- = Skt. √*svid*-.

(2) Orig. *-sv*- internal = Av. *-hv*-, *-h*-, *-vhv*-, *-vuh*-
(Pers. MSS. *-vh*-).

(a) It becomes *hv*,—after *ā*—YAv. *āhva* 'among these' (*āhu* + *a*
postpos.) = Skt. *āsú;* YAv. *ᶦunāhva* 'in empty holes' = Skt. *ūnāsu;*
YAv. *vyarᵉβāhva* 'in separate places' (loc.).—After *a*—GAv. *gūšahvā*
'hear thou' = Skt. *ghóṣasva;* so YAv. *dāmahva* 'among creatures'
(loc. *an*-stem + *a*) = Skt. *dhā́masu*.—After *ō* (= *a* § 39)—YAv. *ba-
ḳšōhva* 'distribute thou' = Skt. *bhákṣasva*.—(b) Becomes *h*,—after *a*—
GAv. *nэmahvaᶦtīš* 'full of homage' = Skt. *námasvatīs;* YAv. *harahvaᶦtīm*
nom. propr. = Skt. *sárasvatīm*.—So (see below under Composition)
YAv. *paᶦriḷhaḳtəm* 'surrounded' = Skt. *pariṣvaktam*.—(c) Becomes *-vuh*-

(-ɴh-, -ɴhv-)—GYAv. vaɴuhīm 'good' (fem.), Pers. MSS. vaɴhīm = Skt. vásvīm; YAv. paᵈdyaɴuha 'set foot, abide' = Skt. pádyasva; YAv. hunaɴuha 'press haoma-juice', cf. Skt. sunuɾvá;—YAv. aojaɴuhaṇt-, GAv. aojōṇghvaṇt-, aojōɴhvaṇt- 'strong' = Skt. ójasvant-. — YAv. vaɴhvqm 'of good things', beside vohunqm; YAv. hₐrᵃnaɴhvaṇta 'glorious', cf. Yt. 15.56, beside hₐrᵃnaɴuhaṇtɔm; YAv. varᵃcaɴhuṇtɔm 'brilliant' Yt. 12.1 = Skt. *varcasvantam.

Note. In rāma hᵃāstrɔm orig. 'having good pastures', h = orig. su + vᵒ (§ 68).

Original sy.

§ 131. This combination, orig. sy preceded by a vowel, becomes somewhat complicated in Av., owing to the varied treatment of y, as y sometimes **remains** after s has become an h-sound, or y sometimes **vanishes**, with or without leaving a trace of epenthesis. In GAv., y is generally retained, in YAv. y generally vanishes.

(A) y remains.

§ 132. Orig. sy = (1) Av. hy (the y remaining);— mostly GAv., more rare YAv.

(a) YAv. hyāṭ 'might be' = Skt. syāt; YAv. uzdāhyamnanqm 'of offerings to be elevated', cf. Skt. dhā-sy-atē; YAv. māhyaēᵇbyō 'to lords of the month' = Skt. māsyēbhyas; YAv. manahyō 'spiritual' (nom. sg.) for *manasyas.—(b) GAv. ahurahyā 'of Ahura, Lord' = Skt. ásurasya; GAv. ahyā 'of this' = Skt. asyá; GAv. vahyō 'better' = Skt. vásyas.

§ 133. Orig. sy = (2) Av. ḥy, mostly GAv., rarely YAv.

(a) YAv. daḥyunqm 'of countries', cf. Skt. dásyu-; and YAv. ḥyaona-, ḥyaonya- nom. propr.—(b) GAv. vaḥyaɴ 'melior' = Skt. vásyān; GAv. aḥyācā 'ejus-que' (beside ahyā) = Skt. asyá. Cf. Geldner, Studien zum Avesta p. 141.

(B) y vanishes.

§ 134. Orig. -sy- internal = (1) Av. -ɴh-, the y vanishing without leaving epenthesis.

YAv. vaɴhō 'melius' = Skt. vásyas; YAv. aēvaɴhɔ gen. sg. fem. (orig. -syās) from aēva- 'one'.

§ 135. Orig. -*sy*- internal = (2) Av. -*iṇh*-, the *y* vanishes but leaves epenthesis.

YAv. *a*ⁱ*ṇhǡ* (also *aṇhǡ*) 'of this' (fem.) = Skt. *asyǡs;* YAv. *da*ⁱ*ṇhǰuš* 'of country', cf. Skt. *dásyu-*.

§ 136. Orig. -*sy*- internal = (3) Av. -*ṇh*-, the *y* with a following *a* becoming *e*.

(a) With. epenthesis—YAv. *a*ⁱ*ṇhe* 'of this' = Skt. *asyá.*—(b) Without epenthesis—YAv. *yeṇhe* 'of whom' = Skt. *yásya.*

§ 137. Orig. -*sy*- internal = (4) Av. *h*, the *y* with a following *a* having become *e*, § 67. Very common in YAv. genitive singular.

YAv. *ahe* 'of this' = Skt. *asyá;* YAv. *ahurahe* (beside GAv. *ahurahyā*) 'of Ahura' = Skt. *ásurasya.*—Isolated GYAv. *vahehīš* 'the better ones' (fem.) = Skt. *vásyasīs.*

Original *sr.*

§ 138. Orig. *sr*- initial = (?) Av. *r*- (the instances are uncertain). GAv. *rǡṇhayǝn* 'they made fall', cf. Skt. *srǝsayan;* YAv. *raṇhǡ* 'the lame', cf. Skt. √*sras-, srǝs-;* Av. *rāmǝm* 'sickness' = Skt. *srāmam.*

§ 139. Orig. -*sr*- internal = Av. -*ŋr*-.

Av. *hazaŋrǝm* 'thousand' = Skt. *sahásram;* Av. *daŋrō* 'cunning, wise' = Skt. *dasrás;* ZPhl.Gloss. *vaŋri-, vaŋra-* 'spring', cf. Skt. *vasantá-;* Av. *aŋrō ma*ⁱ*nyuš* 'the Evil Spirit'.

Note. In GAv. -*ŋgr*- is also written: GAv. *daŋgra-, aŋgra-*.

Original *sm.*

§ 140. Orig. *sm*- initial = Av. *m*, through loss of *h*.

Av. *maṭ* 'with' = Skt. *smáṭ;* YAv. *mahi,* GAv. *mahī* 'sumus' = Skt. *smási.*

§ 141. Orig. *sm*- internal = Av. *hm*.

Av. *kahmāi* 'to whom' = Skt. *kásmāi;* YAv. *ahmi,* GAv. *ahmī* 'sum' = Skt. *ásmi.*

Original *ski*.

§ 142. Orig. sk_1 = Av. *s* (cf. Skt. *ch*).

Av. *jasaⁱti* 'he comes' = Skt. *gáchati,* cf. βάσκει; Av. *isaⁱti* 'he desires' = Skt. *icháti;* Av. *yasaⁱti* 'holds' = Skt. *yáchati.*

Original *ts*.

§ 143. Orig. $t + s$ = Skt. *s* (through intermediate *ss* §§ 185, 186).

GAv. *hšmāvasū* (loc. pl.) 'belonging to you' = Skt. *yuṣmā́vatsu;* GAv. *drəgvasu* 'among the wicked' *(drəgvat + su);* YAv. *masyō* 'fish' = Skt. *mátsyas;* YAv. *ašava.hšnus* 'rejoicing the righteous' (Yt. 13.63 nom. sing. *·t + s*), cf. Av. *hšnūtəm* 'joy'; YAv. *hvīsaṭ* 'he sweated' (*·d* [= *t*] *+ s* § 74), cf. Skt. √*svid-;* YAv. *raose* 'thou growest', cf. Av. *raodahe, raosta;* GAv. *stavas* 'praising' (nom. sg. *stavaṇt-*), cf. Lat. *aman(t)s;* GAv. *dasvā* 'give thou' = Skt. *datsva;* GAv. *pišyasū* loc. plur. stem *pišyaṇt-* 'beholding'.

Original *ps*.

§ 144. Orig. *ps* = Av. *fš,* except before *r, tr.*

YAv. *drafšō* 'spear, banner' = Skt. *drapsás;* GAv. *hafšī* 'thou extendest', cf. GAv. *haptī* from √*hap-* = Skt. √*sap-;* GAv. *nafšū* 'among children', cf. *napātəm, naptyaēšū* § 187 (5); YAv. *hangərəfšāne* 'I will seize' (*s*-aor.), beside *gərəptəm,* √*garw-* = Skt. √*garbh-.*

Note 1. Observe *s* remains unchanged before *r, tr:*—Av. *fsᵊratu-* 'fruit, reward', Av. *hrafstra-* 'noxious creature'.

Note 2. Observe that *s* (= sk_1 cf. § 142) remains unchanged in the examples *tafsaṭ* (YAv.) 'grew warm', *nərᵊfsaⁱtī* (GAv.) 'it wanes'.

2. Older palatal *ś* (Skt. *ś*).

§ 145. **General Remark.** Older palatal *ś* (Skt. *ś*) commonly appears as Av. *s.* In certain combinations it is changed to *š.*

i. Older palatal *ś* (= Skt. *ś*) = Av. *s*.

§ 146. Older palatal *ś* (= Skt. *ś*) = Av. *s* before vowels, semivowels, and most consonants.

Av. *safᵃ̃ṅhō* 'hoofs' = Skt. *śaphā́sas;* Av. *q̊sayā̊* 'of two parties' = Skt. *q̊śayṓs;* GAv. *sā́stī* 'he teaches' = Skt. *śā́sti;* Av. *pasūm* 'pecus' = Skt. *paśúm;* Av. *spasō* 'spies' = Skt. *spáśas;*—Av. *nasyeⁱti* 'he vanishes' = Skt. *náśyati;* Av. *usyāṭ* 'he might wish' = Skt. *uśyāt;* Av. *isvan-* 'having power', cf. Skt. *īśvará;* — Av. *vīspaⁱtiš* 'village-lord' = Skt. *viśpátis;* Av. *usmahi* 'we wish' = Skt. *uśmási;* Av. *sraēšta-* 'fairest' = Skt. *śréṣṭha-.*

Note 1. On Av. *þ* instead of Av. *s* (= Skt. *ś*), see § 77 Note 2.
Note 2. On older palatal *ś* retained in Av. before *n*, see § 160 Note.
Note 3. On older palatal *ś* in *śv* = Av. *sp*, see § 97.
Note 4. On Av. *saēna-* 'eagle' = Skt. *śyēná-*, see § 187 (3).

ii. Older palatal *ś* = Av. *š*.

§ 147. Older palatal *ś* (= Skt. *ś*) before *t* becomes Av. *š* (= Skt. *ṣṭ*). For examples see § 159.

§ 148. Older palatal *ś* (= Skt. *ś*) before *n* generally becomes Av. *š* (= Skt. *śn*). For examples see § 160.

§ 149. Older palatal *ś* (= Skt. *ś*) a f t e r Av. *f* (= orig. *p*) becomes *š*. For examples see § 161.

iii. Older palatal *ś* = Av. *ž.*

§ 150. Older palatal *ś* (= Skt. *ś*) becomes Av. *ž* before sonants. For examples see § 182.

3. Developed Av. *s.*

§ 151. Av. *s* sometimes results from the dentals *t (þ),* *d (d)* becoming *s* before *t.*

Av. *cistiš* 'wisdom' = Skt. *cíttis;* Av. *amavastara-* 'stronger' *(amavaṇt)* = Skt. *ámavattara-;* Av. *iristahe* 'of the dead' *(√iriþ-);* Av. *aⁱwi-šastar-* 'one who sits'

($\sqrt{had}$-) = Skt. *sáttar*-; Av. *raosta* 'has grown up', cf. Av. *raodạnti*, Skt. $\sqrt{rudh}$-.

Note. Sometimes *t* (*ț*) becomes *s* before *c*:—Av. *raɛvaschra*- 'of splendid family' (*raɛvaṇt*- + *cihra*-); Av. *yaśca* 'and when' (*yaṭ* + *ca*).

§ 152. Av. *s* sometimes results from Av. *z* becoming *s* before *m*.

Av. *upasmạm* 'upon earth' (acc. fem.), beside Av. *zạm, zᵊmō*; Av. *rasmanạm* 'of battle ranks', cf. Av. *rāzayeᵊṇte* 'they arrange in ranks' ($\sqrt{rāz}$- = Skt. $\sqrt{rāj}$-); Av. *maēsmana* 'with urine', cf. Av. *maēzaṇti* 'they make urine' ($\sqrt{miz}$- = Skt. $\sqrt{mih}$-); Av. *barᵊsmana* 'with barsom', cf. Av. $\sqrt{barz}$- 'grow up, be high, great' (= Skt. $\sqrt{barh}$-).

§ 153. Av. *s* more rarely results from Av. *z* becoming *s* before *n*. See also § 164 Note 1.

Av. *asnya*- 'belonging to the day' (from *azan*-) = Skt. *tiró-ahnya*- (fr. *áhan*-); Av. *yasnạm* 'worship' ($\sqrt{yaz}$- = Skt. $\sqrt{yaj}$-).

Av. *š, ṣ̌, ṣ̌*.

§ 154. General Remark. Av. *š* (*ṣ̌, ṣ̌*) stands either for an original *s* after *i, u* and certain consonants; or for an earlier palatal *ś* under special conditions.

Av. *š* (*ṣ̌, ṣ̌*) = Skt. *ṣ*.

§ 155. Av. *š* (*ṣ̌, ṣ̌*) answers to Skt. *ṣ* after *i, u*, and their strengthenings, and after *ḥ* and *ṙ*. Cf. Whitney, *Skt. Gram.* § 180.

Av. *išavō* 'arrows' = Skt. *iṣavas*; Av. *vahištō* 'best' = Skt. *vásiṣṭhas*; Av. *raēṣ̌ayāṭ* 'may wound' = Skt. *rēṣ́dyāt*; Av. *sraēṣ̌yeᵊti* 'it clings', cf. Skt. *śliṣyati*.— Av. *duš.kᵊrᵊtᵊm* 'ill-done' = Skt. *duṣ-kṛtám*; Av. *mušti*- 'fist' = Skt. *muṣṭi*-; Av. *gaoṣ̌ᵊm* 'ear' = Skt. *ghóṣam*; Av. *taoṣ̌ayeⁱti* 'makes still' (Yt. 10.48) = Skt. *tōṣáyati*. —Av. *uḥṣ̌ānᵊm* 'bull' = Skt. *ukṣánam*; GAv. *vaḥṣ̌yā*

'I will speak' = Skt. *vakṣyā́mi.*— Av. *varṣnōiš* 'of a ram' = Skt. *vṛṣṇḗs;* Av. *tarṣnō* 'thirst' = Skt. *tfṣṇā-.*

Note 1. Before *r* we find *s* not *š* though *i* or *u* precede:—GAv. *þwisra-* 'glancing', cf. Skt. √*tviṣ-;* YAv. *kusra-, pisra-.* Similarly in Skt. *usra-, tamisra-,* cf. Whitney, *Sanskrit Grammar* § 181 a.

Note 2. Sometimes, *š* is written for *ṣ́* before *y:*—GAv. *fraššyāmahī* 'we send forth' = Skt. *prḗṣyāmasi;* YAv. *büšyaṇtqm* 'of those to be' = Skt. *bhaviṣyátām,* etc.

§ 156. Av. *-š́* from orig. *s,* appears similarly (§ 155) when final after *i-, u-*vowels and their strengthenings, also after *ḥ* and *r,* cf. § 192 (3).

Av. *ažiš́* 'Dragon' (nom. sg.); *gaⁱriš́* 'mountains' (acc. pl.); *tanuš́* 'body'; *vaṇhūš́* 'good' (acc. pl.); *rašnaoš́* 'of Rashnu, Justice'; *vaṇhə̄uš́* 'of the good'; *barōiš́* 'thou shouldst bear'; *gāuš́* 'cow'; *uḥdāiš́* 'with words'. — *druḥš́* 'fiend'; *ānuš́.haḥš́* 'following'; *parō-darᵊš́* 'Fore-seer' § 192 (3).

§ 157. On Av. *fš́* from orig. *ps,* see § 144.

§ 158. Av. *š́* (= older palatal *š́* + *s* = Indog. *kₗs*) = Skt. *kṣ.*

Av. *vaš́i* 'thou wilt' = Skt. *vákṣi* (√*vaš́-*); Av. *dīš́yāṭ* 'should show' (opt. aor.), cf. Skt. *adikṣat*(√*diš́-*); Av. *nāš́āⁱti* 'may vanish' (aor. subj.), √*nas-*; Av. *parōdarᵊš́* 'Fore-seer, the cock' (*-dars* + *s* nom. sg.); GAv. *nāš́ū* loc. pl. from *nās-* 'loss, mishap'.—So Av. *š́aēti* 'he dwells' = Skt. *kṣḗti;* Av. *moš́u* 'quickly' = Skt. *makṣú,* cf. Lat. *mox.*—Similarly Av. *daš́ina-* 'right, dexter' = Skt. *dákṣina-;* Av. √*taš́-* 'to fabricate' = Skt. *takṣ-.*

Note 1. Indog. *kₗs* appears in Av. as *ḥš́.*—In Skt. orig. *kₗs* and *kₗs* fell together in *kṣ;* but Av. still holds them apart as respectively *ḥš́* and *š́.* See Hübschmann, *Z.D.M.G.* 38 p. 428. The same distinction between the two original sounds is to be remarked in Prakrit and Pali as observed by Pischel, *Gött. gel. Anz.* 1881, p. 1322.

Note 2. On *ḥšmākəm* 'of you' and *āḥšnūš́* 'up to the knees', cf. §§ 77 Note 1, 188.

§ 159. Av. š appears for older palatal ś (= Skt. ś) before t (= Skt. ṣṭ), cf. § 147.

Av. naštō 'made to vanish' = Skt. naṣṭás (√naś-); GAv. vaštī 'he wishes' = Skt. váṣṭi (√vaś-); Av. darští- 'seeing, sight' = Skt. dṛṣṭi-; Av. paršta- 'question' = Skt. pṛṣṭá- (√praś-); GAv. daēdōišt redupl. aor. 3 sg. mid. Av. √diš- 'show' = Skt. √diś-.

§ 160. Av. š appears for older palatal ś (= Skt. ś) before n = Skt. śn, cf. § 148.

Av. ašnaoiti 'he attains' = Skt. aśnóti; Av. frašnō 'question' = Skt. praśnás; Av. spašnaoṭ 'he espied' √spas- = Skt. √spaś-.

Note. Sometimes Av. s appears instead of the above š before n, cf. § 146, and Note 2:—Av. snaþa- 'smiting, wounding', to √snaþ- = Skt. śnath-; Av. vasna 'by will', √vas- = Skt. √vaś-.

§ 161. Av. š appears for old palatal ś (= Skt. ś) after Av. f (= orig. p), cf. similarly, orig. ps (dental) § 144.

Av. fšōiš 'with fetters', cf. Skt. 2 paś- 'to bind'; Av. haᵘrva-fš-avō 'having whole flocks' (pasu- = Skt. paśú-).

Note. On Av. tafsaṭ, nərəfsaiti see § 144 Note 2.

§ 162. Av. šy (or sometimes simply š) appears for older cy. In GAv. the y is mostly retained; in YAv. the y is mostly dropped.

YAv. šyaoþnəm, GAv. šyaoþᵃnəm 'deed' = Skt. cyáutnám; GAv. ašyō, YAv. ašō 'worse', comparat. to aka- (superl. acišta-), cf. Skt. aka-; YAv. šāvayōiṭ 'might cause to go' (√šu-) = Skt. cyāváyēt (√cyu-); GAv. šyeṇtī 'they abide, repose', YAv. šāitīm 'repose, joy', cf. Lat. quies; GYAv. fraša- 'forward, prone, ready' = Skt. prācyá-; GAv. vašyeitē 'is spoken' = Skt. ucyátē. See Hübschmann, Z.D.M.G. xxxviii. p. 431.

§ 163. Av. š (ṣ̌) = Skt. rt. See Bartholomae, A.F. ii. p. 39.

Av. aməšəm 'immortal' = Skt. amŕtam; Av. pəšanå 'battles' = Skt. pŕtanās; Av. mašyehe 'of mortal' = Skt. mártyasya; Av. bāšārəm 'rider' = Skt. bhártāram. —Likewise Av. ašavanəm 'the righteous' = Skt. ṛtá-

vānam; Av. *aǯǝm* 'Right, righteoúsness', beside Av.
an-arᵊtāiš = Skt. *r̥tám;* Av. *þwāǯǝm* 'quickly' = Skt.
tūrtám, et al.

Note. As a rule, Av. *ǯ* = Skt. *árt,* 'ft (observe accent), and Av. *ʒrᵊt*
= Skt. *r̥t* (observe unaccented): — e. g. Av. *mǝrᵊtō* 'dead' = Skt. *mr̥tás;*
Av. *bǝrᵊtǝm* 'carried' = Skt. *bhr̥tám;* Av. *fra-bǝrᵊtārǝm* title of priest =
Skt. *-bhartáram.* Allowing a s h i f t of accent would explain a number of
apparent anomalies where the law as to accent appears not to hold.

§ 164. Av. *ǯ* results from Av. *z* changed to *ǯ* before *n.*

Av. *rāǯnǝm* 'of ordinances', from stem *rāzan-;* Av.
raǯnūm 'Justice', beside *raz-ištǝm* 'most just', Skt.
ráj-iṣṭham; Av. *barᵊǯnavō* 'heights' beside *bǝrᵊz-atō*
'of the high', Skt. *br̥hatás;* Av. *dužvarᵊǯnavhō* 'evil-
doers' *(varz-);* Av. *ā-ḫ-ǯnūš* 'up to the knees', beside
zanva 'knees', cf. Skt. *abhi-jñú* § 188.

Note 1. Observe, however, that sometimes Av. *s* instead of *ǯ* (for
Av. *z*) before *n* is found, cf. § 153:—Av. *asni* 'by day' *(azan-)* = Skt. *áhni*
(áhan-); Av. *parō.asna-* 'beyond the day, future', cf. Skt. *aparāhṇá-* 'after
mid-day'; Av. *yasnǝm* 'worship' (beside *yaz-aᵢtē*) = Skt. *yajñám;* Av. *āsna-*
'in-born' *(ā + √zan-* 'to bear').

Note 2. Observe * š* in Av. *šnātar-* (√*zan-* 'know') = Skt. *jñātár;*
Av. *šnūm* 'knee', *āšnubyascit* 'even to the knees'.

§ 165. Av. *ǯ* sometimes results from Av. *z* (= Skt. *j*
or *h*) being changed to *ǯ* before *s.*—See §§ 185, 186.

GAv. *ᵘrvāǯat* 'shall proceed' (*s*-aor.), √*vraz-* = Skt. *vraj-;* GAv.
varᵊǯaitī 'may do' (*s*-aor.), √*varz-,* cf. Skt. √*varj-;* GAv. *varᵊǯ-cā*
2 sg. aor. (•*z* + *s*); Av. *hvarᵊǯ* 'well-doing' nom. sg. (•*z* + *s*); Av.
harᵊǯyamna- 'about to be imbrued' (•*z* + *s*√*harz-* = Skt. *sarj-*).

Note. Perhaps here Av. *aǯaᵢta* 'might be led' beside Av. *azaᵢti,*
Skt. *ájati.*

§ 166. Av. *ǯ* sometimes results from Av. *z* (= Skt. *j*)
being changed to *ǯ* before *t* (cf. Skt. *ṣṭ*).

Av. •*marǯtō* 'rubbed' (√*marz-*) = Skt. •*mr̥ṣṭás* (√*marj-*); Av.
•*harǯta-* 'imbrued' (√*harz-*) = Skt. •*sr̥ṣṭá-* (√*sarj-*); Av. *yaǯtar-*
'worshipper' (√*yaz-*) = Skt. *yaṣṭár-* (√*yaj-*).

Av. z.

§ 167. **General Remark.** Av. z appears either as the representative of Skt. *j* or *h*, see § 88; or it is the corresponding sonant to *s*, §§ 106, 74.

§ 168. Av. z = Skt. *j*.

Av. *zaoẑəm* 'wish' = Skt. *jóṣam*; Av. *zātō* 'born' = Skt. *jātás*; Av. *zəmbayadwəm* 'ye knock together' = Skt. *jambháyadhvam*; Av. *zināṭ* 'may take violently' = Skt. *jināt*; Av. *zrayō* 'sea' = Skt. *jráyas*. — Av. *azaiti* 'he drives' = Skt. *ájati*; Av. *yazaite* 'he worships' = Skt. *yájatē*; Av. *harᵉzaṇti* 'they send forth' = Skt. *sṛjánti*; Av. *vazrəm* 'club' = Skt. *vájram*.

§ 169. Av. z = Skt. *h*.

Av. *zasta-* 'hand' = Skt. *hásta-*; Av. *zarōiš* 'of the golden' = Skt. *háres*; Av. *zī* 'for' = Skt. *hí*. — Av. *azəm* 'ἐγώ' = Skt. *ahám*; Av. *mazištō* 'μέγ-ιστος' = Skt. *máhiṣṭhas*; Av. *bāzuš* 'πῆχυς' = Skt. *bāhús*; Av. *bərᵉzaṇtəm* 'great, high' = Skt. *bṛhántam*; Av. *maēzaṇti* 'mingunt' = Skt. *méhanti*; Av. *izyeiti* 'he seeks', cf. Skt. *íhatē*.

§ 170. Av. z results often from *s* being sonantized before sonant consonants.

Av. *azgatō* 'unmatched, unconquered' Yt. 13.107, √*hag-*, orig. *sag-* = Skt. √*sagh-*; Av. *vaṇhazdā* 'giving the best' (comparat. to *vaṇhu-* + √*dā*), cf. Anc. Pers. *vahyazdāta-* nom. propr.; Av. *māzdrājahya-* 'a month long', cf. Skt. *más-*; Av. *azdᵉbiš* 'with bones' = (stem *ast-*); GAv. *zdī* 'be thou', cf. Av. *as-ti* 'he is'. Cf. Brugmann, *Grundriss der vergl. Gram.* §§ 589 seq.

§ 171. Av. z (similarly § 170) in combination *zd* = Skt. *(ī)dh*, *(ā)dh*. See above (Bartholomae's Law) § 89; and Brugmann, *Grundriss der vergl. Gram.* §§ 476, 591.

Av. *mazdōh-* 'wisdom, Mazda' = Skt. *•médhas*; GAv. *prāzdūm* 'ye protected' (*s*-aor. from √*prā-*) = Skt. *trādhvam*; et al.

Original Av. * s* changed to *s*, *š*.

§ 172. Av. *z* before *n* becomes *s* (*š*), see §§ 153, 164 for examples.
§ 173. Av. *z* before *m* becomes *s*, see § 152 examples.
§ 174. Av. *z* before *t* becomes *š*, see § 166 examples.
§ 175. Av. *z* before *s* becomes *š*, see § 165 examples.

Av. *ž*.

§ 176. **General Remark.** Av. *ž* is the corresponding sonant to *š* as Av. *z* is to *s*. Sometimes (though more rarely) it answers like *z* to Skt. *j*, *h*.

§ 177. Av. *š* (more rarely) = Skt. *j*. See § 88 Note 1.

Av. *°taēžəm* 'sharpness, edge', cf. Skt. *tējas* ($\sqrt{tij}$-); Av. *bažat* 'he distributed, offered' = Skt. *bhájat*.

§ 178. Av. *š* (more rarely) = Skt. *h*. See § 88 Note 1.

Av. *ažiš* 'Dragon' = Skt. *áhis*; Av. *dažaiti* 'it burns' = Skt. *dáhati*.

§ 179. Av. *ž* most commonly results from Av. *š* being sonantized before sonant consonants.

GAv. *asrūždūm* 'ye were heard of' (Ys. **32**.3, *s*-aor. mid.-pass. $\sqrt{sru}$-) = Skt. *asrōḍhvam*, beside Av. *s°raošānē*, *sraoša*-; Av. *snaiᵖižbya* 'with two weapons' from stem Av. *snaiᵖiš*-; Av. *awždāta*- 'laid in the waters', beside Av. *afšciᵖra*- 'having the seed of waters'; Av. *yaoždaᵖəntəm* 'making pure', beside Av. *yaoš* = Skt. *yós*. — Av. *dužūḫtəm* 'ill-spoken' = Skt. *duruktám*; Av. *dužvacaṅhō* 'ill-speaking', beside Av. *duškər°təm* 'ill done' = Skt. *durvacas, duṣkṛtám*; Av. *dušmanaṅhe* 'to the evil-minded' (here *m*-surd) = Skt. *durmanasē*.

Note. Exceptions occur: GAv. *ər°žvacə* 'true-speaking' et al.; cf. Bartholomae, *B.B.* xiii. p. 77.

§ 180. Av. *wš* (= orig. *bh* + *s*) = Skt. *ps*. See § 89.

YAv. *diwžat* 'from deceit', GAv. *diwžaidyāi* 'to deceive', cf. Skt. *dipsati*.

§ 181. YAv. *š* (= Av. *z* [= Skt. *h*] + *s*) = Skt. *kṣ*. Cf. § 165.

YAv. *uz-važat* 'he carried forth' (*s*-aor. from $\sqrt{vaz}$-) = Skt. *vákṣat* ($\sqrt{vah}$-).

Note 1. On *š* in GAv. *ažžōnvamnəm* 'unharmed' cf. Skt. √*kṣan-*, see § 89.
Note 2. GAv. *āžuš* Ys. 53.7 is uncertain. Uncertain also GYAv. *īža-*
'zeal, striving' to √*īz-* = Skt. √*īh-* (?).

§ 182. Av. *ž* appears for old palatal *ǰ* (= Skt. *ś*) before sonants.

GAv. *āždyāi* 'to attain', √*as-* = Skt. √*aś-;* GYAv. *vīžibyō* 'to, from villages' *(vīs-)* = Skt. *viḍbhyás (viś-).*

§ 183. Av. *žd* = Skt. *ḍh,* or *ḍ.* See Brugmann, *Grundriss* § 591.

Av. *mīždəm* 'μισθόν' = Skt. *mīḍhám;* Av. *mərəždikəm* 'mercy' (if from √*marž-,* cf. § 179) = Skt. *mṛḍīkám.* Here again GAv. *asrūždūm* Ys. 32.3 (§ 179) = Skt. *asrōḍhvam.*

Aspiration.

Av. ⲱ, ⳤ, ⲙ.

h, ḥ, hʷ.

§ 184. These are all derived from an original *s*-sound, and have been treated, in particulars, under the sibilants § 110 seqq.

Some Additional Rules as to Consonants.

§ 185. In Av., assimilation of consonants is sometimes found.

YAv. *nmānəm* 'house' = GAv. *dəmānəm;* Av. *kamnəm* 'few' (for **kabnəm* or *kambnəm* § 186), cf. *kambištəm.*— Total assimilation, Av. *bunəm* 'foundation' (for *bunnəm* § 186) = Skt. *budhnám;* Av. *sanaṯ* 'it appeared' Yt. 14.7 (i. e. *sannaṯ, sad-naṯ*).

§ 186. In Av., double consonants (i. e. the same consonant repeated) are not allowed. If owing to total assimilation § 185 they should occur, the combination is then reduced in writing to a single consonant.

Av. *masyō* 'fish' (for *massyō* § 185) = Skt. *mátsyas;* Av. *usnāⁱti-* 'ablution' (for *ussnāⁱti-,* i. e. *ud-snāⁱti-* § 185, cf. Av. *us tanūm snayaēta*); Av. *dušiti-* 'distress' (i. e. *duš-šiti-,* cf. Skt. *sukṣiti-*); Av. *həmiþyāṯ* from *həm* + √*miþ-* 'to change', Ys. 53.9; GAv. *drəgvasū* 'among the wicked' (for *drəgvassu*); Av. *uṣ̌ahva* 'at dawn' (for *uṣ̌ah-hva*); Av. *ajāvarᵊš* 'evil-doing' (nom. sg. *varᵊz-š*, from √*varz-* § 165); Av. *bunəm* § 185 end.

§ 187. A consonant sometimes falls out. See § 186.

(1) *g* before *v* falls out in YAv.

YAv. *drīvyå̄s-ca* 'poor' (gen. fem.), beside YAv. *drijaoš* (gen. masc. *driju-*); YAv. *drvaṇtəm* 'wicked', beside GAv. *drəgvaṇtəm*, cf. Skt. *drúhvan-*; YAv. *hvōvō* nomen propr. beside GAv. *hvōgvō*.

(2) *d* between consonants falls out.

Av. *bərᵊzaṇbya* 'great' (dat. dual for older *°andbhy°*).

(3) *y* after initial older *ś*-palatal (= Skt. *ś*) sometimes falls out.

Av. *sāmahe* 'of black' = Skt. *śyāmásya*; Av. *saēnō* 'eagle' = Skt. *śyēnás*.

(4) *h* (= original *s*) is dropped before *m* (initial) and *r* §§ 140, 138 seq.

(5) *k* (*ḳ*) seems sometimes to fall out.

Av. *tūiryа-* 'quartus' for **kturya-* cf. *ā-ḳtūirya-* 'four times'; Av. *avaṣ̌ata* 'he spake', if these forms are from √*vac-*.

(6) *t* seems sometimes to fall out.

GAv. *nafṣ̌ū* loc. pl. for **napt-su* from Av. *napāt-*, *napt-* 'offspring', cf. § 185 seq.

§ 188. Av. *ḳ* is sometimes introduced before *ṣ̌*.

Av. *āḳṣ̌nūš* 'knee-high', cf. Skt. *abhi-jñu*; Av. *ḳṣ̌mākəm*, *ḳṣ̌maṭ* 'of, from you'.

§ 189. On *s* (= Skt. *ś*, *s*) retained before *-ca* etc., see §§ 120 Note; 124 Note; 129.

§ 190. In Av., *y* takes the place of *v* between *u* and *e*.

Av. *duyē* 'two' = Skt. *dvé*; Av. *upa.mruyē* 'I invoke' = Skt. *upa-bruvé*; Av. *tanuyē* 'for the body' = Skt. *tanvè*; Av. *°buye* 'to be' = Skt. *bhuvé*.

Note. Similarly Av. *uye* 'both' (for **uve*, *uwe* § 68 Note 1) = Skt. *ubhé*.

§ 191. In Av., m e t a t h e s i s of *r* often takes place;
—Skt. *vr (vl)* becomes with prothesis § 71, Av. *ᵘrv.*

Av. *āþrava* 'priest' = Skt. *átharvā*; Av. *caþrudasō*
'fourteenth' = Skt. *caturdaśás*; Av. *brātᵘⁱryō* 'uncle'
(for *brātvryō* § 62) = Skt. *bhrátṛvyas*; Av. *ᵘrvātāiš*
'with doctrines', cf. Skt. *vrátāiš*; Av. *ᵘrvaþō* 'faithful,
friend' (√ *var-*).

§ 192. As f i n a l c o n s o n a n t s in Av., the following
may stand: (1) nasal, *n* and *m*, (2) dental *ţ* (or *t* when
preceded by developed *s* or by *š*), (3) sibilant *š* and *s.*—
Two consonants may stand in the case of *hš, fš, št, st*
and GAv. *ṇg.*

(1) *barən* 'they carried'; *azəm* 'I'; (2) *pərᵊsaţ* 'he
asked'; *amavaţ* 'strong'; (3) *hizubīš* 'with tongues';
tanuš 'body'; *haᵘrvatās* 'perfection' (nom. sg. *-tāt-s*);
hšayąs 'ruling' (nom. sg. *-ant-s*).— *druhš* 'fiend, Druj';
āfš 'water'; *kərᵊfš* 'corpse'; *cōišt* 'he promised, an-
nounced'; *aⁱbī.mōist* 'he turned toward'.— GAv. *ma-
šyąṇg* 'mortals' acc. pl.

Note. When orig. *s* precedes f i n a l *t* the latter is dropped:—e. g.
Av.· *ås* (i. e. *°ås-t*) 'was' = Skt. *åsīt*; Av. *cinas* (i. e. *°cinast* § 109) 'thou
didst promise', opp. to *cōišt* or to *mōist (miþ-).*

§ 193. Av. *m* appears instead of f i n a l *n* in voca-
tives of *an*-stems.

Av. *ašāum* 'O righteous one' = Skt. *ŗtāvan*; Av.
āþraom 'O priest' = Skt. *átharvan*; Av. *yum* (for
*yuvən) 'O youth' = Skt. *yúvan*; Av. *þrizafəm* 'O
triple-jawed' (cf. acc. *þrizafanəm*).

Note 1. The MSS. often fluctuate between final *m* and *n* in endings,
ą, ąn, ąm, e. g. *haomą, haomąn, haomąm* 'haoma-offerings' (acc. pl.) Yt. 10.92
= Skt. *sómān*, cf. § 45 Note 2.— So apparently, Av. *caṣmqm* 'in eye', cf.
Skt. *jánman.*

Note 2. Observe other MS. fluctuations (cons. and vowel):— *c j;
j s; þ d; d ω; ω āu; ω āţ; ai aē; ə u* — *daþqm, dadqm; mazdā, mazdω;
ḳratω °tāu; vastrω °trāţ.*

§ 194. Av. avoids generally a repetition of the same syllable.

Av. *maⁱdyāⁱryehe* 'of Mid-Year' (for *maⁱdya-yāⁱryehe*); *huyāⁱryå* 'of good harvest' (for *huyāⁱryayå*); Av. *fra-ziṇte, fraziṇta* 'they are, were plundered' (for **fra-zinaṇte, *frazinaṇta), cf. Skt. *prajindte;* Av. *hvarᵊna hacimnō* for **hvarᵊnaṽha hacimnō* attended with glory Yt. 10.121.

Resumé.
Principal differences between Sanskrit and Avesta in Phonology.
Vowels.

§ 195. GAv. lengthens all final vowels, YAv. lengthens them in monosyllables, shortens them in polysyllables (§§ 24—26).

§ 196. Original *ĭ* and *ŭ* are lengthened before final *m* in Av. (§ 23).

§ 197. Av. *ı ᵊ* generally answers to Skt. *a* before *m* or *n.* — Av. *ɹrᵊ (arᵊ)* = Skt. *r* (§§ 29, 47).

§ 198. Av. *ↄ e*, commonly a modification of internal *a* after *y.* — Sometimes equals final *ya* (§§ 34, 67).

§ 199. Av. ↂ *ŏ* chiefly equals final Skt. *as (ŏ)* § 120.

§ 200. Av. ↦ *åˢ* chiefly equals Skt. *ās;* — more rarely Skt. *ā* + stop-sound (§§ 121—124, 44).

§ 201. Av. ↠ *q* is a nasalization of *a (ā)* before *m* or *n*. It often equals Skt. *a* with anusvāra (§§ 45, 46).

Diphthongs.

§ 202. The Skt. *ē* is represented by Av. *aē, ōi*, or (when final) *e;* the Skt. *ō* by Av. *ao, ɜu*, or (when final) *ō* (§§ 55—58, 35, 41).

§ 203. A striking peculiarity in Av. is Epenthesis (§ 70) and Anaptyxis (§ 72) and the frequent Reductions (samprasāraṇa etc.) § 63 seq.

Consonants.

§ 204. The voiceless spirants Av. *ḫ, þ, f* are chiefly sprung from old tenues *k, t, p* before consonants; — sometimes they represent old voiceless aspirates (§ 77 seq.).

§ 205. The original voiced aspirates *gh, dh, bh* fell primarily together with the m e d i a e in Av. (§ 82).

§ 206. The v o i c e d s p i r a n t s Av. *j, d, w* are d e v e l o p m e n t s from these earlier two-fold mediae (§ 83).

§ 207. Skt. *j* is often represented by Av. *z* (§ 168).

§ 208. Skt. *h* is represented sometimes by Av. *j*, sometimes by Av. *z* (§§ 88, 169).

§ 209. Skt. *s* generally becomes *h* in Av. (§ 110 seq.).

§ 210. Skt. *as* (internal) becomes *avh, ah;* or (final) *ŏ* (§§ 111—120).

§ 211. Av. *ăs* (internal) becomes *ávh, ăh;* or (final) *á* (§§ 121—124).

§ 212. Skt. *š* is represented in Av. by *s* (§ 146).

§ 213. Skt. *šv* is represented in Av. by *sp* (§ 97).

§ 214. Skt. *ch* is represented in Av. by *s* (§ 142).

§ 215. Dentals before dentals are changed to *s* in Av. (§ 151).

§ 216. Av. *z* and *s* (= Skt. *š*) before voiceless consonants generally become *š* (§§ 164—166, 160).

§ 217. Skt. *rt* is often represented in Av. by *š* (§ 163).

§ 218. Skt. *kš* is represented by Av. *hš* or *š* (§ 158 Note 1).

INFLECTION.

DECLENSION,

NOUNS AND ADJECTIVES.

§ 219. Nominal declension includes nouns and adjectives; these may be conveniently taken together in Avesta and divided into two great classes of declension—(a) the vowel class, and (b) the consonant class—according as the stem ends in a vowel or in a consonant.

For a summary of Avesta declension in a tabular form, see opposite page.

§ 220. **Case, Number, Gender.** The Avesta agrees with the Sanskrit in its eight cases, nominative, accusative, instrumental, dative, ablative, genitive, locative, vocative; three numbers, singular, dual, plural; and in the three genders, masculine, feminine, and neuter.

The uses of the cases are in general the same as in Skt., but see § 233. The Av. dual is interesting as showing a distinct form for the locative case, see §§ 223, 236, 262. In Avesta, a substantive has commonly the same gender that it has in Sanskrit.

Note 1. As to gender, however, some individual peculiarities occur, as a few words in Av. show a different gender from that which they have in Skt.:—e. g. Av. *vāc-* (masc.) 'vox' = Skt. *vā́c* (fem.)—but observe the compound *paítivac-* is fem.; Av. *tarṣna-* (masc.) 'thirst' = Skt. *tṛṣṇā-* (fem.); Av. *eaṇga-* (masc.) 'leg' = Skt. *jáṅghā-* (fem.); Av. *sti-* (fem.) 'existence, creation' = Skt. *sti-* (masc.) — This occasional phenomenon is sometimes important to observe in the matter of exegesis.

Note 2. On fem. and neut. plur. forms interchanging with each other, see § 232.

SYNOPSIS OF DECLENSION.

B. Consonant Stems.   A. Vowel Stems.

1. Stems in *a*.

2. Stems in *ā* { a. Derivative stems in -*ā*.
       b. Radical stems in -*ā*.

3. Stems in *i* and *ī* { a. Derivative stems in original -*i*.
       b. Derivative stems in original -*ī*.
       c. Radical stems in original -*ī*.

4. Stems in *u* and *ū* { a. Derivative stems in original -*u*.
       b. Derivative stems in original -*ū*.
       c. Radical stems in original -*ū*.

5. Diphthongal stems { a. Stems in -*āi*.
       b. Stems in -*āu*.

6. (A) Stems without suffix.

7. (B) Derivative stems in -*vaṇṭ*, -*maṇṭ*, -*vaṇṭ*.

8. (C) Derivative stems in -*an*, -*man*, -*van*.

9. (D) Derivative stems in -*in*.

10. (E) Radical stems in -*n* and -*m*.

11. (F) Stems in original -*r* { a. Derivative stems in original -*tar*, -*ar*.
       b. Radical stems in original -*r*.
       c. Neuters (derivative) in original -*ar*.

12. (G) Stems in original -*s* { a. Derivative stems in -*h* (original -*s*) — { α. -*ah*. β. -*yah*. γ. -*vah*.
       b. Radical stems in -*h* (original -*s*) — { α. -*ah*. β. -*īh*.
       c. Derivative stems in -*iḥ*, -*uḥ*. β. Those resembling them.

§ 221. **Endings.** Here may be enumerated the normal e n d i n g s which are added to the stem in formation of the various cases. The s t e m itself, moreover, s o m e t i m e s v a r i e s in assuming these endings, as it often appears in a stronger form in certain cases, and in a weaker form in others. Connecting elements as in Skt. seem at times to be introduced between stem and ending.

The normal endings (but observe §§ 25, 26) are:

i. MASCULINE—FEMININE.

	Av.	Singular:	cf. Skt.
N.	-s (-š),—		-s,—
A.	-(a)m		-(a)m
I.	-ā		-ā
D.	-ē		-ē
Abl.	-(a)ṭ		-at
G.	(-as) -ō; -s (-š); -he, -hyā		-as; -s; -sya
L.	-i		-i
V.	—		—

		Dual:	
N.A.V.	-ā		-ā (Ved.)
I.D.Abl.	-byā		-bhyām
G.	-ā̊		-ōs
L.	-ō		see gen.

		Plural:	
N.V.	(-as) -ō, ā		-as
A.	(-ṇs), (-as) -ō; ā		(-ns) -as
I.	-biš		-bhis
D.	(-byas) -byō		-bhyas
G.	-ạm		-ām
L.	-su, šu, hu		-su

ii. NEUTER (Separate Forms).

Sg.	N.A.V.	—, -m		—, -m
Du.	N.A.V.	—, -ī		-ī
Pl.	N.A.V.	—, -i		-i

General Remarks on the Endings.

i. MASCULINE—FEMININE.

§ 222. Singular:—

Nominative: The typical ending -*s* is disguised by entering into euphonic combinations with vowels and consonants; it assumes especially often the form -*š*, § 156.—Often it is wanting—e. g. cf. derivative stems in orig. *ā* and *ī*.

Accusative: The typical ending -*m* appears after vowels; the ending -*әm* (= -*am* = -*ṃm*) after consonants. Cf. also § 23.

Instrumental: Regularly *ā*, *a*, § 25.—This is sometimes disguised by combining with a preceding *y* to *ē*, § 67.—The fem. *ā*-declension, as in Skt., shows a fuller form, making the case end in -*ayā* (-*aya*) beside the simpler normal form in *ā*.

Dative: YAv. -*e* (orig. -*ai*), GAv. -*ē*, -*ōi*, § 56.—Notice of course Av. -*aē-ca*.—In the *a*-declension, the *ē* (orig. *ai*) unites with the stem vowel into *āi*, cf. Gr. φ, § 60.—The feminine derivative *ā*-stems and *ī*-stems show a fuller ending *āi*, which in the *ā*-stems is preceded by a *y*, as in Skt. also.

Ablative: The typical ending is -*t*, or -*(a)t* (consonant decl.), -*āt* (in *a*-decl.). Observe, this is not confined, as in Skt., simply to the *a*-declension, but appears in all the declensions (*ā*, *ī*, *u* and cons.). Instances of interchanges between -*at* and -*āt* are not infrequent.— Observe before -*ca*, the form -*āatca*, § 53 iv.—The ending -*(a)t* is often followed by the enclitic postposition *a*, thus giving -*(a)ta*.—In GAv., the *t*-ablative is found, as in Skt., only with the *a*-declension, e. g. *ḫǰaprāt*, *akāt*; otherwise, as in Skt., the genitive is used with ablative force.—The feminine *ā*- and *ī*-stems, unlike the Skt., both show -*āt* which in the *ā*-stems is preceded by *y*.

Genitive: The common ending, as in Skt., is *ō*, -*asca*; it occurs chiefly in the consonant declension.—The ending, simple (*s*) *š* is also found, e. g. throughout the *i*- and *u*-stems, the stem vowel being generally strengthened before it.—In the *a*-stems, the ending -*he* (Skt. -*sya*, § 67), GAv. -*hyā*, -*hyācā* (on *ḫ* cf. § 133) is regularly found. — In feminine *ā*- and *ī*-stems a fuller ending -*ǣ*, -*ǣsca* (= Skt. *ās*) is found, which in the *ā*-declension is preceded by *y* as in Skt.— see dative above.

Locative: The normal form, as in Skt., is -*i*.—In the *a*-declension, this coalesces with the stem vowel to -*e*, -*aē-ca*.—Sometimes the loc. is without ending—the stem being simply strengthened, e. g. cf. *u*-stems and some *an*-forms.—To the locative ending, an enclitic postpositive *a* is often attached, giving rise to forms in -*ya* (-*aya*),

5

-ava.—The feminine *ā*-stems show *-aya* (perhaps orig. instr., or *ya*-suffix advl.) answering to Skt. *-āyām*.

Vocative: Commonly, simple stem without ending. — Often the nom. stands instead of the vocative.

§ 223. **Dual**:—

Nom. Acc. Voc.: The prevailing form for the consonant and the *a*-declension is *ā (a)*, cf. Vedic Skt. *ā*.—The *ā*-stems show *e (e)*.—The masc. fem. *i*- and *u*-stems simply lengthen (then YAv., cf. § 25 and Note, shorten) their stem vowels.

Instr. Dat. Abl.: The normal ending in Av. is *-byā (-bya)*.—The form *-byqm*, which exactly corresponds to Skt. *-bhyām*, is only once found, in Av. *brvaṯbyqm* 'both brows'.—Instead of YAv. *-bya*, the form written *-we* (§§ 67, 87) often appears.

Genitive: Regularly *-ð*, *-ðsca* answering to Skt. *-ōs*—a preceding vowel being treated as in Skt.

Locative: The ending *ō* occurs in *zastayō* (YAv.) from *zasta-* 'hand', in *ubōyō* (GAv.) from *uba-* 'both', and *aŋhvō* (GAv.) Ys. 41.2 from *aŋhu-* 'world, life'.

§ 224. **Plural**:—

Nom. Voc.: The typical form orig. *as* occurs both in the vowel and the consonant classes of declension.—But beside this, in the masculine of both classes t h e e n d i n g *ā (a)* is common, especially in YAv.—Its occurrence in the consonant, declension is probably due to borrowing from the *a*-decl.—In the *a*-declension, the normal orig. *-as* unites, as in Skt., with the stem vowel, thus giving *-ð* (= orig. *-ās*, § 124) which is, however, less common than the ending *ā (a)*.—Often the *a*-stems have *-ðuhō*, cf. Vedic Skt. *-āsas*.—In the *ī*-stems, the usual nom. pl., as in Vedic Skt., is *-īš* instead of *-yō*, *-yasca*.

Accusative: The original ending *-ns* (seen in *-qsca* from *a*-stems) appears in the consonant stems as *-ō*, *-as°* (i. e. orig. *-ŋs*).—Beside this, in the masculine of both classes t h e e n d i n g *ā (a)* is found, cf. nom. above. —In the *a*-declension the normal orig. *-ns* combines with the *a* of the stem into YAv. *-q(n)*, *-qsca*, GAv. *-ŋg*, *-qsca*—sometimes also YAv. *-š*, *-šŝca*.—The fem. *ā*-stems show *-ð*, *-ðsca*.—The masc. fem. *i*- and *u*-stems show generally *-īš*, *-ūš*.

Instrumental: Everywhere the ending *-bīš*, *-bīš* (§ 21 Note), except in the *a*-stems which show *-āiš*.

Dat. Abl.: The regular form is *-byō*, *-byasca*, or written *-wyō*, *-ṯyō*, *-uyō*, §§ 83 (4), 87, 62 Note 3.

Genitive: Universally *-qm*, which is often dissyllabic as in Vedic Skt. —In the vowel stems an *n* is usually inserted before this *-qm*.

Locative: The normal form is *-hu, -ǰu.*—To this ending, an enclitic postpositive *a* in YAv. is óften attached, thus giving *-hva, -ǰva*, cf. Skt. *vánəṣu å* RV. 9.62.8.

ii. NEUTER (Separate Forms).

The neuter shows in general the same endings as the masculine. Its special forms, however, are worthy of note in the following cases:

§ 225. Singular:—

Nom. Acc. Voc.: In general no ending—the case is simply the bare stem in its weak form, if the stem have a weak form. The *a*-stems have *m* as in the accusative masculine.

§ 226. Dual:—

Nom. Acc. Voc.: The ending orig. *-ī* is to be recognized in the *a*-stems, where it is combined with the stem vowel preceding it, into *e*, e. g. *duy-e saḯt-e* 'two hundred'.—Sometimes the simple stem (or like nom. sing.) seems to be used, e. g. *va, dąma* Yt. 15.43, *aǰi* 'two eyes' Yt. 11.2.

§ 227. Plural:—

Nom. Acc. Voc.: Commonly the ending is w a n t i n g i. e. the case-form is the simple stem, or if consonantal it is the strongest form of the stem (cf. *afsmanivąn* i. e. orig. *°ánt;* or again *manæ* from *ah*-stem). —Seldom the ending is *-i: nåmǰni*, cf. Skt. *nåmåni.*—Sometimes in the consonant declension, the endings *-a, -æ* of the vowel *(a-* or *å-)* declension are found, cf. § 234, e. g. *daźmåna, masanæ, maźsma* to stems *daźman-* 'eye, glance', *masan-* 'greatness', *maźsman-* 'urine', but see § 308.

§ 228. General Plural Case.

The plural in Av. occasionally shows a certain· instability which is exhibited in the transfer or rather generalization of some of its case-forms. This is especially true of the neuter plural; and in general it may be added that the tendency to fluctuation increases in proportion to the lateness of the text.—See also, Johannes Schmidt, *Pluralbildungen der indogermanischen Neutra* pp. 259 seq., 98 seq.

§ 229. (1) The instrumental plural in *-bǰ, -åǰ* is occasionally used in YAv. as g e n e r a l p l u r a l case, e. g. *aṣdbǰ* (as acc. neut. Vd. 6.49)— *vīspåǰ* (nom. Yt. 8.48), *sraēǰtåǰ* (Yt. 22.9), *ḳrafstråǰ* (as acc. Ys. 19.2), etc.

§ 230. (2) The *an*-stems have also the neuter plural in *q(n)* sometimes used as g e n e r a l p l u r a l case, see § 308.

§ 231. (3) An ending *-īǰ, -aǰ* (like orig. fem. pl.) is sometimes employed in nouns and adjectives as g e n e r a l p l u r a l case, acc. as well as instr., e. g. GYAv. *nåmǰnīǰ* (as acc.) Yt. 1.11 and (as instr.) Ys. 51.22

= Ys. 15.2, YAv. *aȝaontī* Vsp. 21.3, *savaŋhaitī* Vd. 19.37; *vaŋhū̆ī* Vsp. 6.1,
GAv. *avaŋhū̆ī* (as instr.) Ys. 12.4, *yātū̆ī* Ys. 12.4.

§ 232. **Interchange of Neuter with Feminine forms.**
Closely connected with this instability in the plural (especially neuter) is the interchange between neuter and feminine forms, as the neuter plural (occasionally also the singular) often shows the closest analogy to the feminine.
Instances of this interchange are abundant, e. g. *a*-decl.
nmānəm (nom. acc. sg. neut.) 'house', beside which *nmānā̊*
(acc. pl., cf. fem.), *nmānāhu* (loc. pl., cf. fem.); *awrəm* (nom.
acc. sg. neut.) 'cloud', *awrā̊* (nom. pl., cf. fem.).—*ah*-stem
avaŋhō (gen. sg.) 'of aid', GYAv. *avaŋhyāi* (dat. sg. fem.).—
Similarly stem *barəzah-* (neut.) beside *barəzā-* 'height', et al.
—Adjective combinations *tišarō sata* 'three hundred', *vīspāhu*
karšvōhu 'in all climes', *sⁱrascaⁱṇtīš lvarᵊþā̊* 'steaming viands'.
See also, Johannes Schmidt, *Pluralbildungen* p. 29 seq.

§ 233. **Interchange of cases in their functions.** The
cases in their usage are not always so sharply distinguished
in YAv. as in Sanskrit. Sometimes a case may take upon
itself the functions that belong properly to another, e. g.
dative in genitive sense, etc. A discussion of the question,
however, belongs to Syntax.

§ 234. **Transition in Declension.** Transfers of inflection in parts of some words from one declension to
another, especially in general from the consonant declension to the *a*-declension, are not infrequent in Avesta. A
word may thus follow one declension in the majority of
its cases, but occasionally make up certain of its forms
quite after another declension. Examples are numerous
and are of two kinds.

(a) The simple unchanged s t e m is u s e d, b u t given
the endings of another declension—much the commonest
case, e. g. stem *jaⁱdyaṇt-* 'imploring' with dat. sg. *jaⁱdyaṇt-āi*
(*a*-decl.) instead of **jaⁱdyaṇt-e; tacⁱṇt-ąm* acc. sg. f., et al.

(b) The stem itself is remodelled and made to con-
form to another declension, thus really giving a new stem,
e. g. *sravah-* 'word' with instr. pl. *sravāiš* (stem *srava-*)
instead of **sravɔbiš* cf. gen. pl. *sravavhąm*. The case is
much less common.

§ 235. **Stem-gradation.** In Avesta, as in Sanskrit—
cf. Whitney, *Skt. Gram.* § 311—the stem of a noun or adjective, especially in the consonant declension, often shows
vowel-variation, strongest, middle or strong, and weak
forms,

$$\bar{a}, a, —,$$
$$\text{-}\bar{a}y\text{-}, \text{-}ay\text{-}, \text{-}i\text{-};$$
$$\text{-}\bar{a}u\text{-}, \text{-}ao\text{-}, \text{-}u\text{-};$$
$$\text{-}\bar{a}r^{\jmath}\text{-}, \text{-}ar^{\jmath}\text{-}, \text{-}r\text{-}, \text{-}\partial r^{\jmath}\text{-};$$
$$\text{-}\bar{a}nt\text{-}, \text{-}\partial nt\text{-}, \text{-}at\text{-} \ [=nt] ;$$
$$\text{-}\bar{a}n\text{-}, \text{-}\partial n\text{-}, \text{-}n\text{-}; \text{ etc. (cf. § 60)}.$$

The strong and strongest forms appear commonly in
S i n g u l a r Nom. Acc. Loc., in D u a l Nom. Acc., and in
P l u r a l Nom., of the Masc. and Fem., and in the P l u r a l
Nom. Acc. of the Neuter. The remaining cases are weak,
but there is much overlapping in this matter of stem-
gradation. The distinctions are not always so sharply
drawn as in Sanskrit. _____

A. STEMS IN VOWELS.

1. Stems in *a*.

Masculine and Neuter (cf. Whitney, *Skt. Gram.* § 330).

i. MASCULINE.

§ 236. Av. -ᴍᴜᴙᴠ *yasna-* m. 'worship, sacrifice' = Skt.
yajñá-.

Av. *mazda-yasna-*,[1] *daēva-yasna-*[1] 'worshipper of Mazda, of
Demons'; *ahura-* 'Lord, Ahura'; *vīra-* 'man'; *haoma-* 'haoma-plant'.

---

[1] The forms with ° e. g. °*yasna* are from *mazda-yasna-*, *daēva-yasna-*.
The forms in parentheses do not actually occur, but are made up after
the forms beside them — so throughout below.

	Av.	Singular:	cf. Skt.
N.	*yasn-ō*		*yajñ-ás*
A.	*yasn-əm*		*yajñ-ám*
I.	*yasn-a*		*yajñ-á* (Ved.)
D.	*yasn-āi*		*yajñ-āya*
Abl.	*yasn-āṭ*		*yajñ-āt*
G.	*yasn-ahe*		*yajñ-ásya*
L.	*yesn-e* [1]		*yajñ-é*
V.	(*yasn-a*) *ahura*		*yájñ-a*

Dual:

N.A.V.	(*yasn-a*) *vīra*		*yajñ-á* (Ved.)
I.D.Abl.	(*yasn-aēibya*) *vīraⁱibya* .	. .	*yajñ-ábhyam*
G.	(*yasn-ayå*) *vīrayå*		*yajñ-áyōs*
L.	(*yasn-ayō*) *zastayō*		—

Plural:

N.V.	°*yasn-a*	. .	*yajñ-ás*
	°*åvhō*		*-ásas*(Ved.)
A.	(*yasn-ą*) *haomą*		*yajñ-án*
I.	*yasn-āiš*	. .	*yajñ-āis*
D.Abl.	°*yasn-aēibyō*		*yajñ-ébhyas*
G.	*yasn-anąm*		*yajñ-ánãm*
L.	(*yasn-aēṣu*) *vīraⁱṣu*		*yajñ-éṣu*
	°*-aēṣva*		—

ii. NEUTER (Separate Forms).

§ 237. Av. *vastra-* 'garment' = Skt. *vástra-;* Av. *havuharᵊna-* 'jaw'.

	Av.		cf. Skt.
Sg. N.A.V.	*vastr-əm*		*vástr-am*
Du. N.A.V.	(*vastr-e*) *havuharᵊne*		*vástr-ē*
Pl. N.A.V.	*vastr-a*		*vástr-ā* (Ved.)

Forms to be observed in GAv. and YAv.

§ 238. In general, GAv. has the same forms as above, with long final vowel, cf. § 26.

---

[1] cf. § 34.

i. MASCULINE.

§ 239. **Singular**:—

Nom.: YGAv. *yasnas-ca.* — Quite late, the forms of nom. sg. in *-a, -e*
Yt. 1.8,12 seqq. and occasionally in the Vd.

Acc.: YAv. also *maṣim* 'mortal' (i. e. *-ya-m*, § 63); *daēūm* 'demon' (i. e.
-va-m § 63).—GAv. also *maṣīm* 'mortal' (i. e. *-ya-m*); also *anyām*,
§§ 32, 29, beside *aīnīm* 'alium'; *fraṣ̌m* 'prone, ready'.

Instr.: YAv. also *haēpaiþe* 'with own' (*-e = -ya*, § 67).

Abl.: YAv. *yasnāaṭ-ca* (§ 53 iv).—Also *miþrāda* 'from Mithra' (*-āṭ+a*, § 222)
Yt. 10.42; *sraoṣāda* 'from obedience'; *h̥ṣaþrāda* 'by the sovereignty'
Ys. 9.4.—Also *hupah̥tāṭ haca panvanāṭ* 'from well-drawn bow' § 19.

Gen.: YAv. *vāstryehe* 'of a husbandman' (§ 34). — GAv. has only *-hyā* e. g.
yasnahyā, vāstryehyā, or *-hyā* (before *-ca* 'que' § 133) e. g. *aṣahyā-cā*.

Loc.: YAv. *zqbaē-ca* 'and in birth' (§ 55).—With postpos. *a* § 222, *umānaya*
'in the house' (*-aē+a*).—Also (sporadic) *raiþya* 'in a chariot' Yt. 17.17.
—Again (rare) *maidyōi* 'in medio' Vd. 15.47; — but (often in compounds § 56) *maidyōiᵒ.* — GAv. *yesnē*, as above.—Also (common) *zqþōi*
'in birth' § 56.

§ 240. **Dual**:—

N.A.V.: YAv. also (but not common) *gavō* 'both hands', *yaskō* 'two sicknesses', § 42.

I.D.Abl: YAv. also *gaoṣaiwe* beside *gaoṣaēwe* 'with both ears' (§§ 85, 67),
pādave 'with both feet' (§§ 87, 67).—GAv. *rānōibyā* 'with both allies'.

Gen.: YAv. *hāvanayāos-ca* 'of both haoma-mortars'.

§ 241. **Plural**:—

Nom.: YAv. also (not common) *amiṣā* 'immortals' (*-ā = Skt. -ās*).— Observe YAv. *aire* 'Aryans' (*-e = -ya*, § 67).

Acc.: YAv. *yasnqs-ca;* also *daēvqn* 'Demons'.—Sometimes *yazatā* 'divinities'
(§ 33); *daēvās-ca* 'and Demons'.—Again like nom. *yazata* 'divinities',
mqþrā 'words'. — GAv. (regularly) *maṣyṇg* mortals'; also *yasnqs-cā*
'and sacrifices'. Like nom. (rare) *mqþrā* 'words'. ·

Instr.: YAv. also (rare) *āfrivanaēibiỹ* 'with blessings'.

Dat. Abl.: YAv. *mazdayasnaēibyas-ca.* — GAv. also *yasnōibyō* 'with sacrifices'.

Gen.: YAv. also (isolated) *maṣyānqm* 'of mortals' *(ā).*—Occasionally without
inserted *n* *varᵊsqm* 'of hairs' (*ᵒqm* for *ᵒanqm*), *suh̥rqm, mūþrqm*.

Loc.: GAv. (only *ū*) *maṣyaēṣū* 'among mortals'.

ii. NEUTER (Separate Forms).

§ 242. **Plural**:—

N.A.V.: YAv. also *vastrā* (*ā*-decl., § 232).

Loc.: YAv. also *umānāhu* 'in houses' (*ā*-decl., § 232).

2. Stems in *ā*.

Feminine (cf. Whitney, *Skt. Gram.* § 364).

§ 243.   Av. ـﻮﻳﻦﺝ *daēnā-* f. 'conscience, religion'.

Av. *urvarā-* 'tree', *grīvā-* 'neck', *nāirikā-* 'woman', *gāþā-* 'hymn'.

A. Derivative Stems in *ā*.

FEMININE.

	Av.	Singular:		cf. Skt.
N.	*daēn-a*	. . .	.	*sĕn-ā*
A.	*daēn-ąm*	.	.	*sĕn-ām*
I.	*daēn-aya*	. .	.	*sĕn-ayā*
D.	*daēn-ayāi*	. . .	. .	*sĕn-āyāi*
Abl.	*(daēn-ayāţ)* urvarayāţ	.	. .	see gen.
G.	*daēn-ayā̊*	. . . . . .	. .	*sĕn-āyās*
L.	*(daēn-aya)* grīvaya	.		*sĕn-āyām*
V.	*daēn-e*	. .		*sĕn-ĕ*

Dual:

			cf. Skt.
N.A.V.	*(daēn-e)* urvaᵢre . . .		*sĕn-ĕ*
I.D.Abl.	*(daēn-ābya)* vaþwābya .		*sĕn-ābhyām*
G.	*(daēn-ayā̊)* nāirikayā̊ [1] .		*sĕn-ayōs*

Plural:

			cf. Skt.
N.V.	*daēn-å*	. .	*sĕn-ās*
A.	*daēn-å*	. . .	*sĕn-ās*
I.	*daēn-ābīš*	. . . .	*sĕn-ābhis*
D.Abl.	*daēn-ābyō*	. . . . . .	*sĕn-ābhyas*
G.	*(daēn-anąm)* urvaranąm	.	*sĕn-ānām*
L.	*(daēn-āhu)* urvarāhu	.	*sĕn-āsu*
	-āhva gāþāhva .		—

Forms to be observed in GAv. and YAv.

§ 244.   In general, GAv. has the same forms as above, with the long final vowel, cf. § 26.

§ 245.   Singular:—

Nom.: YAv. also *naᵢre* 'manly' (fem. adj., *-e* = *-ya*, § 67) = Skt. *nā́ryā.*—

---

[1] See Haug, *Zand-Pahlavi Glossary* p. 100 l. 23.

Again some adjs. and nouns, like the pronominal declension, have
-*e* for -*a*: Av. *nāirike* (nom.) beside *nāirika* 'woman', *apərənāyūke*
'maiden', *pərəne* 'plena' beside acc. *pərənqm*. — GAv. also *bərəhdə*
'dear, welcome'.

Instr.: YAv. also *daēna*. — Also (isolated) *suwrya* 'with a ring' beside acc.
suwrqm, cf. Skt. *śubhráyā*, *śubhrām*. — GAv. *daēnā*; — also *sāsnayā*
'by command'.

Dat.: YAv. also (rare) *gaēþyāi* 'for the world' Ys. 9.3 seq.

Abl.: In GAv. wanting — its place supplied by gen.

Gen.: YAv. *daēnayās-ca* § 124 Note. — GAv. (exceptional) *vairyā* Ys. 43.13
from *vairya*- 'desirable' (for *vairyayā* § 194 trissyllable).

Voc.: GAv. *pōurucistā* 'O Pourucista', *spəntā* 'O holy one'.

§ 246. **Dual:** —

Acc.: YAv. (rare) *vaþwa* 'flocks' (*a*-decl.).

§ 247. **Plural:** —

N.A.V.: YGAv. *daēnās-ca*.

Dat. (Abl.): YAv. *urvarābyas-ca* 'and from trees'. — Also *gaēþāvyō* 'from
beings', *vōiṇdāuyō* 'from plagues' Ys. 68.13, § 62 Note 3. — Again
(but uncommon) *haēnbyō* 'from hosts' Yt. 10.93 (analogy to the
following word *draomžbyō*).

Gen.: YAv. (not common) *jənqnqm* 'of woman' (-*q*- § 45). — Without inserted *n* (-*qm* for -*anqm*) *nāirikqm* 'of woman'.

Loc.: GAv. (only -*hū*) *adāhū* 'in rewards'.

B. Radical Stems in *ā*.

§ 248. Stems with radical *ā*, so far as they have not
gone over to the ordinary *a*, *ā* declension, are represented
by a few forms (a) masculine and neuter, (b) feminine.

(i) **Masculine and Neuter** (cf. Lanman, *Noun Inflection in the Veda*
p. 443 seq.).

§ 249. Declension of Av. *rapaēštā*- m. 'warrior standing in chariot'
= Skt. *rathēṣṭhá*- (part of its forms, however, are from the stem *rapaēštar*-,
cf. Skt. *savyēṣṭhár*-). — The forms from radical *rapaē-štā*- are: — **Singular.**
Nom. *rapaēštā*; Acc. *rapaēštqm*; Dat. *rapōište* (cf. Skt. *dhiyq-dhē*, and on
ōi cf. § 56), *rapaēštāi* (*a*-decl., cf. Skt. *rathēṣṭhāyā*); Gen. *rapaēštā*. —
Plural. Acc. *rapaēštās-cā*.

Note 1. The forms from stem *rapaēštar*- are enumerated at § 330.

Note 2. Similar, dat. sg. neut. *pōi* 'for protecting'; cf. also *vōi*.

(ii) F e m i n i n e (cf. Whitney, *Skt. Gram.* § 351).

§ 250. Here belong a few forms: — Singular. Nom. *ɟæ* 'joyous', *ákæ* 'judgment'; Acc. *mqm* 'measure' Vd. 5.61; Yt. 5.127; Instr. *jya* 'with bowstring'. — Plural. Nom. *jyæ* 'bowstrings'.

---

3. Stems in *i* and *ī*.

Masculine, Feminine and Neuter (cf. Whitney, *Skt. Gram.* §§ 339, 364).

A. Derivative Stems in original *i*.

i. MASCULINE—FEMININE.

§ 251.   Av. ـڛ͡ـڡ *gairi-* m. 'mountain' = Skt. *giri-*.

Av. *aḵti-* f. 'sickness', *paitištáiti-* f. 'opposition', *nmānō.paiti-* m. 'lord of house', *aēþra.paiti-* m. 'teacher', *aši-* f. 'Rectitude, Blessing', *aši-* n. 'eye'.

Av.	Singular:	cf. Skt.
N.	*gair-iš*	*gir-is*
A.	*gair-īm*	*gir-im*
I.	*(gair-i) aḵti*	*gir-ī* (Ved.)
D.	*(gar-ōe) paitištāiše*	*gir-áyē*
Abl.	*gar-ōiṭ*	see gen.
G.	*gar-ōiš*	*gir-ēs*
L.	*gar-a*	*gir-ā* (Ved.)
V.	*(gair-e) nmānō.paite* . . .	*gir-ē*
	-i aši	—

	Dual:	
N.A.V.	*(gair-i) aēþra.paiti* . .	*gir-ī*
I.D.Abl.	*(gair-ibya) ašibya* . .	*gir-ibhyām*

	Plural:	
N.	*gar-ayō*	*gir-áyas*
A.	*gair-īš*	*gir-īn* m., *-īs* f.
D.Abl.	*gair-ibyō*	*gir-ibhyō*
G.	*gair-inqm*	*gir-īṇ́ám*

ii. NEUTER (Separate Forms).

§ 252.   Av. *būiri-* n. 'richness', *zaraþuštri-* (adj.) 'Zoroastrian'.

Sg. N.A.V.	*būir-i*	cf. Skt. *bhūr-i*
Pl. N.A.V.	*(būir-i) zaraþuštri*	*bhūr-i*

Forms to be observed in GAv. and YAv.

§ 253. In general, GAv. has the same forms as above, with the long final vowel, cf. § 26.

§ 254. Singular:—

Acc.: In metrical passages, *-īm* (cf. § 23) is sometimes dissyllabic, cf. Geldner, *Metrik* p. 15.

Dat.: YAv. *paitištātayaē-ca* 'and for withstanding'.—GAv. has *-ayōi* (= YAv. *-aye-* § 56) e. g. *ałtōyōi* 'for sickness' (on *ō* see § 39 Note).—Also from weak stem GAv. *paiþyaē-cā* (YAv. *paiþe* Yt. 17.58) 'and to the husband' = Skt. *pátyē*, cf. Lanman, *Noun Inflection* p. 400.—Also inf. GAv. *mruˀitē* 'to speak', *stōi* 'for being', YAv. *stē* 'for being', *tarōidītē* and *tarōidīti* 'for despising'.

Abl.: In GAv. wanting i. e. its place supplied by gen.

Gen.: YAv. seldom *āhityā* 'of sickness' (like *ī*-decl., but variant *āhitayā*). — Also *darŝyōiš* 'of daring' Yt. 14.2.

Loc.: YAv. likewise *garō* 'on the mountain' Vd. 21.5 = Skt. *girāu* (on *ō* see § 42). — GAv. regularly *vīdātā* 'at the judgment'.

§ 255. Plural:—

Nom.: YAv. also (from strongest stem) *staomāyō* 'praises'.

Acc.: YAv. also (*-īš* for *-īš*, § 21 Note 1) *ištiš-ca* 'and wishes' et al.—Also (from middle stem) *garayō*. — GAv. also (from middle stem) *ārmatayō* —likewise (with *-īš*) *uštiš* 'desires'.

Gen.: YAv. also (from weak stem without inserted *n*) *kaoyqm* (i. e. *kav-y-qm, § 224) 'of Kavis'.

§ 256. Observe also the declension of *haχi-* m. 'friend' = Skt. *sákhi-*, cf. Whitney, *Skt. Gram.* § 343 a. — Strong stem *-āy-*, mid. st. *-ay-*, wk. st. *-y-*.

Singular. Nom. *haχa;* Acc. *haχāim (i. e. *-āyəm*, § 65) Ys. 46.13; Instr. *haχa* (§ 162); Dat. *haχē.*—Dual. N.A.V. *haχa.*—Plural. Nom. *haχayō, haχaya;* Acc. *haχayō, haχaya;* Gen. *haχqm* (§ 162).

Note. Transfers from the *i*-declension to the a-declension occur: e. g. from Av. *vi-* m. 'bird' = Skt. *ví-*, Du. Instrum. *vayaēibya.*— Pl. Abl. *vayaēibyas-ca;* Gen. *vayanqm* (beside the regular *i*-decl. forms *vīš, viš* nom. sg. Yt. 13.3; Vd. 2.42; *vayō* nom. pl. and *vayqm* gen. pl.).

B. Derivative Stems in original *ī*.

(Cf. Whitney, *Skt. Gram.* § 364.)

FEMININE.

§ 257. Av. -ﺍﯾﺴﻮﻥ *ašaonī-* fem. to *ašavan-* 'righteous'.

Av. *ərəjaiti-* f. 'dark, dreadful' *(ərəjant-)*, *barəþrī-* f. 'bearer, mother', *fšaonī* f. 'fatness', *āzīzanāiti* f. 'giving birth', *ẖšaþrī-* f. 'female'.

	Av.	Singular:	cf. Skt.
N.	*ašaon-i*	. .	*dēv-ī*
A.	*ašaon-īm*	. . .	*dēv-īm*
I.	*(ašaon-ya)* *ərəjaitya*	.	*dēv-yā*
D.	*ašaon-yāi*	. . . .	*dēv-yāi*
Abl.	*(ašaon-yāt̮)* *barəþryāt̮*		see gen.
G.	*ašaon-yā̊*	. . .	*dēv-yā̊s*
L.	*ašavan-aya* (?) [1]		*dēv-yā̊m*
V.	*ašaon-i*	. . . .	*dēv-i*

		Dual:	
N.A.V.	*(ašaon-i)* *fšaoni*	. . .	*dēv-ī* (Ved.)
I.D.Abl.	*(ašaon-ibya)* *fšaonibya*	.	*dēv-ībhyam*

		Plural:	
N.	*ašaon-īš*	. . . . .	*dēv-īs* (Ved.)
A.	*ašaon-īš*	. . . . .	*dēv-īs*
I.	*(ašaon-ibiš)* *āzīzanāitibiš*		*dēv-ībhis*
D.Abl.	*ašaon-ibyō*	. . .	*dēv-ībhyas*
G.	*ašaon-inąm*	. .	*dēv-īnām*
L.	*(ašaon-išu)* *ẖšaþrišu*	. . .	*dēv-īṣu*
	-*išva* *ẖšaþrišva*	. . . . . .	—

Forms to be observed in GAv. and YAv.

§ 258. In general, GAv. has the same forms as above, with the long final vowel, cf. § 26.

§ 259. Singular:—

On varying *ī, i* see § 21 Note 1.

Nom.: GAv. has *ašāunī* Ys. 53.4.

Instr.: So GAv. *vaṅhuyā* 'with good', *vahehyā* 'with better', and *mainyā* 'with thought', cf. Dat. *mainyāi* Ys. 43.9.

---

[1] Yt. 5.54, uncertain, cf. § 68 Note 3.

Gen.: YAv. *drvatyās-ca* 'and of the wicked' (fem.);—also *astvaifyō* 'of the corporeal' (according to cons. decl.).

Voc.: YAv. sometimes (*e* according to *i*-decl.): *ašaone; ahurāne* 'O Ahuran'.

§ 260. Plural:—

Nom. Acc.: YAv. also -*īš* (cf. § 21 Note) *barəṇtīš* 'bearing' Yt. 8.40, *hrvi-iyeitīš* 'havocking, bloody' Yt. 10.47.—Also (like Skt. *dēvyàs*) *tištryenyō, tištryenyas-ca* 'wives of Tishtrya'.

Gen.: YAv. *vavuhīnąm* 'of the good' (observe *ī*) is sometimes written.

C. Radical Stems in original *ī*.

Feminine Nouns and Adjective Compounds m. f. n. (cf. Whitney, *Skt. Gr.* §§ 351, 352).

§ 261. Here belong a few words chiefly monosyllables—mostly mere roots: Singular. Nom. *bərəzai-dīš* 'high-spirited', *ərəž-jīš* 'right-living'; Acc. *yavaē-jīm* 'ever-living'; Instr. *sraya* 'by beauty'; Dat. *ərəž-jyōi* 'for the right-living'; Gen. *srayā* 'of beauty', *ḫšyō, ḫšayas-ca* 'of destruction'; Loc. *ayaoi-dya* (?) 'in impurity'.—Plural. Nom. *fryō* 'blessings'; Acc. *varša-jīš* (m.) 'buds', *yavaē-jyō* 'ever-living'; Dat. *yavaē-jibyō*.

---

4. Stems in *u* and *ū*.

Masculine, Feminine and Neuter (cf. Whitney, *Skt. Gr.* § 341, 364).

A. Derivative Stems in original *u*.

i. MASCULINE—FEMININE.

§ 262. Av. *ma*i*nyu-* m. 'Spirit' = Skt. *manyú-*.

Av. *zaṇtu-* m. 'tribe', *rašnu-* m. 'justice', *vaṇhu-* 'good', *pasu-* m. 'small cattle', *aṇhu-* m. 'life', *baršnu-* f. 'head, top', *gātu-* m. 'place, bed'.

	Av.	Singular:					cf. Skt.
N.	*ma*i*ny-uš*						*many-úš*
A.	*ma*i*ny-ūm*						*many-úm*
I.	*(ma*i*ny-u) zaṇtu*						*many-únā, -vā*
D.	*ma*i*ny-ave*						*many-ávē*
Abl.	*ma*i*ny-aoṭ*						see gen.
G.	*ma*i*ny-ōuš* / -*aoš rašnaoš*						*many-ōs*
L.	*(ma*i*ny-āu) vaṇhāu* (GAv.)						*many-āú*
V.	*ma*i*ny-ō*						*mány-ō*

	Av.	Dual:	cf. Skt.
N.A.V.	*maⁱny-ū, -u*	.	*many-ā*
I.D.Abl.	*(maⁱny-ubya) pasubya* .	. .	*many-úbhyām*
G.	*maⁱni-vā*[1]	. .	*many-vōs*
L.	*(maⁱni-vō) avhvó* (GAv.) .	.	—

Plural:

N.	*(maⁱny-avō) barₑnavō*	.	. *many-ávas*
A.	*(maⁱny-ūš) barₑnūš* .	. .	*many-ūn* m., -*ūš* f.
D.Abl.	*(maⁱny-ubyō) gātubyō* .	. . .	*many-úbhyas*
G.	*(maⁱny-unąm) zaₑtunqm*	. . .	*many-ūnām*
L.	*(maⁱny-ušu) vavhuₑu* .	.	*many-úṣu*
	-ušva barₑnušva .	.	—

ii. NEUTER (Separate Forms).

§ 263. Av. *vohu-* 'good' = Skt. *vásu-*.   cf. Skt.

Sg. N.A.V.	*voh-u*	. . .	*vás-u*
Pl. N.A.V.	*voh-u*	.	*vás-u, -ū*

Forms to be observed in GAv. and YAv.

§ 264. In general, GAv. has the same forms as above, with the long final vowel, cf. § 26.

i. MASCULINE—FEMININE.

§ 265. Singular:—

Nom.: YAv. also (from strongest stem) *uₑra.bāzāuš* 'strong-armed' Yt. 10.75; *darₑjō.bāzāuš* 'long-armed' Yt. 17.22.

Acc.: YAv. also (from strongest stem) *nasāum* (i. e. -*āvəm*, § 65) 'corpse', *garₑmāum* 'heat';—again (from strong stem) *daⁱɣhaom* (i. e. -*avəm*, § 64) 'nation, country'.

Instr.: Less common instr. (weak stem +) ending *ā:* YA. *ẖraþwa*, GAv. *ẖraþwā* 'by wisdom'; YAv. *pərəþwa* Vd. 9.2; GAv. *ciciþwā* 'through the wise one' = Skt. *cikitvā* (fr. *cikitú-*).—Also (orig. gen. or cf. § 39) YAv. *ẖrvī.drvō* 'with spear of havoc'; *raₑnvō* 'with Rashnu' Yt. 14.47.

Dat.: YAv. also (from weak stem) *raþwe, raþwaē-ca* 'to the Master';— observe (also from weak stem) YAv. *avuhe* (i. e. orig. *•asv-ē*) 'for

---

[1] See §§ 68 b, 62.

life' Ys. 55.2, GAv. *ahuyē* (i. e. orig. *asu-v-ē*, § 190) 'for life' Ys. 41.6.
—Observe also GAv. *haētaovē* variant *haētaoē* Ys. 53.4 beside *haē-tavē* Ys. 46.5, cf. YAv. variant *haētaoe* beside *haētave* 'for kindred' Ys. 20.1, cf. § 61.

Abl.: In GAv. wanting—i. e. its place is supplied by the gen. as in Skt.

Gen.: (a) Also (from strongest stem) YAv. *bāzāuš* 'of the arm', GAv. *mǝrǝθyāuš* 'of death'.—Again (from strongest stem +) ending *ō:* YAv. *nasāvō* 'of a corpse';—and (from weak stem + *ŏ*) YAv. *raθwō* 'of the Master'. —(b) The interchange in the gen. ending *-ǝuš*, *-aoš* is connected perhaps with an original difference of accent: e. g. observe Av. *vavhǝuš*, *avhǝuš* = Skt. *vásōs*, *ásōs* (unaccented ultima), and Av. *tāyaoš*, *garǝnaoš* = Skt. *tāyós*, *gṛdhnós* (accented ultima) et al. Exceptions depend perhaps upon a shift of the accent.

Loc.: (a) The above loc. in *-āu* is Gatha locative, cf. also Ys. 62.6 *vavhāu* (Gatha reminiscence).—Similarly, GAv. *pǝrǝtā* 'at the bridge' Ys. 51.13; *hratā* 'in judgment' Ys. 48.4. The regular YAv. loc. is formed in *ō* (weak stem + *ō*, orig. gen.?), e. g. *ahmi zaṇtvō* 'in this tribe' Ys. 9.28, *gātvō* 'on a couch', *daiŋhvō* 'in the country', *avhvō* 'in the world'. —(b) Observe Vsp. 12.5 *daiŋhō* = Skt. *dásyāu*, cf. § 42 (but see variants), Av. *haētō* 'at the bridge' = Skt. *sētāu;* Av. *varǝtafšō* Vd. 8.4 — and GAv. *pǝrǝtō* Ys. 51.12.—With postpositive *a* and strong stem: YAv. *anhava* 'in the world' Yt. 6.3; *gātava* 'in place' Ys. 65.9.

Voc.: YAv. occasionally *ratvō* 'O Master', *ǝrǝzvō* 'O righteous one', *rašnvō* 'O Rashnu, Justice'.

§ 266. Dual:—

I.D.Abl.: YAv. also *bāzuwe* 'with both arms', cf. §§ 67, 85 a.

§ 267. Plural:—

Nom.: YAv. also with ending *a*, § 224 (from strong stem) *gātava* 'couches'. —With regular ending *ō* (from strongest stem) *nasāvō* 'corpses', (from weak stem) *pasvas-ca* 'small cattle'.—Observe Yt. 14.38 *duš.mainyuš* 'enemies' (nom. pl.).

Acc.: YAv. also (*-āš*, § 21 Note 1) *barǝšnuš* 'heights'; *pauruš* 'many' Yt. 8.49; *daiŋhuš* 'countries' Yt. 8.9.—Again with ending *a*, § 224 (from strong stem) *barǝnava*,— Ending *ō* like nom. (from strongest stem) *nasāvō* 'corpses', (from strong stem) *gātavō* 'places', (from weak stem) *pasvō* 'small cattle'.

Dat. Abl.: YAv. *hinūiwyō* 'from fetters' Yt. 13.100 = Yt. 19.86.

Gen.: YAv. also (without inserted *n*) *vavhvqm* 'of the good', *raθwqm* 'of Masters'; *yāθwqm* 'of sorcerers'.—Observe the variant *-ūnqm* for *-unqm* (§ 21 Note 1) occurs, e. g. variant *vohūnqm* Ys. 65.12 etc.

Loc.: GAv. (only *-ū*) *pourušū* 'among people'.

ii. NEUTER.

§ 268. **Plural**:— N.A.V. YAv. with *a: asrū* 'tears'. — Also *zanva* 'knees' occurs. — Observe *a* in *asrū* 'tears' Yt. 10.38, cf. § 25 Note.

§ 269. Occasional t r a n s f e r s to the *a*-d e c l e n s i o n are found: — e. g. Sg. Gen. *gātvahe* 'of the place'; Dat. *hiškvāi* 'for the dry'.

§ 270. D e c l e n s i o n of Av. *daiŗhu-, dahyu-* f. 'nation, country', cf. Skt. *dásyu-* §§ 135, 133:— Singular. Nom. *daiŗhuš;* Acc. *daiŗhaom* (i. e. -*avṃ* § 64), *dahyūm* (GYAv.); Instr. *daiŗhu;* Dat. *daiŗhave;* Abl. *daiŗhaoṭ;* Gen. *daiŗhṣuš* (YAv.), *dahyṣuš* (GAv.); Loc. *daiŗhvō.*—Dual. Nom. *daiŗhu* (Yt. 10.8,47), *dahyu* (Yt. 10.107).—Plural. Nom. Voc. *daiŗhāvō, daiŗhavō;* Acc. *daiŗhuš, daiŗhāvō;* Gen. *dahyunąm* (GYAv.).

B. Derivative Stems in original *ū*.
(Cf. Whitney, *Skt. Gram.* § 356.)

These are not sharply to be distinguished from A in Avesta, nor are they numerous. As example may be taken

FEMININE.

§ 271. Av. -ﮊﺮﻭ *tanū-* f. 'body' = Skt. *tanū-*.

	Av. Singular:	cf. Skt.
N.	*tan-uš*	*tan-ús*
A.	*tan-vṣm* (GAv.), *tan-ūm* (GYAv.).	*tan-vàm, tan-úm* .
I.	*tan-va* [1]	*tan-vā́*
D.	*tan-uye* (GYAv.)	*tan-vè́*
Abl.	*tan-vaṭ*	see gen.
G.	*tan-vō*	*tan-vàs*

	Plural:	
N.A.	*tan-vō*	*tan-vàs*
I.	*(tan-ubiš)* *hizubiš* (GAv.)	*tan-úbhis*
D.Abl.	*tan-ubyō*	*tan-úbhyas*
G.	*tan-unąm*	*tan-únām*
L.	*tan-ušu*	*tan-úṣu*

Forms to be observed in GAv. and YAv.

§ 272. Metrically, the *v* in *tanvṣm* etc. is to be resolved into *u* as in Sanskrit.

---

[1] See *Aogamadaēcā* 48 p. 25 ed. W. Geiger.

§ 273. Singular:—

Dat.: Observe *tanvaž-ca* Haug, *Zand-Pahlavi Glossary* p. 52. 9.
Abl.: YAv. also *tanaoṭ* like *u*-decl.
Gen.: G(Y)Av. *tanvas-čiṭ;*—also GAv. *hizvō* 'of the tongue' Ys. 45. 1, cf.
Skt. *vadhvās.*

§ 274. Plural:—

N.A.V.: YAv. *tanvas-ca.*

C. Radical Stems in original *ū*.

Masculine Nouns and Adjective compounds (cf. Whitney, *Skt. Gram.*
§ 355 c end, § 352.)

§ 275. Here belong a very few root words:—Singular. Nom. (without *s*) *ahū* (GAv.), *ahu* (YAv.) 'Lord'; *āyū* (neut. GAv.) 'duration'; Acc.
ahūm.— Plural. Acc. *avhvas-čā* (GAv.). — Similarly (nom. sg. without *s*)
apərənāyū 'youth', *framrū* or *°mrū* 'pronouncing'. — Add dative *-buye* 'to
become'.

§ 276. Declension of *yū.* n. 'duration, ever':—Singular. Instr. (adv.)
yava (YAv.), *yavā* (GAv.); Dat. *yave, yavaž-ca* (YAv.), *yavē* or *yaovē, yavōi*
(GAv.); Gen. *yāuš.*

---

5. Diphthongal Stems.

(Cf. Whitney, *Skt. Gram.* § 360 seq.)

i. Stems in *āi.*

§ 277. Av. *rāi, raē*- f. 'splendor' = Skt. *rāi-*.

Singular. Acc. *raēm* (i. e. *ray-əm* § 64); Instr. *raya.*—Plural.
Acc. *rāyō* (GAv.), also *raēš-ca* (YAv. § 64 Note); Gen. *rayqm.*

ii. Stems in *āu.*

§ 278. Av. *gāu-*, *gao*- m. f. 'cow' = Skt. *gāu-*.

Singular. Nom. (Voc.) *gāuš, gaoš;* Acc. *gqm,* or rare *gāum, gaom*
(i. e. *gāv-əm* §§ 64, 65); Instr. *gava;* Dat. *gave* (YAv.), *gavōi* (GAv.);
Abl. *gaoṭ;* Gen. *gəuš.*—Dual N.A.V. *gavā* (GAv.); Gen. *°gavą.*—
Plural. Nom. *gavō*[1]; Acc. *gā;* Instr. *gaobīš;* Gen. *gavqm.*

Note. Similarly Sg. Nom. *hipšuš,* Acc. *hipqm* 'ally' Ys. 48.7, 34.10.

---

[1] See *Aogemadaēčā* 84 p. 28 ed. W. Geiger.

B. STEMS IN CONSONANTS.
6. (A) Stems without Suffix.
Root-words and those inflected like them.

Masculine, Feminine and Neuter (cf. Whitney, *Skt. Gr.* §§ 383, 391).

§ 279.   Av. -ﺱﻭ *vīs-* f. 'village' = Skt. *víś-*.

Av. *spas-* m. 'spy', *amərətāṱ-* f. 'Immortality', *ast-* n. 'bone', *nās-* 'misfortune'.

	Av.		Singular:			cf. Skt.
N.V.	(*vīš*) *spaš*					*viṱ*
A.	*vīs-əm*					*viš-am*
I.	*vīs-a*					*viš-ā*
D.	*vīs-e*					*viš-ē*
Abl.	*vīs-aṱ*					see gen.
G.	*vīs-ō*					*viš-ás*
L.	*vīs-i*					*viš-í*

Dual:

				cf. Skt.
N.A.V.	(*vīs-a*) *amərətāta*			*viš-āu*
I.D.Abl.	(*vīži-bya*) *amərətadbya*			*viḍ-bhyā́m*
G.	(*vīs-ā̊*) *amərətāṱā̊*			*viš-ós*

Plural:

				cf. Skt.
N.V.	(*vīs-ō*) *spasō*			*viš-as*
A.	*vīs-ō*			*viš-as*
I.	(*vīži-bīš*) *azdᵇīš*			*viḍ-bhís*
D.	*vīži-byō*			*viḍ-bhyás*
G.	*vīs-ąm*			*viš-ā́m*
L.	(*vīžu*) *nāṱu* (GAv.)			*vik-ṣú*

Forms to be observed in GAv. and YAv.

§ 280.   In general, GAv. has the same forms as above, with the long final vowel, cf. § 26.

§ 281.   Singular:—

Nom.: GYAv. *druḫš* 'Fiend' § 192, *haᵘrvatās* 'Perfection, Salvation' (*-tās* i. e. *-tāt-s* § 192); *ābərəs* title of priest (*-t + s*), Nirangistan.

Acc.: YAv. also *drujim* 'Fiend' (*-im* = *-əm* § 30).—GAv. also *drujim* § 30 and *kəhrpəm* 'body' (*-ǰ-* § 32).

Dat.: YAv. *yavaētātaē-ca* 'and for eternity'.—GAv. also (*-ōi* more common than *-ē* § 56) *mazōi* 'for the great'.

Abl.: In GAv. wanting—i. e. its place supplied by the gen. as in Skt.

Gen.: GAv. also *mazō* 'of the great' (*-ō* = orig. *-as* § 32).

Loc.: YAv. also *aⁱpya* 'in water' (*aⁱpi* + *a* § 222), *uḷtatāⁱtya* 'in the word *uḷta*' (*•tāⁱti* + *a* § 222).—GAv. has simply *ī: amərətāⁱtī* 'in Immortality'.

§ 282. Dual:—

I.D.Abl.: Solitary YAv. *bruuaḷḅyąm* 'both brows'.

§ 283. Plural:—

Nom. Acc.: YAv. also (with e n d i n g *-a* § 224) *vāca, vaca.* Neut. pl. acc. *asti* 'bones' Yt. 13.11 (variant *asta*, but see § 283 Note).

Loc.: GAv. as above *nāḷā* and (§ 26 Note) *naḷḷu-cā* 'among descendants'.

Note. T r a n s f e r s to the *a*-d e c l. are numerous:—e. g. **Sg.** Nom. *hvarə.darəs-ō* 'sun-like', Skt. *svar-dṛṣ;* Acc. (neut.) *ast-əm* 'bone'; Abl. *vīsāṭ* or *vīsāda* 'from a village' Yt. 13.49.—Pl. Acc. (neut.) *asta* 'bones'; Loc. like *ā*-d e c l. *barəzāhu* 'on the heights'.

With stem-gradation (Strong and Weak).

Cf. Whitney, *Skt. Gram.* § 385 seq.

§ 284. The strong and weak forms are distinguished by a v a r i a t i o n in the quantity of the s t e m - v o w e l (as long or short) or by its elision, again by the presence (strong) or absence (weak) of a n a s a l. For examples see the following declensions.

§ 285. (i) Declension of Av. *vak/c-* m. 'voice, word' (strongest stem *-ā-*, strong *-a-*) = Skt. *vāk/c-* f. (no vowel variation), cf. Whitney, *Skt. Gram.* § 391:—

Singular. Nom. *vāḵṣ;* Acc. *vācəm, vācim;* Instr. *vaca;* Gen. *vacō* (Ys. 31.20).—Dual. *vāxẓibyā-ca.*—Plural. Nom. *vācō, vaca* (ending *a* cf. vowel decl. § 224); Acc. *vācō, vacas-ca, vāca;* Dat. Abl. *vāxẓibyō;* Gen. *vacąm.*

Note. (a) The dat. du. and pl. (pada-endings) seem to derive their *s* (*ẓ*) from the nom. sg. *vāḵṣ.*— (b) Observe the form *vāḵṣ* as gen. Ys. 8.1.

§ 286. (ii) Declension of Av. *ap-* f. 'water' (strongest stem *āp-*, strong stem *ap-*) = Skt. *áp-* f. (stems *āp-, ap-*) Whitney, *Skt. Gram.* § 393:—

Singular. Nom. *āfš;* Acc. *āpəm, apəm-ca* § 19; Instr. *apā-ca;*
Abl. *apaṭ, apāaṭ-ca* (*a*-decl.); Gen. *apō, apas-ca, āpō;* Loc. *aᵢpya*
(*-i + a* § 222).—Dual. *āpa, āpe* (Gah 4.5 *ā*-decl.).—Plural. Nom.
āpō, apas-ca § 19; Acc. *apō, apas-ca, āpō;* Dat. *aᵢwyō;* Gen. *apąm.*
Note.   The dat. pl. *aᵢwyō* is for orig. **abbhyās* § 186.

§ 287.   (iii) Declension of *aŋc*-stems (cf. Whitney,
Skt. Gram. §§ 408, 409):—

Singular. Nom. *frąš* 'forward'; Acc. *°nyāŋcəm* 'down'; Instr.
fraca (? Yt. 10.118 *fraca āiti* [√*i-+ā*] cf. Skt. *prācā*), *tarasca* 'across',
cf. Skt. *tirasćā* instr. advbl. (Whitney § 309 d), *paᵘrvąŋca* 'advancing'; etc.

§ 288.   Av. *paþ-* m. 'path'=Skt. *path-* belongs partly
here and partly under *an*-stems § 310—which see.

---

7. (B) Derivative Stems in *aŋt, maŋt, vaŋt.*

Participial Adjectives and Possessives (see Bartholomae, in *K.Z.*
xxix. p. 487 seq. = *Flexionslehre* p. 68 seq.—Whitney, *Skt. Gram.* § 441 seq.,
§ 452 seq.)

§ 289.   This subdivision of consonant stems includes:
—(i) participial (and adjective) stems in *aŋt;* and (ii) possessive adjective stems in *maŋt, -vaŋt.* They are masculine and neuter; the corresponding feminine is made in
aⁱ(ŋ)tī-. The stem shows vowel-gradation, strong stem
aŋt, weak stem *at* (from *ŋt;* also GAv. *āt,* see § 18 Note).

§ 290. · As to stem-gradation, (1) the adjective *aŋt-*
stems generally show *at* in the weak (= Skt. weak) cases,
(2) the participial (thematic) *aŋt-*stems show *aŋt* in almost
all forms. (3) The *maŋt-, vaŋt-*stems agree with the adjective stems in showing *at* in the weak cases. A number
of interchanges, however, between all three occur—
these interchanges are found chiefly in YAv. e. g. dat. du.
bərᵊzanbya (from str. st.) Ys. 1.11; 3.13.

I. MASCULINE.

§ 291.   (1) Adjective, Av. ·ᴖᵉᵘᵘᶠⁱᵘ *bərᵊzaŋt-* 'great'
= Skt. *bṛhánt-;* (2) Participial, Av. ·ᴖᵉᵘᵘᵘᵍᵈ *fšuyaŋt-*

'thrifty, raising cattle'; (3) P o s s e s s i v e, Av. ـﻤﻮﺳﺮﻛ
astvaṇt- 'possessing bones, corporeal'; ـﺮﻜﺴﺮ dᵊ *drᵊgvaṇt-*
(GAv.) 'belonging to the Druj, follower of Satan'.

(1—2) *aṇt*-stems: Av. *haṇt-* 'being'; *stavaṇt-* 'praising'; *ṭbiṣyaṇt-*
'hating'; *aṣaohṣayaṇt-* 'increasing Righteousness'; (3) *maṇt-*, *vaṇt*-
stems: *drᵊgvaṇt-* (GAv.), *drvaṇt-* (YAv.) 'belonging to the Druj',
* þwāvaṇt-* 'like thee', *amavaṇt-* 'mighty', *satavaṇt-* 'hundred-fold',
pourumaṇt- 'multitudinous', *daēvavaṇt-* 'belonging to the Daevas',
cazdōṇvhvaṇt- 'wise-in-heart'.

(a) *aṇt*-Stems.

(1) Adjective.   (2) Participial.

Av.	Singular:		cf. Skt.
N. { 1. *bᵊrᵊz-ō*			} *bṛh-án*
2. *fšuy-ās*			
-*as slav-as*			
A. *bᵊrᵊz-aṇt-ᵊm*			*bṛh-ántam*
I. *bᵊrᵊz-ata*			*bṛh-atā́*
D. { 1. *bᵊrᵊz-aⁱte*			} *bṛh-atḗ*
2. *fšuy-aṇte*			
Abl. { 1. *(bᵊrᵊz-ataṭ)*			} see gen.
2. *(fšuy-aṇtaṭ)* *ṭbiṣyaṇtaṭ*			
G. { 1. *bᵊrᵊz-atō*			} *bṛh-atás*
2. *fšuy-aṇtō*			
V. *berᵊz-a*			*bṛh-an*

Dual:

N.A.V. *bᵊrᵊz-aṇta*			*bṛh-ántā* (Ved.)
I.D.Abl. *1. bᵊrᵊz-aṇbya*			*bṛh-ádbhyām*
G. *2. (fšuy-aṇtā̆)* *aṣaohṣayaṇtā̆*			*bṛh-atós*

Plural:

N.V. *bᵊrᵊz-aṇtō*			*bṛh-ántas*
A. { 1. *(bᵊrᵊz-atō)* *hatō*			} *bṛh-atás*
2. *fšuy-aṇtō*			
I. *(bᵊrᵊz-adbīš)* *hadbīš*			*bṛh-ádbhis*
D.Abl. { 1. *(bᵊrᵊz-adbyō)*			} *bṛh-ádbhyas*
2. *(fšuy-aṇbyō)* *ṭbiṣyaṇhyō*			

G. { *1. bərᵊz-atąm* . . . . . . } *bṛh-átǔ̄m*
   { *2. (fšuy-antąm) ṯbiỿyantąm* . . . }

L.   *(bərᵊz-asu) fšuyasū* (GAv.)   .   *bṛh-átsu*

(b) *mant-, vant-*Stems.
(3) Possessives.

Av.	Singular:		cf. Skt.
N.	*ast-vā*		
	-vąs ṗwā̆vąs	. . .	*bhága-vā̆n*
	-va amava . .		
A.	*ast-vantəm* . .	.	*bhága-vantam*
I.	*(ast-vata) satavata*	. .	*bhága-vatā̆*
D.	*ast-vaᶦte*		*bhága-vatě*
Abl.	*ast-vataṯ*	.	see gen.
G.	*ast-vatō*	.	*bhága-vatas*
L.	{ *ast-vaᶦṇti* . . .	. . }	*bhága-vati*
	{ *-maᶦti poᵘrumaᶦti* .	. }	
V.	*(ast-vō) drvō*		*bhága-van*

	Plural:		
N.V.	*drəg-vantō*		*bhága-vantas*
A.	*drəg-vatō*		*bhága-vatas*
I.	*drəg-vōdᵊbīš* and *daēvavaṯbīš* . .		*bhága-vadbhis*
D.Abl.	*drəg-vōdᵊbyō* and *cazdōṇẇhvadᵊbyō*		*bhága-vadbhyas*
G.	*drəg-vatąm*		*bhága-vatām*
L.	*drəg-vasū*		*bhága-vatsu*

ii. NEUTER (Separate Forms).

§ 292. Av. *haṇt-* 'being', *astvaṇt-* 'corporeal', *afsmanivaṇt-* 'metrical'.

Sg. N.A.V. (a) *haṯ* (b) *ast-vaṯ* . . cf. Skt. *bhága-vat*
Pl. N.A.V.   —   *afsmani-vąn* . . *bhága-vanti*

Forms to be observed in GAv. and YAv.

§ 293. In general, GAv. has the same forms as YAv., with the long final vowel, cf. § 26.

§ 294. (a) According to § 29, *-əṇt-* or (after palatals § 30) *-iṇt-* may be found instead of *-aṇt-*:—Av. *pat-əṇt-əm* 'falling', *druž-iṇt-əm* 'deceiving', *raoc-iṇt-aṭ* (abl.) 'shining' et al. — (b) According to § 63, -*iṇt*-, -*uṇt*- may be found instead of -*yaṇt*-, -*vaṇt*-: — Av. *varəz-iṇt-əm* beside *varəz-yaṇt-ō* 'working', *harənaŋh-uṇt-əm* 'glorious', *təmaŋh-uṇt-əm* 'dark' Yt. 5.82, cf. Skt. *támasvantam*.

i. MASCULINE.

§ 295. Singular:—

Nom.: In YAv., the *aṇt*-stems generally have nom. -*ō*, and the *vaṇt*-stems have nom. -*vǡ* or -*va* or sometimes -*vō*. In GAv. the nom. is -*qs* or -*as* (for -*at-s*). — Observe YAv. *perənavō, astavō* 'possessing a feather, possessing a bone' Yt. 14.36; also *hą* 'being' Yt. 13.129, *vyąsca* 'driving'. — GAv. *fšuyąs* 'thriving, prospering', *stavas* 'praising', *þwāvąs* 'like thee'. — On *təmavuhǡ* 'dark', *harənavuhǡ* 'glorious' (for orig. -*sv*-) see § 130 (2) c.

Instr.: GAv. also *drəgvåtā* (observe *ā* § 18 Note 3) 'with the wicked'.

Dat.: GYAv. also *drəgvåitē, drvåite* (observe *ā* § 18 Note 3) 'for the wicked' Ys. 31.15 etc., Ys. 71.13. — On GAv. *drəgvåtaē-cā*, see § 19.

Gen.: On *harənavuhatō* 'of the glorious', see § 130 (2) c.

Loc.: Sometimes variant *astvaiti*. See furthermore below § 297.

Voc.: YAv. *drvō* above is like nom. (see Nom.).

§ 296. Plural:—

Nom.: YAv. with e n d i n g *a* § 224: *bərəzaṇta* 'great' Yt. 5.13, *yātuməṇta* 'belonging to sorcery'; — also (isolated) weak stem nom. pl. *mrvatō* 'speaking' Ys. 70.4.

Acc.: YAv. also (observe strong stem) *bərəzaṇtō* 'great'.

Gen.: YAv. also (2 from weak stem) *þbišyatąm* 'of those hating' Yt. 10.76. — Also GYAv. *hātąm* 'of beings' (observe *ā*) § 18 Note 3.

§ 297. T r a n s f e r s to the *a*-d e c l e n s i o n are not infrequent. Here belong:

    i. MASCULINE. Singular. Nom. *bərəzō* above in paradigm, also Voc. *bərəza;* Dat. *zbayaṇtāi* 'for him invoking'; Abl. *saošyaṇtāṭ* 'from Saoshyant'; Gen. *raēvaṇtahe* 'of the radiant'; Loc. *bərəzaṇtaya* or *bərəzaṇtaya* (uncertain see § 257) Yt. 5.54,57. — Plural. Dat. Abl. *saošyaṇtaēibyō* 'for the Saoshyants', *drvataēibyō* 'from the wicked'. — ii. NEUTER. Singular. Acc. *varəcavhaṇtəm* et al. Yt. 19.9.

§ 298. D e c l e n s i o n of Av. *mazaṇt*- 'great' = Skt. *mahánt*-. This word shows a strongest stem *mazǡṇt*-, like Skt. *mahā́nt*-. i. MASC. Singular. Nom. *maza*, Acc. *mazǡṇtəm;* ii. NEUT. *mazaṭ*, cf. Skt. *mahā́n, mahā́ntam, mahát*, Whitney, *Skt. Gram.* § 450 b.

8. (C) Derivative Stems in *an, man, van.*

Masculine, (Feminine) and Neuter (cf. Whitney, *Skt. Gr.* § 420 seq.).

§ 299. The stem has a triple form:—strongest stem *ān*, strong stem *an*, weak stem *n* (before vowels) or *a* (= *ṇ*) before consonants. Cf. Brugmann, *Grundriss der vergl. Gram.* ii. § 113.—The strong and weak forms do not always agree with the Sanskrit in its sharp division; cf. also Whitney, *Skt. Gram.* § 425 f.

(a) *an-, man*-Stems.
i. MASCULINE.

§ 300. Av. ـڊـڊـوـیـلـ *aⁱryaman-* m. 'friend' = Skt. *aryamán-* m.

Av. *maⁱsman-* n. 'urine', *ḫṣapan-* f. 'night', *marᵉtan-* m. 'mortal', *caṣman-* n. 'eye', *p̌rizafan-* 'triple-jawed', *aṣavan-* 'righteous', *asan-* m. 'stone', *rasman-* m. 'rank, column', *dāman-* n. 'creature', *arṣan-* m. 'male', *vyāḫman-* n. 'council'.

	Av.	Singular:		cf. Skt.
·N.	*aⁱryam-a*			*aryam-ā*
A.	*aⁱryam-anəm*			*aryam-áṇam*
I.	{ *aⁱryam-na*			} *aryam-ṇā*
	-*ana maⁱsmana*			
D.	{ (*aⁱryam-aⁱne*)[1]			} *aryam-ṇē*
	-*ne ḫṣafne*			
Abl.	{ (*aⁱryam-naṭ*) *marᵉpnaṭ*			} see gen.
	-*anaṭ caṣmanaṭ* . . .			
G.	{ (*aⁱryam-nō*)[2]			} *aryam-ṇás*
	-*anō*[3]			
L.	(*aⁱryam-aⁱni*) *caṣmaⁱnī* (GAv.) .		.	*aryam-áṇi*
V.	{ *aⁱryam-a*			} *áryam-an*
	-*əm p̌rizafəm* § 194 . . .			
	Dual:			
N.A.V.	*aⁱryam-ana*		.	*aryam-áṇā* (Ved.)
I.D.Abl.	(*aⁱryam-anǣ*) *caṣmanǣ*			*áryam-aṇōs*

---

[1] See Vd. 22.13. — [2] Thus, metrically *aⁱryamnas-cā* Ys. 33.4; 46.1.
— [3] Vsp. 1.8 etc.

Plural:

N.V.	(a*ryam-anō)	*aṣavanō*	. . . . .	*aryam-ánas*	

A. $\begin{cases}$ (a*ryam-nō) *ḫẓafnō* . . . . . . $\\$ -anō *rasmanō* . . . . . $\end{cases}$ *aryam-ṇás*

I.	(a*ryam-ǝbīš)	*dāmǝbīš*	.	. .	*aryam-ábhis*
D.Abl.	(a*ryam-abyō)	*dāmabyō* .		. . .	*aryam-ábhyas*

G. $\begin{cases}$ (a*ryam-naṃ) *arǝnqm* . . . $\\$ -anaṃ *rasmanqm* . . . . $\end{cases}$ *aryam-ṇám*

L. $\begin{cases}$ (a*ryam-ōhu) *vyāḫmōhu* [1] . . . $\\$ -ōhva *dāmōhva* . . . . . $\end{cases}$ *aryam-áhu*

ii. NEUTER (Separate Forms).

§ 301. Av. *nāman-* n. 'name', *cinman-* n. 'attempt'.

Sg. N.A.V. *naṃ-a* . . . . *nām-a*

Pl. N.A.V. $\begin{cases} nām\text{-}a(n) \quad . . . . . . \\ nām\text{-}ǝni \quad . . . . \\ cinm\text{-}ānī \text{ (GAv.)} [2] . . . . . \end{cases}$ *nām-āni*

Forms to be observed in GAv. and YAv.

§ 302. In general, GAv. has the same forms as above with the long final vowel, see § 26.

§ 303. Occasionally (1) instead of Av. *ā* we find *ạ* before the *n* (§ 45) or (2) instead of *a* we find GAv. *ǝ* (§ 32): — e. g. (1) Av. *urvạnō* 'souls'; — (2) GAv. *mazǝnā* 'with greatness'; GAv. *asǝnō* 'stones, heavens'.

§ 304. On the interchange of strong *(an)* and weak *(n)* forms see § 299.

i. MASCULINE.

§ 305. Singular:—

Nom.: YAv. *fravrase* 'Franrasyan' (= •sya cf. § 67, acc. *fravrasyānǝm*).

Acc.: YAv. also (from strongest stem) *hāvanānǝm* title of priest; and (from weak stem) *arǝnǝm* 'male'.

Instr.: GAv. also *mazǝnā* § 303.

Dat.: Similar *(-aіne)* infin. dat. n. YAv. *ḫǝnūmaіne* 'to rejoice', *staomaіne* 'for praise'; GAv. *ḫǝqnmǝnǝ* 'to be content' § 303. — Observe *aіwi.ǰōiᵽne* Vd. 3.24. — From strongest stem YAv. *puᵽrāne* 'having a child'.

Gen.: GYAv. also (from strongest stem) *mar•tānō* 'of mortal', *hāvanānō*.

---

[1] Yt. 13.16, cf. § 39. — [2] Ys. 12.3.

Abl.: YAv. isolated (undeclined abl.) *barᵊsmᵊn* (neut.) 'with barsom'.
Loc.: YAv. also (from weak stem) *asni* 'by day' § 164 Note 1;—and (from strongest stem) *husravāni* 'in good word' (?) Ny. 4.8.—GAv. also *caš-mᵊng*, *cašmqm* (neut.) 'in eye' Ys. 31.13; Ys. 50.10, cf. Whitney, *Skt. Gram.* § 425 c.
Voc.: YAv. *aᵢryama* (cf. Vd. 22.9) above in paradigm is like nom. or after *a*-decl.

§ 306. Dual:—

N.A.V.: YAv. also (from strongest stem § 314 Note 1 b) *spāna* 'two dogs'.

§ 307. Plural:—

Nom.: YAv. also (from strongest stem) *asānō* 'stones'. With ending *a* § 224 (from strongest stem) *aršāna* 'males', and (from weak stem) *asna* 'stones'.
Acc.: YAv. also (from strongest stem) *asānō* 'stones'; GAv. *asᵊnō* Ys. 30.5 cf. § 303.—With ending *a* § 224 (from strongest stem) *aršāna* 'males'.
Dat. Abl.: YAv. also *draomᵊbyō* 'from assaults' § 33.

ii. NEUTER.

§ 308. Plural:—

Nom. Acc.: The common ending is *q(n)* § 45 Note 2: Av. *nāmq(n)*, *dāmqn*, *dāmqm* cf. Ys. 48.7, 46.6, etc. — Less frequent is the ending -*āni* (-*ᵊni*), cf. Skt. -*āni*. — Observe as d u a l and p l u r a l (like sing.) *dqma* Yt. 15.43; Ys. 71.6. — Perhaps here belong likewise *maᵉsma* Vd. 8.11,12, et al., cf. Johannes Schmidt, *Neutra* pp. 89, 316, but see § 227 above.

As g e n e r a l p l u r a l case, *qn* is also used: e. g. (as instr.) Av. *srīrāiš nāmqn* 'by fair names' Ys. 15.1, Vsp. 6.1; so *damqn* (as nom. pl.) Yt. 8.48, (as gen. pl.) Ys. 57.2, (as instr. pl.) Yt. 22.9. — As acc. pl. and gen. loc. s i n g u l a r *ayqn*.

As g e n e r a l p l u r a l case, *iš* (§§ 228, 331) is also used: e. g. (as instr.) *hāiš nāmᵊniš* 'by their own names' Ys. 15.2.

§ 309. T r a n s f e r s t o t h e *a*- d e c l e n s i o n are found. Here belong:

Singular. Dat. *syāvaršānāi* 'to Syavarshan'; Gen. *aršānahe* 'of a male'; Abl. *ḳšafnāᵗca* 'night'.—Plural. Loc. *asānaᵉšva* m. 'on stones'.

§ 310. Declension of Av. *paṇtan-*, *paþ-* m. 'path' = Skt. *pánthan-*, *path-* m. cf. Whitney, *Skt. Gram.* § 433. This word follows partly the *an*-declension (strongest stem *paṇtān-*, strong stem *paṇtan-* § 299), partly the suffixless consonant declension (weak stem *paþ-* § 288).

Singular. Nom. *paṇta, paṇtǣ* Ys. 72.11; Acc. *paṇtānǝm, paṇtqm;* Instr. *paþa;* Abl. *paṇtaṭ;* Gen. *paþō;* Loc. *paiþī* (GAv.). — Plural. Nom. *paṇtānō;* Acc. *paþō, paþa;* Gen. *paþqm.*

Note. Transfers to the *ā*-declension (fem.) are Sg. Acc. *paþqm;* Gen. *paþayǣ.* — Pl. Acc. *paþǣ.*

§ 311. Often, a neuter stem in *an* stands parallel with one in *ar*, see § 237, and Brugmann, *Grundriss der vergl. Gram.* ii. § 118.

(b) *van*-Stems.

§ 312. The *van*-stems are declined like those in *an, man*, but in the weak case-forms the *va* becomes (by samprasāraṇa § 63) *u*, which coalesces with a preceding *a* into *ao* (*āu* § 62) or with a preceding *u* into *ū* (*u* § 51 Note 1).

§ 313. (i) Declension of Av. *aṣavan-* m. 'righteous' = Skt. *ṛtávan-* shows in weak cases *aṣaon-, aṣāun* (i. e. GAv. and cf. § 62 Note 1).

Singular. Nom. *aṣava;* Acc. *aṣavanǝm;* Dat. *aṣaone, aṣaonaē-ca, aṣāunē* (GAv. § 62 Note 1); Abl. *aṣaonaṭ;* Gen. *aṣaonō, aṣaonas-cā* (GAv.), *aṣāunō* (GAv.); Voc. *aṣāum* § 193. — Dual. Nom. Acc. Voc. *aṣavana;* Gen. *aṣaonǣ.* — Plural. Nom. *aṣavanō;* Acc. *aṣavanō* (str. stem YAv.), *aṣāunō* (wk. stem GAv.), *aṣavana* (ending *a* § 224); Dat. *aṣavabyō* (GYAv.), *aṣavaoyō* (YAv. § 62 Note 3); Gen. *aṣaonqm, aṣāunqm* (§ 62 Note 1).

Note 1. Similar to *aṣavan-* is (a) the declension of GAv. *magavan-* (str. st.), *magāun-* (wk. st.) m. 'member of the community', cf. Skt. *maghávan-, maghón-* Whitney, *Skt. Gram.* § 428; — and (b) the declension of Av. *āþravan-* (str. st.), *aþaᵘrun-* (wk. st. §§ 62, 191) m. 'priest' = Skt. *átharvan-*. Observe Av. voc. sg. *āþraom* § 193.

Note 2. Transfers to the *a*-decl. are not infrequent: e. g. Dat. Du. *aṣavanaēibya.*

§ 314. (ii) Declension of Av. *ᵘrvan-* (i. e. *ᵘruvan-* §§ 68 b and 71 end) m. 'soul'. This has in weak case-forms *ᵘrun-* (*ū* § 51 Note 1).

Singular. Nom. *ᵘrva;* Acc. *ᵘrvānǝm;* Instr. *ᵘruna;* Dat. *ᵘrune, ᵘrunaē-ca;* Gen. *ᵘrunō.* — Plural. Nom. *ᵘrvqnō* (§ 45); Acc. *ᵘrunō, ᵘrunas-cā* Ys. 63.3, *ᵘrvqnō* (str. st.); Dat. *ᵘrvōibyō* (a-decl.).

Note 1. (a) Similar to *ᵘrvan-* is the declension of Av. *yvan-* (i. e. *yuvan-* § 68 b, str. st.), *yūn-* (wk. st.) m. 'youth' = Skt. *yúvan-, yūn-* m., cf. Whitney, *Skt. Gram.* § 427.—Observe Av. voc. sg. *yum* opp. to Skt. *yúvan* (§ 193).—(b) Similar also in Av. *span-* (triple stem *spān-, span-, sūn-* § 20) m. 'dog' = Skt. *śván- (śvān-, śván-, śún-)* m., cf. Whitney, *Skt. Gram.* § 427.—(c) Likewise Av. *srvan-* n. 'time', dat. sg. *srūne* Yt. 5.129.

Note 2. Transfers to the *a*-decl. are found:—e. g. gen. sg. *sūnahe* beside *sūno;* again gen. sg. *srvānahe* (stem *srvāna-*), loc. *srūne* Vd. 19.9 (stem *srūna-*, but cf. § 35 Note 2 or § 233). So above dat. pl. * urvōibyu* (variant *urvaẑibyō*, after *a*-decl. instead of *°urvabyō*).

§ 315. (a) Forms to be observed are: YAv. nom. sg. *taurvā* (van-stem) 'overpowering', cf. Bartholomae, in *K.Z.* xxix. p. 561 = *Flexionslehre* pp. 141, 142. So sg. nom. *þrizafā*, acc. *°anəm*, voc. *°əm* (stem orig. *°zapvan-* § 95.—GAv. nom. sg. *advā* (variant *advā*) m. 'way'.—(b) As general plural case with ending *-ąn* §§ 230, 308: YAv. *karśvąn* 'climes'.—As general plural case with ending *-īś* §§ 231, 308: Av. *aŝaonīś* (as acc. pl. neut. Ys. 71.6 *dāma aŝaonīś;* as instr. pl. masc. Vsp. 21.3).

---

9. (D) Derivative Stems in *in*.

Masculine, Feminine and Neuter, (derivative adjectives), cf. Whitney, *Skt. Gram.* § 438 seq.

§ 316. The *in*-stems (few in number) are declined like those in *an;* cf. Brugmann, *Grundriss der vergl. Gram.* ii. § 115:—e. g. Av. *kainin-* f. 'maiden', et al.

I. MASCULINE—FEMININE. Singular: Nom. *kaini;* Acc. *kaíninəm;* Dat. *pərənine* 'having a feather'; Gen. *kaínīnō, kaínīnō.*—Dual: Nom. *hąmina* 'belonging to summer'.—Plural: Nom. *kaínīnō, kaínīnō, kaínina;* Acc. *aśīlacinō* 'having running waters'; Dat. *kaínibyō;* Gen. *drujinąm* 'belonging to the Druj' Yt. 4.7.—II. NEUTER. Sg. Nom. Acc. *raokṣni* 'shining'.

Note. On the interchange of *i, ī,* see § 21 Note 1.

---

10. (E) Radical *n-* and *m*-Stems.

§ 317. Here belongs the root *jan-* 'slay' as final element of a compound: Av. *vərəþrajan-* 'victorious' = Skt. *vṛtrahán-*, cf. Whitney, *Skt. Gram.* § 402. The stem shows triple forms *-jān-, -jan-, -ʒn-*.

Singular: Nom. *vərəþraja, vərəþrəm.jā* (GAv.), *vərəþrajā* (i. e. *-ā* [= *an*] + *s* § 222); Acc. *vərəþrājanəm;* Abl. *vərəþrajnaṭ;* Gen. *vər-þrajnō, vərəþrājnō.*—Plural: Nom. *vərəþrājanō;* Acc. *aŝava-janō.*

§ 318. Radical *m*-stem is Av. *zam- z²m-* f. 'earth' = Skt. *kṣám- jm-*, cf. Brugmann, *Grundriss der vergl. Gram.* ii. § 160.

Singular: Nom. *zå;* Acc. *zqm;* Instr. *z²må* (§ 24); Dat. *z²mē* (cf. also § 233); Abl. *z²maṭ, z²måda* Yt. 7.4 (§ 222, *a*-decl.); Gen. *ů²mō;* Loc. *z²mi.* — Plural: Nom. *z²mō;* Acc. *z²mō, z²mas-ca;* Gen. *z²mqm.*

Note 1. The nom. sg. *zå* is *zā* (=? *zam-* = *zm̄̄i*) + *s* § 222; similarly acc. *zqm* (=? *zm̄̄i* + *m*).

Note 2. Similar to *z²m-* is Av. *zyam-* m. 'hiems', Sg. Nom. *zyå, zyås-ciṭ;* Acc. *zyqm;* Gen. *zimō;* cf. Brugmann, *Grundriss* ii. § 160. Likewise Av. *dam-* 'domus', cf. GAv. gen. sg. *d²ng,* loc. sg. *dqm* — see Brugmann, *Grundriss* ii. § 160. _____

11. (F) Stems in original *r*.

Masculine (Feminine and Neuter), cf. Whitney, *Skt. Gram.* § 369 seq.

§ 319. Here belong a limited number of nouns: (a) Derivative stems in orig. *-tar, -ar* — nouns of a g e n c y and nouns of r e l a t i o n s h i p; (b) Radical stems in orig. *-ar;* (c) Derivative stems (indeclinable) in orig. *-ar.*

§ 320. S t r o n g and w e a k case-forms.—Nouns of this declension show three stem-forms: strongest stem *ār*, strong stem *ar*, weak stem *r* (before vowels), *ər²* (before consonants). The (1) nouns of a g e n c y show the s t r o n g e s t form *ār* in acc. sg., nom. du., and nom. pl.; the (2) nouns of r e l a t i o n s h i p show simply the s t r o n g form *ar* in those cases. — The strong and weak case-forms, however, do not always agree with the Skt. in its sharp division, cf. also Lanman, *Noun-Inflection in the Veda* p. 420 fin.

(a) Derivative Stems in *-tar, -ar.*

§ 321. These are divided with reference to the acc. sg., nom. du., and nom. pl. *ār* or *ar* into two classes:

1) N o u n s o f A g e n c y. — 2) N o u n s o f R e l a t i o n s h i p.
Chiefly Masculine (cf. Whitney, *Skt. Gram.* § 373).

§ 322. 1) Av. ᴫᴗᴘᴧᴜᴎ *dātar-* m. 'giver, creator' = Skt. *dātár-, dhātár-.* 2) Av. ᴫᴗᴘᴧᴜᴎ *patar-* m. 'father' = Skt. *pitár-.*

Av. *frabər*tar-* m. title of priest, *ātar-* m. 'fire', *nar-* m. 'man',
nipātar- m. 'protector', *zāmātar-* m. 'son in law', *sātar-* m. 'persecutor'.

	Av. Singular:		cf. Skt.
N.	*dā-ta* .		*dā-tá*
A.	*1. dā-tārəm*		*dā-táram*
	2. pi-tārəm		*pi-táram*
I.	*(dā-þra)* aþrā (GAv.)		*dā-trá*
D.	*(dā-þre)* frabərəþre		*dā-trḗ*
Abl.	*(dā-þraṭ)* aþraṭ .		see gen.
G.	*dā-þrō* .		*dā-túr*
L.	*(dā-tari)* naⁱri .		*dā-tári*
V.	*dā-tarə* .		*dá-tar*

Dual:

N.A.V.	*1. (dā-tāra)* nipātāra		*dā-tárā* (Ved.)
	2. (pi-tāra) zāmātara		*pi-tárā* (Ved.)
I.D.Abl.	*(dā-tərəbya)* nərəbya		*dā-tŕ̥bhyām*
G.	*(dā-þrā̊)* narā̊		*dā-trós*

Plural:

N.	*1. dā-tārō* .		*dā-táras*
	2. pi-tārō .		*pi-táras*
A.	*1. dā-tārō* .		*dā-tŕ̥n*
	2. fə-drō		*pi-tŕ̥n*
D.Abl.	*(dā-tərəbyō)* ātərəbyō		*dā-tŕ̥bhyas*
G.	*(dā-þrąm)* sāþrąm		*dā-tṝṇā́m*

Forms to be observed in GAv. and YAv.

§ 323. In general, GAv. has the same forms as above,
with the long final vowel, see § 26.

§ 324. On the occasional interchange of strong *(ar)*
and weak *(r, ər°)* case-forms see § 320, and § 47 Note.

§ 325. Singular:—

Nom.: YGAv. observe *pita, pᵃta, ptā* 'father'.

Acc.: YAv. also (from weak stem) *brāþrəm* 'brother'.—Observe Av. *haᵛhā-rəm* 'sister' opp. to Skt. *svásāram (-ār-).*— GAv. also (*ȝm* §§ 22, 32) *pⁱtarəm* 'father'.

Gen.: YAv. *sāþras-cit* 'of the persecutor'.—Also (isolated) from strong stem + *s, sāstarš* 'of the tyrant' Ys. 9.31, like gen. *narš* § 332.

Dat.: GAv. also *fədrōi* 'father' (i. e. *-ōi = -ē,* § 56) Ys. 53.4.

§ 326. Dual:—

N.A.V.: YAv. also (from weak stem) *brāþra* 'two brothers'.

§ 327. Plural:—

Nom.: YAv. also *dātāras-ca* see § 19.—Also ending *a: vaštāra* 'coursers'.
Acc.: YAv. also acc. pl. in *-ʒuš, -ʒš* (like *strʒuš, strʒš, nərʒuš*, §§ 329, 332)
pairi.aētrʒuš Vd. 9.38, cf. Skt. *paryētár-*, see *American Journal of
Philology* x. p. 346.—GAv. also (from strong stem) *mātarō* 'mothers'.
—Also *mātərqš-cā* § 49.
Dat.: YAv. observe *ptərəbyō* 'for fathers' Vd. 15.12.

§ 328. T r a n s f e r s to the *a*-decl. occur: e. g.:

　　Singular. Gen. *sāstrahe* 'of the persecutor' (i. e. stem *sāstra*-
　　beside *sāstar-*).—Plural. Gen. *sāstranqm* 'of persecutors'.

(α) Like nouns of agency.

§ 329. (i) Declension of Av. *star-* m. (strongest stem
stār-, strong stem *star-*, weak stem *str-*, *stərə-*) = Skt. *stár-*
(cf. Whitney, *Skt. Gram.* § 371):—

　　Singular. Acc. *stārəm*; Gen. *stārō*.—Plural. Nom. Acc *stārō*,
staras-ca (§ 19 on *ə*), *strʒuš* (acc. YAv. cf. § 327); Dat. Abl. *stərəbyō*;
Gen. *strqm, stārqm, starṃt-cā* (GAv.).

§ 330. (ii) Declension of Av. *raþaēštar-* 'warrior standing in charriot'.—This word shows also a parallel stem
raþaēštā according to the radical *ā*-decl., see § 249. The
forms from stem *raþaēštar-* are:—

　　Singular. Acc. *raþaēštārəm*; Gen. *raþaēštārahe* (*a*-decl.); Voc.
raþaēštāra (*a*-decl.).—Plural. Nom. *raþaēštārō*; Acc. *raþaēštārīs-ca*
(§ 327, or perhaps here *a*-decl. § 129).

Note. The forms from stem *raþaēštā-* are enumerated at § 249.

(β) Like nouns of relationship.

§ 331. (iii) Declension of Av. *ātar-* m. 'fire' (strong
stem *ātar-*, wk. st. *āþr-*, *ātr-* [§ 79 Note], *ātərə-*):—

　　Singular. Nom. *ātarš* (= str. st. + *s*); Acc. *ātrəm* (YAv.), *ātrīm*
(GAv.); Instr. *āþrā* (GAv.); Dat. *āþre, āþraē-ca*; Abl. *āþraṭ*; Gen.
āþrō, āþras-ca; Voc. *ātar* (YAv.), *ātarə* (GAv.), *ātarš* (YAv. same
as nom.).—Plural. Acc. *ātarō*; Dat. Abl. *ātərəbyō*; Gen. *āþrqm*.

§ 332. (iv) Declension of Av. *nar-* m. 'man' = Skt.
nár- (cf. Whitney, *Skt. Gram.* § 371):—

Singular: Nom. *nā;* Acc. *narəm;* Dat. *naᵉre* (YAv.), *narōi* (GAv.);
Abl. *nərəf* Phl. Version at Vd. 3.42; Gen. *narš* (YAv.), *nərəf* (GAv.);
Loc. *naⁱri;* Voc. *narə.*—Dual: Nom. *nara;* I.D.Abl. *nərəbyō;* Gen.
narä̊.—Plural: Nom. Voc. *narō, naras-ca, nara* (§ 224); Acc. *nərąš*
(GAv. Ys. 40.3 see § 49), *nəršuš* (acc. YAv. cf. § 327); Dat. Abl.
nərəbyō, nərəbyas-ca, nəruyō, nuruyō, nərəyō (§ 62 Note 3, and § 31
Note); Gen. *narąm* (YAv.), *naršm* (GAv.) Ys. 30.2, see § 32.

Note 1. GAv. *nərąš* at Ys. 45.7 is apparently used as gen. sg. rather
than acc. pl., see Gah 3.6 *narš* citation, cf. Skt. *nɹ́n*, Pischel-Geldner,
Vedische Studien p. 43.

Note 2. Transfers to the a-declension, stem *nara-* occur:—
Singular: Nom. *narō;* Gen. *narahe;* etc.

(b) Radical Stems in original *r*.

§ 333. Here belong a very few nouns and their (adjective) compounds, e. g.:—

§ 334. (i) Av. *hvar-* n. 'sun' = Skt. *svàr-* (cf. Whitney, *Skt. Gram.*
§ 388 d):—Singular: Nom. Acc. *hvarə* (YAv.), *hvarš* (GAv.); Gen *hūrō*
or *hū* (YAv.), *həṇg* (GAv. i. e. *hvan-s*, cf. §§ 337, 318 Note 2).

§ 335. (ii) GAv. *sar-* f. 'association, unity':—Singular: *sarəm, saršm;*
Dat. *sarōi;* Gen. *sarš* (Ys. 49.3); Loc. *saⁱrī* (Ys. 35.8).—Plural: Acc. *sarō*
(Ys. 31.21).

(c) Neuters (derivative) in original *ar*.

§ 336. These neuters (indeclinable) in *arə, arš*
(GAv.) are used chiefly as acc. sg., but they may supply
other cases.

Singular: Nom. Acc. *vadarə* (YAv.), *vadarš* (GAv.) 'weapon'
(= Skt. *vádhar*); as Dat. (and acc.) *dasvarə* 'strength' Ys. 68.2; as
Gen. (and acc.) *karšvarš* 'clime'. Vsp. 10.1.—Dual: N.A.V. (and
acc. sg.) *danarə* 'two D. measures'.—Plural: Acc. (beside acc. sg.)
ayārš (GAv.).

Note. These neuters rarely show declined cases:—e. g. Sg. Instr.
dasvara 'with strength' (Ys. 55.3); Pl. Instr. *baēvarəbīš* 'with thousands'.—
Like a-decl., Dat. sg. *baēvarāi.*

§ 337. These *ar*-neuters commonly show parallel *an*-
stems with which they unite in forming a declension: e. g.
Av. *karšvar-, karšvan-* n. f. 'clime, zone'; *ayar-, ayan-* n.

'day ; *zafar-, zafan-* n. 'jaw'; *panvar-, panvana-* (*a*-decl.) n.
'bow'. See § 311 and Brugmann, *Grundriss der vergl.*
Gram. ii. § 118.

_____

12. (G) Stems in original *s*.

(a) Derivative Stems in -*h* (= orig. *s*).

(α) Stems in -*ah* (= orig. Ind.-Iran. -*as*).

§ 338. These very common stems in -*ah* (= orig. -*as*)
are chiefly n e u t e r nouns; but as adjectives (compound or
with original accent on the ending, cf. Whitney, *Skt. Gram.*
§ 417) they may likewise be m a s c u l i n e or f e m i n i n e.
A feminine substantive *uṣah-* (see § 357 for declension)
also occurs.—Cf. Horn, *Nominalflexion im Avesta* p. 26 seq.;
and Whitney, *Skt. Gram.* §§ 414, 418.

I. MASCULINE — FEMININE (ADJECTIVE),
NEUTER (SUBSTANTIVE).

§ 339. Av. ⟨script⟩ *hvacah-* (adj. m. f.) 'well-speaking'
= Skt. *suvácas-*. Av. ⟨script⟩ *vacah-* n. 'word' = Skt. *vácas-*;
Av. ⟨script⟩ *duž-vacah-* (adj.) 'evil-speaking'= Skt. *durvacas-*.

Av. *anaocah-* (adj.) 'hostile', *raocah-* n. 'light', *sarah-* n. 'head'
(= Skt. *śiras-* n.), *zrayah-* n. 'sea', and m. nom. propr. 'Zrayah',
arᵊzah- n. 'daylight'.

	Av.	Singular:	cf. Skt.
N.	*hvac-ā̊*	.	. *suvác-ās*
A.	*hvac-avhəm*	.	. *suvác-asam*
I.	*vac-avha*	.	. *vác-asā*
D.	*vac-avhe* . . .	.	. *vác-asē*
Abl.	*vac-avhaṭ*	.	. see gen.
G.	*vac-avhō* . . .	.	. *vác-asas*
L.	*vac-ahi*	.	. *vác-asi*
V.	*hvac-ō*	.	. *súvác-as*

Dual:

N.A.V.	(*hvąc-avha*) *anaocavhā* (GAv.) .	.	. *suvác-asā* (Ved.)
G.	(*vac-avhā̊*) *zrayavhā̊*	.	. *vác-asōs*

7

	Av.	Plural:	cf. Skt.
N.V.	*dužvac-avhō*		*suvắc-asas*
A.	*dužvac-avhō*		*suvắc-asas*
I.	*vac-ɔ̄biš* [1]		*vắc-ōbhis*
D.Abl.	*(vac-ɔ̄byō)* *raocɔ̄byō* [1]		*vắc-ōbhyas*
G.	*vac-avhąm*		*vắc-asām*
L.	*(vac-ahu)* *sarahu*		*vắc-asu*
	-ahva *arᵊzakva*		—

ii. NEUTER (Separate Forms).

		Av.		cf. Skt.
Sg.	N.A.V.	*vac-ō*		*vắc-as*
Pl.	V.A.N. *vac-ā̆*		*vắc-ą̄si*

Forms to be observed in GAv. and YAv.

§ 340. In general, GAv. has the same forms as above with the long final vowel, see § 26.

i. MASCULINE—FEMININE—NEUTER.

§ 341. **Singular:**—

Nom.: YAv. also u n c o m p o u n d e d adj. (see § 338) *aojā̆* 'strong' Ys. 57.10 beside substantive *aojō* n. 'strength', GAv. *dvaẹ̄jā̆* 'hating' beside *ɣbaẹ̄jō* n. 'hatred', cf. Skt. *yaśắs* 'beauteous' (observe accent) beside *yắśas* n. 'beauty'.—Add *hᵊrᵊnas-ca* n. 'and glory'.

Acc.: On *uṣā̆whᵊm, uṣą̆m* f. 'dawn', see. § 357.

Dat.: YAv. *rafnavhaẹ̄-ca* 'and for support'.—GAv. infin. dat. *srāvayeⁱhⁱ* 'to announce' (see § 118 Note on *-ye- = -ya-*).

Abl.: YAv. also (+ postpositive *a* § 222) *zrayavhāḍa* 'from the sea' Yt. 8.47. —After *a*-decl. (+ postpos. *a* § 222) *tᵊmavhāḍa* 'from darkness'.

Gen.: YAv. *hᵊrᵊnavhas-ca* 'and of glory'.

Loc.: YAv. peculiar *zraya* (Yt. 5.38; 8.8), *zrayā̆* (Ys. 65.4), *zrayāi* (Yt. 5.4; 8.31) 'in the sea'.—See also § 357 Note 2.

§ 342. **Plural:**—

Nom.: YAv. *framanavhas-ca* 'kindly-minded'.

Instr.: YGAv. also (with variant *-biš* § 21) *vacɔ̄biš*.

Loc.: YAv. also (*-ōhu, -ōhva* § 39) *ravōhu* 'in freedom', *tᵊmōhva* 'in darkness'.

ii. NEUTER (Special Forms).

§ 343. **Plural:**—N.A.V.: YAv. add *aojā̆s-ca* 'powers', GAv. *tᵊmā̆s-cā̆* 'and darkness'.

§ 344. **Transfers to the *a*-declension are very frequent:**—

---

[1] See § 33.

Singular. Nom. *arĭ.vacô* (masc.) 'rightly-speaking' ; Acc. (fem. *ā*-decl.) *ravô.vacavhqm* 'whose words go with freedom' Vsp. 7.2 ; Instr. *hvarᵉna* 'with glory' Yt. 10.141, see § 194; Abl. *təmavhāda* 'from darkness' (postpositive *a* § 222). — Dual. Dat. *aⁱþyajavhaðⁱbya* 'for the two imperishable ones'. — Plural. Nom. *anaoʃðvhô* 'undying' (§ 124 Nom. end, stem •*aoʃa*- beside *aoʃah*-), *maⁱnyavasð* (nom. pl. masc.) 'following the will *(vasah-)* of the Spirit' Yt. 10.128, beside *maⁱnivasavhô*; Instr. *sravôiʃ* 'with words'.

(β) Stems in *-yah.* — Comparative Adjectives.

§ 345.　The stems in *-yah* (Skt. *-yas* or *-īyas* § 68) are found in the comparative degree of adjectives.　They show an original double form of stem for masculine and neuter: strongest stem *-yāh*, strong stem *-yah*.　The superlative *-iš-ta* presents the weak stem.　The Skt. has *-yąs*, *-yas*, *-iṣ-ṭha*, cf. Brugmann, *Grundriss* ii. § 135 Anm. 5. — The corresponding feminine form has *-yehī-* (i. e. strong stem + *ī*-declension § 257) e. g. Av. *aspô.staoyehīš* (nom. pl. fem.) 'greater than a horse'. — Cf. Whitney, *Skt. Gram.* § 463 seq.

I. MASCULINE.

§ 346.　Av. -ﺳﯿﻨﯿﺪ *nāⁱdyah-* 'weaker', *masyah-* 'greater', *kasyah-* 'less', *āsyah-* 'swifter', *frāyah-* 'more', *vahyah-* 'better'.

	Av. Singular:	cf. Skt.
N.	*(nāⁱd-yð) masyð*	*śrĕ-yān*
A.	*nāⁱd-yðvhəm*	*śrĕ-yąsam*
D.	*(nāⁱd-yavhe) kasyavhe*	*śrĕ-yasĕ*
G.	*nāⁱd-yavhô*	*śrĕ-yasas*
	Dual:	
N.A.V.	*(nāⁱd-yavha) āsyavha*	*śrĕ-yąsōu*
	Plural:	
N.V.	*(nāⁱd-yavhō) masyavhō*[1]	*śrĕ-yąsas*
I.	*(nāⁱd-yebīš) frāyebīš*	*śrĕ-yôbhis*
G.	*(nāⁱd-yavhqm) vavhavhqm*[2] . .	*śrĕ-yasām*

II. NEUTER (Separate Forms).

Sg. N.A.V. *mas-yō* . . . . *śrĕ-yas*

---

[1] See Haug, *Zand-Pahlavi Glossary* p. 48, 16. — [2] See § 134.

Forms to be observed in GAv. and YAv.

§ 347. **i. MASCULINE.** Singular: Nom. GAv. observe *vahyą̄* 'melior' (see § 133 on *h*); Acc. (from strong stem) *vaṇhaṇhǝm* 'meliorem' (see § 134 on *ṇh* = orig. *sy*), cf. Skt. *kanīyāsam* 'younger', Whitney, *Skt. Gram.* § 465 c. — Observe in paradigm Dual, Plural Nom. *•yaṇha, •yaṇhō* (i. e. s t r o n g stem) opposed to Skt. *•yą̄sāu, •yą̄sas* (i. e. strongest stem). — **ii. NEUTER.** Singular: Nom. YAv. observe *vaṇhō* 'melius' § 134, GAv. *vahyō* 'melius' § 132. On YAv. *aʃ̌ō*, GAv. *aʃ̌yō* 'worse', see § 162.

(γ) Stems in -vah.—Perfect Active Participles.

§ 348.   The stems in *-vah* are perfect active participles used adjectively. They show a double form of stem for m a s c u l i n e and n e u t e r: strongest stem *-vah*, weak stem *-uš*. The Skt. has *-vą̄s, -uṣ*, cf. Brugmann, *Grundriss* ii. § 136 Anm. 6.—The corresponding feminine form has *-uš̌ī-* (i. e. weak stem + *ī*-declension § 257) e. g. Av. *vīḅuš̌i* (nom.), *vīḅuš̌īm* 'knowing', see § 86 on *ḅ*.—Cf. Whitney, *Skt. Gram.* § 458 seq.

MASCULINE—NEUTER.

§ 349.   Av. -ᘓᘓᘓ YAv. *vīdvah-*, GAv. *vīdvah-* 'knowing' = Skt. *vidvás-*.

Av. *dadvah-* 'creator', *iririḅwah-* 'having died'.

	Av.	Singular:	cf. Skt.
N.	*vīd-vā̊*		*vid-vā́n*
A.	*•vīd-vāǝṇhǝm* [1]		*vid-vą́sam*
I.	*vīḅ-uš̌a* [2]		*vid-úṣā*
D.	*vīd-uš̌ē* (GAv.)		*vid-úṣē*
Abl.	*(vīḅ-uš̌aṭ) daḅuš̌aṭ* [3]		see gen.
G.	*vīd-uš̌ō* (GAv.)		*vid-úṣas*
		Plural:	
N.	*vīd-vāǝṇhō*		*vid-vą́sas*
I.	*(vīḅ-ūž̌biš̌) dadǝbiš̌* (GAv.)		*vid-vádbhis*
G.	*(vīḅ-uš̌ą̄m) iririḅuš̌ą̄m*		*vid-úṣą̄m*

Forms to be observed in GAv. and YAv.

§ 350. Singular: Nom. YGAv. also (from weak stem) *mamnuš̌* 'having thought' Yt. 8.39, *vīḅuš̌* 'knowing' Vd. 4.54, *yaētuš̌* 'having striven', Haug,

---

[1] See Vsp. 19.1; Yt. 10.35. — [2] See § 86.

ZPhl. Gloss. p. 16.6; 56.5, *vīduš* (GAv.) 'knowing' Ys. 45.8, *vāunuš* 'having won' Ys. 28.5, cf. Whitney, *Skt. Gram.* § 462 c, and Bartholomae, in *K.Z.* xxix. p. 531 = *Flexionslehre* p. 111; —Voc. YAv. (nom. as voc.) *vīspō.vīdvā̊* 'O all-knowing one' Vd. 19.26. —Plural: Uncertain whether acc. pl. or gen. sg. *daduš̌ō* Ys. 58.6.

Note. On the interchange of *d*, *d̦*, *þ* see §§ 82, 83, 86.

§ 351. Transfers to the *a*-decl. may be found: e. g. dat. pl. Av. *vīþuša̦ibyas-ca*.

(b) Radical Stems in -*h* (= orig. -*s*).

(α) Stems in -*āh* (= orig. -*ās*).

§ 352. To this division (masculine, feminine and neuter) belong simple nouns like Av. *māh-* m. 'moon' (Skt. *mās-*), *āh-* n. 'mouth' (Skt. *ás-*) and the compounds of Av. -*dāh-* 'giving, doing'. The forms have all the long vowel *ā̊* (*ā*). — Cf. Horn, *Nominalflexion im Avesta* p. 4 seq., and Lanman, *Noun-Inflection in the Veda* p. 493 seq.

MASCULINE—FEMININE—NEUTER.

§ 353. Av. -ᵥᵥᵤᵥᵥ YGAv. *hudāh-*, *hudāh-* 'beneficent'. = Skt. *sudās-*.

Av. *yās-* n. (metrically dissyllabic) 'decision', *akō.dāh-* 'maleficent'.

	Av.	Singular:	cf. Skt.
N.V.	*hud-ā̊*		*sud-ās*
A.	*hud-ā̊ṇhəm*		*sud-āsam*
I.	*hud-ā̊ṇhā*		*sud-āsā*
D.	*hud-ā̊ṇhe*		*sud-āse*
Abl.	*hud-ā̊ṇhaṯ*		see gen.
G.	*hud-ā̊ṇhō*		*sud-āsas*
L.	(*hud-āhi*) *yāhi*		*sud-āsi*
		Plural:	
N.V.	*hud-ā̊ṇhō*		*sud-āsas*
A.	*hud-ā̊ṇhō*		*sud-āsas*
I.	(*hud-ā̊bīš*) *akō.dā̊bīš*		—
D.	*hud-ā̊byō*		—
G.	*hud-ā̊ṇhąm*		*sud-āsām*

Forms to be observed in GAv. and YAv.

§ 354. **Plural:** Instr. and Dat. often show MS. authority for *ābīš*, *ābyō;* the form in *-ā-* above, apparently arises from orig. *ās* being treated as if **final**, i. e. before *bīš*, *byō* — pada endings.—Observe Nom. Pl. *za-rᵘzdā* (GAv.).

§ 355. Transfers to the *a*-declension occur: e. g. **Singular:** Nom. *māuhō* 'moon' Yt. 10.142 (cf. Skt. *māsas* nom.); Dat. *māuhāi;* Gen. *māuhahe* beside *māuhō;* Voc. *duzda* 'O malevolent one' § 234b.

Note. The acc. sg. *uši.dąm* 'giving understanding' nom. propr. is perhaps to be explained as formed after the radical *ā*-decl. § 250, cf. Skt. *vayō-dhām* — cf. Brugmann, *Grundriss* ii. § 134, 1², Lanman, *Noun-Inflection* pp. 555, 443, 446.

(β) Like radical *āh*-Stems.

§ 356. Declension of Av. *mazdōh-* f. 'wisdom, Mazda', Anc. Pers. *-mazdāh-* = Skt. *-mēdhas-*. This word like *ušāh-*, *ušah-*, § 357, is after all [1] best considered a contract noun, cf. dat. sg. GAv. (trissyllabic) *mazdāi* (i. e. *mazdā(h)-ē*); acc. sg. GAv. (trissyllabic) *mazdąm* (i. e. *mazdā(h)-am*); gen. sg. GAv. (trissyllabic) *mazdā* (i. e. *mazdā(h)-as*); nom. pl. GAv. (trissyllabic) *mazdās-cā* (i. e. *ā(h)-as*). The forms are as follows:—

Singular. Nom. *mazdā* (dissyllable GAv.); Acc. *mazdąm;* Dat. *mazdāi;* Gen. *mazdā*, *mazdās-ca* (YAv.), *mazdās-cā* (trissyl. GAv.); Voc. (a-decl.) *mazda* (YAv.), *mazdā* (GAv.). — Plural. Nom. Voc. *mazdās-cā* (GAv.).

§ 357. Here may be added Av. *ušāh-*, *ušah-* f. 'dawn' = Skt. *ušās-*, *ušás-*. — Singular: Acc. *ušāuhąm*, *ušąm* (cf. Skt. *ušāsam*, *ušásam*, *ušām*). — Plural: Acc. *ušā* (cf. Skt. *ušás*); Gen. *ušauhąm* (cf. Skt. *ušāsām*); Loc. *ušahva*.

Note 1. Parallel, are the sg. nom. acc. Av. *hvāpā*, *hvāpąm* 'beneficent' = Skt. *svápās*, *svápām*.

Note 2. An instance of contraction in orig. *as*-stem § 339 similar to the above, seems to be the loc. sg. *zrayāi* (trissyllabic) 'in the sea' Yt. 5.4; 8.31 (= *zraya(h)e* like *vaṯjahe*, *arᵉzahe*). But another explanation for *zrayāi* may be suggested: viz. mistake in writing *āi* for *ahi* due to Pahlavi script. — See further, § 341.

Note 3. Transfer to the *a*-declension, sg. nom. *hvāpō* 'beneficent'.

(c) Derivative Stems in *-iš*, *-uš*.

§ 358. The examples are not numerous. The words are chiefly **neuter**. There is no vowel-gradation.— Cf. Whitney, *Skt. Gram.* § 414.

§ 359. Av. *snaiþiš*- n. 'weapon'.—Singular: Nom. Acc. (neut.) *snaiþiš;* Acc. (masc. adj.) *nidā.snaiþiþm* 'having weapons laid down'; Instr. *snaiþiţa;* Gen. *hadiţas-ca* 'of the abode'; Loc. *viþiši* 'at the judgment' (Geldner). — Dual: Instr. *snaiþībya.* —Plural: Gen. *snaiþiţqm.*

Note. Transfers to the *a*-decl. occur: e. g. sg. gen. *hadiţahe* 'of the abode'.

§ 360. Similar are the *uš*-nouns: Av. *arəduš*- n. 'assault, battery'. —Singular: Nom. *arəduš;* Instr. *arəduţa;* Loc. *tanuţi* 'in person'. —Plural: Gen. *arəduţqm.*

ADJECTIVES.

FEMININE FORMATION—COMPARISON.

§ 361. The declension of adjectives, as agreeing exactly with that of nouns, is treated above.

§ 362. **Feminine Formation.** The adjective *a*-stems masc. neut. form their corresponding feminine in -*ā* or -*ī*. The consonant stems and *u*-stems show regularly the fem. in -*ī*, before which the adjective stem usually appears in its weak form.

(1) With -*ā*: Av. *haᵘrva*- (m. n.), *haᵘrvā*- (f.) 'whole'; *sūra*- (m. n.), *sūrā*- (f.) 'mighty'; *uţra*- (m. n.), *uţrā*- (f.) 'strong'; *aspa*- (m.) 'horse', *aspā*- (f.) and *aspī*- (f.) 'mare'.

(2) With -*ī*: Av. *rava*- (m. n.), *rəvī*- (f.) 'broad, smooth'; *spitāma*- (m. n.), *spitāmī*- (f.) 'belonging to Spitama'; *daēva*- (m. n.), *daēvī*- (f.) 'devilish'.—*ašavan*- (m. n.), *ašaonī*- (f.) 'righteous'; *bərəzaṇt*- (m. n.), *bərə-zaitī*- (f.) 'high, great'; *vīdvah*- (m. n.), *vīþuši*- (f.) 'knowing'; *dātar*- (m.), *dāþrī*- (f.) 'giving, giver'; *þrā-tar*- (m.), *þrāþrī*- (f.) 'protector, nurturer'; *vaṇhu*- (m. n.), *vaṇuhī*- (f.) 'good'; *driţu*- (m. n.), *drīvī*- (f.) 'poor' § 187.

-----

[1] For different views on the subject see Horn, *Nominalflexion im Avesta* p. 5; Brugmann, *Grundriss der vergl. Gr.* ii. § 133 ², but ii. § 134, 1 ².

§ 363. **Comparison of Adjectives.** In Avesta as also
in Sanskrit, there are two ways of forming the comparative
and superlative degrees of adjectives: —(1) *-tara-*, *-təma-* and
(2) *-yah-*, *-išta-* added to the stem. The corresponding
feminine to these is *-tarā-*, *-təmā-* and *-yehī-* (§ 34), *-ištā-*
according to rule, § 362.

(1) *-tara-* (comparative), *-təma-* (superlative).

§ 364. Before *-tara-*, *-təma-*, adjectives whose stem
ends in *a* appear commonly in the form *ō* as in noun compounds. The *a*-stems may, however, retain *a* unchanged,
as in Sanskrit. Other stems commonly remain unchanged,
appearing in the weak form if they have one.

baēšazya- 'healing',	*baēšazyōtara-*,	*baēšazyōtəma-*
srīra- 'fair',	*srīrōtara-*,	—
aka- 'bad',	*akatara-*,	—
huyašta- 'well-sacrificed',	*huyaštara-*,	—
hubaoⁱdi- 'sweet-scented',	*hubaoⁱditara-*,	*hubaoⁱditəma-*
ašaojah- 'very strong',	*ašaojastara-*,[1]	*ašaojastəma-*
yāskərət- 'energetic',	*yāskərⁱstara-*,[2]	*yāskərⁱstəma-*
amavaṇt- 'strong',	*amavastara-*,[2]	*amavastəma-*
yaētvah- 'having striven',	—	*yaētuštəma-*

(2) *-yah-* (comparative), *-išta-* (superlative).

§ 365. Before *-yah-*, *-išta-*, the adjective reverts to
its original simple crude stem without formative suffix:

maz- 'great',	*mazyah-*,	*mazišta-*
mas- 'great',	*masyah-*,	—
vaṇhu- ⎫ 'good', ⎰ *vahyah-* (GAv.), ⎱	*vahišta-*
vohn- ⎭ ⎱ *vaṇhah-* (YAv.),[3] ⎰	
ās-u- 'swift',	*āsyah-*,	*āsišta-*
ak-a- 'bad',	⎰ *ašyah-* (GAv.), ⎱	*acišta-*
	⎱ *ašah-* (YAv.),[4] ⎰	

---

[1] Cf. § 109. — [2] § 151. — [3] §§ 132, 134. — [4] § 162.

Note 1. Some few adjectives, in appearance at least, show both forms of comparison, as above *aka-* 'bad', *akatara-,* and to this also (cf. Note 2) *ajyah-, aciŝta-;* so superlative *aŝaojiŝta-* beside *aŝaojastara-, aŝao-yastəma-* to *aŝaojah-* 'very strong'.

Note 2. As seen also above, comparatives and superlatives may be more or less mechanically attached to a positive of similar meaning and containing the same crude stem, see § 365: e. g. to *taḵ-ma-* 'strong', the comparative *tqjyah-,* superl. *tanciŝta-* beside *taḵmõtəma-,* et al.

Note 3. The *an*-stems sometimes follow the analogy of *aṇt*-stems in their comparison: e. g. *vərəþravan-* 'victorious', comparat. *vərəþravastara-,* superl. *vərəþravastəma-; aŝavan-* 'righteous', *aŝavastəma-; vərəþrajan-* 'victorious', *vərəþrająstara-, vərəþrająstəma-.*

§ 366. The numerals in Avesta correspond generally in form and in usage to the Sanskrit equivalents.—Cf. Whitney, *Skt. Gram.* § 475 seq.

Cardinals.

Av.	cf. Skt.		Av.	cf. Skt.
1. *aēva-*	—		10. *dasa*	*dása*
2. *dva-*	*dvá-*		20. *vīsaïti*	*viṣati-*
3. *þri-*	*tri-*		30. *þrisat-*	*trịṣát-*
4. *caþwar-*	*catvár-*		40. *caþwarᵃsat-*	*catvārịṣát-*
5. *paṇca*	*páñca*		50. *paṇcāsat-*	*pañcāśát-*
6. *ḫšvaš*	*šáṣ*		60. *ḫšvašti-*	*ṣaṣti-*
7. *hapta*	*saptá*		70. *haptāᵻti-*	*saptati-*
8. *ašta*	*aṣṭá*		80. *aštāᵻti-*	*aśíti-*
9. *nava*	*náva*		90. *navaᵻti-*	*navati-*
10. *dasa*	*dáśa*		100. *sata-*	*śatá-*

Av.	Av.
100. *sata-*	600. *ḫšvaš sata*
200. *duye saᵻte*	700. *hapta sata*
300. *tišᵃrō sata*	800. *ašta sata*
400. *caþwārō sata*	900. *nava sata*
500. *paṇca sata*	1000. *hazavra-*

10000. *baēvar-*

§ 367. The numbers from 11—19, as far as they occur, are made up as in Skt.: e. g. Av. *dvadasa* '12' = Skt. *dvádaśa*; Av. *paṇcadasa* '15' = Skt. *páñcadaśa*. See below under Ordinals, § 374b.

Note. Observe, the common forms Av. *þrisata-* '30' and *caþwarᵃsata-* '40' arise from transfer of *þrisat-* etc. to the *a*-decl. The strong form *þrisaṇt-* is to be sought in *þrisqs* (orig. nom. but crystallized form), etc.

§ 368. In composite numbers the lesser numeral precedes, and *ca—ca* connects the terms: e. g. Av. *paṇcāca vīsatica* '25'; *prayasca prisąsca* '33'; *paṇcāca capwarʼsatɔmca* '45', etc.

Note. The first member is sometimes put in the sociative instrumental case; e. g. Av. *navaṣatɑ̄iš hazawrɔmca* 'one thousand and nine hundred'.

Declension of Cardinals.

§ 369. (1) Declension of Av. *aēva-* (m. n.), *aēvā-* (f.) 'one, alone' (singular):

i—ii. MASC. NEUT. Sg. Nom. *aɛvō;* Acc. *ōyum* (§ 63 Note 2), or (abbreviated spelling) *ōim, aoim;* Instr. *aɛva;* Gen. *aɛvahe;* Loc. *aɛvahmi* (§ 443). —iii. FEM. Sg. Nom. *aɛva;* Acc. *aɛvąm;* Gen. *aɛvaʋhā* (§§ 443, 134).

§ 370. (2) Declension of Av. *dva-* 'two' = Skt. *dvá-* (dual) — cf. Whitney, *Skt. Gram.* § 482 b.

Du. N.A.V. *dva* (m.), *duye* (f. n.); I.D.Abl. *dvaɛibya;* G.L. *dvayą.*

Note. Observe *dvaɛ-ca* Yt. 19.7 beside *duye* § 190.

§ 371. (3) Declension of Av. *pri-* (m. n.), *tišar-* (f.) 'three' = Skt. *tri- tiṣár-* (plural) — cf. Whitney, *Skt. Gram.* § 482 c.

i—ii. MASC. NEUT. Pl. Nom. *prāyō;* Acc. *prāyō;* Dat. Abl. *pribyō;* Gen. *prayąm.* — iii. FEM. Nom. *prāyō;* Acc. *tišⁱarō, tišrō, tišra;* Gen *tišrąm, tišranqm* (ā-decl.).

Note. Observe *prāyō* (above) is from strongest stem, cf. § 235. —Also *prāyas-ca,* on *ā* cf. § 19 b. —Also neut. (like fem. § 232) *tišⁱarō.*

§ 372. (4) Declension of Av. *capwar-* (m. n.), *catawhar-* (f.) 'four' = Skt. *catvár-, cátasar-* (plural) — cf. Whitney, *Skt. Gram.* § 482 d.

i. MASC. Pl. Nom. *capwārō, capwāras-ca* (§ 19 b); Acc. *capwārō.* —ii. FEM. Acc. *catawrō* Yt. 14.44.

§ 373. (5) Declension of numerals from 5—10:—The following instances of gen. pl. occur, Av. *paṇcanqm, navanqm, dasanqm,* cf. Skt. *paṇcānām,* Whitney, *Skt. Gram.* §§ 483, 484.

§ 374. Declension of remaining cardinals:—20 *vīsaⁱti* indeclinable; 30 *prisatɔm* (nom. acc. neut.), *prisatańqm* (gen. pl.); 40 *capwārʼsatɔm-ca* (§ 19 b); 50 *paṇcāsatɔm, paṇcāsaþiš-ca* (§ 19 b); 60—70 *ħšvaštim* (acc. sg.

fem.) etc., also *nava⁴tiš-ca* (acc. pl. fem. beside *nava⁴tīm*). — 100 — 1000 *sata-*, *hazaₐra-* as neut. nouns, *a*-decl. § 237. — 10000 *baₑvarⁱ* (acc. sg.), *baₑvarūi* (dat. sg. *a*-decl. § 237); *baₑvqn* (acc. pl.), *baₑvarᵢbiš* (instr. pl.) cf. 336.

Ordinals.

	Av.	cf. Skt.		Av.	cf. Skt.
1st	*fratəma-* *paoⁱrya-*	*prathamá-* *pūrvyá-*	11th	*aēvaṇdasa-*	—
2nd	*bitya-*	*dvitíya-*	12th	*dvadasa-*	*dvādašá-*
3rd	*þritya-*	*tṛtíya-*	13th	*þridasa-*	*trayōdašá-*
4th	*tūⁱrya-*	*tūrya-*	14th	*caþrudasa-*	*caturdašá-*
5th	*puḥda-*	*pañcatha* ¹	15th	*pañcadasa-*	*pañcadašá-*
6th	*ḥẓtva-*	—	16th	*ḥẓvaš.dasa-*	*šóḍašá-*
7th	*haptaþa-*	*saptátha-*	17th	*haptadasa-*	*saptadašá-*
8th	*aštəma-*	*aṣṭamá-*	18th	*aštadasa-*	*aṣṭādašá-*
9th	*nāuma-* (§ 64)	*navamá-*	19th	*navadasa-*	*navadašá-*
10th	*dasəma-*	*dašamá-*	20th	*vīsqstəma-*	—

    100th Av. *satōtəma-* = Skt. *šatatamá-*.

    1000th Av. *hazaₐrōtəma* = Skt. *sahasratamá-*.

Note 1. The ordinals as adjectives are declined according to the *a*-decl. § 236 seq.

Note 2. Av. *ḥẓtva-* 'sixth' has fem. *ḥẓtvī-*, cf. § 362.

Note 3. Av. *þrisata-* as 'thirtieth' is found.

Numeral Derivatives.

§ 375. Numeral Adverbs: Av. *hakərⁱţ* 'once' = Skt. *sakṛt;* Av. *biš* 'twice' = Skt. *dvís;* Av. *þriš* 'thrice' = Skt. *trís;* Av. *caþruš* 'four times', cf. Skt. *catús*, Whitney, *Skt. Gram.* § 489. — Also with *ā:* Av. *āⁱbitīm* 'for the second time', *āþritīm* 'for the third time, thrice'; *āþtūⁱrīm* 'for the fourth time'. — Likewise some others.

§ 376. Multiplicative Adverbs: Suffix -*vaṇţ* — Av. *bižvaţ* 'two-fold'; *þrižvaţ* 'three-fold'; *vīsaⁱtivₐ* 'twenty-fold' (nom. masc.); *þrisaþwₐ* 'thirty-fold'; etc. — Suffix -*þwa:* e. g. *þrisata-þwəm* 'thirty-fold'; etc.

Note. Here also might be added a number of other words *þrišva-* 'a third' et al.; but they belong rather to the dictionary.

¹ Cf. Whitney, *Skt. Gram.* § 487.

§ 377. Pronominal declension in Avesta agrees in its main outlines with the Sanskrit. A synopsis of the Pronouns in Avesta may be given as follows:—

SYNOPSIS OF PRONOMINAL-DECLENSION.

1. **Personal** — A. Gender not distinguished. .
  a. First person *azəm*.
  b. Second person *tūm*.
  c. Third person, *hē* and other forms.

B. Gender distinguished.

2. **Relative** — Pronoun *ya-*.

3. **Interrogative** — Pronoun *ka-*.
  (Indefinite.)

4. **Demonstrative**
  a. Demonstrative *ta- (hvō)*.
  b. Demonstrative *aēta-*.
  c. Demonstrative *aēm (a-, i-, ima-, ana-)*.
  d. Demonstrative *ava- (hāu)*.

5. **Other pronominal Words and Derivatives.**
  (Possessive).
  (Reflexive).
  (Adjectives declined pronominally).

§ 378. **General Remark.** Most of the pronouns in Avesta are closely parallel with those in Sanskrit, and like the latter they show also many marked peculiarities. They are generally made up by combining a number of different stems. The principal points to be observed in regard to their inflection are the following:

i—ii. MASCULINE—NEUTER.

§ 379. **Singular:**—

Nom. Acc. Neut.: Commonly the suffix *-ṭ* = Skt. *-t (d)*.—Sometimes in later texts of the YAv. instead of *-ṭ*, the ending *-m*, like the neuter ending of the noun-declension, is found: e. g. *yim, aom*.

Dat. Abl. Loc.: Show an inserted element *-hm-* = Skt. *-sm-*.—The dat. sg.
of the two personal pronouns ends in *-bya (-vya)*, *-byō* = Skt. *-bhya(m)*,
Whitney, *Skt. Gram.* § 492 a.—The loc. sg. in YAv. may take **postpositive** *a* as in the noun-declension, see § 222.

§ 380. **Plural:**—

Nom. (Acc.): The pronominal *a*-stems make this case end in *e*. This form
in *e* often serves also as **accusative**.

Gen.: Shows *-ịqm* = Skt. *-ṣām*.—The 'genitives' *ahmākəm*, *yūṣmākəm*, *yavākəm*, as in Skt., are really crystallized cases nom. acc. neut. of
possessives.

Loc.: In YAv. the loc. pl. may take **postpositive** *a* as in the noun-
declension, see § 224. Similarly also in fem. loc. pl.

iii. FEMININE.

§ 381. **Singular:**—

Dat. Abl. Gen. Loc.: Show an inserted element *-hy- (-hy-)*, *-ŋh-* = Skt. *-sy-*.

§ 382. **Plural:**—

Gen.: Shows *-ŋhqm* = Skt. *-sām*.

§ 383. Interchange of Neuter with Feminine Forms.

As in the nouns § 232, so also in the pronouns the neuter
plural often assumes the form of the feminine or rather
interchanges with it.—See also Johannes Schmidt, *Pluralbildungen der indogerm. Neutra* pp. 21, 260, etc.

Note. In formulaic passages, especially in the Yashts (e. g. Yt. 5.13,15),
masc. forms *yeŋhe*, *aịŋhe*, *ahmāi* are sometimes used instead of the proper
fem. forms. This arises from the mosaic character of such passages.

§ 384. General Relative Case is found in YAv. in

the instances of *yāiš* as plural, cf. § 229.—For the treatment of *yō, yaṭ, yim* as stereotyped case (plural and singular) see under Syntax.

A. GENDER NOT DISTINGUISHED.

1. Personal Pronouns.

§ 385. The first and second personal pronouns,
as in Skt., show many peculiarities and individulities of
inflection. Some cases also use two forms, a fuller and a
briefer form, according to the position of the pronoun in

the sentence, whether accented, unaccented, or enclitic.
Furthermore, on the third personal pronoun, see § 394 seq.

§ 386. (a) **First Person**, Av. ⟨ᵭᶠᵘ⟩ *azəm* 'I' = Skt. *ahám*.

	Av.	Singular:	cf. Skt.
N.	*azəm* . . . . . . :		*ahám*
A.	*mąm; mā* (encl.)		*mām; mā*
D.	*māvᵒya*[1]; *mē* (encl.)		*máhyam; mē*
Abl.	*mat*		*mát*
G.	*mana; mē* (encl.)		*máma; mē*
		Plural:	
N.	*vaēm*[2]		*vayám*
A.	*ahma*[3]; *nō* (encl.)		*asmān; nas*
D.	*ahmaⁱbyā* (GAv.); *nō* (encl.) . . .		*asmábhyam; nas*
Abl.	*ahmat*		*asmát*
G.	*ahmākəm; nō* (encl.)		*asmākam; nas*

Forms to be observed in GAv. and YAv.

§ 387. GAv. has in general the same forms as YAv.,
but shows also a number of peculiarities to be marked;
these are likewise occasionally found in YAv., perhaps
borrowed.

§ 388. **Singular**:—

Nom.: GAv. *azəm*, § 32.—Also once (unaccented or proclitic) *as-cīt* Ys. 46.18.

Dat.: YAv. the form *māvᵃya* before *-ca*, *-cit*, § 386 Note 1.—GAv. *maⁱbyā*, *maⁱbyō*, and (encl.) *mōi*.

Gen.: Observe gen. Av. *mana* (note *-n-*) contrasted with Skt. *máma* (*-m-*).

§ 389. **Plural**:—

Nom.: GAv. (sporadic) nom. pl. unaccented (second place in sentence) *və̄*
Ys. 40.4,˙ cf. Skt. *va-yám*, cf. § 393.

Acc.: GAv. regularly *nə̄*, cf. also at Vsp. 15.2 = Ys. 15.3 *nə̄*, Gāthā reminiscence, see § 387.

Dat.: GAv. *ahmaⁱbyā* (above), *ahmāi*, and (encl.) *nə̄*, cf. also at Vsp. 12.4
nə̄, see § 387.

Gen.: GAv. also (unaccented) *ahmā*, *əhmā*, and (encl.) *nə̄*.

---

[1] Also before *-ca*, *-cit* written *māvᵃya*. See also § 388.

[2] i. e. *vayəm*, § 64.

[3] Yt. 1.24 variant; i. e. Av. *ahma* = Skt. *asmān*; Av. *aspa* = Skt. *átvān*

§ 390. **(b) Second Person,** Av. ᨑᨓᨑ *tūm* 'thou' = Skt. *tvám*.

	Av.	Singular:	cf. Skt.
N.	*tūm*[1]; *tū*		*tvám*
A.	*þwąm*; *þwā* (encl.)		*tvām*; *tvā*
I.	*þwā*[2]		*tvā* (Ved.)
D.	*taibyā* (GAv.); *tē* (encl.)		*túbhyam*; *te*
Abl.	*þwaṭ*		*tvát*
G.	*tava*; *tē* (encl.)		*táva*; *te*

Dual:

G.	*yavākəm*[3]		—

Plural:

N.	*yūžəm*		*yūyám*
A.	*vō* (encl.)		*vas*
D.	*yūšmaoyō, hšmāvōya*; *vō* (encl.)		*yuṣmábhyam*; *vas*
Abl.	*yūšmaṭ*		*yuṣmát*
G.	*yūšmākəm*; *vō* (encl.)		*yuṣmākam*; *vas*

Forms to be observed in GAv. and YAv.

§ 391. GAv. has in general the same forms as YAv., but shows also a number of peculiarities to be marked; these are likewise sometimes found in YAv., perhaps borrowed.

§ 392. Singular:—

Nom.: GAv. *tvəm* (cf. §§ 32, 93 Note 1), *tū*.

Dat.: GAv. *taibyā* (above), also *taibyō*, and (encl.) *tōi*.

Gen.: GAv. *tavā*; *tōi* (encl.) see § 56.

§ 393. Plural:—

Nom.: GAv. also *yūš* i. e. Av. *yūž*: Skt. *yū-yám*:: Av. *vš* (§ 389): Skt. *va-yám*.

Acc.: GAv. regularly *vå*.

Dat.: GAv. *yūšmaibyā, hšmaibyā*; *vš* (encl.), cf. also YAv. (Gāthā reminiscence) *vš* Ys. 14.1, etc.

Abl.: GAv. also *hšmaṭ*.

Gen.: GAv. *hšmākəm* and (encl.) *vš*.—Also *hšmā* Ys. 43.11.

---

[1] i. e. *tvəm*, see § 63.

[2] Ys. 43.10.

[3] Fr. 6.1 and Haug, *ZPhl. Glossary* pp. 3, 46, see § 68 Note 3, cf. Skt. *yuvāku*, see § 380.

§ 394. (c) **Third Person**, Av. ꣖ (꣖) *hē̆ (šē̆)* and other forms.

The proper third personal pronoun *hīm, hē̆* etc. (enclitic) is defective; its deficiencies are partly supplied by the demonstrative pronoun, and partly by enclitic forms of *di-, i-* used with personal force. These latter show distinction of gender, but they may best be included here.

§ 395. The following forms of the proper third personal (often used anaphorically, sometimes used reflexively, see also § 416) occur in GYAv.; they are all enclitic:

> Singular. Acc. *hīm* (GYAv.); Dat. Gen. *hē̆* or *ẜ* § 155 (YAv.), *hōi* (GAv.).—Dual. N.A.V. *hī* (GAv.).—Plural. Acc. *hīš* (GYAv.).

> Note 1. The form *hē̆* dat. gen. sg. seems in some passages in YAv. to serve as plural. See under Syntax.

> Note 2. With the above Avesta forms compare Skt. acc. sg. *sīm;* Prakrit dat. gen. *sē*—all enclitic. See Wackernagel in *K.Z.* xxiv. p. 605 seq.

§ 396. Similar to *hē̆* in usage are the forms from stem YAv. *di-*—likewise enclitic:—

> Sg. Acc. *dim* m. f.; *dit* n.—Pl. Acc. *diš* m. f.; *dī* n. Ys. **65.8.**

§ 397. Of like usage (cf. also § 422), is stem G(Y)Av. *i-* enclitic—sometimes employed almost pleonastically:—

> Sg. Acc. *im* m.; *it* n. (GAv.), *ī̆* (YAv., particle).—Du. N.A.V. *ī.* —Pl. Nom. *ī* n.; Acc. *īš* m.; *ī* n.

§ 398. On *hvō, hvāvōya* used as personal (and reflexive) see §§ 416, 436 Note 3.

B. GENDER DISTINGUISHED.

2. Relative Pronoun.

§ 399. **Relative** Av. ꣖ *ya-* 'who, which' = Skt. *yá-*.

The relative stem *ya-, yā-* = Skt. *yá-, yā-*, shows the following forms.—Cf. Whitney, *Skt. Gram.* § 508.

8

i. MASCULINE—NEUTER.

	Av.	Singular:	cf. Skt.
N.	*y-ō*		. *y-ás*
A.	*y-im*[1]		*y-ám*
I.	*y-ā*		*y-éna*
D.	*y-ahmāi*		. *y-ásmāi*
Abl.	*y-ahmāṯ*		*y-ásmāt*
G.	*y-ehe, y-eŋhe*[2] . . .		. *y-ásya*
L.	*y-ahmi*		. *y-ásmin*

Dual:

N.	*y-ā* . . .		. *y-ā́* (Ved.)
G.	*y-ayā̊* . .		. *y-áyōs*

Plural:

N.	*y-ōi*		*y-é*
A.	*y-ą*		. *y-ā́n*
I.	*y-āiš*		. . *y-āís*
D.Abl.	*y-aēⁱbyō*		. *y-ébhyas*
G.	*y-aēšą̇m*		. *y-éṣām*
L.	*y-aēšū* (GAv.)		. *y-éṣu*

ii. NEUTER.

Sg. N.A.V.	*y-aṯ*		. . *y-át*
Pl. N.A.V.	*y-ā*		. . *y-ā́* (Ved.)

iii. FEMININE.

Singular:

N.	*y-ā*		. *y-ā́*
A.	*y-ąm*		. *y-ā́m*
Abl.	*y-eŋhāṯ, -āda* . .		. see gen.
G.	*y-eŋhā̊* . . .		. *y-ásyās*
L.	*y-eŋhe*[3] . . .		. *y-ásyām*

Plural:

N.A.	*y-ā̊*		. *y-ā́s*
D.Abl.	*y-ābyō*		. *y-ā́bhyas*
G.	*y-ā̊ŋhą̇m* . . .		. . *y-ā́sām*
L.	*y-āhu, y-āhva*		. *y-ā́su*

---

[1] cf. § 30. — [2] cf. §§ 137, 136, 34. — [3] i. e. *ᵒyasyā(m)*, uncertain
Ys. 9.32, cf. *aⁱŋhe* § 422.

Forms to be observed in GAv. and YAv.

§ 400. GAv. has generally the same forms as YAv., but shows also some peculiarities to be marked; these are occasionally found likewise in YAv., perhaps borrowed.

I. MASCULINE—NEUTER.

§ 401. Singular:—

Nom.: YAv. *yas-ca*, *yas⁰ īt.*—In YAv. (commonly in late passages, but cf. Yt. 10.119) the form *yō* is sometimes found as general relative case, cf. § 384, and under Syntax.—GAv. *yž*, *yas-cā* (also YAv. borrowed *yž*, cf. § 400).

Acc.: GAv. *yžm*, *yim*, see §§ 32, 30.

Abl.: YAv. also *yahmāt*, on *ā* see § 19 (b).—GAv. once adverbial *yāt* Ys. 36.6 = Ys. 58.8, like Skt. *yāt*, cf. Whitney § 509 a.

Gen.: GAv. *yehyā*, see § 132.

Loc.: YAv. also (with postpos. *a* § 380) *yahmya.*—GAv. only *yahmī.*

§ 402. Plural:—

Nom.: YGAv. *yaž-ca*, *yaž-cā.*—In YAv. (late) a form *yā* as nom. 'acc. pl. (cf. *tā*, § 413) occurs, cf. noun-inflection *a*-stems § 236.

Acc.: GAv. *yžng*, *yžngs-tū*, *yqs-cā.*

Instr.: YAv., *yāiš* commonly occurs as general plural case, cf. § 384.

Dat. Abl.: GAv. *yažibyas-cā.*

II. NEUTER.

§ 403. Singular:—

Nom. Acc.: YAv. also *yim* like neut. noun-declension, but generally in late passages.—On *yas-ca* = *yat-ca* see § 151 Note.—GAv. *hyat* (variants *yat*, *yiat*, e. g. Ys. 28.9, 30.6 etc.).

§ 404. Plural:—

Nom. Acc.: YAv. also neut. (like fem. § 383) *yā.*

III. FEMININE.

§ 405. Plural:—

Nom. Acc.: YAv. *yās-ca.*—Also rare (like neut.) *yā*, cf. Ys. 10.78.—GAv. *yās-cā.*

---

3. Interrogative Pronoun.

§ 406. Interrogative Av. ⟶ *ka-* 'who, which, what?' = Skt. *ká-*.

The interrogative *ka-*, *kā-* = Skt. *ká-*, *kā-*, is identical in inflection with the relative and requires no full paradigm to be given.—Cf. Whitney, *Skt. Gram.* § 504.

I. MASCULINE—NEUTER.

	Av.	Singular:	cf. Skt.
N.	*k-ō*		*k-ás*
A.	*k-əm* etc.		*k-ám*

II. NEUTER.

Sg. N.A.V. *k-aṯ* etc. . . . . *k-áṯ*

III. FEMININE.

Sg. N. *k-ā* etc. . . . . *k-ā*

Note. YAv. also an instr. sg. *kana* = Skt. *kḗna* beside Av. *kā*.— YAv. also dat. *cahmāi* (indef.) beside *kahmāi*; GAv. *cahyā* beside *kahyā*. —YAv. as gen. pl. (or perhaps fem. sg. form = neut.) *kəm* m. f.

§ 407. Some special forms of interrogative are worthy of note.

1) S t e m *ki-*, *ci-* 'quis':—Sg. Nom. (m. f.) *ciš*, cf. Skt. *ná-kis*; Acc. (m. n.) *cim*, *cīm*, cf. Skt. *kím.*—Pl. Nom. (m. n.) *kaya*, *cayō.*—N e u t. also Sg. Nom. Acc. *ciṯ*, *cīṯ*.

2) S t e m *kati-*, *cati-* 'what, how much':—Sg. Acc. (neut.) *ca¹ti* = Skt. *káti*.

Note. Here also Av. *cina-* 'what'.—Likewise some forms of the inter- rogative used adverbially: — e. g. *kaṯ* 'how, nonne?'.— *cū* 'how'. Perhaps *kəm* Vd. 17.1 (?). — Uncertain *cyaṇhaṯ* 'how' Ys. 44.12 abl. (?) or *ci-aṇhaṯ* doubtful.

Indefinite.

§ 408. The indefinite force is usually given in Av., as in Skt., by combining a particle *-ciṯ*, *-cīṯ* = Skt. *-cit*, *-ca*, *-caṯ* etc., with the interrogative or relative. Sometimes it is added by the particle *-cina* (*-cana* Afr. 3.7 = Skt. *-cana*), which is likewise attached to nouns and adjectives; some- times, again, reduplication of the pronoun (rel. interrog.) gives an indefinite or a distributive force.

Av. *kahmāicit* 'to whomsoever' = Skt. *kásmāicit*; Av. *kaþacina* 'howsoever, in any way'; *cayascā* 'qui-

cunque' Ys. **45.**5, *cīcā* 'quaecunque' Ys. **47.**5 (fr. *ci +
ca*); *yaþa kaþaca* 'even as', *kahmi kahmiciţ* 'in any
case whatever', et al.

Note.   Indefinite negatives are Av. *naē-ciš* 'no one' = Skt. *ná-kis;*
Av. *mā-ciš* (imperative) 'no one' = Skt. *mā-kis.*

---

4. Demonstrative Pronouns.

§ 409.   (a) **Demonstrative** Av. ـﯩﺮﭖ *ta-* 'this' = Skt. *tá-*
The demonstrative stem *ha-*, *hā-*, *ta-* 'ὁ, ἡ, τό' = Skt.
sá-, *sá-*, *tá-*, serves also as personal of the third person.—
Cf. Whitney, *Skt. Gram.* § 495.

i. MASCULINE—NEUTER.

	Av.	Singular:	cf. Skt.
N.	*h-ō* .	. . . .	*s-ás*
A.	*t-əm*	. . . .	*t-ám*
I.	*t-ā* .	. . . .	*t-éna*
G.	*t-ahe*[1]	. . . .	*t-ásya*

		Dual:	
N.A.V.	*t-ā*[2], *t-æ*[2]	. . . .	*t-ā, t-āú*

		Plural:	
N.	*t-ē* .	. . . .	*t-ē*
A.	*t-ą* .	. . . . .	*t-án*
I,	*t-āiš*	. . . .	*t-áis*
D.Abl.	*t-aēᵇyō*	. . . .	*t-ēbhyas*

ii. NEUTER.

Sg.	N.A.V.	*t-aţ* .	. . . .	*t-át*
Pl.	N.A.V.	*t-ā* .	. . . .	*t-á* (Ved.)

iii. FEMININE.

		Singular:	
N.	*h-ā* . .	. . . . . .	*s-á*
A.	*t-ąm* .	. . . .	*t-ám*

		Plural:	
N.A.	*t-æ* .	. . . .	*t-ás*

---

[1] See Vd. 6.29 with v. l. *ca he.* — [2] Yt. 8.22

Forms to be observed in GAv. and YAv.

§ 410. GAv. has in general the same forms as YAv., but shows also some peculiarities; these are occasionally found likewise in YAv., perhaps borrowed.

i. MASCULINE—NEUTER.

§ 411. Singular:—

Nom.: YAv. *has-cit̮.*—Observe *hā* Vsp. 12.1 = Skt. *sá*, Whitney, *Skt. Gram.* §§ 498, 176a, also Av. *aēṣa* § 418.—GAv. *hē* Ys. 58.4, *hī-cā* Ys. 46.1; cf. also at Vsp. 12.1, Ys. 27.6; YAv. (Gāthā reminiscence?) *hī-ca.*

Acc.: GAv. *tīm,* see § 32 for *ī.*

§ 412. Dual:—

Nom.: GAv. *tōi* Ys. 34.11 is probably used as fem. du.

§ 413. Plural:—

Nom.: YAv. *taē-ca.*—Also rare (like neut. or *a*-decl.) *tā,* cf. § 236.—GAv. *tōi, taē-cīt̮.*

Acc.: YAv. also (see nom.) *tē,* cf. § 380.—Late *tā.*—GAv. *tṇg, tąs-cā,* and later dialect *tą* Ys. 63.1 = Ys. 15.2.

ii. NEUTER.

§ 414. Plural:—

Acc.: YAv. also (like fem., see § 383) *tā, tās-ca.*

iii. FEMININE.

§ 415. Plural:—

Acc.: YAv. rarely (like neut., cf. § 383) *tā* Yt. 10.79, cf. similarly *yā* § 405. —GAv. *tās-cā.*

§ 416. Here is to be added also G(Y)Av. nominative singular *hvō* 'ille, ipse', dative *hvāvōya* (like *māvōya*) properly originally reflexive, see §§ 398, 436 N. 1, 3.

Note. In oldest GAv., *hvō* takes the place of demonstr. *hō,* which form does not occur in the metrical Gāthās.

---

§ 417. (b) **Demonstrative** Av. ⟶⟶ *aēta-* 'this' = Skt. *etá-.*

The demonstrative *aēṣa-, aēṣā-, aēta-* 'this, here' = Skt. *ēṣá-, ēṣā́-, ētá-,* is identical in declension with *ha-, hā-, ta-* from which it is derived by prefixing *aē-* which makes it the nearer demonstrative. The only GAv. form noted is nom. sg. fem. *aēšā* 12.9 (later GAv.).— Cf. Whitney, *Skt. Gram.* § 499 b.

i. MASCULINE—NEUTER.

Av.	Singular:	cf. Skt.
N. *aēš-ō*		*ēš-ás*
A. *aēt-əm*		*ēt-ám*
I. *aēt-a*		*ēt-ḗna*
D. *aēt-ahmāi*		*ēt-ásmāi*
Abl. *aēt-ahmāt̰*		*ēt-ásmāt*
G. *aēt-ahe*		*ēt-ásya*
L. *aēt-ahmi*		*ēt-ásmin*

Dual:

G. *aēt-ayå*		*ēt-áyōs*

Plural:

N.(A.) *aēt-e*		*ēt-ḗ*
G. *aēt-aēšąm.*		*ēt-ḗṣām*
L. *aēt-aēšva*		*ēt-ḗṣu*

ii. NEUTER.

Sg. N.A.V. *aēt-at̰*		*ēt-át*
Pl. N.A.V. *aēt-a*		*ēt-ā́*

iii. FEMININE.

N. *aēš-a*		*ēš-ā́*
A. *aēt-ąm*		*ēt-ā́m*
I. *aēt-aya*		*ēt-áyā*
G. *aēt-aṅhå* [1], *aēt-ayå*		*ēt-ásyās*

Forms to be observed in GAv. and YAv.

i. MASCULINE—NEUTER.

§ 418. **Singular:**—

Nom.: YAv. also *aēša* = Skt. *ēšá*, Whitney, *Skt. Gram.* § 176 a, cf. *hā* above § 411.

§ 419. **Plural:**—

Nom. Acc.: YAv. notice that *aēte* like *tē* above §§ 413, 380 serves as both nom. and acc. masc. and also neut.

---

[1] See § 134.

ii. NEUTER.

§ 420. Plural:—

Nom. Acc.: YAv. also (like fem., § 383) *aētå*.—On *aētē* see § 380.

Gen.: YAv. also (contaminated with fem.) *aētaŋhąm*.

iii. FEMININE.

§ 421. Singular:—

Nom.: GAv. (only occurrence) *aēṣ̌å* Ys. 12.9.

Gen.: YAv. the form *aētayå*, *aētayås-cit̰* follows the noun-inflection, *ā*-decl.

§ 422. (c) **Demonstrative** Av. ᚺᚢᚢ *aēm* 'this' = Skt. *ayám*.

The demonstrative *aēm*, as in Skt., is made up from defective stems *a-*, *i-*, *ima-*, *ana-* = Skt. *a-*, *i-*, *ima-*, *ana-* combined to fill out a complete declension.

It is to be observed (in GAv. it is evident) that beside the accented forms, there occur likewise unaccented forms (not found at beginning of a pada). These forms generally come from the brief stem.

i. MASCULINE—NEUTER.

	Av.	Singular:	cf. Skt.
N.	*aēm* [1]	. . . .	*ayám*
A.	*imǝm*	. . . .	*imám*
I.	*ana*	. . . .	*anéna*
D.	*ahmāi*	. . . .	*asmāi*
Abl.	*ahmāt̰*	. . . .	*asmāt̰*
G.	*ahe, aiŋhe* [2]	. . . .	*asyá*
L.	*ahmi*	. . . .	*asmin*

Dual:

N.A.V.	*ima*	. . . .	*imā* (Ved.)
G.	*ayå*	. . . .	*ayós* (Ved.)
	anayå [3]	. . . .	*anáyòs*

Plural:

N.	*ime*	. . . . . .	*imé*
A.	*imą*	. . . .	*imán*
I.	*aēibiš* (YAv.), *anāiš* (GAv.)	. . .	*ēbhis*
D.Abl.	*aēibyō*	. . . .	*ēbhyás*
G.	*aēšąm*	. . . .	*ēṣām*
L.	*aēšu, aēšva*	. . . .	*ēṣú*

---

[1] i. e. *ayǝm*, § 64. — [2] See §§ 136, 137. — [3] Uncertain, see Vd. 4.48.

	Av.	ii. NEUTER.	cf. Skt.
Sg. N.A.V.	*imaţ*	. . . .	*idám*
Pl. N.A.V.	*ima*	. . . .	*imā* (Ved.)

iii. FEMININE.

Singular:

N.	*īm*[1] .	. . . .	*iyám*
A.	*imąm* . . .	. . . .	*imām*
I.	*āya, aya* . . .	. . . . . .	*ayā* (Ved.)
D.	*aⁱŋhāi* . . .	. . .	*asyāi*
Abl.	*aⁱŋhāţ* . . .	. . . .	see gen.
G.	*aⁱŋhā* . . .	. . . . . .	*asyās*
L.	*aⁱŋhe*[2] . . .	. . . .	*asyām*

Dual:

I.D.Abl.	*ābyā* (GAv.) .	. . . . . .	*ābhyām*

Plural:

N.A.	*imā*	. . . .	*imās*
I.	*ābīš*	. . . .	*ābhís*
D.Abl.	*ābyō*	. . . . . .	*ābhyás*
G.	*āŋhąm*	. . . . .	*āsām*
L.	*āhū* (GAv.), *āhva*	. . . .	*āsú*

Forms to be observed in GAv. and YAv.

§ 423. GAv. has in general the same forms as YAv., with lengthened final wherever possible. There are also some peculiarities worthy of note.

i. MASCULINE—NEUTER.

§ 424. Singular:—

Nom.: GAv. also *ayām* beside *aēm*, see § 32.
Abl.: YAv. also *ahmāţ*, on *ā* see § 19(b).
Gen.: GAv. *ahyā, ahyā-ca,* cf. §§ 132, 133.
Loc.: YAv. also (with postpos. *a*, § 379) *ahmya.*

---

[1] i. e. *iyəm,* see §§ 63, 51. — [2] i. e. orig. *asyā(m).*

§ 425. **Dual**:—

Gen.: GAv. also (from stem *a-*, § 431) *ōs-cā.*

§ 426. **Plural**:—

Nom. (Acc.): YAv. *ime* serves also as acc. pl., see § 380.

Instr.: GAv. observe the form *anāiš* above from stem *ana-*, and *āiš* below § 431 from stem *a-*.

Dat. Abl.: YAv. *aēibyas-cit̰.*

ii. NEUTER.

§ 427. **Singular**:—

Nom. Acc.: YAv. observe *imat̰* above as opposed to Skt. *idám.*

§ 428. **Plural**:—

N.A.V.: YAv. also (like fem., § 383) *imā.*—GAv. regularly *imā* which is the only GAv. instance noted of this stem *ima-*.

Loc.: YAv. also (see fem. § 383) *aēšąm.*

iii. FEMININE.

§ 429. **Singular**:—

Instr.: GAv. *ōyā* cf. YAv. *ayā* above in paradigm.

Dat.: GAv. *ahyāi*, cf. § 133.

Abl.: YAv. also *aiŋhāt̰*, on *ā* see § 19 (b).

Gen.: YAv. *aiŋhās-ca*, see § 124 Note.

Loc.: YAv. also, identical with instrumental, *aya.*

§ 430. **Plural**:—

Nom. Acc.: YAv., also a form *imāsᵉ* before *t̰*, see § 124 Note.

Dat. Abl.: YAv., also *ābyas-cit̰, ābwyas-ca*, on *ā* see § 19 Note.

§ 431. Directly from stem *a-* come:—Singular. Acc. Neut. (as particle) *at̰* (GYAv.); Dat. (uncertain?) *āi* Vd. 3.23 (neut. fem.); Abl. (as particle) *āt̰* (GAv.), *āat̰* (YAv.).— Dual. Gen. *ōs-cā* (GAv.).—Plural. Instr. (also used advbl.) *āiš* (GAv.).

---

§ 432. (d) **Demonstrative** *hāu, ava-* 'that' = Skt. *asāú, —.*

The remote demonstrative in Av. *ava-* 'that, yonder' (cf. Old Pers. *ava-*), combined with *hāu*, is to be contrasted with Skt. *amú-, asāú-*. The Av. shows *ava-* throughout where the Skt. has *amú-*.—Cf. Whitney, *Skt. Gram.* § 501.

i. MASCULINE — NEUTER.

	Av.	Singular:		cf. Skt.
N.	*hāu*	. . . .		*asău*
A.	*ao-m* [1]	. . . .		—
I.	*av-a*	. . . .		—
G.	*av-aⁱ**ŋhe*	. . . .		—

Plural:

N.(A.)	*av-e*	. . . .	—
I.	*av-āiš*	. . . .	—
G.	*av-aēšąm*	. . . .	—

ii. NEUTER.

Sg. N.A.V.	*av-aṯ, ao-m*	. . . . . .	—
Pl. N.A.V.	*av-a*	. . . . . .	—

iii. FEMININE.

Singular:

N.	*hāu*	. . . .	—
A.	*av-ąm*	. . . .	—
Abl.	*av-aⁱŋhāṯ*	. . . .	—
G.	*av-aⁱŋhā̊, av-avhā̊*	. . . . . .	—

Plural:

N.A.	*av-å*	. . . .	—
D.Abl.	*av-abyō*	. . . .	—

Forms to be observed in GAv. and YAv.

§ 433. Plural. Acc. Neut.: YAv. also (neut. like fem. § 383) *avå*.

Note. For the derivatives *avaṇt-, avavaṇt- (avaṇt-)* from *ava-* see § 441.

---

5. Other Pronominal Words and Derivatives.

Possessive — Reflexive,
Pronominal Derivatives and Adverbs.

§ 434. Under the above head belong the possessives and a number of words which have chiefly the nature of

---

[1] i. e. *avəm*, § 63.

adjectives and are inflected partly according to the pronominal declension, partly according to the nominal. They
answer in general to corresponding forms in Sanskrit.—
Cf. Whitney, *Skt. Gram.* § 515 seq.

Possessive — Reflexive.

§ 435. Here may be enumerated as connected with
the personal pronoun, the following p o s s e s s i v e (and reflexive) forms: — Av. *ma-* 'meus', *þwa-* 'tuus', *hva-*, *hva-*,
hava- (reflexive) 'suus', *ahmāka-* 'our', *yūṣmāka-*, *h̥ṣmāka-*
'your'.—*mavaṇt-* 'like me', *þwāvaṇt-* 'like thee', *yūṣmāvaṇt-*,
h̥ṣmāvaṇt- 'like you'.—*hvaēpaiþya-* 'own'.

Other Pronominal Derivatives and Adverbs.

§ 436. The following d e r i v a t i v e s may further be
noted:—Relative, *yavaṇt-* 'how much', *yatāra-* 'which of
two'.—Interrogative, *cvaṇt-* 'how much?', *katāra-* 'which of
two?'.—Demonstrative, *aētavaṇt-* 'so much', *avaṇt-* 'that,
such', *avavaṇt-* (*avaṇt-* § 194) 'so much'.—Likewise here,
numerous pronominal a d v e r b s *ya-þa* 'how, as', *ka-da*
'how, when?', *cū* 'how?', *i-da* 'here', etc.

Note 1. Here observe Av. *hvatō* 'reciprocally, each other' = Skt. *svátas*.

Note 2. On *hvō* 'ipse, ille' as personal pronoun, see §§ 398, 416.

Note 3. From same stem as *hvō* (in Note 2) comes the interesting
reflex. dat. *hvavōya* 'self' (like *māvōya* § 388), cf. Lat. *s(v)ibi*.

Note 4. From an assumed demonstrative stem *tva-* comes the neut.
adverb *þwaţ* 'then again' Ys. 44.3 = Skt. *tvat*.

Note 5. Instances of GAv. *ahyā* gen. of demonstr. (= pers.), from
aēm § 422, instead of the r e f l e x. possessive, occur.

Declension of Pronominal Derivatives.

§ 437. In regard to inflection, the pronominal derivatives follow partly the pronominal declension and partly
the nominal. The following forms of the p o s s e s s i v e s
(reflexive), and of the d e m o n s t r a t i v e d e r i v a t i v e s declined according to the pronominal declension are worthy
of note.

§ 438. i. Declension of the possessive pronoun GAv. *ma-* 'meus'.

i—ii. MASC.—NEUT. Sg. Nom. *m3;* Dat. *mahmāi;* Gen. *mahyā.*—Pl. Acc. (Neut.) *mā.*—iii. FEM. Sg. Gen. *mahyā* (§ 133).

§ 439. ii. Declension of the possessive pronoun GAv. *þwa-* 'tuus'.

i—ii. MASC.—NEUT. Sg. Nom. *þw3;* Instr. *þwā;* Dat. *þwahmāi;* Abl. *þwahmāt;* Gen. *þwahyā;* Loc. *þwahmī.*—Pl. Nom. *þwōi* (masc.); Acc. *þwā* (neut.).—iii. FEM. Sg. Nom. *þwōi;* Gen. *þwahyā.*—Pl. Loc. *þwāhū.*

§ 440. iii. Declension of GYAv. *hva-, ha- (hava-)* 'suus' = Skt. *svá.*—GAv. has only -ᴡ, YAv. -ᴡ (from GAv.), -ᴡ and -ᴡ.

i—ii. MASC.—NEUT. Sg. Nom. *h3* (GAv.), *hvō* (YAv.); Instr. *hā;* Gen. *hahe;* Loc. *hahmi.*—Du. Acc. *hva.*—Pl. Instr. *hāiš;* Loc. *haēšu* (? emended Fn. 4.2).—iii. FEM. Nom. *haē-cā* (GAv.), *hva* (YAv.); Dat. *hahyāi.*

Note 1. From the by-form *hava-* come: Masc. Neut. Sg. Nom. *havō;* Acc. *haom* (§ 64); Instr. *hava;* etc. regularly according to nominal declension (§ 236 *a*-decl.).—Fem. Sg. Nom. *hava;* Acc. *havqm;* Dat. *havayāi* with variant *haoyāi* (§ 62, 2); Gen. *havayā* beside *haoyā* (§ 62, 2).

Note 2. The possessives *ahmāka-* 'our', *þwāvaṇt-* 'like thee' etc. follow the noun-inflection.

Note 3. Observe that *ahmākəm, yavākəm, yūšmākəm* employed as 'genitives' of the personal pronoun §§ 386, 390, are really stereotyped cases of possessive adjectives, as similarly in Skt. *asmākam, yavākú, yuṣmākam.*

§ 441. iv. Declension of the demonstrative derivative *avaṇt-* 'that, such', from stem *ava-* § 430. This is to be distinguished from *avavaṇt- (avaṇt-* § 194) in § 442.

MASC. Sg. Nom. *avā.*—Pl. Dat. Abl. *avaþyō.*—NEUT. Sg. Nom. Acc. *avaþ* above in paradigm.

§ 442. v. Declension of the demonstrative derivative *avavaṇt- (avaṇt-* § 194, cf. variants) 'so great' — to be distinguished from *avaṇt-* § 441.

Sg. Nom. (neut.) *avavaþ;* Acc. (masc.) *avāṇtəm* (§§ 194, 44) and *avavaṇtəm* (neut. adv. *a*-decl.); Instr. *avavata;* Gen. *avavatō.*—Pl. Gen. *avavatqm.*

Adjectives declined pronominally.

§ 443. A few adjectives in Av., like their corresponding Skt. equivalents, also follow the pronominal declension
wholly or in part. Cf. Whitney, *Skt. Gram.* § 522 seq.—
Instances are: Av. *aēva-* 'one, alone'; Av. *anya-* 'other' =
Skt. *anyá-*; Av. *vīspa-* 'all' = Skt. *víśva-*.

For example: Pl. Nom. Acc. m. *vīspe, vīspā* (pronominal)
beside Nom. m. *vīspåṅhō;* Acc. *vīspās-ca* (YAv.), *vīspąs-cā, vīspāṅg*
(GAv.) i. e. nominal declension; — Gen. *vīspaēšąm* (pronominal) beside *vīspanąm* (nominal); et al.

CONJUGATION,

VERBS.

§ 444. The Avesta verb corresponds closely to the Sanskrit in form, character, and in usage. The Av. texts, however, are not so extensive as to give the verb complete in all its parts; some few gaps in the conjugation-system therefore occur.

Modelled after the Sanskrit, the Avesta verbal system may be presented as on the next page.

§ 445. **Voice, Mode, Tense.** The Av. agrees with the Skt. — especially with the language of the Vedas — in v o i c e s active, middle (passive), in t e n s e s present (and preterite), perfect (and pluperfect), aorist, future, and in m o d e s indicative, imperative, subjunctive, optative. In usage likewise these generally correspond with the Sanskrit.

Note 1. The middle voice, as in Skt., is often used with a p a s - s i v e force. A formative passive, as in Skt., however also occurs (cf. V. a).

Note 2. Under tenses, observe that 'injunctive' or 'improper subjunctive' is a convenient designation for certain forms of augmentless preterites used with imperative force. These are enumerated under the simple preterite. Cf. Whitney, *Skt. Gram.* § 563.

§ 446. **Infinitive, Participle.** Like the Skt., the Av. conjugation-system possesses also infinitive forms (abstract verbal nouns) and participial forms (active and middle in each tense-system) and gerundives. See VI below.

§ 447. **Person, Number.** The Av. like the Skt. distinguishes t h r e e p e r s o n s, and t h r e e n u m b e r s.

Note. It is to be observed that the first persons imperat. are supplied by subjunctive forms.

SYNOPSIS

OF

VERB-

SYSTEM

I. Present-System
(10 Classes)

i. ACTIVE—ii. MIDDLE

1. Indicative
   a. Present.
   b. Preterite (Injunctive).
2. Imperative.
3. Subjunctive (Pres. and Pret. Forms).
4. Optative.
5. Participle.

II. Perfect-System

i. ACTIVE—ii. MIDDLE

1. Indicative
   a. Perfect (Present).
   b. Pluperfect (Preterite).
2. Imperative.
3. Subjunctive (Pres. and Pret. Forms).
4. Optative.
5. Participle.

III. Aorist-System
(non -s-, and s-Class)

i. ACTIVE—ii. MIDDLE

1. Indicative (Preterite = Aor.).
2. Imperative.
3. Subjunctive (Pres. and Pret. Forms).
4. Optative.
5. Participle.

IV. Future-System
1. Indicative (Act. and Mid.).
2. Participle.

V. Secondary Conjugations.
   a. Passive.   d. Inchoative.
   b. Causative.   e. Desiderative.
   c. Denominative.   f. Intensive.

VI. Verbal Abstract Forms.
   a. Participles.   b. Gerunds.   c. Infinitives.

VII. Periphrastic Verbal Phrases.

§ 448. **Personal Endings.** These are either (a) p r i-
m a r y (pres. and fut. indic., and partly subjunct.) or they
are (b) s e c o n d a r y (pret. indic., opt., aor., and partly
subjunct.). Some individual peculiarities of form occur in
(c) the i m p e r a t i v e and in (d) the p e r f e c t; the endings,
therefore, of the latter two also are separately enumerated.

The scheme of normal endings in comparison with the
Skt.,—cf. Whitney, *Skt. Gram.* § 553—is as follows:

(Observe the Av. 3 du. forms often identical with Skt. 2 du.)

a. Primary Endings.

i. ACTIVE.			**ii. MIDDLE.**		
Av.	Singular:	cf. Skt.	Av.	Singular:	cf. Skt.
1. -*mi*	. . .	-*mi*	-*e*		-*ē*
2. -*hi* (-*ši*)	. .	-*si* (-*si*)	-(*v*)*he* (-*še*) .	.	-*sē* (-*sē*)
3. -*ti*	. . . .	-*ti*	-*te*		-*tē*
	Dual:			**Dual:**	
1. -*vahī* (GAv.)		-*vas*	—		-*vahē*
2. —	. . . .	-*thas*	—		-*āthē*
3. -*tō, -þō*	. .	-*tas*	-*āþe*		-*ātē*
	Plural:			**Plural:**	
1. -*mahi*	. . .	-*masi* (Ved.)	-*maide*	. . .	-*mahē*
2. -*þa*	. . . .	-*tha*	-*þwe* .	. . .	-*dhvē*
3. -*ṇti*	. . . .	-*nti*	-*ṇte*	. . .	-*ntē*

b. Secondary Endings.

i. ACTIVE.			**ii. MIDDLE.**		
Av.	Singular:	cf. Skt.	Av.	Singular:	cf. Skt.
1. -*m*	. . . . .	-*m*	-*i, -a*		-*i, -a*
2. -*s* (-*š*)	. . . .	-*s* (-*s*)	-*vha* (-*ša*)	. . .	[-*thās*]
3. -*ţ*	. . . . .	-*t*	-*ta*		-*ta*
	Dual:			**Dual:**	
1. -*va*	. . . .	-*va*	— . .	. . .	-*vahi*
2. —	. . . .	-*tam*	— . .	. .	-*āthām*
3. -*tәm*	. . .	-*tām*	-*ātәm* .	. .	-*ātām*

9

Plural:			Plural:		
1. *-ma*	. . . .	-ma	{ -ma*i*dī (GAv.) . -ma*i*de (YAv.) . }	-mahi
2. *-ta*	. . . . .	-ta	-dwɘm	-dhvanɪ'
3. *-n*	. . . .	-n	-ṇta	-nta

c. Imperative Endings.

i. ACTIVE.			ii. MIDDLE.		
Av.	Singular:	cf. Skt.	Av.	Singular:	cf. Skt.
2. *-di,* —	. . .	-dhi, —	*-vuha (-švā)*	. .	-sva (-ṣva)
3. *-tu*	. . .	-tu	*-tąm*	. . .	-tām

Plural:			Plural:		
2. *-ta, -nā* (GAv.)[1]	-ta		-dwɘm	. . . .	-dhvam
3. *-ṇtu*	. . . .	-ntu	-ṇtąm .	. .	-ntām

d. Perfect Endings.

i. ACTIVE.			ii. MIDDLE.		
Av.	Singular:	cf. Skt.	Av.	Singular:	cf. Skt.
1. *-a*	. . . .	-a	*-e* .	. . .	-ĕ
2. *-ṗa*	. . . .	-tha	— .	. . .	-sĕ
3. *-a*	. . . .	-a	*-e* .	. . .	-ĕ

Dual:			Dual:		
1. —	. . . .	-va	— .	. . . .	-vahĕ
2. —	. .	-athur	— .	. . .	-āthĕ
3. *-atarɘ*	. . .	-atur	*-a*i*tē* (GAv.)	. .	-ātĕ

Plural:			Plural:		
1. *-ma*	. . . .	-ma	— .	. . . .	-mahĕ
2. *-a*	. . .	-a	— .	. . . .	-dhvĕ
3. *-arɘ, -arɘš*	. .	-ur	— .	. . . .	-rĕ

General Remarks on the Endings.

§ 449. In general, GAv. has the same forms as YAv. above, with the long final vowel wherever possible, cf. § 26; but there are also a number of peculiarities to be remarked upon in connection with GAv. as well as with reference to YAv.

---

[1] Sporadic, cf. § 457.

Note. Observe that Av. 3 du. is in form often like Skt. 2 du.:
e. g. Av. -*þō* (beside -*tō*) 3 du. pres. act. = Skt. -*tas* 3 du. (but -*thas* 2 du.);
—again Av. -*təm* 3 du. pret. act. = Skt. -*tām* 3 du. (but -*tam* 2 du.), et
al.— Compare the Homeric interchange of -τον, -την in secondary tenses.

a. Primary Endings (Observations).

§ 450. Singular:—

First Person: i. ACTIVE. Indicative. GYAv. also -*ā*, -*a*—i. e. GAv.
has -*ā* regularly in the thematic or *a*-conjugation pres. indic., and
-*mī* in the unthematic or non-*a*-conj. pres. indic.; but in YAv. this
distinction is not sharply drawn. — Subjunctive. YAv. -*ni*, -*a*,'
GAv. -*nī*, -*ā*.—ii. MIDDLE. Indicative. GAv. also -*ōi* (§ 56, beside -*ē*).—Subjunctive. GYAv. -*nē*, -*ne*, -*āi* (i. e. *ā* + *ē*).
Second Person: i. ACTIVE. Subjunctive. In later texts of YAv. -*ā(h)i*
sometimes drops its *h* and becomes -*āi*, e. g. YAv. *yazāi* 'mayest
thou worship' Yt. 10.140.—ii. MIDDLE. Indicative. YAv., observe
-*se* (after -*d* [-*t*] §§ 151, 186) *raose* 'thou growest' Ys. 10.4.—GAv.
also indic. subjunct. -*whōi* § 56.
Third Person: ii. MIDDLE. GYAv. also (but not common; cf. also perf.
below) like 1 sg. -*e* = Skt. -*ē* beside *tē*.

§ 451. Dual:—

Third Person: i. ACTIVE. YAv., observe -*þō* in *yaidyaþō* 'they both fight'
Yt. 8.22, a 3 du.-form (like Skt. -*thas* 2 du.-form) beside -*tō* above,
see § 449 Note.—ii. MIDDLE. YGAv. occasionally -*te* or -*aite* e. g.
baraite 'they two bring' ZPhl. Gloss. pp. 54. 8 = 107. 13, *varənvaitē*
'both believe' (indic.) Ys. 31.17.—Again -*ītē*, GAv. *jamaētē* 'they
both may come' (aor. subjunct.) Ys. 44.15.

§ 452. Plural:—

First Person: ii. MIDDLE. YAv. only occasionally is the MS. variant
-*maide* (observe *d*) is noted.
Second Person: ii. MIDDLE. GAv. regularly -*duyē* = Skt. -*dhvē* § 190.
Third Person: i. ACTIVE—ii. MIDDLE. Indicative. YGAv. occasionally
have in the 3 pl. of the non-*a*-conjugation (unthematic) the form
-*aiti* (i. e. -*ṇti*) or even -*āiti* = Skt. -*ati* in the active, and -*aitē*
(i. e. -*ṇtē*) = Skt. -*atē* in the mid.; but more commonly in the non-
a-conj. (unthematic) the ending (-*anti*) -*ṇti*, (-*antē*) -*ṇtē* of the
a-conj. (thematic) is assumed instead.—Uncommon in the pres. is
-*re*, cf. indicative *sōire* 'they lie down' Yt. 10.80 = Skt. *śēre* Whitney,
Skt. Gram. § 629, and subjunctive *mravāire* 'they may say'
Yt. 13.64, *nijrāire* 'they may throw' Yt. 10.40, cf. §§ 486, 521.

b. Secondary Endings (Observations).

§ 453. **Singular:—**

First Person: **ii. MIDDLE.** Observe that the normal ending *i* coalesces with the final of an *a*-stem into -*e;* e. g. *aguze* 'I hid myself' opp. to *aojī* 'I spake'.—The ending -*a* is found in the optative.

Second Person: **i. ACTIVE.** The normal ending -*s* unites with *a* in the *a*-conj. and gives -*ō* (-*ɔ̄* subjunct.); the *š*-form occurs according to rule § 156.—**ii. MIDDLE.** YGAv. notice the suffix is -*sa* (cf. Gk. -σο) contrasted with Skt. -*thās.*

Third Person: **i. ACTIVE.** YGAv., orig. *t* is retained (unchanged to -*ţ*) after *s (š)*, e. g. *mōist* 'he turned', *cōišt* 'he promised', §§ 81, 192. —Notice *ās* (i. e. *ās-t*) 'he was' and *cinas* 'he promised' § 192 Note.

§ 454. **Dual:—**

Third Person: **i. ACTIVE.** YAv., observe that the 3 du. Av. -*təm* is in form like the 2 du. Skt. -*tam*—on this interchange in form between 3 du. and 2 du. see § 449 Note.—**ii. MIDDLE.** YGAv., note Av. -*ātəm* opp. to Skt. -*ātām*, see again § 449 Note.—Again (like primary 2 du., but) with secondary meaning YAv. -*ā*ⁱ*pe* = Skt. -*āthē* and some other forms—see Bartholomae, *K.Z.* xxix. p. 286 seq. = *Flexions-lehre* p. 17 seq.

§ 455. **Plural:—**

First Person: **ii. MIDDLE.** Observe that GAv. has a proper secondary end-ing -*ma*ⁱ*dī* (cf. opt. *va*ⁱ*rīma*ⁱ*dī*) = Skt. -*mahi*, but YAv. substitutes for this -*ma*ⁱ*de* drawn from the present.

Second Person: **ii. MIDDLE.** GAv. shows -*dūm* = Skt. -*dhvām*, § 63.

Third Person: **i. ACTIVE.** In redupl. formations GAv. has occasionally an unthematic 3 pl. pret. in -*aţ* (i. e. -*ņt*) corresponding to the oc-casional -*ati* = -*ņti* of the pres., e. g. *zazaţ* 'they drove away', et al. —GYAv., remark also opt. -*ārə̄š*, -*ārə̄*, thus *buyārə̄š* 'they would be', *hyārə̄* beside *hyqn.* Also -*arə* aor. pret. GAv. *ādarə* 'they made' Ys. 43.15 = Skt. *ādur;* YAv. *aškarə* 'they elapsed' Vd. 1.4, cf. Whitney, *Skt. Gram.* §§ 829, 550 — cf. also under perfect endings (Pf. ii, below). — **ii. MIDDLE.** YAv. also sporadic traces of secondary 3 pl. mid. -*rəm* = Skt. -*ram* in Av. *vaozirəm* Yt. 19.69, cf. Whitney, *Skt. Gram.* § 834 b (perhaps best as pluperf.).

c. Imperative Endings (Observations).

§ 456. **Singular:—**

Second Person: **i. ACTIVE.** YGAv., the *a*-verbs (thematic) have no end-ing, the simple stem form in -*a*, -*ā* is used.—The non-*a*-verbs (un-thematic) show -*di* (-*di* § 83, 1), GAv. -*dī*.—**ii. MIDDLE.** YAv. re-

gularly -*wuha* = Skt. -*sva* —GAv. -*svā* (in *dasvā* 'give' = *dad-sva
§ 186), -*şvā*, -*hvā* § 130, 2 a.

Third Person: ii. MIDDLE. A suffix -*qm* = Skt. -*ām*, 3 sg. mid. is found
in GAv. *sr⋅šūcqm* 'let him speak aright' Ys. 48.9, *vīdqm* 'shall decide' *vi* + *dā* Ys. 32.6, Geldner, in *B.B.* xv. p. 261, cf. Whitney,
Skt. Gram. § 618.

§ 457. Plural:—

Second Person: i. ACTIVE—ii. MIDDLE. The forms are undistinguishable
from an augmentless imperfect § 445 Note 2.—A genuine instance
of -*na* cf. Skt. -*tana* 2 pl. active imperat. is GAv. *baranā* Ys. 30.9,
cf. Skt. *bhajatana*, Whitney, *Skt. Gram.* § 740.

Third Person: i. ACTIVE—ii. MIDDLE. The endings -*aŋtu*, -*əŋtu*, -*əŋtqm*
occur in both *a*-verbs and in non-*a*-verbs — (in the latter case by
transfer § 471 to *a*-conj.).

d. Perfect Endings.

§ 458. For observations on the perfect endings see Pf. ii below.

Mode-Formation.

1. Indicative Mode.

§ 459. The indicative has no special mode-sign other
than the use of the present stem itself. The endings are the
primary in the present, the secondary in the preterite.

Note. For special remarks on the strong and weak stem-forms in
the indicative, see below §§ 467, 476 and observe under the different conjugation classes.

2. Imperative Mode.
(Cf. Whitney, *Skt. Gram.* § 569.)

§ 460. The imperative has no characteristic mode-
sign, the stem is identical with that of the indicative, the
special endings are simply added.

Note 1. For special remarks on the strong and weak stem-forms
see below under the imperatives of the various conjugation-classes.

Note 2. For remarks on the endings see § 456.

3. Subjunctive Mode.
(Cf. Whitney, *Skt. Gram.* § 557 seq.)

§ 461. In Av., as in Skt., the subjunctive has as its
characteristic mark an *a* added to the stem to form the

special mode-stem.   In the *a*-conjugation (thematic) this *a* unites of course with the stem-final and forms *ā*:—e. g. (1) thematic *a*-stem, Av. *bar·ā-hi* 'mayest thou bear' (i. e. *bara-a-hi*) = Skt. *bhár-ā-si*;—(2) unthematic, Av. *jan-a-ʲti* 'may he smite' (cf. pres. indicat. *jaⁱŋ-ti*) = Skt. *hán-a-ti*.

§ 462. The endings of the subjunctive are partly primary (i. e. pres. subjunct.), partly secondary (i. e. pret. subjunct.).—the former predominating. Observe in 1 sg. active YGAv. -*ni*, -*nī* (i. e. -*āni*) or also YGAv. -*a*, -*ā*;—and in 1 sg. middle it is -*ne* (i. e. -*āne*) beside -*āi*. Cf. Whitney, *Skt. Gram.* § 562.

Subjunctive Endings combined with Mode-Sign.

	i. ACTIVE.			ii. MIDDLE.	
Av.	Singular:	cf. Skt.	Av.	Singular:	cf. Skt.
1. -*āni*, -*a*		-*āni*, -*ā*	-*āne*, -*āi*		-*āi*
2. { -*ahi*, (-*ā[h]i*)		-*asi*	-*aṅhe*		-*ase*
{ -*ō*, -*ǣ*		-*as*			
3. { -*aⁱti*		-*ati*	-*ate*		-*ate*
{ -*aṱ*		-*at*	-*ata*		—
Dual:			**Dual:**		
1. -*āva*		-*āva*	—		-*āvahe*
2. —		-*athas*	—		-*āithe*
3. { -*atō*		-*atas*	—		-*āite*
{ -*atəm*		—			
Plural:			**Plural:**		
1. -*āma*		-*āma*	-*āmaⁱde*		-*āmahe*
2. -*atha*		-*atha*	—		-*adhve*
3. { -*əŋti*		—	-*əŋte*, -*aⁱre*		-*ante*
{ -*ən*		-*an*			

Note 1. Observe (late) YAv. 2 sg. -*āi* = -*āhi* § 450.

Note 2. On improper subjunctive or imperative see § 445 Note 2.

4. Optative Mode.
(Cf. Whitney, *Skt. Gram.* § 564 seq.)

§ 463. The characteristic mode-sign of the optative in Av., as in Skt., is -*yā*-, -*ī*- added to the weak-stem for the non-*a*-conjugation (unthematic), or it is -*ī*- added to the regular tense-stem of the class for the *a*-conjugation (thematic).

In the *a*-stems (thematic) the mode-sign -*ī*- unites with the stem-final *a* into -*aē*- (-*ōi*-) §§ 55, 56. In the non-*a*-conj. the distinction between -*yā*-, -*ī*- is that -*yā*- was employed in the active and -*ī*- in the middle.

Note. Instead of -*ī*-, instances of -*ī*- (§ 21 Note) occur, e. g. *daᵢpiᵢa* beside *daᵢdᵢyᵢa* 'mayest thou give'.— Similarly occur instances of -*yă*- for -*yā*- (§ 18 Note 1), cf. *buyata*, *buyama* 'may ye, we be'.—Probably also GAv. *daᵢdyat* Ys. 44.10.

§ 464. The endings of the optative are the secondary ones throughout. In YAv., however, the 1 pl. mid. -*maᵢde* (primary, e. g. Ys. 9.21) instead of GAv. -*maᵢdī* (secondary) is found. Observe in the *a*-conj. (thematic) the 3 pl. act. mid. Av. -*ǝn*, -*ǝnta* (cf. Gk. λέγ-οι-εν, λέγ-οι-ντο) is to be contrasted with Av. non-*a*-verbs which show -*arǝ*, -*arǝš* = Skt. -*ur*, -*ran* (act. mid. in both *a*- and non-*a*-stems).

Optative Endings combined with Mode-Sign.

a. *a*-conjugation (thematic).

	i. ACTIVE.			ii. MIDDLE.		
Av.	Singular:	cf. Skt.		Av.	Singular:	cf. Skt.
1.	—	-*ǝyam*		-*aya*[1]		-*ǝya*
2.	-*ōiš*	-*ǝs*		-*aǝša*		-*ǝthās*
3.	-*ōit*	-*ǝt*		-*aǝta*		-*ǝta*
	Plural:				Plural:	
1.	-*aǝma*	-*ǝma*		-*ōimaᵢdī* (GAv.) / -*ōimaᵢde* (YAv.)		-*ǝmahi*
2.	-*aǝta*	-*ǝta*		-*ōiđwǝm*		-*ǝdhvam*
3.	-*ayǝn*	-*ǝyur*		-*ayaṇta*		-*ǝran*

b. Non-*a*-conjugation (unthematic).

	i. ACTIVE.			ii. MIDDLE.		
Av.	Singular:	cf. Skt.		Av.	Singular:	cf. Skt.
1.	-*yqm*	-*yām*		-*ya*		-*īya*
2.	-*yǡ*	-*yās*		-*īṣa*		-*īthās*
3.	-*yāt*	-*yāt*		-*īta*		-*īta*
	Plural:				Plural:	
1.	-*yāma*[2]	-*yāma*		-*īmaᵢdī*		-*īmahi*
2.	-*yāta*	-*yāta*		—		-*īdhvam*
3.	{ -*yqn* / -*yārǝ* / -*yārǝš* }	— / -*yur* / —		—		-*īran*

[1] Cf. Ys. 8.7. — [2] See Yt. 24.58.

Reduplication and Augment.

a. Reduplication.
(Cf. Whitney, *Skt. Gram.* § 588 seq.)

§ 465. (a) Reduplication in Av., as in Skt., is found in certain parts of the v e r b - c o n j u g a t i o n (pres. of 3 r d. class, and in the desiderative, and intensive), in the per-fect, and sometimes in the a o r i s t. The reduplication consists in the repetition of a part of the root.—The rules of reduplication should be noted:—

(b) A long i n t e r n a l or f i n a l vowel of the root is commonly shortened in the reduplicated syllable; sometimes —see desiderative, intensive—it is lengthened or strengthened. Radical *ar* (*r*-vowel) is reduplicated by *i*. An i n i t i a l v o w e l, by repetition of itself, of course merely becomes long in reduplicating.

(c) Roots beginning with a c o n s o n a n t repeat that consonant, but a g u t t u r a l is reduplicated by the cor-responding p a l a t a l; an o r i g i n a l *s* (including *st, sp, sm*) is reduplicated by *h,* an orig. p a l a t a l *š* by *s*, an i n i t i a l s p i r a n t by the corresponding smooth:—e. g. Av. *ja-jm-aṱ* (√ *gam-* 'go'), *hi-šta-ìti* (√ *stā-* 'stand'), *hi-spōs-ǝmna* (√ *spas-* 'see'), *hi-šmar-ǝntō* (√ *mar-,* **smar-* 'remember'), *tu-þru-ye* (√ *þru-* 'nourish').

Note 1. The original guttural instead of palatal is retained in re-duplication before *u*, cf. Av. *ku-ḫīnv-qna* (√ *ḫīnu-* 'rejoice, please').

Note 2. Observe the redupl. form (desiderative participle) *zi-ḫīnⱥvh-ǝmnⱥ* Yt. 13.49, cf. Skt. *ji-jñās-amānás.*

b. Augment.
(Cf. Whitney, *Skt. Gram.* § 585.)

§ 466. In Av. the augment is comparatively rare, the instances of its o m i s s i o n far exceed in proportion those of the Vedic Sanskrit.

The augment, as in Skt., consists of short *a* prefixed to the preterite tense—imperfect, aorist, pluperfect. This *a,* as likewise in Skt., combines with an initial vowel into the corresponding *vṛddhi.*

It is often difficult to decide whether an *a* is the augment *a* or the verbalprefix *a = ā.*

Note 1. For metrical purposes it seems sometimes that augment must be restored in reading where the texts omit it. — See Geldner, *Metrik* p. 38.

Note 2. Instead of *a,* GAv. shows once a form *ɜ* in augment before *v,* cf. GAv. *ɜvaocaṭ* (but written *ɜ. voacaṭ*) § 32.

Note 3. On augmentless preterites ('injunctive') with imperat.-subjunct. force, see § 445 Note.

§ 467. **Vowel-Variation (Strong and Weak).** In Av., quite as in Skt., verb-stems commonly show vowel-variation —strongest, middle or strong, and weak forms, cf. § 235. This phenomenon must of course go hand in hand with an original shift of accent.

I. PRESENT-SYSTEM.

§ 468. The present-system is the most important of the systems, its forms are by far the most frequent in occurrence, and upon the basis of present-formation may be founded in Av., as in Skt., the conjugation-groups and classification of verbs. See the following § 469.

Classes of Verbs.

§ 469. Taking the Sanskrit Grammar as model, we may in the Av. present-system likewise distinguish ten classes of verbs according to the method of forming the present-stem. In Av., however, the phenomenon of accent (§ 2 end) is not always so clearly discernible.

The ten classes fall into two great groups of conjugation according as the endings are attached to the root with or without the (thematic) stem-vowel *a.* The (I) first group, the thematic or *a*-conjugation (Cl. 1, 6, 4, 10), assumes *a* in the formation of its present-stem; the

(II) second group, the unthematic or non-*a*-conjugation
(Cl. 2, 3, 7, 5, 8, 9), attaches the endings directly to the
root (the latter as stem, however, subject to modification)
without this *a* as formative element of the stem.—Cf.Whitney,
Skt. Gram. § 602 seq.

§ 470. The classification of Av. verbs on the basis
of the Sanskrit Grammar is the following:—

I. *a*-Conjugation (thematic).

First Formation—Class 1—see § 478 seq.

(1) *a*-class with strengthened root-form = Skt. first
(*bhū-*) class.

> Av. √*ba-*, *bav-a-ⁱti* 'he becomes'.

Second Formation—Class 6—see § 479 seq.

(6) *a*-class with unstrengthened root-form = Skt. sixth
(*tud-*) class.

> Av. √*druj-*, *druž-a-ⁱti* 'he deceives'.

Third Formation—Class 4—see § 480 seq.

(4) *ya*-class (unstrengthened root-form) = Skt. fourth (*div-*)
class.

> Av. √*nas-*, *nas-ye-ⁱti* 'he vanishes'.

Fourth Formation—Class 10—see § 481 seq.

(10) *aya*-class (strengthened root-form), causal = Skt. tenth
(*cur-*) class.

> Av. √*ruc-*, *raoc-aye-ⁱti* 'he lights up'.

II. Non-*a*-Conjugation (unthematic).

First Formation—Class 2—see § 516 seq.

(2) Root-class—root itself is present stem = Skt. second
(*ad-*) class.

> Av. √*jan-*, *jaⁱŋ-ti* 'he smites'.

Second Formation—Class 3—see § 540 seq.

(3) Reduplicating class—root redupl. is pres. stem =
Skt. third (*hu-*) class.

> Av. √*dā-*, *da-dā-ⁱti* 'he gives'.

Third Formation—**Class 7**—see § 554 seq.

(7) N a s a l - class—inserted *-na-* (str.), *-n-* (wk.) = Skt. seventh
(rudh-) class.

  Av. √*ric-*, *iri-na-ḥti* 'lets go'.

Fourth Formation—**Class 5**—see § 566 seq.

(5) *nu*-class—root adds *nao-* (str.), *nu̧-* (wk.) = Skt. fifth
(su-) class.

  Av. √*kar-*, *kərə-nao-iti* 'he makes'.

Fifth Formation—**Class 8**—see § 577 seq.

(8) *u*-class—root adds *u-* alone = Skt. eigth *(tan-)* class.

  Av. √*āp-*, *āṣ̌ṇte* (i. e. *āp-v-antē* § 95) 'are overtaken'.

Sixth Formation—**Class 9**—see § 584 seq.

(9) *nā-*class—root adds *nā-* (str.), *n-*, *na-* (wk.) = Skt. ninth
(krī-) class.

  Av. √*garw-*, *gərəw-nā-iti* 'he seizes'.

§ 471. **Transfer of Conjugation.** A verb is n o t
a l w a y s inflected according to one and the s a m e c o n-
j u g a t i o n and c l a s s throughout. The majority of the
forms of a verb may be made up after one conjugation
and class of the present system, while a few forms of the
same verb may be made up after another; the same part
of the verb being thus occasionally formed according to
two classes. Instances of such transition in forms from
one class to another are not rare; in general, examples
of the tendency for verbs of the non-*a*-conjugation (unthematic) to pass over to the inflection of the *a*-conjugation,
are not difficult to find.—See §§ 529, 553 etc.

---

i. The *a*-Conjugation (thematic).

§ 472. **General Remark.** The t h e m a t i c or *a*-con-
jugation in the present-system comprises f o u r c l a s s e s
(Cl. 1, **6, 4, 10**), in all which the endings are attached to
the root by means of a thematic vowel *a* (in 1 person

ā, a). The root-vowel may, or may not be strengthened according to the class of the verb; it remains then as in the indicative throughout the other modes of the present-system.—The verbs of the *a*-conj. are numerous.—Cf. Whitney, *Skt. Gram.* § 733 seq.

Note. The 1 plu.r. thematic shows *ă* more often than *ā* (Skt. *ā*): e. g. Av. *yasămaide* commoner than *barămaide*.

Mode Formation—Special Remark.
1. Indicative.

§ 473. The various endings are simply attached by means of the thematic *a* (in 1 person *ā*) directly to the stem formed according to the rules of its particular class.

2. Imperative.

§ 474. The normal endings are attached by means of the thematic *a* directly to the present-stem of the class.

3. Subjunctive.

§ 475. The characteristic *a* of the subjunctive unites with the thematic *a* into *ā* in attaching the subjunctive endings given above, § 462.

4. Optative.

§ 476. In the *a*-verbs the optative sign is -*ī*- (instead of -*yā*-) and it unites with the thematic *a* into -*aē*- (-*ōi* § 56) in attaching the endings.

5. Participle.

§ 477. The participial forms (verbal adjectives) are made in each class by attaching to the present-stem the formative element -*ṇt* (§ 291, -*ṇtī* fem.) for the active, and -*mna* (§ 237, -*mnā* fem.)—also -*āna* (-*ana*), see Note—for the middle.

Note. On middle ptcpl. in -*āna* (-*ana*) see § 507.

Classes of the *a*-Conjugation (thematic).
Cl. 1, 6, 4, 10.

§ 478. **Class 1**—*a*-class with strengthened root-form = Skt. first *(bhū-)* class.—To form the present-stem, the thematic *a* is attached to the root which has the strong (middle) form. Cf. Whitney, *Skt. Gram.* § 734.—Examples are numerous.

Av. √*bar-* 'to bear', *bar-a-iti* = Skt. *bhár-a-ti;* Av. √*hši-* 'to rule', *hšay-e-iti* = Skt. *kšáy-a-ti;* Av. √*bū-* 'to be', *bav-a-iti* = Skt. *bháv-a-ti.*

Note 1. Here for convenience, as in Skt., may be included the roots Av. *stā-, had-* (orig. redupl.) = Skt. *sthā-, sad-,* e. g. Av. *hištaiti* 'he stands' = Skt. *tišthati;* Av. *hidaiti* 'he sits' = Skt. *sídati,* cf. Whitney, *Skt. Gram.* §§ 748, 749 a.

Note 2. Some roots in *a* + cons. show a fluctuation between *ă* and *ā,* cf. Whitney, *Skt. Gram.* § 745 d, e: Av. √*nam-* 'to bow' has *nam-a-* beside *nām-a-* = Skt. *nám-a-;* Av. √*dvar-* 'to run' has *dvar-a-* beside *dvār-a-,* cf. also § 18 Note 1, and Whitney, *Skt. Gram.* § 545 e.

§ 479. **Class 6**—*a*-class with unstrengthened root-form = Skt. sixth *(tud-)* class.—The thematic *a* is simply attached to the root in its weak form to make up the present-stem.—Cf. Whitney, *Skt. Gram.* § 751.

Av. √*iš-* 'to seek, desire', *iš-a-ite* = Skt. *iš-á-tē;* Av. √*vīs-* 'to become', *vis-a-iti* (cf. § 20 on *i*) = Skt. *viš-á-ti;* et al.

Note. With nasal strengthening Av. *hiṇc-a-iti* 'he sprinkles' (√*hic-*) = Skt. *siṇc-á-ti.*

§ 480. **Class 4**—*ya*-class (unstrengthened root-form) = Skt. fourth *(div-)* class.—Also here the Passive, cf. V. a below. —The present-stem is formed by adding *ya-* (*ye-* § 34) to the simple unstrengthened root.—Cf. Whitney, *Skt. Gram.* § 759.

Av. √*nas-* 'to vanish', *nas-ye-iti* = Skt. *nás-ya-ti;* Av. √*prā-* 'to protect', *prā-ye-iṇtē* = Skt. *trá-ya-ntē.*

Note 1. For the Passive formation see V. a below.

Note 2. The strong form of the stem (-*ae-* instead of -*i-*) is to be noted in the verb Av. *sraēš-ye-iti* 'it clings' = Skt. *šliš-ya-ti.*

§ 481. **Class 10**—*aya*-class (strengthened root-form) = Skt. tenth *(cur-)* class.—This class includes in part the secondary formation causative, denominative, see V. b, c, below. The formative element *aya* is added to the strengthened root.—The roots in internal *a* generally, but not always, receive the *vṛddhi* strengthening; the roots in *i, u* commonly receive the *guṇa* increase.

> Av. √*tap*- 'to warm', *tāp-aye-ⁱti* = Skt. *tā́p-áya-ti*;
> Av. √*pat*- 'to fly', *apat-ayə-n* = Skt. *ā́pāt-aya-n*; Av.
> √*riš*- 'to wound', *raēš̤-aya-ṭ* = Skt. *rḗṣ-áya-t*; Av.
> √*ruc*- 'to light up', *raoc-aye-ⁱti* = Skt. *rōc-áya-ti*.

Note 1. Observe that the roots with *a* do not always show the *vṛddhi* stage.

Note 2. Some exceptions to the rule for *guṇa* of *i*- and *u*-roots occur.

Note 3. In Av., as in Skt., a heavy syllable ending in consonant does not take *vṛddhi* or *guṇa*.

Paradigms of the *a*-Conjugation (thematic).
Cl. 1, 6, 4, 10.
(Cf. Whitney, *Skt. Gram.* § 734 seq.)

§ 482.   Av. ᜨ *bar*- 'bear, carry' = Skt. *bhár*-.

Cl. 1. Av. *ḫṣ̌i*- 'rule, possess', *zū*- 'call, bless, curse', *vaēn*- 'see', *yaz*- 'worship', *jas*- 'come', *jīv*- 'live', *ciš*- 'teach, point out', *car*- 'move, go', *ʰvar*- 'eat', *az*- 'drive, win', *yās*- 'desire, seek', *pac*- 'cook', *van*- 'win', *þwars*- 'cut, make', *ram*- 'delight', *miz*- 'make urine'.— Cl. 6. *vaš*- 'speak', *vīs*- 'become'.—Cl. 4. *yud*- 'fight', *zan*-, *zā*- 'give birth, be born', *varz*- 'work', *bud*- 'mark, know'.—Cl. 10. *vid*- 'know', *taᵘrv*- 'overcome', *var*- 'to cover', *ʄar*- 'go, make go', *dar*- 'hold fast', *haƶl*- 'incite'.

§ 483.   1. Indicative.—a. Present.

i. ACTIVE.

Av.	Singular:	cf. Skt.
1. *bar-ā-mi* .	. . . .	*bhár-ā-mi*
2. *bar-a-hi* .	. . . . . .	*bhár-a-si*
3. *bar-a-ⁱti* .	. . . . . .	*bhár-a-ti*

	Dual:	
1.	—	*bhár-ā-vas*
2.	—	ˉ*bhár-a-thas*
3. { *bar-a-tō*	. .	} *bhar-a-tas*
｛ *-a-þō yaⁱdyapō*[1] .	. . . .	

---

[1] Cf. § 449 Note.

Av.	Plural:	cf. Skt.
1. { *bar-ā-mahi* . . . . *-ā-mahi* va*z̆dayamahī*	} *bhár-ā-masi* (Ved.)
2. (*bar-a-þa*) *ḫ̌ayaþā* (GAv.)	*bhár-a-tha*
3. { *bar-ə-ṇti* . . . . *-a-i̯ṇti* zava*i̯ṇti*	} *bhár-a-nti*

ii. MIDDLE.

Av.	Singular:	cf. Skt.
1. . *bai̯r-e*	*bhár-ē*
2. { *bar-a-he*¹ . . . . *-a-vhe* va*ṣ̌avhe*	} *bhár-a-sē*
3. *bar-a-i̯te*	*bhár-a-tē*

Dual:

1.	—	*bhár-ā-vahē*
2.	—	*bhár-ē-thē*
3.	(*bar-ōi̯-þe*) va*z̆nōi̯þe*² . .	*bhár-ē-tē*

Plural:

1. { (*bar-ā-ma*ⁱ*de*) yaza*maⁱde* . . . . . *-ā-maⁱde*	} *bhár-ā-mahē*
2. (*bar-a-þwe*) cara*þwe*³ . . .	*bhár-a-dhvē*
3. *bar-ə-ṇte*	*bhár-a-ntē*

§ 484. b. Preterite (and Injunctive).⁴

i. ACTIVE.

Av	Singular:	cf. Skt.
1. *bar-ə-m*	*á-bhar-a-m*
2. (*bar-ō*) ja*sō*	*á-bhar-a-s*
3. *bar-a-ṯ*	*á-bhar-a-t*

Dual:

1. (*bar-ā-va*) j*vāva*⁴	*á-bhar-ā-va*
2. —	*á-bhar-a-tam*
3. (*bar-a-təm*) ta*ᵘrvayatəm*⁵	*á-bhar-a-tām*

---

¹ Cf. § 116. — ² Cf. § 449 Note. — ³ See Yt. 13.34. — ⁴ On augmentless Pret.—Subjunct. Imperat. (Injunctive) see § 445. — ⁵ Cf. § 449 Note.

	Av.	Plural:	cf. Skt.
1.	*bar-ā-ma* . . . . . . *-ā-ma* *bārayama* . .		*á-bhar-ā-ma*
2.	*(bar-a-ta)* *ta^urvayata* . . .		. *á-bhar-a-ta*
3.	*bar-ə-n*		. *á-bhar-a-n*

ii. MIDDLE.
Singular:

1.	*baⁱr-e* [1]		. *á-bhar-ē*
2.	*(bar-a-ɳha)* *zayaɳha* .		. *á-bhar-a-thås*
3.	*bar-a-ta*		. *á-bhar-a-ta*

Dual:

1.	—		. *á-bhar-ā-vahi*
2.	—		. *á-bhar-ē-thaɱ*
3.	*(bar-aē-təm)* *caɛɛaɛtəm* . *(bar-ōi-þe)* *carōiþe* [2] . .		. *á-bhar-ē-tāɱ* —

Plural:

1.	—		. *á-bhar-ā-mahi*
2.	*(bar-a-dwəm)* *vārayadwəɱ* [3] .		. *á-bhar-a-dhvaɱ*
3.	*(bar-ə-ɳta)* *carəɳta* . . .		. *á-bhar-a-nta*

§ 485.   2. Imperative.
i. ACTIVE.

	Av.	Singular:	cf. Skt.
2.	*bar-a*		. *bhár-a*
3.	*bar-a-tu*		. *bhár-a-tu*

Plural:

2.	*(bar-a-ta)* *ɦarata*		. *bhár-a-ta*
3.	*bar-ə-ɳtu* . . . . . . *-a-ɳtu* *pārayaɳtu* . . .		*bhár-a-ntu*

ii. MIDDLE.
Singular:

2.	*bar-a-ɳuha*		*bhár-a-sva*
3.	*(bar-a-tąm)* *vərəzyatąm* [4]		*bhár-a-tām*

---

[1] Yt. 5.6, cf. *apərəse, aguze.* — [2] Ys. 9.5, cf. § 449 Note, cf. Delbrück, *Altind. Vb.* § 106, Bartholomae, *Altiran. Vb.* p. 52, 53. — [3] Cf. § 484 Foot-Note 4. — [4] See Vsp. 15.1, best reading.

	Av.	Plural:			cf. Skt.
2.	*(bar-a-đwəm)* *dārayađwəm*	.	.		*bhár-a-dhvam*
3.	*(bar-ə-ṇtạm)* *jasṇtạm*	. . . . .	.	.	*bhár-a-ntām*

§ 486.　　　3. Subjunctive.

i. ACTIVE.

	Av.	Singular:	cf. Skt.
1.	*bar-ā-ni* .	. . . .	*bhár-ā-ni*
2.	*bar-ā-hi* .	. . . .	*bhár-ā-si*
3.	*(bar-ā-ʲti) carāiti*	. . . . .	*bhár-ā-ti*
	bar-ā-ṯ .	. . . . .	*bhár-ā-t*

Dual:

1.	—	. . . .	*bhár-ā-va*
2.	—	. . . .	*bhár-ā-thas*
3.	*(bar-ā-tō) jasātō*	. . . . . .	*bhár-ā-tas*

Plural:

1.	*bar-ā-ma* [1]	. . . .	*bhár-ā-ma*
2.	*(bar-ā-þa) azāþā* (GAv.)	. . .	*bhár-ā-tha*
3.	*bar-ą-n*	. . . .	*bhár-ā-n*

ii. MIDDLE.

	Av.	Singular:	cf. Skt.
1.	*(bar-ā-ne) vīsāne*	. . . .	—
	(bar-āi) vīsāi	. . . .	*bhár-āi*
2.	*(bar-ā̊-ɯhe) yāsaɯhe*	. . . . .	*bhár-ā-sɛ*
3.	*(bar-ā-ʲte) pacāite*	. . . . .	*bhár-ā-tɛ*

Plural:

3.	*(bar-ā̊-ṇte) yazāṇte*	. . . .	—
	-ā-ʲre mravāire [2]	. . . .	—

§ 487.　　　4. Optative.

i. ACTIVE.

	Av.	Singular:	cf. Skt.
1.	—	. . . .	*bhár-ɛ-yam*
2.	*bar-ōi-š* .	. . . .	*bhár-ɛ-s*
3.	*bar-ōi-ṯ* .	. . . .	*bhár-ɛ-t*

---

[1] Cf. § 484 Note 1. — [2] By transfer to *a*-conj. from rt. cl. 2, √*mra*-
§§ 521, 452.

Av.	Plural:	cf. Skt.
1. *(bar-aē-ma)* vanaēma . .		bhár-ē-ma
2. *(bar-aē-ta)* ßwɔrᵊsaēta . .		bhár-ē-ta
3. *bar-ay-ɔn*		bhár-ē-yus

ii. MIDDLE.

Singular:

1. *(bar-ay-a)* haḷḷaya[1]	.	bhár-ē-ya
2. *(bar-aē-ṣa)* haḷḷaēṣa . .		bhár-ē-thās
3. *bar-aē-ta*		bhár-ē-ta

Plural:

1. *(bar-ōi-maᵢde)* büidyōimaᵢde .		bhár-ē-mahi
2. *(bar-ōi-ḍwɔm)* rāmōiḍwɔm .	.	bhár-ē-dhvam
3. *(bar-ay-aṇta)* maēzayaṇta[2]		bhár-ē-ran

§ 488.   5. Participle.

Av.	i. ACTIVE.	cf. Skt.

bar-a-ṇt- (fem. *-ɔṇtī-*) . . . . . *bhár-a-nt-* (fem. *-antī-*)

ii. MIDDLE.

bar-ɔ-mna- (fem. *-ɔ-mnā-*) . . . *bhár-a-māna-* (fem. *-a-mānā-*)

Forms to be observed in GAv. and YAv.

§ 489. GAv. shows in general the same forms as above, but with the long final vowel, cf. § 26. It has, however, a certain number of individual differences; these as well as other variations in YAv. also may here be noted.

§ 490. (1) The original unmodified forms of 3 pl. act. mid. *-anti, -ante,* cf. *zavaᵢṇte* above, occasionally stand instead of being changed to *-ɔṇti, -ɔṇte,* e. g.:—

GAv. *vanaᵢṇtī*, YAv. *vanaṇti* 'they win' Yt. 13.154, GAv. *hacaᵢṇtē* beside YAv. *haciṇte* 'they follow' (§§ 30, 491).

§ 491. (2) According to § 30, the forms *-iṇti, -iṇte, -in* are often found after palatals, instead of *-ɔṇti, -aᵢṇti* etc., e. g.:—

Av. *frataciṇti* 'they run forth' (variants •tacaᵢṇti, •tacṇti Ys. 65.3, √tac-), *fratacin* 'they ran forth'; *haciṇte* (YAv.) beside *hacaᵢṇtē*

---

[1] Ys. 8.7. — [2] i. e. •maēz-aē-aṇta for •maēz-a-i-aṇtá.

(GAv.) 'they follow'; *yazinti* 'they worship' Yt. **8.**11 beside *yazṇti*
Yt. **8.**24, cf. Yt. 10.54 *yazṇte, yazinti; snaĕžintaĕ-ca* 'and they drop
as snow' (cf. § 55).

§ 492.   (3) GYAv., when *y* precedes the thematic
-a- (-ā-), especially in Cl. **4, 10**, the combination *-ya- (-yā-)*
generally becomes *-ye-* according to § 34, e. g.:—

Av. *sāḍayemi, sāḍayehi, sāḍayeⁱti* 'I, thou, he appear' (√*sad-*
Cl. 10); *jaⁱdyemi, jaⁱdyehi, jaⁱdyeⁱṇti* 'I, thou, they beseech' (√*jad-*
Cl. 4); *ḫšayehī* (GAv.), *ḫšayeⁱti, ḫšayeⁱte, ḫšay.ⁱṇti, ḫšayeni* (subjunct.
-āni) 'thou, he etc. rule, possess' (√*ḫši-* Cl. 1); *zbayemi, zbayehi,
zbayeⁱti* 'I invoke', etc.; *baṇdayeni* 'I may bind' (subjunct.).

§ 493.   (4) Some reductions of *-ya-, -va-* before *m, n*
(§ 63) occur, e. g.:—

Av. *vərⁱzinti* 'they work' (i. e. *vərⁱzyaṇti*, √*varz-* Cl. 4); *irišinti*
'they wound' (i. e. *irišyaṇti*, √*iriš-* Cl. 4); *ᵘrvaĕsinti* 'they turn';
uḫšin 'they grew' (i. c. *uḫšyan*, √*vaḫš* Cl. 4); *fyavhuṇte* 'they shower
sleet' (i. e. *fyavhvaṇte*).—So imperat.- 2 sg. *nase* 'perish' (i. e. *nasya*).

§ 494.   (5) Some reductions of *-aya-, -ava- (-āya-, -āva-)*
before final *m, n* (§ 64) occur, e. g.:—

Av. *daĕsaĕm* 'I showed' (i. e. *daĕsayam*, √*dis-* Cl. 10); *abaom*
'I became' (i. e. *abavam*, √*bū-* Cl. 1) Yt. 19.57,61,63, *baon* 'they
became' Yt. 5.98 etc.

§ 495.   Certain other peculiarities likewise require de-
tailed notice.

1. Indicative.

a. Present.

§ 496.   **Singular**:—

First Person: **i.** ACT. GAv. shows only the ending *-ā* (Gk. -ω), instead
of *-āmi* in the thematic verbs and only *-mī* in the non-*a*-verbs
(unthematic), e. g. GAv. *ufyā* 'I praise', *kayā* 'I discern'.—YAv.
similar but rare (perhaps borrowed) *zbaya* 'I invoke' at Vsp. 6.1 by
the side of *frayeze* which likewise is an indicative.

§ 497.   **Dual**:—

Third Person: **i.** ACT. GAv. add *ĕaratas-cā* 'both come' Ys. **51.**12.—
ii. MID. *ZPhl. Gloss.* p. 54.8 has *baraite·* 'they two bring' cf. *A. O. S.
Proceedings* Oct. 1889 p. 165.

§ 498.   **Plural**:—

First Person: **i.** ACT. YAv., similarly with short *ā* (as above) *zbayāmahi*
'we invoke'.

Second Person: i. ACT. YAv. also isolated (-*t*- like pret. form) *ḥarata*
'ye eat' Vd. 7.57.—ii. MID. GAv. -*duyĕ* (cf. § 190) *dīdraǰẑōduyĕ* 'ye
keep holding' (desiderative)—on -*ō*- for -*a*- of stem, see § 39.
Third Person: See general details above § 490 seq.

b. Preterite.

§ 499. Plural:—
Third Person: ii. MID. GAv., observe *vīšṇtā* 'they entered' (on -*ǰ*-,
cf. § 32).

2. Imperative.

§ 500. Singular:—
Second Person: i. ACT. YAv., note (by reduction §§ 34, 493) *nasē* 'perish
thou' (i. e. *nasya*, √*nas*- Cl. 4).—ii. MID. GAv., only -*hvā*: *gūšahvā*
'hear thou', *baḳšōhvā* 'share thou' (on -*ō*- for -*a*-, see § 39).
Third Person: i. ACT. GAv., observe -*ō*- (cf. § 39) in *vǝrǝzyōtū* 'let him
work' (√*varz*- Cl. 4), *vātayōtū* 'let him announce' (√*vat*- Cl. 10).

§ 501. Plural:—
Second Person: i. ACT. GAv. with ending -*na* (cf. Skt. -*tana*) *baranā*
'bear ye' Ys. 30.9, cf. § 457 above, and Whitney, *Skt. Gram.* § 740.
—ii. MID. GAv. *gūšōdūm* 'hear ye' = Skt. *ghóṣadhvam*.

3. Subjunctive.

§ 502. Singular:—
Second Person: i. ACT. YAv. occasionally -*āi* for -*ā(h)i* § 450: *apa.yasāi*
'thou wilt destroy' (i. e. *yasāhi*); *vazāi, vaṯāhi* (as variants) 'mayest
thou bring' Vd. 5.16.—YAv., a form with secondary ending (but
syntax bad) is *bavǭ* Yt. 24.8.

§ 503. Plural:—
Third Person: i. ACT. GAv. shows also -*ǝn* (for -*ǝn*) in *rapǝn* 'they may
hold'.—ii. MID. YAv. like *mravāire* above § 452, also *niǰrāire* 'they
may strike' Yt. 10.40, so again *ǭuhāire* Yt. 10.45.

4. Optative.

§ 504. Singular:—
First Person: ii. MID. YAv., observe *mainya* 'I would think' Yt. 10.106
(for *mainyaya* § 194).

§ 505. Plural:—
First Person: i. ACT. GAv. (with regular secondary ending -*maidī*, cf.
Skt. -*mahi*) *vāᵘrōimaidī* 'we would cause to believe'.
Third Person: YAv. like *maēzayaṇta* in paradigm is *yazayaṇta* 'they
would sacrifice'.

5. Participle.

§ 506. On the relation of Av. -*mna* (metrically often -*mana*) to Skt. -*mãna*, see § 18 Note 2.

§ 507. In Av. more often than in Skt. (cf. Whitney, *Skt. Gram.* § 741 a) there appear instances of middle (passive) participles of *a*-verbs formed with the participial suffix -*ana*, -*ãna* (= Skt. -*ãna*, § 18) instead of -*mna*, e. g. *barana*- 'bearing', •*azana* 'driving';—*yazãna*- 'worshipping'; *starãna*- 'strewing'.

---

ii. The non-*a*-Conjugation (unthematic).

§ 508. **General Remark.** In Av., as in Skt., the verbs of the non-*a*-conjugation (unthematic) are not so numerous as those of the thematic conjugation. They may be grouped in six classes (Cl. 2, 3, 7, 5, 8, 9), in each of which the endings are attached directly (without an interposed *a*) to the stem which is subject to modification.

The striking characteristic of the entire group is the variation of the root in different forms. The modified root or the suffix assumes now a stronger form, again a weaker form.

§ 509. **Strong and Weak Stem-Forms.** The strong (*guṇa*) forms, as a rule, are:—(1) the Sing. Indic. Act. (Pres. Pret.),—(2) the 3 rd. Sing. Imperat. Act.,—(3) the entire Subjunct.—The remaining forms are weak. Many fluctuations and transfers, however, occur; especially often is the strong stem employed in forms (see 3rd. plurals) modelled after the *a*-conjugation.

Mode Formation.—Special Remark.

1. Indicative.

§ 510. The endings of the non-thematic indicative require some remark. GAv. generally shows the older use of -*mī* (§ 450) and -*aiti̯*, -*aitē*, -*at̯* (for thematic -*anti̯*, -*ante* -*an* § 452). In YAv. this old distinction is not sharply preserved. The stem in general to which the endings are

directly attached shows a variation of str. and wk. forms
according to the preceding rule, § 509.

2. Imperative.

§ 511.   The ending of the Imperat. 2 sing. is *-dī, -di.*
The endings in general are attached directly to the prepared class-stem.   This shows the s t r o n g form in the
3 sg. a c t.; in the other forms it has the weak grade, but
fluctuations occur.

3. Subjunctive.

§ 512.   The endings are attached by means of the
m o d e - s i g n *a* to the prepared class-stem which shows the
s t r o n g f o r m t h r o u g h o u t.

4. Optative.

§ 513.   The regular optative endings are attached by
the m o d e - s i g n *-yā-, -ī- (ī)* in accordance with the rules
given above at § 463.   The stem regularly shows its w e a k
f o r m throughout, but variations from this sometimes occur.

5. Participle.

§ 514.   The participial forms (verbal adjectives) are
made by attaching to the present stem in its w e a k grade
the formative element *-aṇt, -aṭ* (i. e. *-ṇt*) for the active, and
-āna, -ana beside *-mna,* for the middle.

Classes of the non-*a*-Conjugation (unthematic).

Cl. 2, 3, 7, 5, 8, 9.

§ 515.   The six classes of unthematic verbs have
certain characteristics in common but they have also certain
individual peculiarities, these classes will now each be taken
up in detail.

Class 2—Root-Class.

§ 516.   **Class 2—**R o o t - Class—root itself is present
stem = Skt. second *(ad-)* class.—The stem may have the
strong or the weak form according to § 509, the endings

are then attached directly to the stem. Examples are quite numerous:

Av. $\sqrt{p\bar{a}}$- 'to keep, protect', *pā-ʲti* (3 sg. pres.) = Skt. *pá-ti;* Av. $\sqrt{i}$- 'to go', *aēʲ-ti* (3 sg.), *y-eⁱnti* (3 pl. pres. § 34) = Skt. *é-ti, y-ánti;* Av. $\sqrt{stu}$- 'to praise', *staoʲti* = Skt. *stāú-ti* (§ 60 Note c); Av. $\sqrt{jan}$- 'to slay', *jaⁱn-ti* (3 sg. pres. indic.) = Skt. *hán-ti;* Av. $\sqrt{vas}$- 'to wish', *vaš-tī* (3 sg.), *us-mahi* (1 pl. pres. indic.) = Skt. *váš-ti, uš-mási* (Ved.).

Paradigm of Class 2.
(Cf. Whitney, *Skt. Gram.* § 612 seq.)

§ 517. Av. ـﺳﺤ $\sqrt{mr\bar{u}}$- 'to say' = Skt. $\sqrt{br\bar{u}}$-.

Av. *hap-* 'promote', *vas-, us-* 'wish', *āh-* 'sit', *rud-* 'grow', *stu-* 'praise', *i-* 'go', *is-* 'be able'.

§ 518. 1. Indicative.—a. Present:

i. ACTIVE.

Av.	Singular:	cf. Skt.
1. *mraó-mi*		*bráv-ī-mi*
2. *(mrao-ši) hašī* (GAv.) . . .	. .	*bráv-ī-ši*
3. *mrao-ʲti*	.	*bráv-ī-ti*
	Dual:	
1. *(mrvahi¹) usvahī* (GAv.) . .	.	*brū-vasi*
	Plural:	
1. *(mrū-mahi) usmahi*	.	*brū-masi*
3. *(mrv-aⁱnti) mrvhⁱnti²*	.	*brúv-anti*

ii. MIDDLE.

	Singular:	
1. *mruy-ē³*	. .	*bruv-é*
2. *(mrū-še)* cf. *raose⁴* . . .	. .	*brū-šé*
3. ⎰ *mrū-ʲte*	. .	*brū-té*
⎱ *mruy-ē⁵*		*bruv-é*
	Plural:	
1. *mrū-maⁱde*	.	*brū-máhē*
3. *(mrv-ante) mrvhⁱnte⁶*	.	*bruv-átē*

---

¹ i. e. *mru-vahi* § 68.1. — ² Yt. 17.10. — ³ § 190. — ⁴ Strong form § 509. — ⁵ Ys. 19.10, cf. § 450 end. — ⁶ Yt. 17.11; Ys. 9.22.

§ 519. b. Preterite Indicative (and Injunctive).

i. ACTIVE.

Av.	Singular:	cf. Skt.
1. *mrao-m*		*á-brav-am*
2. *mrao-š*		*á-brav-ᴶ-s*
3. *mrao-ṭ*		*á-brav-ᴵ-t*

Plural:

3. *(mrao-n?* [1]*)* *usən*		*á-bruv-an*

ii. MIDDLE.

Singular:

1. *mrav-ī* [2]		*á-bruv-i*
3. ⎰ *mrū-ta*		*á-brū-ta*
⎱ *mrao-tā* (GAv.)		—

Plural:

3. *mrav-aṇta* [3]		*á-bruv-ata*

§ 520. 2. Imperative.

i. ACTIVE.

Av.	Singular:	cf. Skt.
2. *mrū-ᴶdi*		*brū-hí*
3. *mrao-tū* (GAv.)		*bráv-ᴶ-tu*

Plural:

2. *(mrao-ta)* *staota* [4]		*brū-tá*
3. *(mrᵃv-aṇtu)* *yaṇtu*		*bruv-áṇtu*

§ 521. 3. Subjunctive.

i. ACTIVE.

Av.	Singular:	cf. Skt.
1. *mrav-ā-ni* [5]		*bráv-ā-ni*
3. ⎰ *mrav-a-ᴶtī* (GAv.)		*bráv-a-ti*
⎱ *mrav-a-ṭ* [6]		*bráv-a-t*

Plural:

1. *(mrav-ā-ma)* *janāma*		*bráv-ā-ma*
3. *(mrav-ə-n)* *vasən*		*bráv-a-n*

---

[1] § 64. — [2] Observe str. stem; or is it *mrᵃvī* § 68 Note 3? — [3] Cf. § 509 end. — [4] Strong form (!), cf. § 509. — [5] Yt. 15.56; 12.2. — [6] See *ZPhl. Gloss.* p. 111.

ii. MIDDLE.

Av.	Singular:	cf. Skt.
1. { *(mrav-āi) isāi*		*bráv-āi*
{ *mrav-āne* [1]		—
	Plural:	
3. *mrav-ā-ire* [2]		—

§ 522.   4. Optative.

i. ACTIVE.

Av.	Singular:	cf. Skt.
2. *mru-yǡ*		*bru-yā́-s*
3. *mru-yā-ṭ*		*brū-yā́-t*

ii. MIDDLE.
Singular:

2. *mrv-i-ṣa* [3]		*bruv-ī-thā́s*
3. *mrv-ī-tā* (GAv.)		*bruv-ī-tá*

§ 523.   5. Participle.

Av.	**i. ACTIVE.**	cf. Skt.
mrv-at-		*bruv-ánt-*

ii. MIDDLE.

mrav-āna- [4]		*bruv-āná-*
mrao-mna- [5]		—

Forms to be observed in GAv. and YAv.

§ 524. Beside the above paradigm, a certain number of forms in GAv. and YAv. are worthy of note.

1. Indicative.

a. Present.

§ 525. Singular:—

First Person: i. ACTIVE. GAv., notice (from strongest stem) *stǎumī* 'I praise' (but v. l. *staomi*) Ys. 43.8, cf. Skt. *stǎuti* (Ved. 3 sg.).

Second Person: i. ACTIVE. YAv., observe likewise as regular form (§ 122) *ṭāhi* 'thou protectest'.

Third Person: ii. MIDDLE. YAv. also (like 1st.—3rd. sg. pres., above) *ni-ɟne* 'he smites'.

---

[1] Yt. 5.82. — [2] *a*-conj. cf. §§ 486, 452 end. — [3] Cf. § 21 Note. —
[4] Cf. Skt. *stávāna-*, Whitney § 619 d. — [5] i. e. like *a*-conj. ptcpl.

§ 526. Plural:—

First Person: ii. MID. YAv., note (from str. stem) *staomaᵢde* 'we praise'. —GAv., observe (-*ai̯-ca* § 55) *aogᵉmadai̯-cā* 'and we name'.

Third Person: ii. MID. YAv., seldom the plur. ending -*ati̯* (= * n̥ti̯*): Av. *aojaᵢte* 'they say' Yt. 8.51, etc. — Observe also Av. *sōire* 'they lie' Yt. 10.80 = Skt. *śére*.

b. Preterite.

§ 527. Singular:—

Second Person: ii. MID. GAv., note as a regular 2 sing. *aojṯā* 'thou saidst' Ys. 43.12.

Third Person: i. ACT. GAv., observe (with inserted -*ī*- like Skt. *ábravīt*) the form *sāhī̆t* 'he taught' Ys. 50.6.—ii. MID. YAv. also (from str. stem, like *mraotā* above) *staota* 'he praised'.

5. Participle.

§ 528. ii. MID. Observe also -*āna* (for -*āna*) and (like *a*-conj. §§ 514, 477) -*ᵊmna*: Av. *aojāna-*, *aojᵊmna-* 'speaking'.

Transfers to the *a*-Conjugation (thematic).

§ 529. A number of transfers from the Root-Class to the *a*-conjugation are to be found.

1. Indicative. i. ACT. b. Pret. GAv. *mrav-a-t̆* 'he said' Ys. 45.2.
2. Imperative. i. ACT. YAv. *mrav-a*, *mrv-a* 'say thou'.—ii. MID. YAv. *stav-a-ᵥuha* 'praise thou'.
3. Subjunctive. i. ACT. YAv. *mrav-āi* (for -*āhi* § 502) 'if thou say' Ys. 71.15.—ii. MID. YAv. (above in paradigm) *mrav-āᵢre* 'if they say' § 452 end.
4. Optative. i. ACT. YAv. *stav-ōi-t̆* 'he might praise' beside *stuyāt̆*.

---

§ 530. Inflection of Av. √*ah-*, *h-* 'to be'—only act. — = Skt. √*as-*, *s-*, cf. Whitney, *Skt. Gram.* § 636.

§ 531.   1. Indicative.—a. Present.

Av.	Singular:	cf. Skt.
1. *ah-mi*		*ás-mi*
2. *ahi* [1]		*ási*
3. *as-ti*		*ás-ti*
	Dual:	
3. *s-tō*		*s-tás*

[1] i. e. for *ah-hi::* Skt. *ási* for *ás-si*.

	Av.	Plural:	cf. Skt.
1.	*mahi*[1]	. . . .	*s-mási* (Ved.)
2.	*s-tā*[2]	. . . .	*s-thá*
3.	*h-ənti*	. . . .	*s-ánti*

§ 532.   b. Preterite.

Singular:

3.	{	*ās*[3]	. . . .	*ās* (Ved.)
	{	*as*	. . . .	*ās-ī-t*

Dual:

1.	*ahvā* (GAv.)	. . . .	*ās-va*

Plural:

3.	*h-ən*	. . . .	*ās-an*

§ 533.   2. Imperative.

	Av.	Singular:	cf. Skt.
2.	*s-dī* (GAv.)	. . . .	*ē-dhí*
3.	*as-tu*	. . . .	*ás-tu*

Plural:

3.	*h-əntu* (GAv.)	. . . .	*s-ántu*

§ 534.   3. Subjunctive.

	Av.	Singular:	cf. Skt.
2.	*avh-ō*	. . . . .	*ás-a-s*
3.	{ *avh-a-itī* (GAv.)	. . . .	*ás-a-ti*
	{ *avh-a-ţ*	. . . . . .	*ás-a-t*

Plural:

3.	*avh-ə-n*	. . . .	*ás-a-n*

§ 535.   4. Optative.

	Av.	Singular:	cf. Skt.
1.	*h-yš-m* (GAv.)[4]	. . . .	*s-yā-m*
2.	*h-yā* (GAv.)	. . . .	*s-yā-s*
3.	*h-yā-ţ* (GAv.), *h-yā-ţ* (YAv.)[5]	. . . .	*s-yā-t*

Plural:

1.	*h-yā-mā* (GAv.)	. . . .	*s-yā-ma*
2.	*h-yā-tā* (GAv.)	. . . .	*s-yā-ta*
3.	*h-yš-n* (GAv.), *h-yā-n* (YAv.), *h-yārə* (YAv.)	. . . .	*s-yúr*

§ 536.   5. Participle.

Av. *h-ənt-* . . . . cf. Skt. *s-ánt-*

---

[1] Cf. § 140. — [2] For *s-þa*, cf. § 78 a. — [3] See § 192 Note. — [4] Cf. § 32. — [5] Cf. §§ 132, 133.

Forms to be observed.

§ 537. YAv., notice in a late passage Yt. 24.12 (2 pl. opt. with primary ending!) *h-yā-þa* 'might ye be'.

§ 538. Transfers to the *a*-conjugation: — 1. Indic. Pret. 3 sg. *aṷh-a-ṭ*.—3. Subjunct. 3 sg. *aṷh-ā-iti*.

§ 539. Beside all the above paradigm of the present-system, there is made from this root *ah* 'to be', as in Skt., a regular perfect *āṷha* etc. § 606 = Skt. *āsa* etc.

Class 3.—Reduplicating Class.

§ 540. **Class 3.**—Reduplicating Class. The root is reduplicated to form the present stem. The stem then shows a variation of strong and weak forms (§ 509); the endings are attached to it directly.

The general rules for reduplication have been given above § 465. As examples of formation, the following may be taken:—

Av. √*dā*- 'to give, to place' (Stems *dadā-*, *dadā-*; *dad-*, *daþ-*, *dad-*, §§ 82, 83, 86), *da-dā-iti* (YAv.), *da-dā-itī* (GAv.), *da-dą-m*, *da-þą-m* = Skt. *dá-d(h)ā-ti*, *á-da-d(h)ā-m*;—Av. √*ci*- 'to atone' (Stems *ci-kay-*, *ci-ki-*), *ci-kay-aṭ* 3 sg. subjunct. = Skt. *cikayat*;—Av. √*hac*- 'to follow', *hi-šhaḫ-ti*, *hi-šc-a-maidē* (Ys. 40.4) = Skt. *sí-ṣak-ti*;—Av. √*jan*- 'to slay', *ni-ja-ɣn-əṇti* = Skt. *ji-ghn-anti*.

Paradigm of Class 3.
(Cf. Whitney, *Skt. Gram.* § 647 seq.)

§ 541. Av. ⸺ √*dā*- 'to give, to place' (str. stem YAv. *dadā*, GAv. *dadā-*; wk. stem YAv. *dad-*, *daþ-*, GAv. *dad-*) = Skt. √*dā-*, √*dhā-* — stems *dad(h)ā-*, *dad(h)-* —, cf. Whitney, *Skt. Gram.* § 667 seq.

Note. Observe that orig. *dā-*, *dhā-* are practically fallen together in Av. as *dā-*, §§ 82, 83.—On the interchange of *d*, *đ*, *þ*, see §§ 82, 83, 86.

§ 542.　1. Indicative.—a. Present.

i. ACTIVE.

Av.	Singular:	cf. Skt.
1. *dadā-mi*		*dád(h)ā-mi*
2. *dadā-hi*		*dád(h)ā-si*
3. { *dadā-iti*		*dád(h)ā-ti*
{ *das-ti* (YAv.)[1]		—[2]

	Plural:	
1. *dadᵊ-mahi*		*dad(h)-mási* (Ved.)
2. —		*d(h)at-tá*
3. { *dada- itī* (GAv.)[3]		} *dád(h)-ati*
{ *dadā-iti* (YAv.)[4] . . .		

ii. MIDDLE.

Av.	Singular:	cf. Skt.
1. { *daⁱd-e* (YAv.), *dad-ē* (GAv.) . . .		*dad(h)-ĕ*
{ *daⁱp-e*[5]		—
2. —		*d(h)at-sĕ*
3. { *das-te* (GYAv.)[6]		*d(h)at-tĕ*
{ *daz-dē* (GAv.)[5]		—

	Plural:	
1. *dadᵊ-maⁱde*		*dád(h)-mahĕ*

§ 543.　b. Preterite Indicative (and Injunctive).

i. ACTIVE.

Av.	Singular:	cf. Skt.
1. *dadą-m, dapą-m*	. .	*á-dad(h)ā-m*
2. *dadā̊* (GAv.)	. .	*á-dad(h)ā-s*
3. *dadā-ṭ* (YAv.), *dadā-ṭ* (GAv.)	.	*á-dad(h)ā-t*

	Dual:	
3. *daⁱd-ī-tᵊm*[7]	. .	*á-d(h)at-tām*

	Plural:	
2. *das-ta*[8]		*á-d(h)at-ta*
3. *dad-aṭ* (GAv.)[9]		*á-dad(h)-ur*

---

[1] From weak stem *dad-*. On *s*, cf. §§ 151, 170. — [2] Cf. Epic Skt. *dadmi*. — [3] Ys. 46.1, i. e. *-ŋti*. — [4] i. e. *-ŋti*, uncertain, Yt. 10,3. — [5] § 541 Note. — [6] § 542 Foot-Note 1. — [7] Cf. §§ 550, 449 Note. — [8] §§ 151, 445 Note 2. — [9] Ys. 32.14, i. e. *dad-ŋt*.

ii. MIDDLE.

Av.	Singular:	cf. Skt.
3. *das-ta*	. . . .	*á-d(h)at-ta*

§ 544.   2. Imperative.

i. ACTIVE.

Av.	Singular:	cf. Skt.
2. *daz-di*[1]	. . . . . .	*d(h)ī-hí*
3. *dadā-tū* (GAv.)	. . . .	*dád(h)ā-tu*

Plural:

Av.		cf. Skt.
3. *das-ta*[2]	. . . .	*d(h)at-tá*

ii. MIDDLE.

Av.		cf. Skt.
2. *dasva*[3]	. . . . .	*d(h)at-sva*

§ 545.   3. Subjunctive.

i. ACTIVE.

Av.	Singular:	cf. Skt.
1. *dapā-ni* .	.	*dád(h)ā-ni*
3. *dadā-ṭ*[4] .	. . . .	*dád(h)ā-t*

Plural:

Av.		cf. Skt.
1. *dapā-ma*	. . . .	*dád(h)ā-ma*

ii. MIDDLE.

Av.		
1. *dapā-ne*[5]	. . . .	—

§ 546.   4. Optative.

i. ACTIVE.

Av.	Singular:	cf. Skt.
1. *daid-yą-m* .	. . . .	*dad(h)-yā-m*
2. *daip-yāə* . .	.	*dád(h)-yā-s*
3. *daip-yā-ṭ*	. . . .	*dád(h)-yā-t*

Plural:

Av.		cf. Skt.
3. { *daip-yą-n*	. . . .	—
{ *daip-yā-rᵊš* .	. . . .	*dad(h)-y-úr*

ii. MIDDLE.
Singular:

Av.		cf. Skt.
2. *daip-ī-ṣa*[6]	. . . .	*dad(h)-ī-thās*
3. *daip-ī-ta* (YAv.), *daid-ī-tā* (GAv.)	. .	*dad(h)-ī-tá*

---

[1] § 151. — [2] Cf. Injunctive §§ 543, 445 Note 2. — [3] § 186. — [4] Not distinguishable from augmentless imperfect above. — [5] Ny. 4.8. — [6] Yt. 3.1 with variants *daidīša*, *dapīš*.

§ 547.   5. Participle.

i. ACTIVE.   cf. Skt.

Av. •*daþ-ənt-*[1] .   .   .   .   *dád(h)-at-*

ii. MIDDLE.

Av. *daþ-āna-*   .   .   .   .   *dád(h)-āna-*

Forms to be observed in GAv. and YAv.

§ 548.   There are both in GAv. and in YAv. a number of forms beside the above, that deserve special notice.

1. Indicative.

§ 549.   a. Present. i. ACT.—ii. MID. GAv., observe that the forms *dåitī, dåitē, dånṭē* resembling pres. in dic. forms after Class 2, are best regarded as radical aor. subjunct., cf. § 633 below.—Note GAv. *hišcamaᵢdē* (with v. l. *hišcimaᵢdē*) 'we follow' 1 pl. pres. indic. mid. Ys. 40.4—(observe *a*, Bartholomae, *K.Z.* xxix. p. 273 = *Flexionslehre* p. 4).—Add also 3 sg. pres. indic. act. *zazaṇti* 'he produces' Vd. 3.5 = Skt. *jajánti*.

§ 550.   b. Preterite. i. ACT. YGAv., observe with interposed *ī* (like Skt. *ábravīt* etc.) and from weak stem: *daᵢdᵢī* (YAv. 2 sg. pret. indic.), *daᵢdᵢī* (YAv. Yt. 13.12), *daᵢdᵢī* (GAv. 3 sg. pret.), *daᵢdᵢtəm* (3 du. cf. above paradigm).—Remark 3 pl. in -*aṭ* (= -*ṇṭ*) GAv. *jīgərəzaṭ* 'let them lament' (injunctive).—ii. MID. YAv., observe from strong stem, 2 sg. pret. mid. *ji-jaē-ša* 'thou didst live, mayest live' ($\sqrt{gi}$-, *ji*-).

3. Subjunctive.

§ 551.   Sg. Pl. i. ACT. YAv., add (regularly) from $\sqrt{ci}$- 'to atone', *ci-kay-aṭ* (3 sg. subjunct.), *ci-kay-a-tō* (3 du. subjunct. *ZPhl. Gloss.* p. 92, 34), *ci-kaēn* (3 pl. subjunct.) i. e. •*ci-kay-ṇ* § 64.

4. Optative.

§ 552.   Beside the mid. forms with long *ī* (-*īša, -īta*) are found also the variants -*īša, -īta*, cf. § 21 Note.

Transfers to the *a*-Conjugation (thematic).

§ 553.   A number of transitions from the Third Class to the *a*-conjugation occur. The reduplicated wk. stem *daþ-* (YAv.), *dad-* (GAv.) of $\sqrt{dā}$- in Av. as in Skt.—cf. Whitney, *Skt. Gram.* § 672—thus not infrequently assumes the inflection of an *a*-stem, § 483.

---

[1] Ys. 9.1.

1. **Indicative.** i. ACT. a. Pres. YAv. *dap-a-ˀti, dap-ʒ-ŋti.* —
b. Pret. YGAv. *daþ-ʒ-m, daþ-ŏ, daþ-a-ţ, dad-a-ţ; daþ-ʒ-n, dad-ʒ-n*
(beside *dadaţ* § 543 Foot-Note). — ii. MID. YAv. *daþ-a-ˀtɛ.* — GAv.
dad-ʒ-ŋtɛ 'they are placed'.

Note. Similarly transferred Av. *zīzanʒŋti, zīzanʒn, zīzandţ* from
√*zan-* 'beget, bear'. The Skt. shows *jījanat* as redupl. aor. Whitney,
Skt. Gram. § 864.

Class 7.—Nasal Class.

§ 554. The roots of the nasal class all end in a
consonant; the class has for its characteristic feature the
assumption of an internal nasal to form the stem. That
is, the root has a *-na-* (in strong forms), an *-n-* (in weak
forms) inserted immediately before its final consonant to
form the present stem. The root itself retains its weak
grade; the endings are attached directly to the stem.—
Cf. Skt. seventh Class, Whitney, *Skt. Gram.* § 683 seq.

Here belong for example: Av. √*ciš-* 'to announce,
promise' *ci-na-sti;* Av. √*ˀric-* 'to let go' *ˀri-na-ħti* = Skt.
ri-na-kti, and some others—see following paradigm § 555.

Paradigm of Class 7.
(Cf. Whitney, *Skt. Gram.* § 684.)

§ 555. Av. √*ciš-* 'to announce, promise', *cip-* 'to proclaim, think',
mark- (mʒrʒŋc-) 'kill', *kart-* 'to cut', *mis-* 'mingle', *vid-* 'find, receive'. Cf.
Skt. √*chid-* 'to cut'.

§ 556.   1. **Indicative.—a.** Present.

i. ACTIVE.

Av.	Singular:	cf. Skt.
1. *ci-na-hmⁱ* (GAv.)[1]		*chi-ná-dmi*
2. *ci-na-sti*		*chi-ná-tti*

ii. MIDDLE.
Singular:

3. *kʒrʒ-ŋ-tɛ*[2]		*chi-n-tɛ*

Plural:

2. *mʒrʒ-ŋ-gʒ-duyɛ* (GAv.)		*chi-n-ddhvɛ*
3. *mʒrʒ-ŋ-caⁱtɛ* (GAv.)[3]		*chi-n-dátɛ*

---

[1] Cf. § 141. — [2] Vd. 7.38, cf. imperat. *kʒrʒŋtu*, but *kʒrʒŋtaⁱti* a-conj.
as Skt. *kṛntáti.* — [3] Ys. 31.1, *-atɛ* = *-ŋtɛ*.

§ 557.   b. Preterite.

                          i. ACTIVE.

Av.   Singular: cf. Skt.

2. *mi-na-ʃ*[1] . . . . *á-chi-na-t*

3. *ci-na-s*[2] . . . . / . . . . . *á-chi-na-t*

§ 558.   2. Imperative.

                          i. ACTIVE.

Av.   Singular: cf. Skt.

3. *kərᵊ-ŋ-tu*[3] . . . . *chi-ná-ttu*

§ 559.   3. Subjunctive.

                          ii. MIDDLE.

Av.   Plural: cf. Skt.

1. *ci-na-pāmaᵢde*[4] . . . . *chi-ná-dāmahāi*

§ 560.   4. Optative.

i. ACTIVE.   ii. MIDDLE.

Av.   Singular: cf. Skt.   Av.   Singular: cf. Skt.

3. *mərąʃ-yā-ʈ*[5] . . . *chi-n-d-yā-t*   3. *vi-ŋ-dīta*[6] . . . *chi-n-dītá*

§ 561.   5. Participle.

Av.   i. ACTIVE.   cf. Skt.   Av.   ii. MIDDLE. cf. Skt.

vi-ŋ-da(ŋ)t-[7] . . . *chi-n-dánt-*   *vi-ŋ-dəmna-* . . . . *chi-n-dāná-*

Forms to be observed in GAv. and YAv.

§ 562. The form Av. *mərᵊjąŋte* stands perhaps for *°mərᵊ-ŋ-gte* (3 sg. mid.). If so, the formation would be regularly after this (7) class. But the form is quite uncertain.

Transfers to the *a*-Conjugation.

§ 563. The stem *mərᵊŋc-* 'kill' has practically become stereotyped as a root according to the *a*-conj. by transfer; hence the thematic forms:—Pres. Act. 3 sg. *mərᵊncaⁱti*; 3 pl. *mərᵊncinti*;—Mid. 3 sg. *mərᵊncaⁱte*, 3 pl. *mərᵊncaṇte* (above).—Imperat. Mid. 2 sg. *mərᵊncavuha*.

§ 564. The root GAv. *marᵈ-* (as *mōrᵊṇd-* § 39) 'to destroy' has likewise become practically crystallized according to *a*-conj.: ·Pret. Act. 3 sg. *mōrᵊṇdaṭ*, 3 pl. *mōrᵊṇdən* (on -ö-, cf. § 39 end).

---

[1] i. e. *mi-na-s-s*, § 158. — [2] i. e. *ci-na-s-t*, § 192. — [3] Vd. 7.38, weak form I — [4] *a*-conj. by transfer as in Skt. — [5] On -rą- = *r* + *n*, see § 49. On *ʃ*, cf. § 162. — [6] Yt. 17.54, with variant *viṇdīta (i)*. — [7] In compounds.

§ 565. Similar instances of stereotyped forms and transfer to
a-conjugation as also in Skt., are: Av. 2 *vid-* 'find, obtain' *(viṇd-,* like Skt.
vi-n-d-á-ti) vi-ṇ-d-ə-ṇ-ti (3 pl. indic.), *vi-n-d-ā-iti* (3 sg. subjunct. Vd. 13.36)
beside unthematic *vi-na-stī* (GAv.), *vi-ŋ-dīta* (YAv. opt. above).—Likewise
Av. *kart-* 'to cut' *(kərəṇt-,* like Skt. *kṛ-n-t-á-ti) kərə-ṇ-t-aiti* (3 sg. indicative), *kərə-ṇ-t-a-ţ* (pret.).—Also some others.

Note. Peculiar is 2 sing. pret. act. *mərəṇcainiī* 'thou didst destroy'
—weak nasalized root with added *an (= ŋn).* On *-iš = iš* cf. § 527 end.

Class 5.—*nu*-Class.

§ 566. The verbs of this class are not numerous.
The root adds *nao-* (in the strong forms), *nu- nv-* (in the
weak forms) to make the present stem. The root itself
retains its weak grade.

Here belong for example: Av. √*kar-* 'to make'
kərə-nao-iti = Skt. *kṛ-nó-ti;* Av. √*sru-* 'to hear' *suru-*
nao-iti = Skt. *śr-ṇó-ti;* Av. √*as-* 'to attain' *aš-nao-iti*
= Skt. *aś-nó-ti;* and a few others.

Paradigm of Class 5.
(Cf. Whitney, *Skt. Gram.* § 698.)

§ 567. Av. √*kar-* 'to make', *var-* 'cover choose', *dab-* 'deceive',
hu- 'press', *sri-* 'give over', *sru-* 'hear'.—Cf. Skt. √*kr-.*

§ 568.   1. **Indicative.**—a. Present.

i. ACTIVE.

Av.	Singular:		cf. Skt.
1. *kərə-nao-mi*	. . . . . .	. .	*kṛ-ṇó-mi*
2. *kərə-nū-ši*[1]	. . . . . .	. .	*kṛ-ṇó-ṣi*
3. *kərə-nao-iti*	. . . . . .	. .	*kṛ-ṇó-ti*

Plural:

3. *kərə-nav-aṇti*[2]	. . . . . .	. .	*kṛ-ṇv-áṇti*

ii. MIDDLE.

Singular:

3. *varə-nū-ite*	. . . . . .	. .	*kṛ-ṇu-tė*

Dual:

3. *varə-nv-aitē* (GAv.)[3]	. . . . .	. .	*kṛ-ṇv-āitė*

---

[1] On *a,* cf. § 60 Note b. — [2] Yt. 13.26, so metrically. Cf. § 68
Note 3. — [3] Ys. 31.17.

Av.	Plural:	cf. Skt.
3. *vərᵊ-nv-aⁱṇte*[1]		*kṛ-ṇv-átē*

§ 569.   b. Preterite.

i. ACTIVE.

Av.	Singular:	cf. Skt.
3. *kərᵊ-nao-ṭ*		*á-kṛ-ṇŏ-t*
	Plural:	
2. *dᵊbᵊnao-tā* (GAv.)[2]		*á-kṛ-ṇŏ-ta*

ii. MIDDLE.

3. *hu-nū-ta*		*á-kṛ-ṇu-ta*

§ 570.   2. Imperative.

i. ACTIVE.

Av.	Singular:	cf. Skt.
3. *kərᵊ-nū-ᵢdi*		*kṛ-ṇu-hí*
	Plural:	
2. *sⁱri-nao-ta*[3]		*kṛ-ṇŏ-ta*

§ 571.   3. Subjunctive.

i. ACTIVE.

Av.	Singular:	cf. Skt.
1. *kərᵊ-nav-āni*		*kṛ-ṇáv-āni*
	Plural:	
3. *kərᵊ-nāu-n*[4]		*kṛ-ṇáv-an*

ii. MIDDLE.
Singular:

1. *kərᵊ-nav-āne*		*kṛ-ṇáv-ăi*

§ 572.   4. Optative.

i. ACTIVE.

Av.	Singular:	cf. Skt.
2. *sᵘru-nu-yās*		*kṛ-ṇu-yās*
3. *kərᵊ-nu-yāṭ*		*kṛ-ṇu-yāt*

§ 573.   5. Participle.

i. ACTIVE. Av. *hu-nv-a(ṇ)t-*	*kṛ-ṇv-á(n)t-*
ii. MIDDLE. *hu-nv-ana-*	*kṛ-ṇv-āná-*

---

[1] After *a*-conj. — [2] Ys. 32.5, from str. st. form, cf. Whitney, *Skt. Gram.* § 707. — [3] Str. stem form, as Skt. *kṛṇóta*, Whitney, *Skt. Gram.* § 704. — [4] On -*āun*, cf. § 64.

Forms to be observed in GAv. and YAv.

§ 574. Instances of **transfer** to the *a*-conj. (beside the 3 pl. above) are not infrequent:—

1. Indicative. i. ACT. a. Pres. YAv. *vɔrɔ-nav-a-ⁱti* 'he covers'. —b. Pret. *kɔrɔ-nav-ō* 'thou didst make'.

2. Imperative. i. ACT. YAv. *kɔrɔ-nav-a* 'make thou'.—II. MID. YAv. *hu-nv-aʋuha* 'press thou'.

3. Subjunctive. i. ACT. YAv. *kɔrɔ-nav-ā-hi*, *kɔrɔ-nav-āṭ*, *kɔrɔ-nav-ąn* 'if thou, he, they make'.

§ 575. On instances of *kar-* made up after class 9, see below § 591.

Class 8.—*u*-Class.

§ 576. The eigth class (Skt. *tan*-class, Whitney, *Skt. Gram.* § 697 seq.) is hardly more than a variety of the preceding (5) class. It comprises, however, enough roots to be distinguishable. The present-stem is made by adding to the root *ao-, av-* (in the str. forms), *u-, v-* (in the wk. forms).

Included under this class are the roots: Av. √*tan-* 'to stretch' = Skt. √*tan-*; Av. √*in-* 'drive' = Skt. √*in-*. Likewise here, parts of Av. √*āp-* 'to reach' = Skt. √*āp-*; Av. √*jžar-* 'flow' (pres. participle), cf. Skt. √*kṣar-*; Av. √*har-* 'protect'.

Paradigm of Class 8.
(Cf. Whitney, *Skt. Gram.* § 698 b.)

§ 577. Av. √*in-* 'to drive', *tan-* 'stretch', *van-* 'strike', *jžar-* 'flow', *jžan-* 'destroy'.—Cf. Skt. √*tan-* 'to stretch'.

§ 578.   1. Indicative.—a. Present.

i. ACTIVE.

Av.	Singular:	cf. Skt.
3. *in-ao-ⁱti*		*tan-ó-ti*
	Plural:	
2. *spaʃ-u-ʃā* ¹ (?)		*tan-u-thá*

ii. MIDDLE.

	Plural:	
3. *āʃ-ɔŋte* ²		*tan-v-átē*

---

¹ Uncertain; Ys. 53.6. — ² i. e. *°āp-v-ante* after *a*-conj. On *ʃ*, see § 95.

§ 579.   3. Subjunctive.
                                  i. ACTIVE.
              Av.   Singular: cf. Skt.
    1. *tan-av-a*   . . . .   *tan-āv-ā* (Ved.)

§ 580.   4. Optative.
        i. ACTIVE.   ii. MIDDLE.
   Av.   Singular: cf. Skt.   Av.   Singular: cf. Skt.
3. *van-u-yāṭ* . . . . *tan-u-yāt*   1. *tan-u-ya* [1] . . . . *tan-v-īyá*

§ 581.   5. Participle.
   Av.   i. ACTIVE.   cf. Skt.   Av.   ii. MIDDLE.   cf. Skt.
jᵋar-v-a(n)t- . . . *tan-v-á(n)t-*   *jᵋōn-v-amna* [2] . . . *tan-v-āná*

Forms to be observed.

§ 582.   1. Indic. Pres. Act. 3 sg. *haᵘr-v-aⁱti* (after *a*-conjuga-
tion).—Mid. 3 pl. *fyaᵛuṇtaᵈ-ca* 'and they rain' (i. e. *fyaᵛh-v-aṇtē* § 63).

Class 9.—*nā*-Class.

§ 583. In the ninth class *nā*- is added to the root
to form the strong present-stem; *n*-, *na*- (i. e. *n* + *a*-conj.) is
added to make the weak pres. stem. The form *na*- (i. e.
a-conj.) is commoner than *n*-. The endings are attached
directly; the root itself retains its weak grade.

The Skt. ninth class likewise adds *nā*- in the strong
forms, but *n*-, *nī*- (i. e. *nⁱ* before cons.) in the weak. — Cf.
Whitney, *Skt. Gram.* § 717 seq., esp. § 731.

Here belong: Av. √*frī*- 'to love' *frī-nā-mi* = Skt.
prī-nā-mi; Av. √*garw*- 'to seize' *gərᵊw-nā-ⁱti* = Skt.
grbh-nā-ti; Av. √*var*- 'to choose' *vərᵊ-n-tē* = Skt. *vr̥-*
nī-té; Av. √*gar*- 'to sing' *gərᵊ-n-te* = Skt. *gr̥-nī-té*.
Likewise some others—see following paradigm § 584.

Paradigm of Class 9.
(Cf. Whitney, *Skt. Gram.* § 718).

§ 584. Av. √*frī*- 'to love', *garw*- 'seize', *var*- 'choose', *hu*- 'to
press', *par*- 'fight'.—Cf. Skt. √*prī*- 'to please', √*var*- 'to choose'.

---

[1] cf. Skt. *tan-v-ī-ya* § 62. — [2] Like *a*-conj., *-amna*. On *ō*, cf. § 39.

§ 585.   1. Indicative.—a. Present.

i. ACTIVE.

Av.	Singular:	cf. Skt.
1. *frī-nā-mi*	. . . .	*prī-ṇá-mi*
3. *gərᵊw-nā-iti*	. . . .	*prī-ṇd-ti*

	Plural:	
1. *fry-ą-mahī* (GAv.)[1]	. . . .	*prī-ṇī-masi*
3. *frī-n-əṇti*	. . . .	*prī-ṇ-ánti*

ii. MIDDLE.
Singular:

1. *vərᵊ-n-e*	. . . .	*vṛ-ṇ-é*
3. *vərᵊ-ṇ-tē*	. . . . .	*vṛ-ṇī-té*

§ 586.   b. Preterite.

i. ACTIVE.

Av.	Singular:	cf. Skt.
3. *miþ-nā-ṭ*	. . . .	*á-prī-ṇā-t*

ii. MIDDLE.
Singular:

3. *fraorᵊ-ṇ-ta*[2]	. . . .	*á-vṛ-ṇī-ta*

	Plural:	
3. *vərᵊ-n-ātā* (GAv.)[3]	. . . .	*á-vṛ-ṇ-ata*

§ 587.   2. Imperative.

i. ACTIVE.

Av.	Plural:	cf. Skt.
3. *frī-n-əṇtu*	. . . . . .	*prī-ṇ-ántu*

§ 588.   3. Subjunctive.

i. ACTIVE.

Av.	Singular:	cf. Skt.
1. *frī-nā-ni*	. . . . . .	*prī-ṇd-ni*
3. { *hu-nā-itī* (GAv.)	. . . .	*prī-ṇd-ti*
{ *frī-nā-ṭ*	. . . . . .	*prī-ṇā-t*

	Plural:	
3. *gərᵊw-ną-n*	. . . .	*prī-ṇd-n*

---

[1] i. e. *frī-ṇ-mahi* or *fry-ṇn-mahi*. — [2] Ys. 57.24; Yt. 10.92, i. e. *fra-vərᵊ-ṇ-ta*, cf. § 62.2. — [3] i. e. *vərᵊ-n-ạta.

ii. MIDDLE.

Av.	Singular:	cf. Skt.
I. { *pərə-nā-ne*	. . . .	—
{ *frī-nāi* .	. . . . . .	*prī-ṇāi*
3. *pərə-nā-ite*	. . . .	*prī-ṇá-tāi*

	Plural:	
3. *vərə-nǣ-ṇte* [1]	. . . . . .	*vṛ-ṇá-ntāi*

§ 589.   5. Participle.

ii. MIDDLE. Av. *frī-n-əmna-* [2] . . .   *prī-ṇ-āná-*

Forms to be observed.

§ 590. The weak forms in *na-* (i. e. *a*-conjugation by transfer) are frequent; the instances of 3 pl. thus formed are noted above. Other examples of this transfer *(-n-a)* are given in the next section § 591.

§ 591. The transfers to the *a*-conjugation with weak stem *(na)* are:

     1. Indicative. i. ACT. a. Pres. *hu-n-a-hi* 'thou pressest', *frī-n-a-iti*, *frī-n-ā-mahi*, *frī-n-ṇti* (above).—ii. MID. *kərə-n-ṇte* 'they make, cut'.—b. Pret. i. ACT. *kərə-n-əm* 'I made, cut', *sa-n-a-ṭ* 'it appeared' (i. e. *sad-n-aṭ* § 185) Yt. 14.7.—ii. MID. *stərə-n-a-ta* 'he strewed'.

     2. Imperative. i. ACT. GAv. *pərə-n-ā* 'fulfil thou' Yt. 28.10, YAv. *miþ-n-a-tu* 'let him turn', *frī-n-ṇtu* (above).—ii. MID. *brī-n-a-ṇuha* 'cut thou'.

     4. Optative. i. ACT. *kərə-n-ōi-ṭ*, *ᵃra-n-aē-mā* (GAv.) 'we might anger' Ys. 28.9, *stərə-n-ay-ṇ* 'let them strew'.—ii. MID. *stərə-n-aē-ta* 'let him strew'.

II. PERFECT-SYSTEM.
Perfect.
(Cf. Whitney, *Skt. Gram.* § 780 seq.)

§ 592. **General Remark.** The chief characteristic of the perfect is the reduplication; the endings also differ in some respects from those of the present-system; the perfect shows likewise a distinction of strong and weak forms. As to signification, the perfect (and pluperfect) as

---

[1] Vd. 5.59. — [2] *-əmna* like *a*-conj.

in Skt. commonly denotes simple past time; sometimes present time is expressed.

Note 1.   An assumed periphrastic form of the perfect sporadically occurs, see § 623.

Note 2.   On the absence of reduplication, see § 620.

Reduplicated Syllable.

§ 593. The principal points to be observed in regard to reduplication of the vowels (cf. Whitney, *Skt. Gram.* § 783) are:

1. Internal or final *a* or *ā* is regularly reduplicated by *a* (sometimes by *ā*—cf. Whitney, *Skt. Gram.* § 786a), occasionally by *i*. For example—

> Av. *ta-taš-a* 'he has formed' ($\sqrt{taš}$-) = Skt. *ta-tákṣ-a*; Av. *da-dā-ṗa* 'thou hast created' ($\sqrt{dā}$-) = Skt. *da-dhā-tha*; Av. *dā-darᵊs-a* 'I have seen' ($\sqrt{dars}$-) = Skt. *da-dárs-a*; Av. *cā-ḫr-arᵊ* 'they have made' ($\sqrt{kar}$-) = Skt. *ca-kr-úr*; GAv. *vā-vᵊrᵊz-ōi* 'he has worked' (mid.) $\sqrt{varz}$-; Av. *ji-gaᵘrv-a* (observe palatal *j* § 465c) 'I have perceived' ($\sqrt{garw}$-) = Skt. *ja-grdbh-a*.

2. Internal or final *i, u* or *ī, ū* are reduplicated by *i, u* (sometimes *ī, ū*). For example—

> Av. *di-dvaẕ-a* 'I have hated' ($\sqrt{dviš}$-) = Skt. *di-dvẕ-a*; Av. *di-day-a* 'he has seen' ($\sqrt{dī}$-) = Skt. *dī-dhay-a*; Av. *tu-tav-a* 'he has been able' ($\sqrt{tū}$-) = Skt. *tu-tāv-a*.

Note. Worthy of remark is Av. *bā-bv-arᵊ* (with *ā* from $\sqrt{bū}$- 'to be') Yt. 13.150 = Skt. *ba-bhūv-úr*, but Av. *bvāva* (i. e. *bu-vāv-a*, Yt. 13.2, cf. § 68b = Skt. *ba-bhūv-a*.

3. Initial *a* by reduplication with itself becomes *ā*. For example—

> Av. *ā-ṅh-a* 'he has been' ($\sqrt{ah}$-) = Skt. *ā-s-a*.

4. Initial *i* (or *u* if found) is reduplicated by *» y* i. e. *i-y* (or *u* i. e. *u-v*), cf. § 68a.

> Av. *𐬫𐬉𐬫𐬃* *yeyą* (i. e. *iy-ay-ąn*) 'they may have come' Ys. 42.6 ($\sqrt{i}$- subjunct. *a*-inflect. if not redupl. pres.). So also *𐬫𐬀𐬉𐬫𐬀* *yaẕa* i. e. *iyaẕa* Yt. 13.99.

§ 594. The laws for the reduplication of consonants have been sufficiently treated above, § 465c.

Radical Syllable.
Strong and weak Stem-Forms.

§ 595. The strong stem or guṇa-form of the radical syllable, as in the non-*a*-conjugation (unthematic), is found in the perfect-system 1) in the Indicative Act. 1, 2, 3 sg. Pres. Pret.; 2) in the Imperative Act. 3 sg.; 3) in the Subjunctive entire. The remaining forms are weak. But numerous fluctuations in this rule occur.

Note. In GAv., as in Vedic Skt., medial short *a* before a single consonant is lengthened to *ā* in the radical syllable of the 3 sg. pf. act. For YAv. no rule is laid down.—Cf. Whitney, *Skt. Gram.* § 793 c. Thus, GAv. *nə̄-nās-a* 'it is lost' ($\sqrt{nas}$-) = Skt. *na-nāś-a*.

§ 596. With reference to the weak forms, some observations as regards the radical syllable may be made. An internal or final *i, u* remains unchanged e. g. *irī-riþ-arə* 'they lie' ($\sqrt{riþ}$-), *su-sru-ye* 'I have heard' ($\sqrt{sru}$-) Yt. 17.17, yet *sū-srū-ma* 'we have heard' Yt. 13.198; but a number of roots having medial *a* between single consonants (cf. Whitney, *Skt. Gram.* § 794 e) and certain others, by loss of the vowel in weak forms may undergo some change:

1. Roots in -*ar* show weak forms in -*r*- before vowels: Av. *ba-wr-arə* 'they bore' ($\sqrt{bar}$-), beside GAv. *vā-vərəz-ōi* 'he worked' 3 sg. pf. mid. ($\sqrt{varz}$- i. e. two cons.).

2. Roots in -*am*, -*an* show weak forms in -*m*-, -*n*-: Av. *ja-ɣm-yąm* 'I would have come' ($\sqrt{gam}$-); GAv. *cā-ḫn-arə* 'they have desired' ($\sqrt{kan}$-).

3. Roots with initial *ya*-, *va*- by contraction with the reduplicated syllable show in the weak forms *yaē*- (*yōi*-), *vao*- (*vāu*-) i. e. *ya-i*-, *va-u*-: Av. $\sqrt{yat}$- 'to strive' makes 1 pl. act. YAv. *yaēþma*, GAv. *yōiþmā* (i. e. *ya-yt-ma*, *ya-it-ma*); Av. $\sqrt{van}$- 'win' makes 3 pl. act. *vaonarə* (i. e. *va-vn-ar*, *va-un-ar*). Cf. § 63 seq.

4. Roots with radical final *ā* lose this *ā* before endings beginning with a vowel, so also before endings where Skt. shows the union-vowel *i*, Whitney, *Skt. Gram.* § 794 end: Av. $\sqrt{stā}$- 'to stand', *hi-št-a* 1, 3 sg. pf. act.; $\sqrt{dā}$- 'give, place', *da-d-a* 3 sg. act., *da-ið-e* 3 sg. mid.; *da-d-vā* ptcpl. (Skt. *da-d-i-vąs* or *da-d-vąs*).

Personal Endings
and their connection with the Stem.

§ 597. The endings of the perfect, especially in the middle voice, are mostly primary. They are attached directly to the tense-stem as in the unthematic conjugation; sporadic traces of a 'union-vowel' *i, ə* (cf. Whitney, *Skt. Gram.* § 797 seq.) perhaps however exist. See Bartholomae, *A.F.* ii. p. 97.

§ 598. The endings agree with those of the Skt.; some forms however are to be specially observed, see below § 599 seq.

Perfect Endings.

	I. ACTIVE.			II. MIDDLE.	
Av.	Singular:	cf. Skt.	Av.	Singular:	cf. Skt.
1. *-a*	. . . .	*-a*	*-e*	. . . .	*-ə*
2. *-þa*	. . . .	*-tha*	—	. . . .	*-sə*
3. *-a*	. . . .	*-a*	*-e*	. . . .	*-ə*
	Dual:			Dual:	
1. —	. . . .	*-va*	—	. . . .	*-vahə*
2. —	. . .	*-athur*	—	. . . .	*-āthə*
3. *-atarə*	. . . .	*-atur*	*-aitē* (GAv.), *-tē*		*-ātē*
	Plural:			Plural:	
1. *-ma*	. . .	*-ma*	—	. . . .	*-mahə*
2. *-a*	. . .	*-a*	—	. .	*-dhvē*
3. *-arə, -ərəš*	. . .	*-ur*	—	. . . .	*-rē*

Perfect Endings (Observations).

§ 599. Singular:—

First Person: II. MIDDLE. A 1st. sg. mid. form in *-ð* (i. e. *-āu* § 54 = Skt. *-āu*) from a root ending in long *ā* is perhaps to be found in *dadō* 'I have made' Ys. 10.9 = Skt. *dadhāu*, Whitney, *Skt. Gram.* § 800 e.

Second Person: I. ACTIVE. Note the form *-ta* (for *-þa* § 78 end) after *s* in GAv. *vōistā* 'thou knowest'.

§ 600. Dual:—

Third Person: II. MIDDLE. Observe the suffix *-tē* 3 du. mid. in GAv. *dazdē* 'they both created' Ys. 30.4 (i. e. *dhazdhai, dha-dh-tai*), cf. Bartholomae, *K.Z.* xxix. p. 285 = *Flexionslehre* p. 16.

§ 601. **Plural:—**

Third Person: i. ACTIVE. The ending *-ərəš* (above) beside *-arə* is found in GAv. *ci-kōit-ərəš* 'they have thought, taught' Ys. 32.11.

Pluperfect (Preterite).

(Cf. Whitney, *Skt. Gram.* § 817 seq.)

§ 602. The existence of a preterite (pluperfect) indicative corresponding to the present perfect, seems to be shown by a few forms. There is, however, some uncertainty, see Note. The forms here recognized as pluperfect are made by adding the secondary endings directly to the perfect stem. The strong stem appears in the singular active; the weak stem elsewhere. The thematic *a* (transferring to the *a*-inflection) is sometimes found.—Cf. Whitney, *Skt. Gram.* § 817 seq.

Note. There is much difficulty in distinguishing a pluperfect from some other reduplic. forms. Some of the examples may equally well be referred to other forms (impf., aor.) of the redupl. preterite.

Mode-Formation of the Perfect.

§ 603. The perfect like the other tense-systems shows an indicative (pres. perf.; pret. pluperf.), imperative, subjunctive (prim. and sec.), optative and participle (cf. Whitney, *Skt. Gram.* § 808 seq.). These are formed as in the non-*a*-conjugation (unthematic); the subjunctive has the strong stem + mode-sign *a*; the optative has the weak stem + *-yā-*, *-ī-*.

§ 604. A number of transfers to the *a*-inflection instead of the thematic are found in pluperfect, imperat., subjunct., optative, and participle. See § 619.

Paradigm of the Perfect-System.

(Cf. Whitney, *Skt. Gram.* § 800 seq.)

§ 605. Examples of the inflection of the perfect may be taken from the following roots:—

Av. √*garw-* 'to seize' = Skt. √*grabh-;* Av. √*dviš-* 'hate' = Skt. √*dviṣ-;* Av. √ı *rud-* 'grow' = Skt. √ı *rudh-;* Av. √*dars-* 'see'

= Skt. √*darš-;* Av. √*dā-* 'give, make' = Skt. √*dā-, dhā-;* Av.
√*kan-* 'love' = Skt. √*kan-;* Av. √*tu-* 'be able' = Skt. √*tu-;* Av.
√*dar-* 'hold' = Skt. √*dhar-;* Av. √*sru-* 'hear' = Skt. √*sru-;*
Av. √*yat-* 'strain, strive' = Skt. √*yat-;* Av. √*han-* 'earn' = Skt.
√*san-;* Av. √*bar-* 'bear' = Skt. √*bhar-;* Av. √*kar-* 'make' =
Skt. √*kar-;* Av. √*pru-* 'support, nourish'; Av. √*man-* 'think' =
Skt. √*man-;* Av. √*dī-* 'consider, see' = Skt. √*dhī-;* Av. √*2 rud-*
'obstruct' = Skt. √*2 rudh;* Av. √*sac-* 'learn, can' = Skt. *šac-;*
Av. √*qs-, as-* 'attain' = Skt. *qš-, aš-;* Av. √*vaz-* 'carry' = Skt.
√*vah-;* Av. √*ar-* 'go, rise' = Skt. √*ar-;* Av. √*har-* 'protect';
Av. √*ah-* 'be' = Skt. √*as-;* Av. √*vraz-* 'proceed'; Av. √*gam-*
'go, come' = Skt. √*gam-;* Av. √*van-* 'strive, contend, win' =
Skt. √*van-.*

§ 606. 1. Indicative.—a. Perfect (Present).

i. ACTIVE.

	Av. Singular:		cf. Skt.
1.	*ji-gaᵘrv-a, di-dvaēš-a*	. .	*ja-grābh-a, di-dvēš-a*
	ᵘrū-raod-a, dā-darᵊs-a	. .	*ru-rōdh-a, da-darš-a*
2.	*da-dā-þa* [1]		*da-d(h)ā-tha*
3.	*ca-kan-a, tū-tav-a*	. .	*cā-kan-a, tū-tāv a*
	da-dār-a		*da-dhār-a, dā-dhār-a*

Dual:

3.	*yaēt-atarᵊ* [2] .	. . .	*(yēt-atur)*

Plural:

1.	*di-dvīš-ma* [3], *sū-srū-ma*	. .	*di-dviš-i-má, vi-viš-má*
	yaēþ-ma [4]		*(yēt-i-má)*
2.	*ha-vhān-a*		—
3.	*ba-wr-arᵊ, cā-hr-arᵊ*		*ja-bhr-úr, cā-kr-úr*

ii. MIDDLE.
Singular:

1.	*su-sruy-e*		*šu-šruv-ē*
3.	*tu-þruy-e*		*šu-šruv-ē*

Dual:

3.	*ma-man-āitē* [5]		*ma-mn-ātē*
	da-z-dē [6]		

---

[1] Ys. 71.10. — [2] *ZPhl. Gloss.* p. 56.11. — [3] On *ī* after *v* cf. § 20. —
[4] cf. § 596.3. — [5] Ys. 13.4, Bartholomae, *K.Z.* xxix. p. 288 = *Flexionslehre*
p. 17, 19. — [6] GAv. Ys. 30.4, cf. § 600.

§ 607.   b. Pluperfect (Preterite).

i. ACTIVE.

Av.	Singular:	cf. Skt.
1. *di-ḍaē-m*[1]	. . . . . .	*a-ja-grabh-am*[2]
3. *urū-raos-t*[3]	. . . . . .	*a-ci-kǝ-t*

Plural:

3. *sa-šk-ǝn*[4] .	. . . .	—

ii. MIDDLE.
Singular:

3. *ǝn-āḫš-tā* (GAv.)[5]	. . . . .	—

Plural:

3. *vaoz-i-rǝm*[6] .	. . . . .	—

§ 608.   2. Imperative.

i. ACTIVE.

Av.	Singular:	cf. Skt.
3. *ni-ša-vhar-a-tū*[7]	. . . .	—

ii. MIDDLE.

2. *ārǝ-ǧvā* (GAv.).	. . . . . .	—[8]

§ 609.   3. Subjunctive.

i. ACTIVE.
Plural:

1. *ǡvh-āma*[9]	. . . . . .	*ās-āma*
2. *vaorāz-a-þā* (GAv.)	. . . . .	*va-vraj-a-tha*

ii. MIDDLE.
Plural:

3. *ǡvh-a-ire*[10]	. . . .	—

§ 610.   4. Optative.

i. ACTIVE.

Av.	Singular:	cf. Skt.
1. *ja-ɟm-yąm*	. . . . . .	*ja-gam-yām*
2. *tū-tu-yǡ*[11]	. . . . . .	*tū-tu-yās*
3. *vaon-yąṭ*	. . . . . .	*ma-man-yāt*

---

[1] Can as well be redupl. pret. Cl. 3. — [2] cf. Whitney, *Skt. Gram.*
§ 818a. — [3] Skt. √*rudh-*, cf. § 151. — [4] Ys. 53.1 i. e. *saškǝn-cā.* — [5] cf.
Bartholomae, *B.B.* xiii. p. 65. — [6] cf. §§ 455, 616. — [7] Ys. 58.4, *a*-inflect.
by transfer, Whitney, *Skt. Gram.* § 814. — [8] cf. Whitney, *Skt. Gram.* § 813
end. — [9] cf. *a*-inflect. — [10] Ys. 9.23, cf. § 452, v. l. *ǡvhāirǝ.* — [11] Ys. 9.29,
used as 3 sg.

§ 611.   **5. Participle.**   cf. Skt.

i. ACTIVE. Av. *ha-vhan-vah-* . . . . *sa-san-vás-*

ii. MIDDLE. *ha-vhan-ana-* . . . . *sa-san-ãná-*

Forms to be observed in GAv. and YAv.

1. Indicative. a. Perfect.

§ 612.   Singular:—

First Person: ii. MID. GAv., add *ãrõi* 'I have earned' (√*ar-*) Ys. 33.9,
    on -*õi-* cf. § 56.—On a possible 1st. sg. mid. in -*õ* (i. e. -*ãu*) = Skt.
    -*ãu*, from √*dã-*, see § 599 above.

Third Person: i. ACT. Observe radical *ã* in (root with medial *a* before
    one consonant) GAv. *nãnãsã* 'it is lost', YAv. *dadãra* 'he fixed'—
    see § 595 Note, but likewise *ã*, YAv. *cakãna* 'he loved' (√*kan-*),
    yayãta 'he strove' (√*yat-*), *bavãra* 'he bore' (√*bar-*).—Again from
    weak stem (final radical *ã* lost before vowels, § 596.4) *da-ã-a* 'he
    made' (√*dã-*).—ii. MID. GAv. also (with strengthened reduplication)
    vã-vᵊrᵊz-õi 'he has worked', cf. § 56.—Add GAv. *ãraᵉ-cã* 'has been
    earned' (√*ar-*) Ys. 56.3.

§ 613.   Dual:—

Third Person: i. ACT. GAv. (note -*ã*-) *vaocãtarᵊ* 'they both have spoken',
    vãvᵊrᵊzãtarᵊ 'they both have done' Ys. 13.4.

§ 614.   Plural:—

First Person: i. ACT. GAv., note *yõiᵖᵊmã* 'we strive' (-*õi-* § 56) beside
    YAv. *yaᵉpma* above.

Second Person: i. ACT. YAv., note the long *ã* strongest stem in *havhãna*
    above in paradigm.

Third Person: i. ACT. YAv. from weak stem (final radical *ã* lost before
    vowels § 596.4) and str. redupl. *dã-d-arᵊ* 'they made' (√*dã-*) = Skt.
    dadhúr.—Likewise note (§ 62.2) YAv. *vaonarᵊ*, GAv. *vaonarᵊ* 'they
    strove' (i. e. *va-vn-ar* § 596.3).—Long redupl. syl. *cã-ḫr-arᵊ* 'they have
    made' Vd. 4.46.—GAv. also (suffix -*ᵊrᵊʃ*) *ci-kõit-ᵊrᵊʃ* 'they thought'.

b. Pluperfect.

§ 615.   Singular:—

Third Person: ii. MID. GAv. *ᵊnãḫᵗã* (in paradigm, see Foot-Note) pre-
    sents 'Attic reduplication'.

§ 616.   Plural:—

Third Person: ii. MID. YAv. *vaozirᵊm* (i. e. *va-vz-i-rᵊm* √*vaz-*) above in
    paradigm shows 3 pl. ending in -*rᵊm* = Skt. -*ram* (cf. Whitney,
    Skt. Gram. §§ 834 b, 867) with connecting vowel. See above
    § 455 end.

4. Optative.

§ 617. **Plural:—**
First Person: i. ACT. YAv., perhaps here *daidyama* Yt. 24.58.

5. Participle.

§ 618. i. ACT. On inflectional forms of the pf. act. ptcpl. see §§ 349, 350.—ii. MID. Also suffix *-āna* (beside *-āna*) *vavazāna-* 'driven', *dadrāna-*, *dadrāna-* 'held'.

Transitions to the thematic *(a)* inflection.

§ 619. A number of transfers to the *a*-inflection occur cf. § 604.

1. Indicative. i. ACT. b. Pluperf. **Sg.** 3. YAv. *ta-tai-a-ṭ* 'he formed'; *ja-ym-a-ṭ.*

2. Imperative. i. ACT. **Sg.** 3. GAv. *ni-iavhar-a-tū* (in paradigm).

3. Subjunctive. i. ACT. **Sg.** 3. YAv. *āvhāṭ* 'may be'; Du. 3. *āvhātəm* Yt. 13.12; Pl. 3. *iyeyq (iieiiq = °iy-ay-a-an)* 'they may go' (√*i*-) Ys. 42.6 (if not desiderative).—ii. MID. Pl. 3. YAv. *āvhāire* Yt. 10.45, cf. §§ 452, 486.

Absence of Reduplication.

§ 620. In Av., as in Skt., the absence of a reduplicated syllable is met with in a number of cases. This is familiar in *vaēda* 'οἶδα' = Skt. *vēda,* and in some other forms.—Cf. Whitney, *Skt. Gram.* § 790.

§ 621. As example of perf. lacking reduplication may be given G(Y)Av. √*vid-* 'to know' = Skt. √*vid-*.

1. Indic. a. Perf. **Sg.** 1. *vaēdā,* 2. *vōistā,* 3. *vaēdā, vaēda* (YAv.).
2. Imperat. Pl. 2. *vōizdūm* Ys. 33.8.
3. Subjunct. **Sg.** 1. *vaēdā* Ys. 48.9; Pl. 2. *vaēdōdūm* (§ 39).
4. Optat. **Sg.** 3. *vīdyāṭ.*
5. Partic. i. ACT. *vīdvah-* (GAv.), *vīdvah-* (YAv.).—ii. MID. *vaēdəna-* Ys. 34.7, *vaēdəmna-* (themat.).

§ 622. Other examples of pf. wanting redupl. are: GAv. √*cag-* 'grant', *cag°mā* (1 pl. pf. act.), *cag°dō* (3 du. plpf.), *cagvā* (ptcpl.). — Also GAv. *apānō* 'attained' (ptcpl. √*ap-*).

Periphrastic Perfect.

§ 623. In YAv. traces of a periphrasis which may be construed as forming a perfect are found.—Cf. also Whitney, *Skt. Gram.* §§ 1070, 1072. In Av. the acc. sg. fem. of the pres. participle is united with the perfect of the auxiliary *ah-* to be:—

> YAv. *sraēšyeiⁿtīm āṇhāṭ* 'it may have clung' (subjunct.), *āstarayeiⁿtīm āṇhāṭ* 'should have corrupted'.—Perhaps also here *biwivāṇha* 'he had frightened' Yt. 19.48,50 (? nom. sg. ptcpl. $\sqrt{bi}$- + *āṇha*, cf. variants).

III. AORIST-SYSTEM.
Aorist.
(Chiefly found in Gāthā Avesta.)

§ 624. **General Remark.** In regard to form the aorist in Av. may perhaps best be defined as a preterite, whose exact corresponding present is missing and which consequently attaches itself to an analogous present and preterite, and forms a new system subordinate to these.

In regard to meaning the aorist in Avesta commonly denotes a simple past action, usually but not always momentary. It may often, as in Skt., be rendered by our 'have'.

The instances of aorist formation are found chiefly in the Gāthā portions of the literature, but occurences in the later parts are by no means uncommon.

> Note. The resemblance in form which the aorist bears to the preterite (imperfect) sometimes gives rise to question whether certain given forms are to be classed as preterite (imperfect) or as aorist; the decision depends chiefly upon whether or not we assume a present to the form— e. g. cf. Bartholomae, *Verbum* p. 63 seq.

§ 625. Two groups of aorists may conveniently be distinguished; they are 1. non-sigmatic, 2. sigmatic. These comprise several sub-varieties of formation (7 as in Skt.), as follows.—Cf. Whitney, *Skt. Gram.* § 824.

Aorist-System
{
i. Non-Sigmatic
{
1. Root-aorist.
2. Simple *a*-aorist (thematic).
3. Reduplicated aorist.
}

ii. Sigmatic
{
4. *h- (s-)* aorist.
5. *ha- (sa-)* aorist (or *h*-thematic).
6. *iš*-aorist,
7. *hiš*-aorist.
}
}

§ 626. **Augment and Endings.** The a u g m e n t in aorist forms as elsewhere in Av. is commonly m i s s i n g; the augmentless forms, moreover, often have a subjunctive (imperative) signification (cf. § 445 Note 2 injunctive). The e n d i n g s in the indicative are the s e c o n d a r y.

§ 627. **Modes of the Aorist.** The m o d e s—imperative, subjunctive (prim., sec.), optative—of the aorist are formed according to the regular laws of the other systems.

Note. Observe the existence of a form 3 sg. i m p e r a t. mid. in -*q m* = Skt. -*ăm:* GAv. *ᴣrᵊšūcqm* 'speak', *vīdqm* 'it shall decide' Ys. 32.6, cf. Skt. *duhăm*, Whitney, *Skt. Gram.* § 618.

i. Non-Sigmatic Group.

§ 628. The aorists of the non-sigmatic group—1. root-aorist, 2. simple *a*-aorist (thematic), 3. reduplicated aorist—resemble preterites (imperfects) which correspond respectively to the root-class, the *a*-conjugation (thematic), and to the reduplicated class.

1. Root-Aorist.
(Cf. Whitney, *Skt. Gram.* § 829.)

§ 629. The root-aorist is like an imperfect of the root-class without a corresponding present indicative. The endings are attached directly to the root in its strong or its weak form. The distribution of strong and weak stem-forms is in general the same as in the present and perfect systems. The modes show their characteristic mode-signs.

§ 630. Example of root-aorist inflection (almost exclusively G A v.).

12

Av. -ᴖᴖ $\sqrt{}$ *dā-* 'to give, do, make' (str. stem *dā-*, *da-*, wk. stem *d-*) = Skt. $\sqrt{}$ *dā-*, *dhā-*, Whitney, *Skt. Gram.* § 829.

§ 631. 1. Indicative.—Aorist (Preterite).

i. ACTIVE.

(G)Av.	Singular:	cf. Skt.
1. —		*á-d(h)ā-m*
2. *dāo, dāos-cā*		*á-d(h)ā-s*
3. *dā-t̬*		*á-d(h)ā-t*
	Plural:	
1. *dā-mā*		*á-d(h)ā-ma*
2. *dā-tā*		*á-d(h)ā-ta*
3. *d-arᵒ*		*á-d(h)-ur*

ii. MIDDLE.
Plural:

3. *d-ātā*[1] . . . . —

§ 632.   2. Imperative.

i. ACTIVE.

(G)Av.	Singular:	cf. Skt.
2. *dā-ⁱdī*		—
3. *dā-tū*		*d(h)ā-tu*

§ 633.   3. Subjunctive.

i. ACTIVE.
Singular:

2. *dā-hī*		—
3. *dā-ⁱtī*		*d(h)ā-ti*
	Plural:	
2. *dą-mahi*[2]		—
3. *dą-n*		—

ii. MIDDLE.
Singular:

1. *dā-nē̄*[3]		—
2. { *dāo-vhē̄*		—
dāo-vhā		—
3. *dā-ⁱtē̄*		—
	Plural:	
3. *dāo-ṇtē̄*		—

---

[1] i. e. *d-ạ̄ta*. — [2] Ys. 68.1. — [3] Ys. 44.9.

§ 634.　　　　　4. Optative.

i. ACTIVE.

(G)Av.	Singular:	cf. Skt.
1. *d-yąm*		*d(h)ī-yām*
2. *da-yā*[1], *dā-yā*[2]		—
3. *d-yāṭ, da-yāṭ*[3]		—
	Plural:	
2. *dā-yata*[4]		—
	ii. MIDDLE.	
1. *d-yā*[5]		—
2. *d-īṣ̌ā*		—
3. *d-yātąm*		—

§ 635.　　　　　5. Participle.

i. ACTIVE. Av. *daṇt-* . . . . —

Forms to be observed in GAv. and YAv.

§ 636.　Some further examples of inflection in GAv. and some forms also in YAv. may be observed.

1. Indicative.—Aorist.

§ 637.　**Singular:**—

First Person: i. ACT. GAv. *darəsəm* 'I saw'; note *srɯ-ī-m* 'I heard' (observe -*ī*-, like §§ 527, 550).

Second Person: i. ACT. GAv. *varəš* 'thou hast done' (*varə + s* § 165).

Third Person: i. ACT. GAv. *mōist* 'he turned' ($\sqrt{miθ}$-), *corəṭ* 'he made' ($\sqrt{kar}$-, -*ō*- = -*a*- § 39). — Here probably also *yaogəṭ* Ys. 44.4.— Observe GAv. *sāh-ī-ṭ* 'he taught' (*sāh-*), YAv. *vaⁱn-ī-ṭ* 'let conquer' Ys. 60.5 (if not opt. with wk. ending).

§ 638.　**Dual:**—

Third Person: ii. MID. GAv. *asrvātəm* 'they called'.

§ 639.　**Plural:**—

First Person: ii. MID. YAv. *yaoẑmaⁱde* 'we joined', GAv. *varəmaⁱdī* 'we have chosen'.

Third Person: i. ACT. YAv. *a-ⁱk-arə* 'they elapsed' ($\sqrt{sac}$-) Vd. 1.4; also *bun* 'they become'. — GAv. *ᵊjən, ᵊgəmən* 'they came'.—ii. MID. *fracarənta* 'they provided' ($\sqrt{kar}$-) Vd. 2.11.

---

[1] From strong stem. So metrically Yt. 10.114; Ys. 57.26. — [2] From strongest stem. — [3] From str. stem. So metrically Yt. 13.50, cf. Vd. 3.32. — [4] From strongest stem. — [5] i. e. *ᵊdīya*.

2. Imperative.

§ 640. Singular:—

Second Person: ii. MID. GAv. *kər̊ɉvā* 'make thou'.

Third Person: ii. MID. GAv. (ending *-qm* above §§ 456, 627 Note) *ərə̄ū-cqm* 'speak right', *vīdqm* 'shall decide'.

§ 641. Plural:—

Third Person: i. ACT. GAv. *scaᶇtū* 'let them follow' (√*sac-*).

3. Subjunctive.

§ 642. Singular:—

First Person: i. ACT. YAv. *ḫṣtā* 'I will stand'.—GAv. *yaojā* 'I will yoke', *varānī* 'I will choose'.—ii. MID. *gərə̄zē*, *gərə̄zōi* 'I will complain', *sruyē* 'I may be heard', YAv. *buye* 'I may be' (√*bū-*) Afr. 1.10,11.

Third Person: i. ACT. YAv. *bvaṱ* 'will become'.—GAv. *jimaṱ* 'he may come'.

§ 643. Dual:—

Third Person: ii. MID. GAv. *jamaēt ̄ē* 'they may come'.

§ 644. Plural:—

First Person: i. ACT. YAv. *jimama* 'we shall come'.

Second Person: i. ACT. GAv. *vī-cayapā* 'ye distinguish'.

Third Person: i. ACT. GAv. *bvaᶇti-cā* 'and they will be', *jimən* 'may they come'.

4. Optative.

§ 645. Singular:—

Second Person: i. ACT. YAv., similarly *ḫ ̌nuyæ* 'thou mightest rejoice'.

Third Person: i. ACT. YAv. also (from str. stem) *jam-yāṱ* 'he might come'; again (from wk. stem as above) *dis-yāṱ* 'let him show' Afr. 3.7 etc., likewise GAv. *mipyāṱ* 'he might deprive'.—ii. MID. GAv. *drītā* 'he might hold' (√*dar-*).

§ 646. Plural:—

First Person: i. ACT. YAv. *jamyāma* beside *jamyāma* 'we might come'. —GAv. *buyāma* 'we might be'.—ii. MID. GAv. *vairīmaidī* 'we might choose'.

Second Person: i. ACT. YAv. *buyātā* 'might ye be'.

Third Person: i. ACT. YAv. *buyqn*, *buyārə̄ṣ* 'they might be'.

Note. For fuller GAv. lists in regard to the root-aorist see Bartholomae, *K.Z.* xxiv. p. 313 seq. = *Flexionslehre* p. 44 seq.

§ 647. **Transfers to the thematic *a*-inflection** are found, e. g. GAv. *vaḫš-a-ṱ* 'he increased', GAv. *frā-jm-a-ṱ* 'he came' (√*gam-*).

2. Simple *a*-Aorist (thematic).
(Cf. Whitney, *Skt. Gram.* § 846 seq.)

§ 648. The instances of the simple *a*-aorist are not very numerous; in Av. this aorist plays a part similar to that in the Skt. of the Rig Veda. In formation and inflection it is identical with a preterite (imperfect) of the 6th class. The root in its w e a k form simply assumes the thematic vowel *a;* the secondary endings are then added for the indicative.—Cf. Whitney, *Skt. Gram.* § 846.

§ 649. E x a m p l e s of the *a*-aorist (chiefly GAv.) are the following:

1. I n d i c a t i v e. i. ACT. Aor. (pret.) Sg. 3. *vīdaṭ* 'he found' (beside 3 sg. pres. pret. *viṇd-aṭ*), *būjaṭ* 'he absolved' (beside pres. *buṇj-aᵢṇti*).—ii. MID. Pl. 3. *ḫiᵊṇtā* 'they ruled' (√*ḫiᵊā-*).

2. I m p e r a t i v e. i. ACT. Sg. 2. *vīdā* 'find thou'.—ii. MID. Pl. 3. *ḫiᵊṇtąm* 'let them rule'.

3. S u b j u n c t i v e. i. ACT. Sg. 1. *hanānī*, 3. *hanōṭ* 'let me, him earn'.

4. O p t a t i v e. ii. MID. Sg. 3. *ḫᵊaᵉtā* 'might he rule'.

5. P a r t i c i p l e. i. ACT. *vīdat°* (in compounds).

Likewise some other forms might be added.

---

3. Reduplicated Aorist.
(Cf. Whitney, *Skt. Gram.* § 856 seq.)

§ 650. The reduplicated aorist is comparatively rare. The stem is made by r e d u p l i c a t i n g the root which then appears in its w e a k form and assumes the t h e m a t i c *a*. The secondary endings are added for the indicative.—Cf. Whitney, *Skt. Gram.* § 856.

§ 651. E x a m p l e of inflection, Av. -ᵖᵘᵍ √*vac-* 'to speak' (stem *vaoc-a-* i. e. *va-uc-*, *va-vc-*) = Skt. √*vac- (vóca-):*

1. I n d i c a t i v e. i. ACT. Sg. 1. *vaocᵊm, vaocim* (§ 30), 2. *vaocō, vaocas-cā,* 3. *vaocaṭ, ᵊvaocaṭ* (§§ 32, 466).—Pl. 1. *vaocāma, vaocāmā.*

2. I m p e r a t i v e. i. ACT. Sg. 2. *vaocā.*

3. S u b j u n c t i v e. i. ACT. Sg. 1. *vaoca* (Ys. 45.3), 3. *vaocāṭ.*

4. O p t a t i v e. i. ACT. Sg. 3. *vaocōiṭ.*—Pl. 1. *vaocōimā.*

Note 1. Similarly GAv. *nqsaṭ* 'he disappeared' (i. e. *na-ns-aṭ,* √*nas-* = Skt. √*nas-*).

Note 2. To the redupl. aor. possibly belong the obscure forms YAv.
urū-rud-u-ṣa 'thou didst grow' 2 sg.-mid. Ys. 10.3, GAv. *qs-aṣ-u-tā* 'it has
been accomplished'. The *u* may be anaptyctic, or is it from a pres. formation?

§ 652. Instances of the true c a u s a t i v e a o r i s t with
strengthened reduplication (cf. Whitney, *Skt. Gram.* §§ 1046,
856) are: $\sqrt{}$*var-* 'to believe, cause to believe', GAv. *vāurāitē*
(3 sg. subjunct. mid.); *vāurayā* (1 sg. opt. mid.), *vāurōi-
maidī* (1 pl. opt. mid.). On *vāurāite* etc. for *vā-vr-āite*
see § 62, 2 above.

Note 1. The forms *sīzanin, sīzanāṭ* (cf. Skt. *ajījanat,* Whitney, *Skt.
Gram.* §§ 864, 869) are best reckoned under Cl. 3 in Av. on account of
pres. indic. *sīzananti* Yt. 13.15.

Note 2. The form *vaozirim* Yt. 19.69 is reckoned under pluperf.
above § 616.

---

ii. Sigmatic Group.

4. *h- (s-)* Aorist.
(Cf. Whitney, *Skt. Gram.* § 878 seq.)

§ 653. The characteristic mark of this aorist is an
orig. s i b i l a n t *s* (= Av. *h, s, š*) which is added in forming
the stem. The inflection is u n t h e m a t i c, the endings
being attached directly to the root which shows different
degrees of s t r e n g t h e n i n g, see next section § 654.

§ 654. The i n d i c a t i v e sg. act. has the vṛddhi-strengthening;
the indic. plur. act. and generally both numbers of the indic. mid. have
the guṇa form. The i m p e r a t i v e mid. and the entire s u b j u n c t i v e
a c t. show likewise guṇa. The o p t a t i v e and some instances of indic.
plur. mid. generally have the w e a k form.

§ 655. E x a m p l e s of inflection of this aorist are
taken from the following roots:

Av. $\sqrt{}$*dī-* 'regard, think' = Skt. $\sqrt{}$*dhī-;* Av. $\sqrt{}$*dar-* 'hold, hold
back' = Skt. $\sqrt{}$*dhar-;* Av. $\sqrt{}$*sand-* 'show, present, appear' = Skt.
$\sqrt{}$*chand-* § 142; Av. $\sqrt{}$*man-* 'think' = Skt. $\sqrt{}$*man-;* Av. $\sqrt{}$*pwars-*
'shape, create'; Av. $\sqrt{}$*fras-* 'ask' = Skt. $\sqrt{}$*praš-;* Av. $\sqrt{}$*prā-* 'protect' = Skt. $\sqrt{}$*trā-;* Av. $\sqrt{}$*van-* 'win' = Skt. $\sqrt{}$*van-;* Av. $\sqrt{}$*ı nqš-,
nas-* 'cause to vanish' = Skt. $\sqrt{}$*ı nqš-, naš-;* Av. $\sqrt{}$*varz-* 'work'

= Skt. $\sqrt{varj}$-; Av. $\sqrt{pā}$- 'protect' = Skt. $\sqrt{pā}$-; Av. $\sqrt{vac}$- 'speak'
= Skt. $\sqrt{vac}$-; Av. $\sqrt{dā}$- 'give, do, make' = Skt. $\sqrt{dā}$-, *dhā-;* Av.
$\sqrt{2\ nqs}$-, *nas-* 'attain' = Skt. $\sqrt{2\ nqś}$-, *naś-.*

§ 656.   1. Indicative.—A o r i s t (Preterite).

i. ACTIVE.

(G)Av.	Singular:	cf. Skt.
2. *dāi-š, sqs*[1]	. . . .	*bhāi-s*[2], *achān*
3. *dārˀšt, dōrˀšt*[3], *sqs*[4]	. . . . .	*á-bhār*[5], *achān*

ii. MIDDLE.
Singular:

1. *mˠvh-ī*[6], *fraš-ī*	. . . .	*mqs-i*
2. *mˠnghā*	. . . .	—
3. *mqs-tā*	. . . .	*mqs-ta*

Plural:

1. *a-mˠh-maⁱdī*[7], *mˠh-maⁱdī*[7]	. . . .	*á-gas-mahi*
2. *ƀwarˀž-dum*[8]	. . . .	*á-vr̥-dhvam*

§ 657.   2. Imperative.

ii. MIDDLE.
Singular:

2. *fˀrašvā*	. . . .	—

Plural:

2. *ƀrāz-dūm*[9]	. . . .	*trá-dhvam*

§ 658.   3. Subjunctive.

i. ACTIVE.

(G)Av.	Singular:	cf. Skt.
3.{ *vˠnvh-aⁱtī*	. . . .	*vqs-ati*
vˠngh-aṯ	. . . .	*vqs-aṯ*

Plural:

1. *nāš-āmā*[10]	. . . .	*vqs-āma*
3.{ *varˀš-ˠntī*[11]	. . . . . .	—
vˠngh-ˠn	. . . . . .	*vqs-an*

---

[1] Ys. 46.19. — [2] Wh., *Skt. Gram.* § 891. — [3] § 39. — [4] Ys. 43.11. —
[5] Wh., *Skt. Gram.* § 890. — [6] Also *mˠnhī.* — [7] i. e. w k. form, **masmadī* from
mn̥-s-madī. — [8] §§ 71, 179. — [9] § 171. — [10] § 158 *-š + s.* — [11] § 165 *-s + s.*

ii. MIDDLE.

Av.	Singular:	cf. Skt.
1. *pǣvh-ē, mǝ̄ngh-āi*[1]	. . . .	*mqs-āi*[1]
2. *pǣvh-ahe*[2]	. . . .	*mą́s-ase*
3. *var³š-aᶦtē*[3]	. . . .	*mqs-ate*

	Plural:	
2. ᵒ*dǣvh-ōdūm*[4]	. . . . . .	*dās-adhvam*
3. *vahš-ǝ̨tē*[5]	. . . . . .	*vaks-ante*

§ 659.   4. Optative.

i. ACTIVE.

Av.	Plural:	cf. Skt.
1. *nāš-īma* (YAv.)[6]	. . . .	—

§ 660.   5. Participle.

II. MIDDLE. $\begin{cases} \text{(Y)Av. } \textit{mavh-āna-}\,[7] & . . . . \quad —[8] \\ \text{(G)Av. } \textit{dīš-ǝmna-}\,[9] & . . . . . \textit{dhis-amāna-} \text{ (RV.)} \end{cases}$

Forms to be observed.

§ 661. GAv. *rǣ-vhavh-ōi* 'thou wilt give' 2 sg. subjunctive mid. √*rā-*, cf. YAv. *pǣvhahe* (in paradigm).

Note. GAv. *mǝ̄nghēi* (above) is by transfer thematic like Skt. *mqsāi* cf. § 663.

---

5. *ha- (sa-)* Aorist.
(Cf. Whitney, *Skt. Gram.* § 916 seq.)

§ 662. The orig. *sa*-aorist (= Av. *ha, vha*) in Av. is really only a variety of the preceding *s*-aorist. It arises by transfer of the *s*-aorist to the *a*-inflection.

§ 663. Examples of the *ha- (sa-)* aorist inflection are the following:

1. Indicative. i. ACT. Sg. 3. YAv. *asqs-a-ʈ* 'he fulfilled, offered' (√*sand-* above § 656) Vd. 19.15 = Skt. *á-chant-s-at*.

2. Imperative. i. ACT. Pl. 3. YAv. *javhǝ̨tu* 'they will smite' (√*jan-*) Vd. 2.22.

---

[1] themat. § 661. — [2] Yt. 8.1. — [3] § 165. — [4] Ys. 45.1, cf. § 39, *ð = a*. — [5] √*vac-* 'say, call'. — [6] Ys. 70.4, √*2 nas-* = orig. *-s + s*. — [7] Yt. 8.47. — [8] Cf. Whitney, *Skt. Gram.* § 897. — [9] themat. Ys. 51.1.

3. **Subjunctive.** i. ACT. Sg. 3. YAv. *nāš-ā-iti* 'will disappear' Yt. 2.11 (√*ī nas-* = Skt. √*ī naś-* § 158); *jahāt* Ny. 1.1.—ii. MID. YAv. *nāš-ā-ite*. Likewise here 1 sg. subj. mid. *mšnghāi* above § 661.

5. **Participle.** ii. MID. GAv. *ḫšnaoš-əmna-* (√*ḫšnu-* 'to gratify'), *dišəmna* above in paradigm § 660.

6. *iš*-Aorist.
(Cf. Whitney, *Skt. Gram.* § 898 seq.)

§ 664. One or two instances (GAv.) of the *iš*-aorist —see Whitney, *Skt. Gram.* § 898—are quotable. They are from √*kū-, ciū-* 'look for, hope', √*ḫšnu-* 'gratify, delight':—

1. **Indic.** ii. MID. Aor. (pret.). Sg. 1. *civ-iš-ī* (on long *-ī-* after *v* see § 20). 3. *civ-īš-tā*.

3. **Subjunct.** i. ACT. Sg. 1. *ḫšnəv-iš-ā*.

7. *hiš*-Aorist.
(Cf. Whitney, *Skt. Gram.* § 911.)

§ 665. An instance (YAv.) of the *hiš- (siṣ-)* aorist is apparently the following:

1. **Indic.** i. ACT. Sg. 2. *ədā-hiš* 'thou hast made' (√*dā-*) Yt. 3.2 cf. Skt. *glāsīs*, Whitney, *Skt. Gram.* §§ 912, 913.

§ 666. No certain instance of a **precative** seems to be found in Avesta.

Aorist Passive, third Singular.
(Cf. Whitney, *Skt. Gram.* § 842.)

§ 667. In Av. as in Skt. an aor. 3rd. singular in *-i* with passive meaning occurs, though it is not of common use. The form is made by adding *i* to the verbal root which has either the vṛddhi or guṇa strengthening. The form may take the augment as in Skt.

§ 668. Examples of 3rd. sg. Aor. Pass. are the following:—

(a) With vṛddhi.—From Av. √*vac-* 'speak, call' *vācī, avācī* (GAv.) = Skt. *vācī, avācī;* Av. √*sru-* 'hear, call' *srāvī* (GAv.) = Skt. *srāvī;* so Av. *āidi* 'is said, spoken of' √*ad-* (so Geldner) = Skt.

ak-. —(b) With guṇa (or middle) form. — From Av. √*mrū-* 'say'
mraoī (GAv. i. e. *mrav-i*), Av. √*vat-* 'understand' *vaiti* (GAv.),
Av. √*jan-* 'slay' *jaini* (YAv.).

Note. The form YAv. *ərənāvi* 'it was granted, obtained' (√*ar-*) is
made, not directly from the root, but from the prepared stem *ərə-nu-*, *ərə-nāu-*.

IV. FUTURE-SYSTEM.
Future.
(Cf. Whitney, *Skt. Gram.* § 932 seq.)

§ 669. The characteristic mark of the future
in Avesta as in Sanskrit is *-hy-* (*-šy-* § 133) = Skt. *-sy-* (*-sy-*)
added to the root. The root assumes the guṇa-form;
the inflection is thematic (*-hya, -šya*). — Cf. Whitney, *Skt.
Gram.* § 932 seq.

Modes of the Future.

§ 670. The instances of the future are in general not
very numerous; they are confined to the indicative mode
and to the participle. The place of the other modes is
often taken by a subjunctive of other parts of the verb
used in a future sense. Cf. Whitney, *Skt. Gram.* § 938.

Future Formation and Inflection.

§ 671. Examples of future formation and inflection are
taken from the following roots. Cf. Whitney, *Skt. Gram.* § 933.

Av. √*vac-* 'to speak' = Skt. √*vac-;* Av. √*harz-* 'let go, drop'
= Skt. √*sarj-;* Av. √*sū-* 'further, save' = Skt. √*sū-.*

§ 672.　　1. Indicative.—Future.

i. ACTIVE.

Av.	Singular:	cf. Skt.
1. *vah-šy-ā* (GAv.)		*vak-sy-āmi*

ii. MIDDLE.

Singular:

3. *vah-šy-eite* [1]		*vak-sy-átē*

Plural:

3. *harə-šy-eṇte* [2]		*sark-sy-aṇtē* [3]

---

[1] Ys. 19.10; Vsp. 15.3. — [2] Vsp. 12.1. On *z + s* see § 165. — [3] Cf.
Skt. *varkṣyaṇtē* from √*varj-.*

§ 673.   2. Participle.

i. ACTIVE. Av. *sao-šy-aṇt-* . . . . . cf. Skt. *kṣĕ-ṣy-ánt-*

ii. MIDDLE.   *harᵃ-šy-amna-* . . . . . . *yak-ṣy-ámāna-*

Forms to be observed.

§ 674. Notice the long vowel instead of strengthening in the Av. participles *bū-šy-aṇt-* from √*bū-*, opp. to Skt. *bhav-i-ṣyánt-* (§ 61 Note 2), cf. Skt. RV. *sū-ṣy-ant-*. Observe also *hrvī-šy-aṇt-* beside *hrvĭ-šy-aṇt-* from √*hrvī-* 'be raw, bloody'.

V. SECONDARY CONJUGATIONS.

§ 675. The secondary conjugations consist of the following formations (thematic), a. Passive, b. Causative, c. Denominative, d. Inchoative, e. Desiderative, and f. Intensive (unthematic).

A. Passive.

(Cf. Whitney, *Skt. Gram.* § 768 seq.)

§ 676. **General Remark.** The passive force may be given in any tense-system simply by employing the middle voice in a passive sense. In the present-system, however, there is also a for mative passive made by means of the passive sign *-ya-* (cf. Cl. 4) attached to the prepared root.

Note. The connection between this formative passive in *ya* and Cl. 4 of the present-system is generally acknowledged. In Skt. the difference of accent distinguishes the two, the passive having accented *yá*, but Cl. 4 an unaccented *ya*. As no written accent is found in Av., such a distinction cannot always be sharply drawn; it is therefore sometimes doubtful whether a given form is really a passive or merely a middle used with passive sense, e. g. *manyeti* (pass.) Ys. 44.12 identical in form with *manyete* (mid.) Yt. 10.139 = Skt. *manyáte, mányate.*

§ 677. **Formation of the Passive.** The passive sign is *-ya-* (= Skt. accented *-yá-*) attached to the root which then assumes the weak form.

Note. The *ar*-roots require some remark as they frequently show MS. variations as to the way in which the radical *r*-vowel is expressed: e. g. Av. √*mar-* 'to die', *mir-ye-iti, mir-ye-ite, mᵃrᵃ-ye-iti, maᵢr-ye-ite* Vd. 3.33 = Skt. *mriyáte;* again Av. √*kar-* 'to make', *kir-ye-iti* Yt. 10.109, *kir-ye-iṇṭe* v. l. *kaĭr-ye-iṇṭe* Vd. 3.9, cf. § 48 above. The development in such cases evidently is

$$*mṛ-ya-tĕ$$

| Av. *mar-ya-tĕ* (or -*aĭr-* § 48) | Skt. *mṛ-i̯á-tĕ* |
| or *mir-ya-tĕ* (-*ŕ-* § 70) | *mĭr-i-yá-tĕ* |

§ 678. **Endings.** In Skt. the passive form assumes the middle endings, but some exceptions with active endings occur, cf. Whitney, *Skt. Gram.* § 774. In Av. also, the m i d d l e endings are used but the a c t i v e ones likewise are not very uncommon. Observe especially the MS. variants in final *e*, *i* (§ 35 Note 2) *kiryeĭti, kiryeĭte*. The intransitive passive force seems therefore to lie in the *ya*-element.

Note. An undoubted example of act. ending but passive force is *frā-yez-yāṭ* in Yt. 13.50 *kahe vō urvā* (nom. masc.) *frāyezyāṭ* 'of which one of you will the soul be worshipped?' Apparently also with active ending (from √*dā-*) *dayāṭ* (subjunct.) Vd. 3.32, *ni-dayaṭ* (impf.) Yt. 12.17.

Modes of the Passive.

§ 679. The modes of the passive are the usual ones of the present-system; a complete list of forms, however, cannot be gathered from the texts.

Passive Inflection.

§ 680. Examples of passive voice with middle and active endings are the following:

1. I n d i c a t i v e. a. Pres. **Sg.** 3. *baĭr-yeĭte* v. l. *baĭryeĭti* 'he is borne', *kiryeĭti* v. l. *kiryeĭte* 'it is made'; **Pl.** 3. *kiryeĭṇṭe* v. l. *kaĭr-yeĭṇṭe* 'they are made' (§ 48).— Pret. **Sg.** 2. *maĭryaṽha* 'didst die' v. l. *mərⁱyaṽha*, 3. *vī-sruyata* 'was heard', *ni-dayaṭ* 'was placed'.

3. S u b j u n c t i v e. **Sg.** 3. *maĭryāĭte* v. l. *miryaĭte, miryāĭti* 'is destroyed, dies'; *yezyāṭ* 'is worshipped'; **Pl.** 3. *baĭryⱥṇṭe* 'they will be borne', *janyⱥṇṭe* 'they will be slain' Yt. 14.43.

5. P a r t i c i p l e. Av. *suyamna-* 'being advanced, saved'.

Note. From √*var-* 'to cover' is found a form *ni-vōⁱr-ye-ĭte* (v. l. •*ĭti*), —on *ō*, cf. § 39.

§ 681. A Perf. Pass. Participle in -*ta* or -*na* also belongs to the passive conjugation. See § 710 below.

§ 682. A Fut. Pass. Participle (Gerundive) in
ya- is formed according to § 716 below.

§ 683. The Aorist Passive 3rd. Singular likewise
falls under this formation. It is treated above, § 668.

B. Causative.

§ 684. **General Remark.** In Av. as in Skt. the causative *(-aya-)*, like the Denominative is identical in form
with Cl. 10, the latter being originally a causative formation. The causal is found in the Present-System.

Note. In Skt. many of the so-called causatives do not have a strict
causative value and are therefore reckoned as belonging to the Skt. *cur-*
Class (10); similarly in Av., a number of causative forms have been treated
above under Class 10, cf. § 482 seq.

§ 685. **Formation.** The present-stem of the causative is formed by adding the causal formative element *-aya-*
to the root which is usually strengthened. The strengthening of the root is subject to certain variations.

a. Internal or initial *a* before a single consonant is generally
lengthened (vṛddhi), but sometimes it remains unchanged, thus:
Lengthened *ā*, Av. √*vat-* 'to comprehend', caus. 'make known'
vātaya- = Skt. *vātáya-;* Av. √*tap-* 'to warm, be warm', caus. 'make
warm' *tāpaya-* = Skt. *tāpáya-;* Av. √*gam-*, *jam-* 'go, come' *jāmaya-*
= Skt. *gāmáya-* (Whitney, *Skt. Gram.* § 1042 g).—Unchanged *a*,
Av. √*pat-* 'to fall, fly' *pataya-* = Skt. *patáya-;* Av. √*sad-* 'appear'
sadaya- = Skt. *chadáya-;* Av. √*ap-* 'obtain', *āpaya-*, opp. to Skt.
āpáya-.

b. Internal and initial *a* before two consonants (i. e. long
by position) remains unchanged: Av. √*dakš-* 'to know, cause to
know' *dakšaya-* = Skt. *dakṣáya-;* Av. √*vakš-* 'grow, cause to grow'
vakšaya- = Skt. *vakṣáya-;* Av. √*band-* 'bind' *bandaya-* = Skt. *ban-*
dháya-; Av. √*zamb-* 'crush' *zambaya-* = Skt. *jambháya-*.

c. Final long *ā* disappears: Av. √*stā-* 'to stand, cause to stand'
staya- opp. to Skt. *sthāpáya-*, cf. Whitney, *Skt. Gram.* § 1042 i.

d. Internal or initial *i, u* before single consonants (i. e. in
light syllables) have the guṇa-strengthening: Av. √*vid-* 'to know',
caus. 'inform' *vaēdaya-* = Skt. *vēdáya-;* Av. √*ruc-* 'light up' *rao-*
caya- = Skt. *rōcáya-*.

e. Final *u* (or *i*) receives the vṛddhi-strengthening: Av. √*sru-* 'to hear' *srāvaya-* = Skt. *śrāváya-*.

Note 1. The nasal of the present-stem (Cl. 9) appears in Av. *kərəṇtaya-* from √*kart-* 'to cut' as in Skt. *kṛntáya-*, cf. Whitney, *Skt. Gram.* § 1042 h. So also Av. *buṇjaya-* from √*buj-* 'to release'.

Note 2. The root *zā-* 'to let go' makes *zayaya-*, cf. Whitney, *Skt. Gram.* § 1042.

Note 3. Observe with lengthening instead of strengthening of root (§ 61 Note) GAv. *ᵘrūpayeiṇtī* 'they cause pain' (√*rup-*) = Skt. *rōpáyanti*; GAv. *ᵘrūdōyatā* 'he caused to lament' = Skt. *rōdháyata*.

Modes of the Causative.

§ 686. The Causative shows the same modes, 1. Indicative, 2. Imperative, 3. Subjunctive, 4. Optative, including also 5. Participle, as the present-system naturally does.

Inflection of the Causative: Present-System.

§ 687. The causal in the present-system is inflected after the *a*-conjugation (thematic), see Cl. 10 above, §§ 481, 482 seq.

Other Causative Formations.

§ 688. To the causal formation belongs not only the causative of the present-system, but also a causal aorist (see § 652); possibly likewise a causative perfect (pluperfect), and some other parts.

§ 689. On the reduplicated Causative Aorist, see § 652 above.

§ 690. Possibly here belongs as Periphrastic Perfect (Plupf.), Av. *biwivåŋha* 'he had frightened', see § 623.

§ 691. A causal derivative from √*hvap-* 'to sleep' is made by attaching the root *dā-* 'to make, do' in its causal form directly to the radical element; thus, Av. *hvabdayeⁱti* 'puts to sleep'.

§ 692. Other causative derivatives made with root *dā-* (cf. § 691) but without causal form, are *ava-ŋhab-daēta* 'he would cause to sleep' (√*hvap-*), *xraoždat̰* 'caused to howl' (√*xrus-*), *yaoždāⁱti* 'makes pure' (√*yaoš-*).

§ 693. Some forms with causal signification but without the *-aya-* formation occur: Av. *vaxšat̰* 'he caused to grow' Ys. 48.6 opp. to *vaxšaya-tō* 'they both cause to grow' Ys. 10.3.

§ 694. An occasional verbal noun (infinitive) or adjective (participle) is likewise to be noted under the causal formation: Av. *frasrūta-* 'made

famous, renowned', *rvaêîta- 'turned' Ys. 11.2. Cf. Whitney, *Skt. Gram.*
§ 1051 seq.

C. Denominative.
(Cf. Whitney, *Skt. Gram.* § 1053 seq.)

§ 695. Denominative verbs are formed from a noun-stem (substantive or adjective) by adding *-ya* or *-a* = Skt. *-yá* or *-a* to the stem. In Skt. the *-yá* is accented, but as there is no written accent in Av., it is sometimes hard to decide whether a certain given verb-form in *-aya* be really a denominative from an *a*-stem or not rather simply a causative. As to meaning, the denominative usually signifies 'to make, use, cause, be, or practise' that which the noun-stem itself denotes.

§ 696. Formation and Inflection. The denominative is found in the Present-System and is made 1. by adding *-ya* (= Skt. *-yá*), or more rarely 2. *-a* (= Skt. *-a*) directly to a noun-stem. The inflection is therefore that of the present-system *a*-conjugation (thematic).—Cf. Whitney, *Skt. Gram.* §§ 1054, 1068.

1. *ya* added: Av. *aṣa-* n. 'holiness' (*a*-stem) denom. *aṣa-ya-* 'to gain by holiness', *aṣayeîti* = Skt. *r̥tayá-;* Av. *vâra-* m. 'rain' denom. *vâra-ye-mi* 'I rain down';—Av. *avhu-* m. 'lord' (*u*-stem) denom. *avhu-ya-* 'to become lord of', *avhuyôîte;*—Av. *nəmah-* n. 'homage' (cons. stem) denom. *nəmah-ya-* 'do homage' *nəmahyâmahî* = Skt. *namasyá-;*—Av. *iṣud-* f. 'debt' (cons. stem) denom. *iṣud-ya-* 'incur a debt', *iṣnîdyâmahî* = Skt. *iṣudhyá-*.

2. Simple *a* added: Av. *paîti-* 'lord' (*i*-stem) denom. *paîþy-a-* 'to possess as lord', *paîþyeîti* = Skt. *pátya-;*—Av. *ḳratu-* m. 'wisdom' (*u*-stem) denom. *ḳraþw-a-* 'be wise', ptcpl. mid. *ḳraþwəmnahe* 'of him that is wise';—Av. *fyavhu-* m. 'mist' (*u*-stem) denom. *fyavhv-a-* 'to fall as mist', *fyavhuṇtaê-ca* (§§ 63, 493, 582);—Av. *aênah-* n. 'sin' (cons. stem) denom. *aênavh-a-* 'to commit sin', *aênavhaîti* Ys. 9.29 opp. Skt. *ênas-yá-*.

Note. Final *a* of a noun-stem seems occasionally to disappear (cf. in Skt. after *n* or *r*, Whitney, *Skt. Gram.* § 1059 e). Thus, Av. *baêṣaz-ya-ti* etc. 'he practises healing' Yt. 8.43 (*baêṣaza-* n.), *vâstryaê-ta* 'let him pasture' (*vâstra-* n.), *parꞌsan-ye-îti* 'he asks' Yt. 8.15. So probably also

Av. *pǝǰanaᶦti* 'he fights' (*pǝǰana-* n., *pǝǰanā-* f.), cf. Skt. *pṛtanyati*, Whitney, *Skt. Gram.* § 1060.

_____

D. Inchoative.
(Cf. Whitney, *Skt. Gram.* §§ 608, 747.)

§ 697. The existence of the inchoative in Av., as in Skt., is shown by a few verbs. The i n c h o a t i v e s i g n is *s* = Skt. *ch* (§ 142) added directly to the root in its weak stage. The t h e m a t i c *a*-inflection is then assumed. The instances of inchoative are comparatively so few that these inchoative *s*-forms have sometimes been reckoned as independent roots.

§ 698. E x a m p l e s o f I n c h o a t i v e s. The formation and inflection is shown by the following instances.

Av. √*gam-, jas-* (i. e. *gm̥-s-*) 'to go, come' *ja-s-a-ᶦti*, cf. βάσκει = Skt. *gá-ch-a-ti;* Av. √*yam-, yas-* (i. e. *ym̥-s-*) 'come, reach' *ya-s-a-ᶦte* = Skt. *yá-ch-a-tē;* Av. √*fras-, pǝrǝs-* (i. e. *parś-s-*) 'ask' *pǝrǝ-s-a-ᶦte,* cf. Lat. *po(r)scit* = Skt. *pṛ-ch-a-ti;* Av. √*vah-, us-* (i. e. *us-s-*) 'to light up' *us-a-ᶦti* = Skt. *ucháti;* Av. √*tap-, tafs-* 'to warm, grow warm' *taf-s-a-ṭ,* cf. Lat. *tepesco.* Also a few others.

Note. Observe the assimilation and loss of consonants before *s* in the following examples: Av. *tǝrǝsaᶦti* 'he trembles' (i. e. **tǝrǝs-s-a-ᶦti*), cf. Skt. √*tras-;* Av. *usaᶦti* just above § 698. So Av. *ᵂisaṭ* 'he began to sweat' √*ᵂid-* = Skt. √*svid-.* See §§ 184, 185 above.

_____

E. Desiderative.
(Cf. Whitney, *Skt. Gram.* § 1026 seq.)

§ 699. The desiderative in Av. resembles the Skt. in formation and signification. The root is r e d u p l i c a t e d and the f o r m a t i v e e l e m e n t *-ha (-ʮha, -ṣa, -za)* = Skt. *-sa* as desiderative sign is added. The vowel of the re-d u p l i c a t e d s y l l a b l e is always *-i- (-ī-* § 21 Note); the initial consonant of the root in reduplicating follows the usual rules above § 465.

The root of the desiderative appears ordinarily in its weak grade; sometimes, however, in its strong (middle)

form. The desiderative is confined to the present-system;
the inflection *(-ha, -sa)* is thematic.

§ 700. Examples of Desiderative Formation.
The instances of the desiderative are not very numerous;
the following may be noted.

Av. √*ji-* 'to conquer, win', desid. *jī-ji-ṣa-* 'seek to win over' = Skt.
ji-jī-ṣa; Av. √*ḫšnu-* 'gratify, rejoice', desid. *ci-ḫšnu-ṣa-;* Av. √*žnā-*
'know', desid. *zi-ḫžnā-ṇha-* (§§ 164, 465 Note 2) = Skt. *ji-jñā-sa-;*
Av. √*dab-* 'deceive', desid. GAv. *di-w-ža-* (i. e. *di-ᵈbh-ža* § 89) 'seek
to deceive' = Skt. *dipsa-;* Av. √*sac-* 'teach, learn, can', desid. *siṣa-*
(i. e. *ˣsi-ˢk-sa-*) = Skt. *śi-k-ṣa-.* Likewise a few other forms, e. g.
dīdərˀ²ža- from √*darz-* 'make firm', *mimaʒža-* from √*maṇj-* 'magnify',
vīvarˀža- from √*varz-* 'do'.

§ 701. Examples of Inflection. These are confined to the present-system thematic.

    1. Indicative. a. Pres. i. ACT. Pl. 3. GAv. *jī-ji-ṣəṇṭī* Ys. 39.1.
—ii. MID. Pl. 2. *dī-draʒ-žōduyē* Ys. 48.7.—b. Pret. i. ACT. Sg. 2. *ci-
ḫšnu-ṣō* Ys. 45.9.—ii. MID. Sg. 3. *dī darˀ-ṣatū* 'he held back' (√*dar-*).
    2. Imperative. i. ACT. Sg. 3. GAv. *vī-vəṇgha-tū* 'let him seek
to surpass' (√*van-*). — ii. MID. Sg. 2. YAv. *mi-marˀḫ-ṣavuha.*
    3. Subjunctive. i. ACT. Sg. 1. GAv. *ci-ḫšnu-ṣa* Ys. 49.1;
3. YAv. *ji-ji-ṣā-iti.*—ii. MID. Sg. 3. *mi-marˀḫ-ṣā-itē.*
    5. Participle. i. ACT. GAv. *ci-ḫšnu-ṣaṇṭ-* Ys. 43.15. — ii. MID.
YAv. *zi-ḫžnā-ṇhəmna-* § 465 Note 2.

    Note. A Perf. Participle of the desid. Act. is *jaḫžavū* 'having the
desire to slay' (√*jan-*) ZPhl. *Glossary* p. 92.

_____

F. Intensive.
(Cf. Whitney, *Skt. Gram.* § 1000 seq.)

§ 702. The characteristic features of the Intensive are
reduplication and the unthematic inflection. In formation, the Intensive in Av., as in Skt., closely resembles
the reduplicating class (Cl. 3) of the present-system; it is
distinguished from Cl. 3 by having a strengthened reduplicated syllable.

§ 703. As regards the reduplication, the formation of the Intensive in Av. is twofold.

1. The reduplicated syllable is made by repeating the initial conso-
-nant followed by the radical vowel in a strengthened form (*a* being strengthened to *ā;*—*i* to *ai̯*, *ōi̯;*—*u* to *ao*). — Cf. Whitney, *Skt. Gram.* § 1002.

2. The reduplicated syllable is made by repeating the entire root.
—Cf. Whitney, *Skt. Gram.* § 1002 ii.

§ 704. As regards the radical syllable itself, this
assumes sometimes the strong form, sometimes the weak
grade, according to the person or the mode in which it
is found. The inflection as stated above is unthematic.

§ 705. Examples of Formation. As instances
to illustrate the Intensive formation the following may
be taken:

1. Strengthened Reduplication: Av. √*part*- 'to fight', intens. *pā-pərət*-;—Av. √*dis*- 'show, teach' *dai̯-dōis*-, *dai̯-dis*- = Skt. *dī-deś*-, *dī-diś*-; Av. √*vid*- 'find' *vōi̯-vid*- = Skt. *vī-vid*-;—Av. √*sū*- 'call' *zao-zao*- = Skt. *jō-hav*-.

2. Repeated Root: Av. √*dar*- 'to tear' *dar-dar*- = Skt. *dar-dar*-; Av. √*kar*- 'make' *car-kərə*- = Skt. *cár-kr*-; Av. √*ǰi̯ar*- 'stream, flow' *ǰi̯ar-ǰi̯arə*- (in participle) opp. Skt. *cā-kṣar*-.

Note. An intensive with the *ya*-inflection (Cl. 4 thematic) is to be
found in the following instance: Av. √*rai̯*- 'to wound-, GAv. *rā-rəǰ-yei̯ṇtī*
(indic.) Ys. 47.4; *rā-rəǰ-yąn* (subjunct.) Ys. 32.11; YAv. *rā-rəǰ-ya-ṇtō* (nom.
pl. ptcpl.) Yt. 11.6; but un-thematic GAv. *rā-rəǰ-ō* (ptcpl.) Ys. 49.2—cf.
Skt. *rā-rakṣ*-; see also Whitney, *Skt. Gram.* § 1016. Similarly, Av. √*yah*-
'be heated, boil' *yaei̯ya*- (i. e. *yā-i̯-ya*-) in the ptcpl. *yaei̯yaṇt*- = Skt. *yā-yas*-.

§ 706. Examples of Inflection. These are confined to the present-system unthematic, and they are mostly
from GAv. Thus:

1. Indicative. a. Pres. i. ACT. Sg. 1. GAv. *zao-zao-mī;* Pl. 1.
GAv. *carə-kərə-mahī* Ys. 58.4. — ii. MID. Sg. 1. GAv. *vōi̯-vīd-ē*. —
b. Pret. Sg. 3. *dai̯-dōiš-t*.

4. Optative. i. ACT. Sg. 3. YAv. *darə-dai̯r-yāṯ* (with str. rad.
stem *-dar*- instead of expected wk. *-dərə*-).

5. Participle. i. ACT. YAv. *ǰi̯arə-ǰi̯ar-əṇt*- (*a*-inflect.).

§ 707. Transfers to the *a*-inflection are found, e. g.
Indic. Pres. 3 sg. act. YAv. *naē-niž-aiti* 'it removes', et al.

VI. VERBAL ABSTRACT FORMS.

Participle, Gerund, Infinitive.

§ 708. To the verbal system there also belong the
Participle or verbal adjective, the Gerund, with Gerundive, and the Infinitive or verbal noun.

A. Participle.

1. Participle in *-aṇt, -at* (Act.); *-mna, -āna* (Mid.).
(Cf. Whitney, *Skt. Gram.* §§ 583, 584 etc.)

§ 709. Participial forms in *-aṇt, -at* (i. e. *-ṇt*),
fem. *-aⁱṇtī, -aⁱtī* in the Active, and forms in *-mna, -āna*
(-āna) in the Middle, are found in each tense-system. As
these attach themselves directly rather to the tense-systems,
they have been discussed above under the respective systems,
cf. §§ 488, 533 etc.

2. Passive Participle in *-ta.*
(Cf. Whitney, *Skt. Gram.* § 952 seq.)

§ 710. A passive participle or past passive participle, is made in Av., as in Skt., by adding the suffix *-ta*
= Skt. *-tá* (accented) directly to the verbal root, which is
subject however to certain euphonic changes. This verbal
adjective in *-ta* (m. n.), *-tā* (f.) is regularly declined according to the *a*-declension §§ 236, 243. Examples of the
formation are Av. *pāta-* 'protected' (√*pā-*) = Skt. *pātá-;*
Av. *gərəpta-* 'grasped' (√*garw-* § 74) = Skt. *gr̥bhītá;* Av.
druhta- 'deceived' (√*druj-* § 90) = Skt. *drugdhá-.*

§ 711. Treatment of the Root before *-ta.* The
form of the root is subject to modification and is liable
to vary before the added suffix. The following points
may be noted:—

1. The root very commonly (but not always) shows the weak
form, if it has one, before *-ta;* a penultimate nasal is accordingly
dropped. Thus, with weak form, from Av. √*vac-* 'to speak'
ptcpl. •*uxta-* = Skt. *uktá-;* Av. √*hu-* 'press out' *huta-* = Skt. *sutá-;*
—Av. √*panj-* 'draw, drive' *paxta-;* Av. √*hvanj-* 'encircle' *hvaxta-* =

Skt. *svakta-;* Av. √*baṇd-* 'to bind' *basta-* (§ 151) = Skt. *baddhā-*.
—Strong form or unchanged, Av. √*dā-* 'to place' *dāta-* opp. Skt.
hitā-; Av. √*taš-* 'cut, form' *tašta-* = Skt. *taṣṭá-*.

2. Roots in final *-ā* retain this. Thus, Av. √*stā-* 'to stand'
stāta- opp. Skt. *sthitá-;* Av. √*dā-* 'place' opp. Skt. *hitá-;* Av.
√*snā-* 'bathe' = Skt. *snātá-;* Av. √*pā-* 'protect' = Skt. *pātá-*.

3. Roots in *-ar* often show MS. variations between *-ərᵊta* and
-arᵊta, cf. § 47 Note. Thus, Av. √*bar-* 'to bear' *bərᵊta-, barᵊta-*
(e. g. Ys. 62.9) = Skt. *bhṛtá-;* Av. √*star-* 'stretch, strew' *frastərᵊta-,
frastarᵊta-*.

4. Roots in *-an*, *-am* in Av., as in Skt., often form *-ata* (i. e.
-ṇtá, -ṃtá); sometimes they show *-āta*. Thus, Av. √*jan-* 'to slay'
jata- = Skt. *hatá-;* Av. √*man-* 'think' *mata-* = Skt. *matá-;* Av.
√*gam-* 'go' *gata-* = Skt. *gatá-;* Av. *zan-* 'beget, bear' *zāta-* =
Skt. *jātá-*.

5. But roots in *-an*, *-am* often retain the nasal (*m* being assimilated to *n* before *t*). Thus, Av. √*kan-* 'to dig' *•kaṇta-* (cf. also
kata-) opp. Skt. *khātá-;* Av. √*zan-* 'know' *•zaṇta-;* Av. √*gram-*
'be angry' *graṇta-*.

6. Sometimes a radical short *ŭ* appears as long *ū* before *-ta*,
cf. § 20. Thus, Av. √*sru-* 'to hear' *srūta-* = Skt. *srūtá-;* Av.
·√*dru-* 'run' *drūta-* = Skt. *drūtá-*.

§ 712. The past participle in *-ita,* although common
in Skt., hardly appears in Av.; the instances Av. *daršita-*
Ys. 57.11 = Skt. *dhṛṣitá-*, Av. *raoḍita-*, *zairita-* are best
treated under Suffixes below, § 786 Note 1.

3. Passive Participle in *-na*.
(Cf. Whitney, *Skt. Gram.* § 952.)

§ 713. The *na*-formation of the passive participle is
very rare in Avesta. The instances are hardly distinguishable from adjectives. As examples may be given, Av.
√*tan-* 'to stretch' *us-tāna-* 'upstretched' = Skt. *uttāná-;*
Av. √*ū-* 'be wanting' *ūna-* = Skt. *ūná-;* Av. √*par-* 'fill'
pərᵊna- = Skt. *pūrṇá-*.

4. Perfect Active Participle in *-vah*.
(Cf. Whitney, *Skt. Gram.* § 802.)

§ 714. The formation of the Perf. Act. Participle has been
treated above under the Perfect-System, see §§ 611, 618, 399.

5. **Perfect Middle Participle in -āna, -ăna.**
(Cf. Whitney, *Skt. Gram.* § 806.)

§ 715. On the formation of the Perf. Mid. Participle, see above under Perfect-System, §§ 611, 618.

B. Gerundive and Gerund.

1. Gerundive: (a) Fut. Pass. Participle in -ya (declined).
(Cf. Whitney, *Skt. Gram.* § 961.)

§ 716. A d e c l i n e d derivative adjective with verbal force is made from some verbs by attaching the formative element -*ya* to the root. Such an adjective is regularly inflected according to the *a*-declension. In meaning, it often corresponds to the Latin form in -*ndus;* it is therefore commonly called a gerundive or future passive participle.

> Examples are from Av. √*iš-* 'to wish', a gerundive (vbl. adj.) *iṣya-* = Skt. °*iṣya-;* Av. √*karš-* 'draw furrows, plow' *karṣya-* = Skt. °*kṛṣya-;* Av. √*var-* 'choose, believe' *vairya-* = Skt. *várya-*. Other instances occur.

2. Gerundive: (b) Fut. Pass. Participle in -tva, -ṭwa (declined).
(Cf. Whitney, *Skt. Gram.* § 966 a.)

§ 717. A d e c l i n e d derivative adjective of like signification (-*ndus)* with the preceding (§ 716) is made by adding -*tva*, -*ṭwa*, -*dwa* (§§ 94, 96; see also under Suffixes) directly to the root in its strong form. Such a verbal adjective is regularly inflected after the *a*-declension.

> Examples are: Av. *jaṭwa-* 'worthy to be killed' (√*jan-*) = Skt. *hántva-;* Av. *ḳṣnaoṭwa-* 'worthy to be satisfied' (√*ḳṣnu-*); Av. *varštva-* 'to be done' (√*varz-*), *maṭwa-* 'to be thought', *vaḳdwa-* 'to be spoken'.

3. Gerund (Absolutive) in -ya (indeclinable).
(Cf. Whitney, *Skt. Gram.* § 989 seq.)

§ 718. A species of Gerund or Absolute (i n d e c l i n a b l e) in -*ya* seems to occur in the following instances with *daîpe:* Av. *aîbigaîrya* 'seizing' = Skt. °*gīrya;* Av. *paîtiricya* 'throwing away'. But cf. Bartholomae in *B.B.* xv. 237.

C. Infinitive.

(Cf. Whitney, *Skt. Gram.* §§ 538, 968.)

§ 719. The Infinitive is a verbal noun, an abstract derived from a verb. It is formed either directly from the root, or sometimes from a tense-stem. Such a derivative noun is used with an infinitival or a semi-infinitival force. The noun form is found most often in the dative case; sometimes, however, in other cases. The abstracts used as infinitives are most commonly cases of a substantive stem made by means of the suffix *-di, -ti, -ah;* less often they are formed from stems in *-man, -van, -a;* or they are from suffixless stems.

§ 720. Examples of Infinitives or Verbal Nouns so used, are the following. Cf. also Whitney, *Skt. Gram.* § 970.

1. Ending Av. *-dyāi, -dyāi* dative = Skt. *-dhyāi.*
   (Chiefly GAv.; rare YAv.)

From root: GAv. *dərədyāi* 'for holding'· ($\sqrt{dar}$-).—From pres. stem: GAv. *vərəzyeïdyāi* 'to work', YAv. *vazaïdyāi* 'for driving' ($\sqrt{vaz}$-) Yt. 15.28, *srāvayeïdyāi* 'to proclaim' Yt. 24.46.

2. Ending Av. *-tʒe, -tayaē-ca* dative = Skt. *-tayē.*
   (Only YAv., but frequent.)

From root: YAv. *anu-matʒe, anu-matayaē-ca* (§ 254) 'to think, according to' ($\sqrt{man}$-) = Skt. *ánu-matayē;* Av. *kərətʒe* 'for making' ($\sqrt{kar}$-) = Skt. *kŕtayē;* Av. *bərətʒe* 'for bearing', etc.

3. Ending Av. *-aŋhe* dative = Skt. *-asē.*
   (Chiefly GAv.)

From pres. stem: GAv. *vaēnaŋhē* 'to see' ($\sqrt{vaēn}$-), *srāvayeŋhē* 'to repeat' ($\sqrt{sru}$-, causal), GAv. *avaŋhē*, GAv. *avaïŋhe*, *avaŋhaē-ca* 'to aid' ($\sqrt{av}$-). — From aor. stem redupl., GAv. *vaocaŋhē* 'to speak' ($\sqrt{vac}$-).

4. Ending Av. *-maïne, -vaïne* dative = Skt. *-manē, -vanē.*
   (GAv. and YAv.)

From pres. stem: YAv. *staomaïne* 'for praising' ($\sqrt{stu}$-), GAv. *vīdvanōi* 'to know' ($\sqrt{vid}$-) § 56. Also a couple of others.

5. Ending Av. -ăi dative (a-decl.) = Skt. ăi.
(GAv. and YAv.)

From root: YAv. *jayāi* 'to win' ($\sqrt{ji}$-).—From stem: GYAv. *fradapāi* 'to promote' ($\sqrt{dā}$-).

6. Ending Av. -ĕ dative (radical) = Skt. -ĕ.
(Chiefly GAv.)

From root: GAv. *darᵊsōi* 'to see' ($\sqrt{dars}$-), *suyĕ*, *savōi* 'to profit, save' ($\sqrt{su}$-), *pōi* 'to protect'.

7. Ending -te locative.
(GAv. and YAv.)

From root: GAv. *āitĕ* 'to go to' ($\sqrt{i}$-) Ys. 31.9.—From stem: YAv. *daste* 'to put, make' Vsp. 15.1.

§ 721. A number of other formations in the acc., gen., loc., cases of abstract nouns may be regarded as infinitives. For examples, see Geldner, in *K.Z.* xxvii. p. 226; Bartholomae, in *K.Z.* xxviii. p. 17, *B.B.* xv. p. 215 seq.

VII. PERIPHRASTIC VERBAL PHRASES.

§ 722. In the Av., there is an inclination occasionally to use periphrastic phrases made up by means of an adj., a participle or a noun, with a copula verb or auxiliary, instead of a regularly formed tense-stem. The auxiliary may sometimes even be omitted. The periphrastic phrase is chiefly found in YAv.; its presence, however, is recognized in GAv.—Cf. Whitney, *Skt. Gram.* § 1069 seq.

§ 723. The possible existence of a Periphrastic Perfect has been noted above, § 623.

§ 724. A number of Periphrastic Expressions made by means of an adjective, a participle, or a noun combined with a verb, deserve special mention.

1. Periphrastic with Av. $\sqrt{i}$- 'to go' = Skt. $\sqrt{i}$-, cf. Whitney, *Skt. Gram.* § 1075 a. GAv. *stavas ayenī* 'I shall praise' Ys. 50.9.

2. With Av. $\sqrt{āh}$- 'sit' = Skt. $\sqrt{ās}$-, and Av. $\sqrt{stā}$- 'stand' = Skt. $\sqrt{sthā}$-, cf. Whitney, *Skt. Gram.* § 1075 c. YAv. *upa.maiⁱtīm āste* 'remains', *tĕ hištᵊnti jᵊarᵊjᵊarᵊntiĭ* 'they keep flowing'.

3. With Av. √*ah-* 'be' = Skt. √*as-*, and Av. √*bū-* 'be' =
Skt. √*bhū-*, cf. Whitney, *Skt. Gram.* § 1075 d. GAv. *ahvā frī-
nəmnā* 'let us both pray to', 1 du. injunct. Ys. 29.5; GAv. *hyāṯ
cihṣnuṣō* 'let one be gratifying' Ys. 43.15; GAv. *isvā hqs* 'being able,
possessed of'; YAv. *paⁱrikərⁿntiš aŋhən* 'may be looking about';
YAv. *yaoždayqn aŋhən.* Cf. also *fraoⁱristā* Yt. 13.25.—YAv. *yaṯ
bavāni aⁱwi.vanyā* 'that I may be conquering'; YAv. *yaoždāta būn*
'they become cleansed', *vavanə buye* 'become victorious'.

4. With √*dā-* 'give, make, do'. So apparently YAv. *aⁱbīgaⁱryā
daⁱbē* 'I do accept', *paⁱtiricya daⁱbē* 'he does throw away' cf. § 718.

———

INDECLINABLES.

§ 725. **General Remark.** The indeclinable words in
Avesta, correspond in general to those in Sanskrit and in
the other Indo-Germanic languages. Under Indeclinables
are comprised Adverbs, Prepositions, Conjunctions, and
Interjections. These may be taken up in detail.

A. Adverbs.

§ 726. The adverbs in Av., as in Skt., may be made
either from a pronominal stem or from a noun-stem by
means of a suffix, or their forms are merely crystallized
cases of old or abandoned nouns.

1. Adverbs made by Suffix.
(Cf. Whitney, *Skt. Gram.* § 1097.)

§ 727. A number of adverbs are made by adding
suffixes to a noun or an adjective stem, or especially to
a pronominal stem. Their meaning is various.

a. Adverbs of Place.
(Cf. Whitney, *Skt. Gram.* §§ 1099, 1100.)

§ 728. The principal adverbs of place made by means
of a suffix are:

Suffix Av. *-tō* = Skt. *-tas*, Av. *aⁱwitō* 'around' = Skt. *abhitas*.
—Suffix *-ṛra* = Skt. *-tra*, Av. *kuṛra* 'where' = Skt. *kútra;* Av.
haṛra 'along, with' = Skt. *satrá.*—Suffix *-da* = Skt. *-ha*, Av. *ida*
'here, now' = Skt. *ihá.* Likewise a number of others.

b. Adverbs of Time.
(Cf. Whitney, *Skt. Gram.* § 1103.)

§ 729. The number of temporal adverbs that are
made by means of a suffix is not extensive but corresponds
in proportion to the Sanskrit. Examples are:

Suffix GYAv. -*dā*, -*da* = Skt. -*dā*, -*dhā*, -*dha*, Av. *yadā*, *yada* 'when' = Skt. *yadā̆*; Av. *kada*, *kadā* 'when?' = Skt. *kadā̆*. So Av. *aδa* 'then' = Skt. *ádha*, *ádhā*.

c. Adverbs of Manner and Degree.
(Cf. Whitney, *Skt. Gram.* §§ 1101, 1104 seq.)

§ 730. The adverbs of manner and degree made by means of a suffix are numerous.

Suffix Av. -*þa* = Skt. -*thā*, GYAv. *yaþā*, *yaþa* 'as' = Skt. *yáthā̆*; Av. *aþa*, *aþa* 'so' = Skt. *átha* (*áthā*).—Suffix -*š* = Skt. -*s* (Whitney, § 1105), Av. *þriš* 'thrice' = Skt. *tris*.—Suffix -*ti* = Skt. -*ti* (Wh., § 1102), Av. *aⁱti* 'thus'.—Suffix -*vaţ* (acc. sg. advbl.) = Skt. -*vat* (Wh., § 1106), Av. *vacastaštivaţ* 'after the manner of the text'. Similarly Av. *hakərəţ* 'once' = Skt. *sakŕt*.

2. Case-forms as Adverbs.
(Cf. Whitney, *Skt. Gram.* § 1110 seq.)

§ 731. Many adverbs in Av., as in Skt., are really only stereotyped cases of nouns, adjectives, or pronouns, used with an adverbial force.

1. Accusative as Adverb — frequent (cf. Whitney, § 1111): (a) From pron. stem, Av. *iţ* 'even' = Skt. *it*; Av. *kaţ* 'how' = Skt. *kát*; Av. °*ciţ* particle = Skt. °*cit*; Av. *cōiţ* (cpd. w. *iţ*) particle = Skt. *cět*; Av. *nōiţ*, *naēda* 'not' = Skt. *nět*.—(b) From adj. stem, Av. *nūrqm* (acc. sg. f.), *nūrəm* (acc. sg. n.) 'now, quick', cf. Skt. *nūnám*; Av. *aparəm* 'hereafter' = Skt. *áparam*.—(c) From noun-stem, Av. *nqma* 'by name' = Skt. *nåma*.

2. Instrumental as Adverb (cf. Wh., § 1112): (a) From pron. stem, Av. *yavata* 'as long' = Skt. *yāvatā̆*; Av. *tā* 'by this, therefore', *yā* 'by which, whereby', *āiš* 'thereby' (§ 431).—(b) From adj., Av. *daššina* 'to the right' = Skt. *dákšiņ̄ena*; Av. *yesnyata* 'praiseworthy' (cf. Wh., § 1112 d); Av. *tarasca* 'across' (§ 287 above) = Skt. *tiraścá*; Av. *fraca* 'forth' Ys. 9.8 (cf. § 287), cf. Skt. *prácā*.

3. Dative as Adverb (cf. Wh., § 1113): Av. *bityāi*, *þrityāi* 'for second, third time', Vd. 16.15, v. l.

4. Ablative as Adverb (cf. Wh., § 1114): (a) From pron. stem, *āţ* (GAv.), *āaţ* (YAv.) 'then' cf. § 431 above = Skt. *āt*.—(b) From noun-stem, *aṇtarᵉ.naēmāţ* 'within'.—(c) From adj. stem, Av. *dūrāţ* 'from afar' = Skt. *dūrāt*; Av. *paskāţ* 'behind' = Skt. *paścāt*.

5. Genitive as Adverb—in temporal sense (cf. Wh., § 1115): Av. *xšapō* 'at night'.

6. Locative as Adverb (cf. Wh., § 1116): From noun and adj. stems, Av. *dūi̯re, dūraē-ca* 'afar' = Skt. *dūré*; Av. *asne, asnaē-ca* 'near'.

3. Miscellaneous Adverbs and Particles.
(Cf. Whitney, *Skt. Gram.* § 1122.)

§ 732. A number of adverbial words, chiefly mono-syllabic forms, deserve mention here. Examples are:

a. Place. Av. *kva (kᵃva)* 'where' = Skt. *kvà;* Av. *haca* 'with, forth' = Skt. *sáca;* Av. *parᵑtarᵉ* 'outside'. Likewise some others; see § 728 above.

b. Time. Av. *nū* 'now' = Skt. *nú, nū́;* Av. *mošu* 'soon, quickly' (§ 38) = Skt. *makṣú;* Av. *pascaētā* 'after'.

c. Manner. Av. *aēva* 'so' = Skt. *ēvá;* GAv. *nanā* 'differently, specially' (§ 17) = Skt. *nānā;* Av. *ca* 'how'.

d. Negative. Av. *mā* 'not' (prohibitive) = Skt. *mā́.*

e. Asseverative. Av. *bā* 'indeed, truly', *bādā* 'even, indeed, always'.

4. Adverbial Prefixes.
(Cf. Whitney, *Skt. Gram.* § 1118 seq.)

§ 733. Here belong the verbal prefixes treated below (§ 749), some of which however show at times more or less distinctly their original adverbial value. Examples are:

Av. *aⁱpi, aⁱpī* (GAv.) 'even, for, afterward' = Skt. *ápi;* GAv. *aⁱbī,* YAv. *aⁱwi* 'to, unto' (occasionally advbl.) = Skt. *abhí;* Av. *ava, avā* (GAv.), *avō* (Ys. 30.10 extra metrum) 'down' = Skt. *áva, avás;* Av. *parō* 'forth, before, beyond' = Skt. *parás;* Av. *haca* 'with, forth' = Skt. *sácā;* Av. *upaⁱri* 'above' = Skt. *upári.*

B. Prepositions.
(Cf. Whitney, *Skt. Gram.* § 1123 seq.)

§ 734. Prepositions in the sense of words that 'govern' oblique cases do not strictly exist in Avesta, any more than in Sanskrit. There are, however, a number of adverbial words which are used with the oblique cases and which define such cases more precisely. Their office is thus directive. These are termed Prepositions, and sometimes they seem really to govern the cases with which they stand.

§ 735. A fuller discussion of the Prepositions and of the cases with which they are used, belongs rather to Syntax. A mere enumeration of these forms in comparison with the Skt. is here given. Some of the words are case-forms used adverbially with a prepositional value; see under Syntax.

Principal Avesta Prepositions.

aipi (with acc., loc.) 'upon, after, for', cf. Gk. *ἐπί* = Skt. *ápi*

aiwi, GAv. *aibī* (w. acc., dat., loc.) 'to, unto, upon', cf. *ἀμφί* = Skt. *abhí*

adairi (w. acc.) 'under, beneath', cf. Skt. *adhár* (adv.)

ana (w. acc.) 'along, upon', cf. Gk. *ἀνά*

anu (w. acc.) 'along, after, according to' = Skt. *ánu*

antarə (w. acc., instr., loc.) 'between, among', cf. Lat. *inter* = Skt. *antár*

apa (w. dat.) 'away, off', cf. Gk. *ἀπό* = Skt. *ápa*

arəm (w. abl., Ys. 51.14) 'without', opp. Skt. *áram*

avi, aoi (w. acc., dat., gen.) 'to, upon'; (w. abl.) 'from'; (loc.) 'in'

ā (w. acc., dat., abl., gen., loc.) 'hither, from, to, until' = Skt. *ā*

upa (w. acc., loc.) 'unto, in', cf. Gk. *ὑπό* = Skt. *úpa*

upairi (w. acc., instr.) 'above, over', cf. Gk. *ὑπέρ* = Skt. *upári*

tarō, tarasca (w. acc.) 'through, across', cf. Lat. *trans* = Skt. *tirás, tiraścā*

paiti (w. acc., instr., dat., abl., gen., loc.) 'to, at, for, with', cf. *ποτί* = Skt. *práti*

pairi (w. acc., abl.) 'around, from around', cf. *περί* = Skt. *pári*

para (w. acc., instr., abl., gen.) 'before, from', cf. *πέρᾱ* = Skt. *párā*

parō, GAv. *parə* (w. abl., gen., loc.) 'before, beside', cf. *πάρος* = Skt. *parás*

pasca (w. acc., instr., abl., gen.) 'after, behind' = Skt. *paścā*

pascaēta (w. acc.) 'after, following'

pasne (w. acc., gen.) 'behind, on the other side of', cf. Lat. *pōne*

mat (w. instr., abl., gen.) 'with' = Skt. *smát* (§ 140 above)

haca (w. acc., instr., abl., gen.) 'with, in consequence of' = Skt. *sácā*

haþra (w. acc., instr., dat.) 'with, along with' = Skt. *satrā*

hada (w. instr., dat., abl.) 'with, along with' = Skt. *sahá*.

§ 736. The Prepositions, as in other languages, are not infrequently placed after the case which they determine, instead of before it; they thus become 'Postpositions'. Examples are numerous:

Av. *apəm ā* 'to the water', *raocanəm paiti* 'at the window', *aṣ̌āt haca* 'in accordance with righteousness', etc. Similarly in the loc. case *-hva, -ꝑva* = *•su + a;* so *ahmya* 'therein' = *ahmi + a.* Others likewise.

§ 737. The abl. phrase YAv. *aṇtarāṭ naēmāṭ* 'within' is employed, in addition to its adverbial use, also with a force that is practically equivalent to a preposition: Av. *aṇtarāṭ naēmāṭ yārⁿdrājō* 'within a year's time'; *aṇtarāṭ naēmāṭ barⁿpriᵩva* 'within the wombs'.

C. Conjunctions.

(Cf. Whitney, *Skt. Gram.* § 1231 seq.)

§ 738. The conjunctions and particles of adverbial value have in part been treated above under Adverbs. It remains only to emphasize the conjunctive force of some of the most important Co-ordinates and Subordinates. They are mostly postpositive in position.

1. Co-ordinate Conjunctions.

§ 739. The chief co-ordinate conjunctions, copulative, adversative, etc. are here noted.

a. Copulative. Av. *ca* 'and, que' = Skt. *ca;* Av. *ca ... ca* 'both ... and' = Skt. *ca ... ca;* Av. *uta* 'also' = Skt. *utá;* Av. *uta ... uta* 'both ... and' = Skt. *uta ... uta.* Negative, Av. *nōiṭ* 'not' = Skt. *nḗd;* Av. *nōiṭ ... nōiṭ, nōiṭ ... naēda, nava ... nōiṭ* 'neither ... nor'.

b. Adversative. The only one in use seems to be Av. *ta* 'but, however' = Skt. *tú.*

c. Disjunctive. Av. *vā* 'or, else', e. g. Vd. 12.1 = Skt. *vā;* Av. *vā ... vā* 'either ... or' = Skt. *vā ... vā.*

d. Causal. Av. *zī* 'for' (orig. asseverative, and often so used in Av. as in Skt.) = Skt. *hí.*

e. Illative. Here may be noticed Av. *aþa* 'so, therefore' = Skt. *átha.* Perhaps also some others.

2. Subordinate Conjunctions.

§ 740. The subordinate conjunctions, temporal, modal, final, etc., with adverbial force, have been noted above under Adverbs (§ 728 seq.), e. g. Av. *yada* 'when', *yaþa* 'as, that', etc. To these may be added the conditional conjunction Av. *yezi, yedi* 'if' = Skt. *yádi.*

D. Interjections.

§ 741. A few exclamations are worthy of notice; they are, in part, remnants of cases of unused words crystallized as Interjections. Examples are not numerous.

§ 742. The most important Interjections are: Av. *āi* 'O' (w. voc.) = Skt. *āi*; Av. *ušta* 'hail' (an old loc.). Likewise a few others, probably originally case-forms of nouns or adjectives, e. g. Av. *āvōya* 'alas' (old instr.), cf. *āvōya mē bāvōya* 'woe, woe indeed to me' Yt. 3.14; Av. *inja* 'ha, here', *tinja* 'ho, there'.

WORD-FORMATION.

FORMATION OF DECLINABLE STEMS.

§ 743. **General Remark.** Words are made from roots either directly without an affix, or they are more commonly formed by means of added suffixes, or again by composition.

(1) Only a small proportion of declinable stems, however, are made directly from verbal or pronominal radicals in their bare root-form without any affix. The simple root does sometimes serve as a declinable stem (see discussion below, § 744), but this happens chiefly in compounds.

(2) The great majority of words, in Av. as in other tongues, is derived from radicals by assuming an affix (suffix or prefix). The root-part of the word contains the fundamental idea; the prefix or suffix modifies its meaning.

(3) A third method of making new words is by combining words already formed so as to build up a compound.

The formation of verbs and pronouns has been sufficiently treated above; attention is here given to the formation of noun-words.

1. Suffixless Formation.

Root-Words.

(Cf. Whitney, *Skt. Gram.* § 1147.)

§ 744. A limited number of declinable stems, nouns and adjectives, in Av. as in Skt, are made directly from a simple root without assuming any suffix. The suffix-

less stems have been discussed above, under Declension
§§ 248, 261 etc. They occur oftenest as finals of compounds; they are therefore frequently made up with verbal
prefixes.

As to signification, the root-words, as in Skt.
(cf. Whitney, *Skt. Gram.* § 1147a), are action-words, especially infinitives; or they may be nouns of agency. Some-
times· they are adjectives.

§ 745. As examples of Root-Words without Suffix
may be given:

Av. *vac-* 'voice, word' = Skt. *vâc-*; Av. *druj-* 'deceit, Fiend' = Skt. *drúh-*; Av. *adruh-* 'undeceiving'
= Skt. *adrúh-*; Av. *aⁱwi-ṣac-* 'following' = Skt. *abhi-ṣâc-*.

Note 1. In Av., as in Skt., root-words at the end of a compound
are subject to some variation. (a) Internal *a* is often lengthened, *anuⁱ-
hāc-* 'attending'. — (b) Radical *i, u* remain unchanged. — (c) Roots ending
in a short vowel including *-ar* usually assume a *t*, as in Skt. (cf. Whitney,
Skt. Gram. § 1147 d), Av. *âbᵊrᵊt-* title of a priest (√*bar-*), cf. Skt. *ᵒbhṛt-*,
Whitney, *Skt. Gram.* § 383 h. Similarly in the prior member of a compound, Av. *sruṭ.gaoṣa-* 'of listening ears' (√*sru-*), cf. Skt. *ṡrút-karṇa-*; Av.
jiṭ.aṣa- (√*ji-*), cf. Whitney, *Skt. Gram.* §§ 1147 e, 383 h.

Note 2. Reduplication is perhaps to be sought in Av. *tū-tuc-*, cf.
loc. pl. *tᵃtuḳìva* Vd. 6.51, cf. Skt. *tvâc-*.

---

2. Derivation by Prefix and Suffix.
(Cf. Whitney, *Skt. Gram.* §§ 1118, 1136.)

§ 746. Words are derived from radicals chiefly by
the addition of prefixes and suffixes. The Prefixes and
Suffixes may now be taken up in detail.

PREFIXES.
a. Nominal Prefixes, Substantive and Adjective.
(Cf. Whitney, *Skt. Gram.* § 1121.)

§ 747. A number of prefixes are used in making new
words of substantival or adjectival value out of words already formed; these may be called **nominal** or **noun-**

prefixes. The most important Nominal Prefixes (subst. and adj.) in Av. are: *a-* negative, *hu-* 'well', *duš-* 'ill'.

§ 748. Examples of nouns and adjectives formed with modifying nominal prefixes are:

> Av. *a-* negative (*an-* before vowels, *ə-* before *v;* rare *ana-*) = Skt. *a-, an-:* e. g. Av. *a-srušti-* 'disobedience'; Av. *an-arəþa-* 'wrong' = Skt. *anartha-;* Av. *ə-visti-* 'ignorance' = Skt. *dvitti-;* Av. *ana-marždika* 'unmerciful'.
>
> Av. *hu-* (occasionally *hao-*) 'well' = Skt. *su-:* e. g. Av. *hu-šiti-* 'prosperity' = Skt. *sukṣiti-;* Av. *hao-zqþwa-* 'friendship'.
>
> Av. *duš-* (sporadic *dᵃuš-*) 'ill' = Skt. *dus-:* e. g. Av. *dušiti-* (i. e. *duš-šiti-* § 186) 'distress'; sporadic Av. *dᵃuš-sravah-* 'inglorious'. Likewise a few others.

b. Verbal Prefixes.
(Cf. Whitney, *Skt. Gram.* § 1076 seq.)

§ 749. A number of verbal prefixes or so-called 'prepositions' occur in combination with verbs; they modify or define the meaning of these more clearly. Some of these prefixes were originally stereotyped cases of nouns that have assumed an adverbial character.

§ 750. The most important verbal prefixes in Av. are the following. The meanings given are of course only general and approximate. See Whitney, *Skt. Gram.* § 1077.

> Av. *aⁱti* 'past, over, beyond', √*bar-* + *aⁱti* 'bring over to' = Skt. *áti*
> *aⁱpi* 'upon, on', √*jan-* + *aⁱpi* 'smite upon' = Skt. *api*
> *aⁱwi,* GAv. *aⁱbī* 'to, upon, against',√*gam-* + *aⁱwi, aⁱbī* 'come upon'=Skt. *abhí*
> *anu* 'after, along', √*i-* + *anu* 'go after' = Skt. *ánu*
> *aⁿtarə* 'between, among', √*mrū-* + *aⁿtarə* 'interdict' = Skt. *antár*
> *apa* 'away, forth, off', √*bar-* + *apa* 'bear away' = Skt. *ápa*
> *ava* 'down, upon', √*jan-* + *ava* 'strike down' = Skt. *áva*
> *avi, aoi* 'to, upon', √*bar-* + *avi* 'bring to'
> *ā* 'to, unto', √*bar-* + *ā* 'bring to' = Skt. *ā*
> *upa* 'to, unto, toward', √*bar-* + *upa* 'bring up' = Skt. *úpa*
> *us, uz* 'up, forth, out', √*bar-* + *us, uz* 'bring forth' = Skt. *úd*
> *nī* 'down, in, into', √*jan-* + *nī* 'smite down' = Skt. *ní*
> *niš, niž* 'out, forth, away', √*bar-* + *niš, niž* 'bring away' = Skt. *nís*
> *para* 'away, forth', √*bar-* + *para* 'bear away' = Skt. *párā*
> *paⁱri* 'round about, around', √*bar-* + *paⁱri* 'bear around' = Skt. *pári*

frā 'forth, fore, forward', √*bar-* + *frā* 'bring forth' = Skt. *prá*
pai̯ti 'towards, against, back', √*bar-* + *pai̯ti* 'bring towards' = Skt. *práti*
vī 'apart, away, out', √*bar-* + *vī* 'bear asunder' = Skt. *ví*
hąm, haŋ-, GAv. *hə̄m, hə̄ŋ-* 'together', √*bar-* + *hąm* 'bear together' =
Skt. *sám*.

Note. Instances of stereotyped case-forms of a noun entering into
verbal combination as prefix, are to be found: e. g. Av. *yaoš* + √*dā-*,
yaoš-dā̊i̯ti 'makes pure', cf. Av. *yaoš* Ys. 44.9 = Skt. *yṓs*.

§ 751. The connection between the prefix and the
verb, in Av. as in Vedic Skt. (Whitney, *Skt. Gram.* § 1081)
is very loose; several words, therefore, often intervene between the prefix and the predicate, so that sometimes it
is difficult to tell whether the prefix is to be connected
directly with the verb or is to be regarded merely as an
adverb: e. g. *apa haca ązahibyō | miþra barōiš* 'mayest
thou, O Mithra, bring us away from distresses' Yt. 10.23,
beside *apa-bara̡i̯ti* 'he brings away' Vd. 5.38.

§ 752. A repetition of the prefix is not uncommon,
that is, the prefix may stand at some distance before the
predicate and then be repeated in combination with the verb:

As an example of such repetition compare, Av.
hąm ida šaētəm hąm.bārayən 'let them c o l l e c t
possessions t o g e t h e r there' Vd. 4.44.

Note 1. In GAv., the m e t r e shows that the second prefix is re-
gularly to be expunged: e. g. GAv. *hya̡t hə̄m vohū || mazdā [hə̄m⁰]-fraštā
manaŋhā* 'when he c o n f e r r e d w i t h Vohu Manah' Ys. 47.3. Again *hya̡t
þwā hə̄m cašma̡i̯nī [hə̄ŋ]-grabəm* 'when I conceived thee in mine eye'
Ys. 31.8. Similarly *us . . . [uz]-jən* Ys. 46.12; et al.

Note 2. In the case of a long predicate, when several subjects or
objects belong to the same verb, the verb itself is sometimes expressed
but once, the prefix being then repeated each time with the subject or
object as the case may be: e. g. *aya daēnaya fraorəṇta | ahurō mazdā̊
ašava | frā vohu manō, frā . . . frā . . . frā . . .* 'Ahura Mazda professed
his faith according to this law, Vohu Manah professed it, so did' etc.
Ys. 57.24.

§ 753. When the prefix immediately precedes the verb
to which it belongs, the form of the prefix is sometimes

made subject to the rules of sandhi (see Sandhi, below); sometimes, however, it undergoes no change but is allowed to remain unaltered, cf. §§ 51, 52 above. Thus:

(a) With Sandhi. Av. √az- 'to drive' + *ava, upa, para* may give *avāzōiṭ (ava + az), upāzaiti (upa + az), parāzaṇti (para + az)*;—Av. √i- 'to go' + *upa, para* gives *upaēta- (upa + ita), parāiti (para + aēiti)*;—Av. √vac- 'to speak' shows *paityaoḥta* 'he spoke' Ys. 9.2, and *aipyūḥda- (aipi + uḥda)*, cf. § 52 Note 1;—Av. √hac- 'follow', *upavhacaiti (upa + hac)*; —Av. √harz- 'let go', *upavharᵊzaiti, fravharᵊzaiti*.

(b) Without Sandhi. Av. √as- 'to reach, obtain', *ava.aṣnaoiti, paiti.aṣnaoiti* (beside *frāṣnaoiti* with sandhi). Also many other examples.

Note 1. The metre sometimes determines whether sandhi is to take place, or whether the hiatus is to be allowed to remain; compare instances like *paiti.apayaṭ* Yt. 8.38, *pairi.apaya* Yt. 10.105, et al.

Note 2. The forms *us, niš* (with voiceless *s*) are used chiefly before voiceless consonants, the forms *uz, niž* are used before voiced; but this rule is likewise by no means without exception. Thus Av. *uzharᵊṇti, uzuḥṣyqn, nižbᵊrᵊta*, so *ᵊrᵊžuḥda-* (*z* before voiced sounds); but *usaᵤa-, nišqsya* Ys. 50.12, *arᵊšuḥda-* (*s* before voiced).

Note 3. The preposition Av. *hqm* 'σύν' = Skt. *sám* appears in various forms, the form being assimilated to the sound following: thus, *ham-* (before vowels), *hqm* (before labials and some other consonants), *haŋ* (before gutturals, palatals, dentals), also *hᵊm-, hᵊŋ-* occur in GAv.—Examples are Av. *hamarᵊna-, hqmbārayᵊn, haŋkārayemi, haṇjasᵊṇṭe, haṇlacaiti*. Some exceptions to the law of assimilation occur, e. g. *mainyuhqm.taṣta-* 'constructed by the spirit'; et al.

§ 754. Specially to be observed in compounds is the treatment of an original *s* after a prefix ending in *i, u*.

1. The original *s*, as expected, becomes *š* after *i, u*, cf. Whitney, Skt. Gram. § 185. Thus, YAv. *nišṭaiti* (√stu-) Yt. 14.42; YAv. *nišṭayeiti* (√stā-) Yt. 10.109 (but GAv. *paitistavas* with *s* Ys. 50.9); Av. *aⁱvišāc-* 'accompanying' Ys. 52.1 = Skt. *abhiṣāc-*; Av. *paitišmaramna-* (v. l. *paiti.šmarᵊmna-, paiti.marᵊmna-*) 'thinking upon' (Av. √mar- = Skt. √smar- § 140) Yt. 10.86.—Similarly in internal

reduplication, unless followed by *p* §§ 155, 109. Thus, Av. *hišma-rəŋt-* 'remembering'. But (with *sp*) Av. *hispōsəṇtəm*, *hispōsəmna* 'spying' Yt. 8.36, Yt. 10.45.

2. Frequently the peculiar writing *šh*, *šh* is found after *i*, *u*. It seems to be an attempt at etymological restoration. Thus, Av. *ānuš.hac-* 'attending' Ys. 31.12 = Skt. *ānuṣác-*; Av. *aiwišhuta-* (v. l. *aiwiš.huta-*) 'pressed haoma-juice' (Av. √*hu-* = Skt. √*su-*) Ys. 11.3; Av. *pairišhaḫta-* 'encircled' Ys. 11.8 = Skt. *pariṣvakta-*; Av. *hušhafa* 'soundly sleeping' (§ 95) Ys. 57.17. — Similarly in internal reduplication, Av. *hišhaḫti* 'it clings' (√*hac-*).

3. Complicated are the following formations: GAv. *niš-a-vharatū* 'let him protect' Ys. 58.4 (beside Av. *nī ... harai̯te* Ys. 19.10); YAv. *niš-a-vhasti* 'he settles down' Ys. 57.30 (beside *nišādaya̯t* Ys. 9.24); Av. *pairiavharšta-* 'imbrued' (beside v. l. *pairivharšta-*.)

SUFFIXES.

§ 755. Most derivatives, in Av. as in other languages, are made by means of suffixes. These resemble the corresponding suffixes in Skt., and they may likewise be divided into two general classes:

a. Primary Suffixes, or those added directly to original roots or to words resembling such.

b. Secondary Suffixes, or those added to derivative stems which have already been formed with a suffix.

These two classes may now be taken up in detail.

A. Primary Derivatives.
(Cf. Whitney, *Skt. Gram.* § 1143.)

§ 756. A Primary Derivative is a word that is formed by adding one of the so-called Primary Suffixes directly to an original root.

§ 757. Form of the Root. The root to which the primary suffix is added may undergo more or less change in its form. Most generally the root is strengthened either to the *guṇa* or the *vṛddhi* stage. Such variations for the most part answer to corresponding changes in Skt.; they will n o t be taken up in detail here; reference may be made to Justi, *Handbuch der Zendsprache* pp. 366—383.

§ 758. Some g e n e r a l r e m a r k s, subject to exceptions, however, may be made with regard to the strengthening of the root.

(a) In Av., as in Skt., internal radical *a* is commonly vṛddhied before the suffix *a;* but it commonly remains unchanged before the suffix *i*.

(b) Internal and initial *i, u* are guṇated before the suffix *a* and *i*.

(c) Internal and final *i, u* are guṇated before the suffixes *-ana, -ah, -pra, -pwa, -man*.

(d) The root generally remains unstrengthened before the suffixes *-ta, -ti, -u, -pu, -ra, -van*, and in some other cases.

The Principal Primary Suffixes.
(Cf. Whitney, *Skt. Gram.* § 1146 a.)

§ 759. A list of the principal primary suffixes may here be given in connection with the Sanskrit, see Whitney, *Skt. Gram.* § 1146 a. One or two of these here given might perhaps be further resolved and regarded as secondary, but it is found convenient to include them here.

1 -*a*	17 -*uš*	33 -*ma*
2 -*an*	18 -*u*	34 -*man*
3 -*ana*	19 -*ka (-ika)*	35 -*mi*
4 -*aini*	20 -*ta (-da)*	36 -*mna, -mana*
5 -*ant (-ant)*	-*ita, -ata*	37 -*ya*
6 -*ar*	21 -*tar (-dar)*	38 -*yah, -išta*
7 -*ah*	22 -*ti*	39 -*yu*
8 -*a*	23 -*tu*	40 -*ra*
9 -*ana (-ana)*	24 -*tra (-pra, -dra)*	41 -*ri*
10 -*i*	25 -*tva (-pwa)*	42 -*ru*
11 -*in*	26 -*pa (-da)*	43 -*va*
12 -*ina*	27 -*pi*	44 -*van (-pvan)*
13 -*iš*	28 -*pu*	45 -*vant (-pwant)*
14 -*iští*	29 -*na (-ana)*	46 -*vah*
15 -*i*	30 -*nah*	47 -*var (-vara)*
16 -*u*	31 -*ni*	
-*una*	32 -*nu*	

A few other Primary Suffixes.

§ 760. A few other suffixes occur sporadically and may also for convenience be classed under the primary division, though their secondary origin may be possibly traced. As examples may be taken:

Suffix, Av. -*aya* in *zarᵊdaya-*; Av. -*āra* in *daḳṣāra-*; Av. -*ura* in *razura-*; Av. -*tah* in *parṣtāh-* (Whitney, § 1152 a). Likewise some others.

Discussion of the Primary Suffixes.

1. Av. -*a* = Skt. -*a* (Whitney, § 1148).

§ 761. With this suffix a great number of derivatives are formed. Their signification is various; they are adjectives, action-nouns, agent-nouns. The root is generally strengthened by *guṇa* or *vṛddhi*. Examples are very numerous:

Noun (masc., neut.). Av. *vāza-* 'strength' = Skt. *vája-*; Av. *maēja-* 'cloud' = Skt. *mēghá-*; Av. *gaoṣa-* 'ear' = Skt. *ghóṣa-*; Av. *caḳra-* 'wheel' (neut.) = Skt. *cakrá-*.—Adjective. Av. *ama-* 'strong' = Skt. *áma-*; Av. *asāra-* 'headless'; Av. *aməṣa-* 'immortal' = Skt. *amṛta-*; Av. *draoja-* 'deceitful' = Skt. *drógha-*. Also many others.

2. Av. -*an* = Skt. -*an* (Whitney, § 1160).

§ 762. This suffix forms a limited number of neuter and masculine nouns of action and agency, including also a few adjectives. Examples are:

Noun. Av. *uḳṣan-* m. 'ox' = Skt. *ukṣán-*; Av. *taṣan-* m. 'shaper' = Skt. *tákṣan-*; Av. *ᵘrvan-* m. 'soul'; Av. *masan-* n. 'greatness' = Skt. *mahán-*.—Adjective. Av. *aviṇdan-* 'not receiving'; Av. *ᵒtaᵘrvan-* 'conquering'.

3. Av. -*ana* (-*əna*) = Skt. -*ana* (Whitney, § 1150).

§ 763. This suffix, as in Skt., forms many derivatives, nouns and adjectives of varied value. Roots in *i*, *u* commonly receive the *guṇa*-strengthening before this suffix.

Some of the adjectival derivatives made with this element can hardly be distinguished from participles. Examples are:

Noun. Av. *vaᵥhana-* n. 'clothing' = Skt. *vásana-;* Av. *hanja-mana-* n. 'assembly' = Skt. *sqgámana-;* Av. *bajina-* n. 'dish' = Skt. *bhājana-,* § 17, 30; Av. *maᵉhana-* n. 'dwelling'; Av. *raocana-* n. 'light, window' = Skt. *rôcana-.* — A d j. Av. *zayana-* 'wintry'.

§ 764. After an *r*, the Av. form *-ᵊna* answers in some instances to orig. *-ana*, while in others it corresponds to *-na* (i. e. *-ᵊna*, see § 802). These must be distinguished. As examples after *r* :

(a) Av. *-ᵊna* = Skt. *-aᵥa* (i. e. *-ᵃna*), Av. *varᵊna-* m. 'choice, belief' = Skt. *varaṇá-;* Av. *hamᵊrᵊna-* n. 'battle, conflict' = Skt. *samáraṇa-.* Likewise some others. But observe Av. *karana- (-ana)* 'side, shore' Yt. 5.38 etc. opp. to Av. *karᵊna- (-na)* 'ear' Yt. 11.2 = Skt. *kárṇa-;* yet consult the variants.

(b) Examples of Av. *-ᵊna* (i. e. *-ᵊna*) = Skt. *-na*, after *r*, are given below under *-na* § 802.

4. Av. *-aᶦni* = Skt. *-ani* (Whitney, § 1159).

§ 765. Sporadic traces of the suffix *-ani* in Av., as in Skt., are to be found. As example may be quoted:

Av. *duᶎ-aᶦni-* adj. 'evil' Vd. 14.5.

5. Av. *-aṇt (-ᵊṇt, -iṇt)* = Skt. *-ant* (Whitney, § 1172).

§ 766. This is the suffix which forms the pres. and fut. participles. It has been sufficiently treated above, §§ 477, 514.

6. Av. *-ar (-ara)* = Skt. *-ar* (Whitney, §§ 169 a, 1151 l).

§ 767. This suffix forms a limited number of nouns; they are almost all of the neuter gender. It occurs likewise in adverbs and prepositions, probably there representing old case-endings. In some nouns the form becomes *-ara* by the *a*-transfer. The prefix *-ar* must be connected with *-an,* cf. § 337. Examples:

Av. *vaᵈar-* n. 'weapon' = Skt. *vádhar-;* Av. *zafar-* n. 'jaw'; Av. *baᵉvar-, baᵉvara-* (a-inflection) 'thousand'; Av. *nar-, nara-* m. 'man' = Skt. *nár-, nara-.* Observe the adverbs Av. *aṇtarᵊ* 'between, inter' = Skt. *antár;* Av. *iᵉarᵊ* 'immediately'.

7. Av. *-ah* = Skt. *-as* (Whitney, § 1151).

§ 768. From this very common suffix, in Av. as in Skt., a great number of derivatives are made. They are

chiefly abstract neuter nouns and some adjectives (probably
originally distinguished from the latter by a difference of
accent, cf. Whitney, *Skt. Gram.* § 1151 e). The roots in
i, u show *guṇa*-strengthening before this suffix. Examples are:
Noun. Av. *avah-* n. 'aid' = Skt. *ávas-*; Av. *aēnah-*
n. 'sin' = Skt. *énas-*; Av. *təmah-* n. 'darkness' = Skt.
támas-; Av. *raocah-* n. 'light'. — Noun, Adjective.
GAv. *dvaēṣah-* n. 'hate', *dvaēṣah-* adj. 'hateful' Ys. 43.8
= Skt. *dvéṣas-*; Av. *vasah-* n. 'will', *vasah-* adj. 'willing' Ys. 31.11, cf. Whitney, *Skt. Gram.* § 1151 e. A
feminine noun in Av., as in Skt., is Av. *uṣah-* f.
'dawn' = Skt. *uṣás-*, cf. § 357 above.

8. Av. -ā = Skt. -ā (Whitney, § 1149).

§ 769.   This suffix makes feminine adjectives
answering to masculine and neuter *a*-stems. It also makes
a considerable number of feminine action-nouns. Its form
is often obscured, as it frequently appears as *ă* §§ 25, 17, 18.
Examples have been given under declension of fem. nouns
and adjectives §§ 362, 243.

9. Av. -āna (-ăna) = Skt. -āna (Whitney, § 1175).

§ 770.   This suffix is used in forming middle and
passive participles; it has therefore been treated under
the different tense-systems, §§ 477, 507 etc. Examples of
participles mid. and pass. are:
Av. *isāna-* 'ruling' = Skt. *iśāna-*; Av. *mavhāna-*
'thinking' (aorist ptcpl.); Av. *yazāna-* 'worshipping',
pāpərətāna- 'fighting'. Also others.

Note. A few noun-stems in -*an* also show -*ăna* as a sporadic heavy
form with *a*-transfer, e. g. *arṣăna-* 'male' § 310.

10. Av. -i = Skt. -i (Whitney, § 1155).

§ 771.   With this suffix a considerable number of derivatives are formed. They are adjectives and substantives.

The masculines are chiefly agent-nouns; the feminines are abstracts; there is an occasional neuter. The root generally shows the *guṇa* stage. Examples are:

Nouns. Av. *aži-* m. 'dragon' = Skt. *áhi-*; Av. *kavi-* m. 'Kavi, king' = Skt. *kaví-*.—Av. *karši-* f. 'circle, circuit' = Skt. *kṛṣí-*; Av. *dāhi-* f. 'creation' = Skt. *dhāsi-*; Av. *maēni-* f. 'wrath, punishment' Ys. 31.15, 44.19 = Skt. *mēni-*.—Av. *aši-* n. 'eye' = Skt. *ákṣi-*. —Adjective. Av. *zairi-* 'yellow, golden' = Skt. *hári-*; Av. *darši-* 'bold', etc.

§ 772. On Av. *-ita* = Skt. *-ita*, see § 786 below.

§ 773. On Av. *-iti* = Skt. *-iti*, see § 789 below.

11. Av. *-in* = Skt. *-in* (Whitney, § 1183).

§ 774. Only a few undoubted instances of this suffix as a primary derivative are noted; its use in secondary formation of possessives is more familiar (§ 835), though not so common as in Sanskrit. Quotable examples of the primary usage of this suffix are:

Noun. Av. *kainin-* f. 'maiden'.—Adjective. Av. °*tacin* (in *afštacinō*) 'flowing, running'.

12. Av. *-ina* = Skt. *-ina* (Whitney, § 1177 c).

§ 775. There are a few quotable derivatives that show this suffix. Examples are:

Adjective. Av. *dašina-* 'right' = Skt. *dákṣiṇa-*; Av. *zairina-* 'golden' = Skt. *hariṇá-*.

13. Av. *-iš* = Skt. *-is* (Whitney, § 1153).

§ 776. A small number of neuter nouns are made by means of this suffix. Instances are:

Noun. Av. *barᵊziš-* n. 'cover, mat', cf. Skt. *barhís-*; Av. *hadiš-* n. 'abode'; Av. *vipiš-* n. 'judgment', *snaipiš-* n. 'weapon', cf. § 359 above.

14. Av. *-iši* = Skt. *-iṣī* (cf. Whitney, §§ 1153, 1156 a).

§ 777. This suffix belongs perhaps rather under secondary derivation than under primary endings. It occurs in only one or two words and may best be mentioned here. It seems to answer as a corresponding feminine formation

(-iži) to the preceding *-iš*. The root is strengthened before it. Examples are:

Noun. Av. *təviži-* f. 'power, might' = Skt. *távišī-;*
Av. *hāⁱriži-* f. 'mother'.

§ 778. On *-išta* in superlatives see § 813 below.

15. Av. *-ī* = Skt. *-ī* (Whitney, § 1156).

§ 779. This suffix is to be sought in feminine nouns and adjectives, cf. also Whitney, *Skt. Gram.* § 1156 b. Such feminines correspond for the most part to masc. and neut. stems in *-a, -i* or a consonant. Sometimes it is doubtful whether it would not be better to regard some of the nouns and adjectives as secondary in origin.

Noun. Av. *mahžī-* f. 'fly', *vaⁱdī-* f. 'stream, river'. —Adjective. Av. *daēvī-* 'fiendish' = Skt. *dēvī-;* Av. *drīvī-* f. 'poor' (§ 187, fem. to *driju-* m. n.). Likewise certain others, cf. § 362.

16. Av. *-u* = Skt. *-u* (Whitney, § 1178).

§ 780. This suffix which closely resembles the corresponding one in Skt., forms derivative nouns and adjectives. The nouns are chiefly masculine. Examples are:

Noun. Av. *ąsu-* m. 'branch, twig' = Skt. *ąśú-;* Av. *išu-* m. 'arrow' = Skt. *išu-;* Av. *pasu-* m 'small cattle' = Skt. *paśú-;* Av. *tanu-, tanū-* f. 'body' = Skt. *tanú-, tanú-;* Av. *madu-* n. 'honey' = Skt. *mádhu-.* —Adjective. Av. *poᵘru-* 'full' = Skt. *purú-;* Av. *vaŋhu-, vohu-* 'good' = Skt. *vasu-;* Av. *driju-* 'poor'. Likewise others.

§ 781. On Av. *-una* = Skt. *-una,* see § 802 below.

§ 782. On Av. *-ura* = Skt. *-ura,* see § 816 below.

17. Av. *-uš* = Skt. *-us* (Whitney, § 1154).

§ 783. This suffix forms a few derivatives; they are chiefly neuter nouns. As examples may be quoted:

Av. *arᵉduš-* n. 'assault, battery', *garᵉbuš-* n. 'milk', *tanuš-* n. 'person' Ys. 43.7, cf. § 360. Add also *manuš-* masc. nom. propr.

18. Av. -ū = Skt. -ū (Whitney, § 1179).

§ 784. With this suffix only an occasional feminine noun is made. As an example may be quoted Av. *tanū- (tanu-)* f. 'body' = Skt. *tanū- (tanú-).*

19. Av. -ka = Skt. -ka (Whitney, § 1186).

§ 785. This suffix forms a few primary derivatives; they are nouns and adjectives. Its use in secondary derivation, as in Skt., is more common. Examples of -ka as primary suffix are:

Noun. Av. *adka-* m. 'garment, robe' Yt. 5.126 = Skt. *átka-;* Av. *mahrka-* m. 'death' = Skt. *marká-.*—Adjective. Av. *huška-* 'dry' = Skt. *śúṣka-.*

20. Av. -ta (-ita, -ata) = Skt. -ta (-ita, -ata), Whitney, § 1176.

§ 786. The suffix -ta is used chiefly (1) in forming past-passive participles directly from the conjugation-stem as explained above under Participles, § 710 seq. It appears also (2) in a few general nouns and adjectives which show more or less of a participial character. The feminine form shows -tā. Examples are:

(1) Past-Passive Participles in -ta, see § 711 above.—(2) Nouns and Adjectives: Av. *dūta-* m. 'messenger' = Skt. *dūtá-;* Av. *aŋgušta-* m. 'toe' = Skt. *aṇguṣṭha-;* Av. *zasta-* m. 'hand' = Skt. *hásta-;* Av. *aṣa-* n. 'right' (-ṣa = -rta, § 163) = Skt. *ṛtá-;* Av. *anāhita-* fem. 'Anahita' nom. propr.

Note 1. The suffix Av. -ita = Skt. -ita (Whitney, § 1176 d) appears in a few adjectives: e. g. Av. *zairita-* 'yellow, green' = Skt. *hárita-;* Av. *masita-* 'great'; perhaps in Av. *raodita-* 'red'. Likewise in the ptcpl. adj. Av. *darṣita-* 'emboldend, daring' (√darš-) Ys. 57.11 = Skt. *dhṛṣitá-,* cf. § 712 above.

Note 2. A suffix -ata (stem a + ta) = Skt. -ata (Whitney, § 1176 e) may be assumed in a few nouns and adjectives which show partly a gerundive force. Av. *ərəzata-* n. 'silver' = Skt. *rajatá-;* Av. *yazata-* m. 'adorable, divinity'.

Note 3. The suffix -ta is sometimes disguised as -da in accordance with certain phonetic changes, cf. § 89 etc. Av. *vərəzda-* 'grown great, mighty' (i. e. vardh + ta) = Skt. *vṛddhá-.* So Av. *drəwda-* Yt. 13.11. Likewise -r-ta is often disguised as -ṣa, cf. § 163.

21. Av. *-tar (-dar)* = Skt. *-tar* (Whitney, § 1182). .

§ 787. This suffix is used in forming masculine, and a few feminine, nouns of a g e n c y and r e l a t i o n s h i p, cf. § 321 seq. The suffix is attached directly to the root; and radical *i, u* are generally strengthened before it. There is a corresponding feminine *-þrī* besides. Examples of *-tar* are:

(1) N o u n s o f A g e n c y. Av. *dātar-* m. 'giver, creator' = Skt. *d(h)ấtar-*; Av. *zaotar-* m. name of priest = Skt. *hốtar-* et al. — (2) N o u n s o f R e l a t i o n- s h i p. Av. *patar-* m. 'father' = Skt. *pitár-*; Av. *mātar-* f. 'mother' = Skt. *mātár-*.

Note 1. The suffix *-tar* is sometimes disguised (cf. § 163): Av. *vāẓar-* m. 'eater'; Av. *bāẓar-* m. 'rider' = Skt. *bhártar-*.

Note 2. Observe the form of the suffix in YAv. *duẓdar-*, GAv. *dugᵉdar-* f. 'daughter' Yt. 17.2, Ys. 45.4 = Skt. *duhitár-*.

Note 3. Observe *-tar* as n e u t e r in infin. YAv. *vīdōiþre* Yt. 10.82 (perhaps here *harᵉþre* v. l. Ys. 62.2).

22. Av. *-ti* = Skt. *-ti* (Whitney, § 1157).

§ 788. This suffix is used in forming a large number of feminine nouns, chiefly abstracts, and also an occasional masculine noun or adjective. The suffix is added directly to the root in its weak form. Examples are numerous:

N o u n. Av. *anumaⁱti-* f. 'thought, agreement' = Skt. *ánumati-*; Av. *cisti-* f. 'wisdom' = Skt. *cítti-*; Av. *stūⁱti-* f. 'praise' = Skt. *stuti-*; Av. *supti-* f. 'shoulder' = Skt. *súpti-*; Av. *paⁱti-* m a s c. 'lord' = Skt. *páti-*.— D i s g u i s e d form, Av. *aṣi-* f. 'Rectitude' = **ar-ti* § 163.

§ 789. A form Av. *-iti* = Skt. *-iti* (Whitney, § 1157 g) is found in a few words: Av. *spaṣiti-* Yt. 19.6, *āskᵉiti-* (cf. § 32) Ys. 44.17.

23. Av. *-tu* = Skt. *-tu* (Whitney, § 1161).

§ 790. With this suffix, in Av. as in Skt., are formed a number of abstract and concrete derivatives. They are prevailingly masculine. The root is commonly strengthened before the *-tu*. Examples are:

Av. *yātu*- m. 'sorcerer' = Skt. *yātú*-; Av. *haētu*- m.
'bridge' = Skt. *sétu*-; Av. *hratu*- m. 'wisdom' = Skt.
krátu-; Av. *pitu*- m. 'food' = Skt. *pitú*-; Av. *vantu*-
masc. 'spouse'; Av. *jyātu*- (fem. ?) 'life' = Skt. *jīvátu*-.

24. Av. -*tra* (-*þra*, -*dra*) = Skt. -*tra* (Whitney, § 1185).

§ 791. The suffix -*tra* (-*þra*, -*dra*, -*dra*) forms numerous nouns, which are chiefly neuter, and a few adjectives. The root usually has the *guṇa*-strengthening, but
sometimes it remains unaltered. The original form (1) -*tra*
of the suffix is preserved only after sibilants or a written
nasal (§ 78); otherwise it becomes regularly (2) -*þra* (§ 77, 2).
The forms (3) -*dra* (in -*f*ˀ*dr*-, -*hdr*-) and -*dra* (in -*zdr*-, -*ždr*-)
appear only under special circumstances, see §§ 79, 89, 90.
The corresponding feminine is -*trā*. Examples are:

Noun. Av. *uštra*- m. 'camel' = Skt. *úṣṭra*-; Av.
vastra- n. 'garment' = Skt. *vástra*-.—Av. *puþra*- m.
'son' = Skt. *putrá*-; Av. *hšaþra*- n. 'rule, kingdom' =
Skt. *kṣatrá*-.—Av. -*yaoh*ˀ*dra*- n. 'girdle' Yt. 15.54 (cf.
§ 79) = Skt. *yôktra*-; Av. *vah*ˀ*dra*- n. 'word', cf. Skt.
vaktrá-; Av. *važdra*- m. 'bearer'.—Adjective. Av.
fraoᵘrvaēštra- 'productive'. — Av. *bröiþra*- 'cutting'
Yt. 10.130 etc. (√ *brī*-).—Av. *mazdra*- 'learned, wise'
(§ 90), *siždra*- Yt. 8.36; Vd. 13.2.

Note. A few feminines with suffix Av. -*trā* = Skt. -*trā* (Whitney,
§ 1185 d) may here be noted: Av. *aštrā*- f. 'goad' = Skt. *áṣṭrā*-; Av.
zaoþrā- f. 'libation' = Skt. *hótrā*-.

25. Av. -*tva* (-*þwa*, -*dwa*) = Skt. -*tva* (Whitney, § 966 a).

§ 792. The suffix -*tva*, (-*þwa*, -*dwa* §§ 94, 96) is used (1) chiefly
in forming the Gerundive, or declinable future-passive participle of adjectival value (Latin -*ndus*) as described above § 717. But it is found
also (2) in a few abstract nouns. The feminine form is -*tvā*, -*þwā*.

1. Gerundive. Examples of the suffix so used have been
given above.—2. Noun. Av. *staoþwa*- n. 'praise'; *daṣtvā*- f. 'skill',
vaþwā- f. 'herd'.

26. Av. -*þa* (-*da*, -*da*) = Skt. -*tha* (Whitney, § 1163).

§ 793. With the suffix -*þa* (-*da*, -*da* §§ 89, 90, 77 Note 3) are made, in Av. as in Skt., a number of action-nouns of different genders, and a few verbal adjectives with passive signification. The root usually appears in its weak form. The feminine is regularly -*þā*. Examples are:

Noun. Av. *raþa-* m. 'chariot' = Skt. *rátha-*; Av. *hamərəþa-* m. 'foe'; Av. *vīciþa-* m. 'decision'; Av. *zaþa-* m. 'birth'.—Av. *arəþa-* n. 'subject, thing' = Skt. *ártha-*.—Av. *gāþā-* f. 'song, hymn' = Skt. *gāthā-*; Av. *gaēþā-* f. 'being, creature'; Av. *ciþā-* f. 'penalty'.—

Adjective. Av. *uḫda-* 'spoken, word' (§ 77 Note 3) = Skt. *ukthá-*; Av. *þrafəda-* 'gratified'; Av. *yūḫda-* 'girt, compact' Yt. 10.127.

Note 1. On Av. -*da* = orig. -*ta*, see § 786 above.

Note 2. The form -*aþa* (probably thematic *a* + *þa*) = Skt. -*atha* (Whitney, § 1163 c) occurs in some words: Av. *vaḫṣaþa-* n. 'growth' = Skt. *vakṣátha-*.

27, 28. Av. -*þi*, -*þu* = Skt. -*thi*, -*thu* (Whitney, §·1164).

§ 794. The suffix Av. -*þi* = Skt. -*thi* occurs in one or two words; it is also disguised as -*ti*. The suffix Av. -*þu* = Skt. -*thu* is likewise quotable. Both of these elements are used in making nouns, the suffix being attached to the weak form of the root. Examples are:

Suffix -*þi*: Av. *ciþi-* f. 'punishment'; Av. *aⁱþi-* f. 'dread, terror'. So Av. *asti-* m. 'minister', cf. Skt. *áti^thi-*; Av. *haḫti-* n. 'thigh' = Skt. *sákthi-*.—Suffix -*þu*: Av. *hiþu-* m. 'dweller, socius'.

§ 795. On the form -*þra*, see -*tra* § 791 above.

§ 796. On the form -*þwa*, see -*tva* § 792 above.

§ 797. On -*þwan*, see -*van* § 820 below.

§ 798. On the form -*þwaṇt*, see below, § 821.

§ 799. On the form -*da*, see -*ta* § 786, and -*þa* § 793 above.

§ 800. On -*da* see above, -*þa* § 793.

§ 801. On the form -*dra* see -*tra*, -*þra* § 791 above.

29. Av. -*na*, (-*una*) = Skt. -*na*, (-*una*), Whitney, § 1177.

§ 802. The suffix -*na* is used (1) in making a few past-passive participles equivalent to those in -*ta*. It is also employed (2) in forming some abstract nouns and likewise adjectives whose verbal character is easily recognized. The root is generally not strengthened.

(1) Passive Participle in -*na*. Examples of this formation have been given at § 713 above.— (2) Noun. Av. *fraṣna-* m. 'question' = Skt. *praśná-:* Av. *yasna-* m. 'sacrifice' = Skt. *yajñá-;* Av. *hvafna-* m. 'sleep' = Skt. *svápna-.*—Av. *parᵊna-* n. m. 'wing' = Skt. *parṇá-.*—Av. *haēnā-* f. 'army' = Skt. *sḗnā-.*— Adjective. Av. *maȝna-* 'naked' = Skt. *nagnd-;* Av. *kamna-* 'few'. See also § 713.

§ 803. The suffix form Av. -*una* = Skt. -*una* (Whitney, § 1177 c), doubtless of secondary origin, is distinguishable in a few words: Av. *taᵘruna-* 'young' = Skt. *táruṇa-;* Av. *aᵘruna-* 'fiery' = Skt. *aruṇá-.*

30. Av. -*uah* = Skt. -*nas* (Whitney, § 1152).

§ 804. The suffix -*uah* is perhaps somewhat more common in Av. than in Sanskrit. It forms neuter abstracts. Radical *i*, *u* are strengthened before it; *a* remains unchanged. Examples are: Av. *raēhnah-* n. 'possession' = Skt. *réknas-;* Av. *hvarᵊnah-* n. 'splendor'; Av. *draonah-* 'offering' = Skt. *dráviṇas-;* Av. *parᵊuah-* n. (in *parᵊnavhuṇtəm*) 'fulness' = Skt. *párīṇas-;* Av. *rafnah-* n. 'help, comfort'.

31. Av. -*ni* = Skt. -*ni* (Whitney, § 1158).

§ 805. With this suffix, as in Skt., are made a small number of nouns and adjectives. Strengthening of the root occurs. Examples are: Av. *varṣni-* m. and adj. 'virile, male' = Skt. *vṛ́ṣṇi-;* Av. *sraoui-* f. 'hip' = Skt. *śróṇi-;* Av. *fṣaoni-* f. 'fatness'.

32. Av. -*uu*, (-*jnu*) = Skt. -*uu*, (-*snu*), Whitney, §§ 1162, 1194.

§ 806. With the suffix -*uu*, as in Skt., a small number of nouns or adjectives are made. Examples are: Av. *bānu-* m. 'light, ray' = Skt. *bhānú-;* Av. *garᵊnu-* m. 'itch' = Skt. *gṛdhnú-;* Av. *tafuu-* m. 'fever' = Skt. *tapnú-.*—Av. *daēnu-* f. 'female, cow' = Skt. *dhēnú-.*

§ 807. The suffix Av. -*jnu* = Skt. -*snu* (Whitney, § 1194) is likewise quotable: e. g. Av. *raoḥjnu-* m. 'light, brightness' = Skt. *róčiṣṇú-;* Av. *pąsnu-* f. 'dust', cf. Skt. *pąsú.*

33. Av. -*ma* = Skt. -*ma* (Whitney, § 1166).

§ 808. With this suffix a considerable number of derivatives are made; they are adjectives and nouns. The nouns are chiefly masculine. The root is often strengthened. Examples are:

Noun. Av. *haoma*- m. 'haoma' = Skt. *sóma*-; Av. *azma*- m. 'fury'; Av. *uruþma*- m. 'growth'. — Av. *garᵊma*- n. 'heat' = Skt. *gharmá*-. — Adjective. Av. *ᵒbāma* 'shining' = Skt. *bhāma*-; Av. *taḫma*- 'strong, swift'; Av. *garᵊma*- 'hot' = Skt. *gharmá*-.

34. Av. -*man* = Skt. -*man* (Whitney, § 1168).

§ 809. The suffix -*man* in Av., as in Skt., forms a number of derivative action-nouns; most of these are neuter; a few are masculine. The root generally shows the guṇa-strengthening. Examples are:

Noun. Av. *asman*- m. 'stone, heaven' = Skt. *áśman*-; Av. *rasman*- m. 'column, rank'.—Av. *nāman*-, *nqman*- n. 'name' = Skt. *nāman*-; Av. *vaēsman*- 'dwelling' (in *vaēsmən-da* Yt. 10.86) = Skt. *vēśman*-; Av. *taoḫman*- n. 'seed' = Skt. *tókman*-; Av. *barᵊsman*- n. 'barsom'.

35. Av. -*mi* = Skt. -*mi* (Whitney, § 1167).

§ 810. This suffix, as in Skt., is found in a very few masculine and feminine nouns. Examples are:

Av. *varᵊmi*- m. 'wave, billow' = Skt. *ūrmi*-; Av. *dqmi*- m. 'creator' Ys. 31.8; Av. *ᵒzāmi*- m. 'birth' = Skt. *jāmi*.—Av. *būmi*- f. 'earth' = Skt. *bhāmi*-, *bhūmī*-.

36. Av. -*mna*, -*mana* = Skt. -*māna* (Whitney, § 1174).

§ 811. This suffix is used in forming the middle (passive) participles of the different systems. It has been discussed above, § 709 etc. Furthermore on Av. -*mna*, -*mana* (Gk. -μενος) opp. to Skt. -*māna*, see § 18 Note 2.

37. Av. -*ya* = Skt. -*ya* (Whitney, § 1213).

§ 812. This suffix is used in making the Gerundive (fut. pass. ptcpl. § 716) and also verbal adjectives; likewise a few nouns. It is sometimes difficult, in Av. as in Skt., to distinguish the primary from the secondary deri-

vatives made with this suffix. The root is usually weak.
The corresponding feminine form is *-yā*. Examples are:

> Gerundive and Adjective (cf. also § 716): Av. *ižya-* 'desir-
> able' = Skt. *ı̄ṣya;* Av. *jīvya-* 'living, fresh' = Skt. *jı̄vya-;* Av.
> *maı̄rya-* 'deadly'; Av. *haiþya-* 'true' = Skt. *satyı̄-;* Av. *maidya-*
> 'middle' = Skt. *mádhya-.* — Noun. Av. *hahya-* n. 'grain' = Skt.
> *sasyá-;* Av. *qiþyā-* fem. 'beam', cf. Lat. *antae.*

38. Av. *-yah, (-išta)* = Skt. *-īyas, (-iṣṭha)*, Whitney, § 1184.

§ 813. These suffixes are used respectively to form
the comparative and superlative degree of a number of
old adjectives The form *-išta* is perhaps more strictly
secondary, but as both forms are practically added directly
to the crude stem (§ 365) it is more convenient to keep
both together under the head of primary derivation. For
examples, see § 365.

39. Av. *-yu* = Skt. *-yu* (Whitney, § 1165).

§ 814. This suffix is attached in forming a very few nouns. The
root remains unstrengthened before it. Examples are:

> Noun. Av. *mainyu-* m. 'spirit', cf. Skt. *manyú-;* Av. *mərəþyu-*
> m. 'death' (√*mar-* + *ı̄* as in Skt.) = Skt. *mṛtyú-;* Av. *dahyu-*
> *daiŋhu-* fem. 'country', cf. Skt. *dásyu-.*

40. Av. *-ra* = Skt. *-ra* (Whitney, § 1188).

§ 815. This suffix is common, in Av. as in Skt.;
numerous adjectives are formed by it; these adjectives
may also be used as nouns of all three genders. The root
is usually weak. Examples are:

> Noun. Av. *vazra-* m. 'club' = Skt. *vájra-;* Av. *caxra-* n. 'wheel'
> = Skt. *cakrá-;* Av. *hurā-* f. 'a drink' = Skt. *súrā-.* — Adjective.
> Av. *uɡra-* 'mighty' = Skt. *ugrá-;* Av. *ciþra-* 'bright' = Skt. *citrá-;*
> Av. *suxra-* 'red' = Skt. *śukrá-;* Av. *ɡufra-* 'deep'.

§ 816. The form Av. *-ura* = Skt. *-ura* (Whitney, § 1188 f) used
apparently as a primary suffix has sporadic traces: Av. *razura-* m. f. 'forest'.
Perhaps also *arəzūra-* n. nomen propr. Mt. Demāvand *(-ūra).*

41. Av. *-ri* = Skt. *-ri* (Whitney, § 1191).

§ 817. This suffix is found in a very few derivatives. Examples
are: Av. *bairi-* f. 'abundance', cf. Skt. *bhári-;* Av. *tiɡri-* m. nomen propr.

15

42. Av. *-ru* = Skt. *-ru* (Whitney, § 1192).

§ 818. This suffix occurs in a very few words. Noun and adjective examples are quotable:

Noun. Av. *asru-* n. 'tear' = Skt. *áśru-*. — Adjective. Av. *vaṇdru-* 'desiring'. Uncertain *amru-, camru-*.

43. Av. *-va (-dwa, -spa)* = Skt. *-va* (Whitney, § 1190).

§ 819. With this suffix are formed a few derivative adjectives and nouns. The root generally appears in its weak form. The suffix is sometimes disguised in *-spa, -dwa* §§ 96, 97. The corresponding feminine form is *-vā*.

Noun. Av. *saᵘrva-* m. nomen propr., cf. Skt. *śarvá-;* Av. *aspa-* m. 'horse' (§ 97) = Skt. *áśva-;* Av. *awhvā-* f. 'soul'; Av. *gadwā-* f. 'bitch'. — Adjective. Av. *haᵘrva-* 'whole' = Skt. *sárva-;* Av. *draoǐdva-* 'hard'; Av. *ərᵊdwa-* 'high, arduus' = Skt. *ūrdhvá-;* Av. *aᵘrva-* 'speedy'.

44. Av. *-van (-þwan)* = Skt. *-van* (Whitney, § 1169).

§ 820. The suffix *-van* is comparatively rare in Avesta. It forms derivative nouns and adjectives. The root remains unstrengthened. A *t* is added, as in Skt., to roots ending in a short vowel, including *-ar;* this gives rise to the form *-þwan* § 94. Examples are:

Noun. GYAv. *advan-, adwan-* m. 'way' = Skt. *ádhvan-;* Av. *kərᵊþwan-* m. 'doer' (√*kar-* + *t*, see just above) = Skt. *kṛ́tvan-;* Av. *karšvan-* f. n. 'clime, zone'. — Adjective. Av. *isvan-* 'able, potent' (√*is-*). With reduplication Av. *yōiþwan-* 'active' (i. e. *ya-it-van* fr. √*yat-*).

45. Av. *-vaṇt (-þwaṇt)* = Skt. *-vant* (Whitney, § 1233 g).

§ 821. The ending *-vaṇt* as primary suffix occurs in a few words, chiefly verbal adjectives. Some of these derivatives bear resemblance to an *aṇt*-participle of Cl. 8. As above (§ 820), a *t* is added after a root ending in a short vowel, including *-ar;* this gives rise to the form *-þwaṇt* § 94. The weak form of the root is the rule. The suffix *-vaṇt* sometimes seems to add the force of possession as it does when secondary. Examples are:

Av. *aᵘrvaṇt-* adj. and noun 'swift, courser' = Skt. *árvant-;* Av. *sᵘrunvaṇt-* 'audible'; Av. *bərvaṇt-* 'advantageous' (§ 31); Av. *vivaᵘhvaṇt-* m. nomen propr. = Skt. *vivásvant-;* Av. *stərᵊþwaṇt-* 'levelling' (√*star-* + *t*, see above); Av. *vibərᵊþwaṇt-* 'divided, having pauses' (√*bar-* + *t* added).

46. Av. -vah (-vāuh-,-uš) = Skt. -vas (-vās, -us), Whitney, § 1173.

§ 822. With the suffix -vah (-vāuh str., -uš wk.) is made the perfect active participle. The root is reduplicated except in a few words which make the perfect without reduplication. For examples, see § 348 seq.

47. Av. -var (-vara) = Skt. -vara (Whitney, § 1171).

§ 823. With the suffix -van (-vara) are made a considerable number of neuter nouns. They commonly show a parallel stem with suffix -van (§ 820). The form -vara arises by transfer to the a-declension. Examples are:

> Av. karfvar- n. f. beside karfvan- 'clime, zone'; Av. zafar- (i. e. *zap-var § 95) n. beside zafan- 'jaw'; Av. baēvar- n. beside baēvan- 'myriad'. So miþwara- n. (-vara) beside miþwan- 'pair'. Observe Av. srvara- (for sruvara- § 68) 'horned, Sruvara'.

B. Secondary Derivatives.
(Cf. Whitney, Skt. Gram. § 1202 seq.)

§ 824. The so-called Secondary Suffixes are those which are added to make new derivatives from primary derivatives or words which already show a suffix. The forms thus arising are termed Secondary Derivatives. The great majority of them are adjectives, but often they are nouns.

§ 825. Form of the Stem. In assuming the secondary suffix the stem, though it is already prepared, may still undergo other changes in form.

> (a) Final -a of a stem disappears before suffixes beginning with a vowel or y.

> (b) Final -i, -u of a stem are generally strengthened before suffixes beginning with a vowel, though u, as in Skt., sometimes remains unchanged, cf. Whitney, Skt. Gram. § 1203 a, b.

> (c) Final -an of the stem appears as -an, -n, depending chiefly upon the difficulty of pronunciation (cf. Whitney, § 1203 c): Av. barᵉsmanya- 'relating to the barsom', vyāḳaᶦnya- 'ruling in the council'; Av. vārᵉþrajni- 'victorious' (from an-stem), cf. Skt. vār- traghna-.

(d) The initial syllable of the stem receives the vṛddhi-strengthening in secondary derivation less often in Av. than in Skt., cf. Whitney, § 1204. Examples of vṛddhi (cf. § 60) are: Av. *āhuⁱri-* 'of the Ahurian', cf. Skt. *āsuri-;* Av. *māzdayasni-* 'belonging to the worship of Mazda'; Av. *gāvya-* beside *gaoya-* 'belonging to the cow', opp. Skt. *gávya-* (§ 60 Note d); Av. *hāvani-* 'relating to Havana'; Av. *ārṣṭya-* 'belonging to a spear'. For guṇa-forms, see above § 60 Note c.

The Principal Secondary Suffixes.
(Cf. Whitney, *Skt. Gram.* § 1207.)

§ 826. A list of the principal secondary suffixes may here be given in connection with the Sanskrit, see Whitney, *Skt. Gram.* § 1207.

1 -*a*	11 -*u*	21 -*na*
2 -*aēna (-aēni, -aini)*	12 -*ka (-aka, -ika)*	22 -*ma*
3 -*aona*	13 -*ta*	23 -*man (-mana, -mna)*
4 -*an*	14 -*tara, -təma*	24 -*maṇt*
5 -*ana (-āna, -āni)*	15 -*tāt*	25 -*ya*
6 -*aṇc*	16 -*ti*	26 -*ra*
7 -*i*	17 -*pa (-ḍa)*	27 -*va*
8 -*in*	18 -*pya*	28 -*van*
9 -*ina*	19 -*pwa*	29 -*vana*
10 -*ī*	20 -*hwana*	30 -*vaṇt*

A few other Secondary Suffixes.

§ 827. A few other secondary suffixes occur sporadically and may for convenience be mentioned here.

Suffix. Av. -*ṣva* in numerals, *priṣva-* 'a third', *capruṣva-* 'a fourth', *pavtavhva-* 'a fifth' Ys. **19.**7. Also Av. -*sa* = Skt. -*sa* (Whitney, § 1229), Av. *navasa-, iṣasa-, aṣṣasa-*.

1. Av. -*a* = Skt. -*a* (Whitney, § 1208).

§ 828. This suffix, in Av. as in Skt., is very common. It forms secondary derivatives from nouns or from adjectives. The derivatives thus made are chiefly adjectives denoting 'relating to', 'of', 'with'; but there are also numerous nouns, including patronymics.

The secondary *a* is especially common in compound words, transferring the whole compound to the *a*-declension; the treatment of that, however, does not really belong here. Examples of *a* as secondary suffix are:

Noun. Av. *haozą̄pwa-* n. 'the goodly company'; Av. *ayaṇha-* m. n. 'iron' Ys. 11.7 = Skt. *āyasá-*; Av. *narava-* m. 'descendant of Naru' (patronym.).—Adjective. Av. *tamaṇha-* 'dark' = Skt. *tāmasa-* (w. vṛddhi); Av. *upa-sm-a-* 'upon the earth' *(z²m-)* § 836.

Note. Final *-i, -u* of the primitive g e n e r a l l y, but not a l-w a y s, appear as *-ay-, -av-* before this suffix. Thus, Av. *kāvaya-* 'kingly' *(kavi-)* = Skt. *kāvyá-*; Av. *dar²ja.ar²taya-* 'long-speared'; Av. *ma²nyava-* 'spiritual' *(ma²nyu-)*. But simple *y, v* in *staomya-* (fr. *staomi-*), *haozą̄pwa-* (fr. *huzaṇtu-*) above § 828.

2. Av. *-aðna (-aðni, -aini)* = Skt. *-ðna* (Whitney, § 1223 e).

§ 829. This suffix in Av. makes adjectives of material, of. Skt. *sāmidhðná-*, Whitney, § 1223 e. The form *-aðni* is found beside it in the same adjectives; the sporadic *-aini* appears to be a mere variation of the latter, cf. § 193 Note 2. Examples are:

Av. *ayaṇhaðna-, ayaṇhaðni-* 'made of iron'; Av. *ər²zataðna-, °aðni-* 'of silver'; Av. *zaranaðna-, °aðni-* 'golden'; Av. *bawraini-* 'of beaver-skin'.

3. Av. *-aona*, cf. Skt. *-ana*.

§ 830. This suffix (perhaps primitive *u*-stem + *ana* § 832) occurs in Av. *þraðtaona-* m. 'Thraetaona' = Skt. *trāitaná-*; Av. *ar²jaona-* m. nomen propr. Yt. 13.117 (? cf. Skt. *arhaṇa-* n.); Av. *pitaona-* m. nomen propr. Perhaps also in Av. *marĵaona-* adj. 'deadly'.

4. Av. *-an* (cf. Skt. *-in*).

§ 831. This derivative suffix forming secondary nouns and adjectives occurs in a few words. It corresponds in part to the Skt. suffix *-in*. A final stem vowel disappears before it. Examples are:

Noun. Av. *maþran-* m. 'prophet', cf. Skt. *mantrín-*; Av. *hāvanan-* m. nomen propr.—Adjective. Av. *puþran-* 'having a son', cf. Skt. *putrín-*; Av. *vīsan-* 'possessing a house'.

5. Av. *-ana (-āna, -ānī)* = Skt. *-ana (-āna, -ānī)*, Whitney, §§ 1175 a, 1223 a, b.

§ 832. This suffix is a patronymic and is found chiefly in proper nouns and adjectives. Before *-ana* a final stem vowel *a* may be dropped, or it may coalesce with the ending, thus giving -*āna*. A final *i* is strengthened before -*ana*. The form -*ānī* (-*ānī*) seems to be a corresponding feminine. The initial syllable is not always strengthened. Examples are:

Noun. Av. *jāmāspāna*- m. 'son of Jamaspa'; Av. *gaorayāna*- m. 'son of Gaori' Yt. 13.118; — Av. *vɔhrkāna*- m. 'Hyrcania'; Av. *ahurānī*- f. 'daughter of Ahura'.— Adjective. Av. *haēcaṭ.aspāna*- 'descended from Haecataspa'; Av. *āpwyāna*-, *āpwyānī*- 'belonging to the Athwyas' (Skt. *āptyá*-).

6. Av. -*aŋc*, -*ac* = Skt. -*añc*, -*ac* (Whitney, § 407 seq.).

§ 833. The ending Av. -*aŋc*, -*ac* (of verbal origin) is combined with prepositions and some other words to make a few derivative adjectives. It may practically be regarded as a secondary suffix. See § 287 above.

Av. *pa^urvaŋc*- 'advancing' (§ 287 above); Av. *fraŋc*-, *frac*- 'forward' = Skt. *prāñc*-, *prāc*-; Av. *nyaŋc*- 'downward' = Skt. *nyàñc*-; Av. *vīīvaŋc*- 'on all sides' = Skt. *viṣvañc*-.

7. Av. -*i* = Skt. -*i* (Whitney, § 1221).

§ 834. With this suffix are made some derivative adjectives and substantives chiefly patronymic. They are formed from noun-stems in -*a*; and most of the examples show the vṛddhi-strengthening.

Noun. Av. *hāvani*- m. nomen propr. (cf. Av. *havana*- = Skt. *sávana*-); Av. *uzdaēzi*- m. beside *uzdaēza*- 'heap'; Av. *hvawhzvi*- m. 'blessedness' Ys. 53.1. — Adjective. Av. *āhu^dri*- 'of the Ahurian' (§ 60), cf. Skt. *āsuri*-; Av. *māzdayasni*- 'Mazdayasnian' (fr. *māzdayasna*-); Av. *vār^əprajni*- 'victorious', cf. Skt. *vārtraghna*-; Av. *zāra-puštri*- 'of Zarathushtra'; Av. *raji*- 'belonging to Ragha' *(raja-)*.

8. Av. -*in* = Skt. -*in* (Whitney, § 1230).

§ 835. The suffix -*in* is used as a secondary ending in Av., as in Skt., in forming possessive adjectives. They are not numerous. A final vowel disappears before the suffix. Examples are:

Av. *pɔr^ənin*- adj. 'having a feather' *(parɔna-)* Yt. 14.38 = Skt. *parṇin*-; Av. *myɛzdin*- 'having offering' Yt. 13.64; Av. *drujin*- 'possessed of a devil' *(druj-)* Yt. 4.7.

9. Av. -*ina* = Skt. -*ina* (Whitney, § 1209 c).

§ 836. A secondary suffix -*ina* (apparently an *a*-inflection of -*in*) may be assumed for a few nouns and adjectives. As examples:

Noun. Av. *rapipwina-* m. nomen propr.; Av. *uʒahina-* m. nomen propr. — Adjective. Av. *vacahina-* 'consisting of a word, verbal' Vd. 4.2. Similarly the ending *-ini* in Av. *maʒʒini-* 'belonging to sheep' (fr. *maʒʒī-*).

          10. Av. *-ī* = Skt. *-ī* (cf. Whitney, § 1156 a).

§ 837. The primary derivatives in *-ī* have been treated above; one or two words however seem to show a more distinctive secondary origin, e. g. Av. *nāirī-* f. 'woman' (observe vṛddhi) = Skt. *nārī-*.

          11. Av. *u.*

§ 838. The suffix *u*, used in forming secondary derivatives, is to be recognized in one or two instances: Noun. Av. *haʒdawhu-* m. 'satisfaction, fill' Ys. 62.9.

    12. Av. *-ka (-aka, -ika)* = Skt. *-ka (-aka, -ika),* Whitney, § 1222 seq.

§ 839. With the suffix *-ka* are made a number of nouns and adjectives. The forms in *-aka, -āka, -ika* may conveniently grouped with it, cf. Whitney, §§ 1186 c, 1181 d. The corresponding feminine is *-kā.* As examples:

    Noun. Av. *araska-* m. 'disorder'; Av. *pasuka-* m. 'cattle, beast'; Av. *drafʃaka-* m. 'banner' (in *drafʃakavaṇt-*); Av. *dahāka-* m. nomen propr.; Av. *maʃyāka-* m. 'man'; — Av *marīdika-* n. 'mercy' (cf. Whitney, § 1186 c) = Skt. *mṛdīká-;* Av. *aᶦnika-* m. n. 'face' = Skt *ánīka-;* — Av. *nāirikā-* f. 'woman'; Av. *paᶦrikā-* f. 'fairy, Peri'. — Adjective. Av. *kasvika-* 'trifling'; Av. *kutaka-* 'small'. Pronominal adj. Av. *ahmāka-* 'ours' = Skt. *asmāka-;* Av. *ʃʃmāka-* 'your' = Skt. *yuṣmāka-,* cf. Whitney, § 1222 c.

    13. Av. *-ta* = Skt. *-ta* (Whitney, § 1245 e).

§ 840. This ending as secondary suffix occurs in a few words, adjectival and substantival. Examples are:

    Noun. Av. *þrita-* m. 'Thrita', cf. Skt. *tritá-;* Av. *bûʃyqstā-* f. 'Bushyansta'. — Adjective. Av. *aʃavasta-* adj. 'righteous', m. 'righteousness'; Av. *paᶦtʒrᵊta-* 'winged'.

    14. Av. *-tara, -tʒma* = Skt. *-tara, -tama* (Whitney, § 1242).

§ 841. These suffixes are used respectively in forming the comparative and superlative degree of adjectives, the latter also in the ordinals *vīsqstʒma-, satōtʒma-, ha-*

zavrōtəma-. The treatment of the stem-final before these endings has already been given. Examples, see §§ 364, 374.

15. Av. *-tāt* = Skt. *-tāt* (Whitney, §§ 1238, 383 k).

§ 842. This suffix makes feminine abstracts. Its independent origin is shown, for example, in Av. *yavaēca.tā*ᵗᵉ beside *yavaētāⁱtaēca* Ys. 62.6, Yt. 13.50, cf. § 893. Examples:

> Av. *uparatāt-* f. 'supremacy' = Skt. *uparátāt-;* Av. *ha*ᵘ*rvatāt-* f. 'completeness, Salvation' = Skt. *sarvátāt-*. Likewise others.

16. Av. *-ti* = Skt. *-ti* (Whitney, § 1157 h).

§ 843. The suffix *-ti* appears as secondary ending in a few words; the most important of these are the numerals. Examples are:

> , Av. *θanwarᵉti-* f. 'bow' (cf. *θanvar-*); Av. *χšvašti-* 'sixty' = Skt. *šašti-;* Av. *haptāⁱti-* 'seventy' = Skt. *saptati-;* Av. *navaⁱti-* 'ninety' = Skt. *navati-*, see § 366 above.

17. Av. *-θa (-δa)* = Skt. *-tha* (Whitney, § 1242 d).

§ 844. The secondary suffix *-θa* is to be sought in one or two numeral and pronominal words. As examples: Av. *haptaθa-* 'seventh' = Skt. *saptátha-;* Av. *puχδa-* 'fifth', cf. Skt. *pañc-a-tha-;*—Av. *avaθa-* 'thus, so'.

18. Av. *-θya* = Skt. *-tya* (Whitney, § 1245 b).

§ 845. This suffix in Av., as in Skt., makes one or two derivative adjectives from prepositions and adverbs. As instances: Av. *aⁱwiθya-* 'away, distant'; Av. *pascaⁱθya-* 'behind'.

19. Av. *-θwa* = Skt. *-tva* (Whitney, § 1239).

§ 846. With this suffix, as in Skt., a few neuter nouns denoting 'condition', 'state' are formed from adjectives and nouns. Examples:

> Av. *aɴhuθwa-* n. 'lordship'; Av. *ratuθwa-* n. 'mastership'; Av. *vaɴhuθwa-* n. 'good deed' = Skt. *vasutvá-*.

20. Av. *-θwana* = Skt. *-tvana* (Whitney, § 1240).

§ 847. This suffix is hardly more than an extension of the preceding, which it resembles in meaning. A quotable example is the abstract noun, Av. *nāⁱriθwana-* n. 'marriage', cf. Skt. *patitvaná-*, Whitney, § 1240.

21. Av. *-na* = Skt. *-na* (Whitney, § 1223 g).

§ 848. With this suffix a very few secondary derivatives are formed. Examples are:

Noun. Av. *ahuna-* m. 'the Ahuna formula'.—Adjective. Av. *hayana-* 'belonging to a well' Yt. 6.2; Av. *zrayana-* 'of the sea'; Av. *vahmana-* 'praiseworthy'; Av. *airyana-* 'Aryan'.

22. Av. -*ma* = Skt. -*ma* (Whitney, § 1224 b).

§ 849. With -*ma* as secondary suffix are made a few superlatives from prepositions, a few ordinal numerals, a small number of adjectives from nouns, and one or two derivative substantives likewise. Examples are:

Noun. Av. *spitāma-*, *spitama-* m. 'Spitama'.—Adjective. Av. *apɔma-* 'last' = Skt. *apamá-*; Av. *upɔma-* 'highest' = Skt. *upamá-*; —Av. *fratɔma-* 'first' = Skt. *prathamá-* (Whitney, § 487 h); Av. *nāuma-* 'ninth' (§§ 64, 374) = Skt. *navamá-*;—Av. *dahyuma-* 'belonging to the country' *(dahyu-)*; Av. *zaṇtuma-* 'belonging to the tribe'.

23. Av. -*man* (-*mana*, -*mna*) = Skt. -*man* (-*mna*), Whitney, §§ 1168 i, 1224 c.

§ 850. A very few words show the suffix -*man*, or its variations -*mana*, -*mna*. The examples are:

Noun. Av. *airyaman-* m. 'connection, family, Airyaman', cf. Skt. *aryamán-*.—Adjective. Av. *yātumana-* 'relating to a sorcerer'; Av. *zaranimna-* 'angered' Yt. 10.47.

24. Av. -*mant* = Skt. -*mant* (Whitney, § 1235).

§ 851. The secondary suffix -*mant*, like -*vant* below, is used in making a number of possessive adjectives from noun-stems. The noun-stems with which it is used, as in Skt., are chiefly *u*-stems. Examples are:

Av. *hratumant-* 'having wisdom' = Skt. *krátumant-*; Av. *gaomant-* 'having milk, flesh' = Skt. *gómant-*; Av. *madumant-* 'rich in sweets' = Skt. *mádhumant-*; —Av. *arɔpamant-* 'right, true to fact' (from *a*-stem); —Av. *afraṣīmant-* 'not progressing' (fr. *i*-stem).

25. Av. -*ya* (-*aya*) = Skt. -*ya* (-*iya*, -*īya*), Whitney, §§ 1210, 1214, 1215.

§ 852. The suffix -*ya* corresponds to Skt. -*ya*, -*iya* (§ 68, 1), and forms a large number of secondary derivatives. These are chiefly adjectives; less often they are nouns. The vṛddhi-strengthening which is often found in Skt. (Whitney, § 1211) is almost wanting in Avesta. The feminine form is *-yā*.

Before this suffix, the stems in *-a, -ā,* drop their final vowel; the stems ending in *-u* retain the *u* unchanged, unless it unites with a preceding *t* into *þw,* § 94.

A few forms in *-aya* occur, either by retention of stem-*a,* or by extension (§ 68 Note 3), compare Skt. *-iya,* Whitney, § 1214. Examples of *-ya* are:

Noun. Av. *aēþrya-* m. 'pupil'; Av. *nãwhaiþya-* n. nomen propr., cf. Skt. *nāsatya-;* Av. *vāstrya-* adj. 'farming', m. 'farmer'; — Av. *awhuyā-* f. 'lordship'. — Adjective. From *a-*stem: Av. *āhūirya-* 'lordly' (observe vṛddhi fr. *ahura-*) Yt. 13.82, 14.39; Av. *agrya-* 'topmost' = Skt. *ágrya-, agriyá-;* Av. *haomya-* 'relating to haoma' = Skt. *sōmyá-;* Av. *ḫšaþrya-* 'kingly' = Skt. *kṣatríya-;* Av. *yesnya-* 'revered' = Skt. *yajñíya-.* — From *ā-*stem: Av. *haēnya-* 'belonging to an army' = Skt. *sénya-;* Av. *gaēþya-* 'material, earthly'. — From *u-*stem: Av. *raþwya-* 'reasonable', cf. Skt. *ṛtviya-;* Av. *pouruya-* 'first' = Skt. *purvyá-;* so Av. *gaoya-, gāvya-* 'belonging to the cow' = Skt. *gávya-.* — From consonant stem: Av. *vīsya-* 'of the clan' = Skt. *viśyà-.*

Note. Observe the few forms that show *-aya* as remarked upon just above § 852 c. Examples are: Noun. Av. *zarᵊdaya-* n. 'heart' = Skt. *hṛdaya-;* Av. *zarᵊmaya-* adj. 'green', n. 'verdure', cf. Skt. *harmyá-.* — Adjective. Av. *aspaya-* (acc. *aspaēm*) 'belonging to a horse' = Skt. *áśvya-;* Av. *nāvaya-* 'flowing, navigable' = Skt. *nāvyà-,* cf. § 68 Note 3.

26. Av. *-ra* = Skt. *-ra* (Whitney, §§ 1226, 474).

§ 853. This suffix occurs in a very few words, chiefly pronominal derivatives. Examples are:

Av. *adara-* adj. 'under, lower' = Skt. *ádhara-;* Av. *apara-* adj. 'later, behind' = Skt. *ápara-;* Av. *upara-* adj. 'further, above' = Skt. *úpara-.* Probably Av. *hazawra-* adj. and n. 'thousand' = Skt. *sahásra-.* Observe Av. *ahura-* m. 'lord, Ahura' = Skt. *ásura-.*

27. Av. *-va, (-vya)* = Skt. *-va, (-vya),* Whitney, § 1228.

§ 854. The ending *-va* as secondary suffix occurs in a very few adjectives. These must be distinguished from orig. *u-*adjectives transferred to the *a-*inflection. Examples of *-va* as secondary suffix are:

Av. *ajrava-* 'belonging to the head' *(ajra-)*; Av. *bûnava-* 'belonging to the tail' *(buna-* § 185).

Note. The suffix Av. -*vya* = Skt. -*vya* (Whitney, § 1228 c) is disguised in one or two words, names of kindred: Av. *brātūirya-* m. 'uncle' § 191, cf. Skt. *bhrātṛvya-*.

28. Av. -*van,* (f. -*vairī*) = Skt. -*van,* (f. -*varī*), Whitney, § 1234.

§ 855. A few secondary derivatives are made with the suffix -*van*. They show also a corresponding feminine -*vairī*. Examples are:

Av. *ašavan-* adj. m., *ašavairī-* (beside *ašaonī-*) adj. f. 'righteous' = Skt. *ṛtāvan-* (f. -*varī*); Av. *āpravan-* m. 'priest' = Skt. *átharvan-*; Av. *haptō.karšvan-* n. 'seven karshvars', Av. *haptō.karšvairī-* 'belonging to the seven karshvars'.

29. Av. -*vana* = Skt. -*vana* (Whitney, § 1245 l).

§ 856. This suffix arises apparently by transfer of the preceding -*van* to the *a*-inflection. It bears also a relation to -*var* § 337. It is to be recognized in a couple of instances: Av. *āfrivana-* n. 'blessing'; Av. *panvana-* m. 'bow'; Av. *hâpravana-* adj. 'splendid'.

30. Av. -*vaṇt* = Skt. -*vant* (Whitney, § 1233).

§ 857. The suffix -*vaṇt* is closely akin to the suffix -*maṇt*, and like the latter it is used in making a large number of possessive adjectives from nouns. The suffix -*vaṇt* is used with *a-*, *i-* and consonant stems, -*maṇt* being employed chiefly with *u*-stems as noted above § 251. Examples are numerous:

From *a*-stem: Av. *amavaṇt-* adj. 'strong' = Skt. *ámavant-*; Av. *puþravaṇt-* 'having a son' = Skt. *putravánt-*; Av. *haomavaṇt-* 'having haoma' = Skt. *sómavant-*.—From *i*-stem: Av. *frazaiṇtivaṇt-* 'having offspring'; Av. *nāirivaṇt-* 'having a wife'; Av. *raēvaṇt-* 'radiant' = Skt. *rēvánt-*.—From consonant stem: Av. *aojavhvaṇt-, aojōvhvaṇt-* 'mighty' Ys. 57.11, Ys. 31.4 = Skt. *ójasvant-*; Av. *təmavhvaṇt-* 'dark' = Skt. *támasvant-*; Av. *paēmavaṇt-* 'with milk' *(paēman-)*; Av. *aršnavaṇt-* 'possessing a stallion' *(aršan-)*.

Note 1. A trace of the l e n g t h e n i n g of the final vowel before
-*vaṇt* (cf. Whitney, § 1233 d) is to be found in Av. *zairimyāvaṇt*- 'producing verdure' Yt. 7.5, cf. Skt. *vṛṣṇyāvant*-. So Av. *yuṣmāvaṇt*-, *ḥṣmāvaṇt*-.

Note 2. A few words, chiefly pronominal derivatives in -*vaṇt*, have
the meaning 'like to', 'resembling', cf. Whitney, *Skt. Gram.* § 1233 f.
Examples are: Av. *mavaṇt*- 'like me' = Skt. *māvant*-; Av. *pwāvaṇt*- 'like
thee, your Grace' = Skt. *tvāvant*-. So also Av. *vīsaᵢtivaṇt*- 'twenty-fold';
Av. *satavaṇt*- 'hundred-fold', § 376.

FORMATION OF COMPOUND STEMS.

§ 858. **General Remark.** Compounds, Verbal and
Nominal, occur in Avesta as in Sanskrit, but in Av. since
most words are written s e p a r a t e l y in the MSS. and each
is followed by a point, the compounds are not always so
easily recognized as in Skt., nor are the rules of Sandhi
so rigorously carried out.

Verbal Composition has been sufficiently treated above,
§ 749 seq.; it is necessary here to take up only the Noun-
Compounds.

Note. In printed texts the compounds are differently marked in
different editions; Geldner's Avesta has the compound united in printing
and retains the separating point (.); Westergaard likewise but a small
dash (-) is used; Spiegel's edition does not designate the compounds.

Noun-Composition.

§ 859. Noun-compounds have either a substantival or
an adjectival force. They consist usually of two members,
more rarely of three (§ 894), e. g. *drva-aṣa-ciþra* 'the sound
offspring of righteousness'. The members which enter into
composition may be nouns, adjectives, or indeclinables;
or they may be parts of a verb, either radical or participial. The final member of the compound receives the
inflection. The first member is subject to some modification in form, generally assuming the weak grade.

§ 860. E x a m p l e s of different combinations, nouns,
adjectives, etc., entering into composition are:

Av. *vīspaⁱti* (subst. + subst.) m. 'lord of the clan' = Skt. *viṣpáti-;* Av. *darᵊjō.bāzu-* (adj. + subst.) adj. 'longimanus' = Skt. *dīrgha-bāhu-;* Av. *vīspō.bāmya-* (adj. + adj.) adj. 'all-shining'; Av. *hvaspa-* (indecl. + subst.) adj. 'well-horsed' = Skt. *sváśva-;* Av. *rapaⁱštā-, rapaⁱštar-* (subst. + rad.) m. 'warrior standing in chariot' = Skt. *rathēṣṭhā́-;* Av. *nidāsmaⁱpiš-* (rad. + subst.) adj. 'having weapons laid down'; Av. *starᵊtō.barᵊsman-* (ptcpl. + subst.) adj. 'with out-spread barsom'. Likewise some other combinations.

Union of the Members of Compounds.

a. Contraction and Hiatus.

§ 861.   The rules of Sandhi for concurrent vowels and consonants are in great measure carried out, though some-times they are disregarded. Hiatus, for example, is at times allowed to remain between concurrent vowels.

§ 862.   Examples of the different methods of treat-ment of vowels are:

With Contraction or Resolution. Av. *aᵘruⱼāspa-* 'having white horses' *(aᵘruⱼa + aspa);* Av. *aⁱwyāma-* 'over-mighty' *(aⁱwi + amᵊ);* Av. *paⁱtyāsti-, paⁱtyasti-* (v. l. *paⁱpi.asti-*), *paⁱpyesti-* 'repetition' *(paⁱti + asᵊ)* Ys. 53.3, Afr. 1.8, Vd. 22.13; so Av. *uⁱtyaojana-* beside *uⁱti aojana-* 'thus speaking'; Av. *paⁱtyaohta* beside *paⁱti aohta* 'he an-swered'; Av. *mazdaohta-* 'spoken by Mazda' *(ᵊa + uhta)* Ys. 19.16. — With Hiatus. Av. *āsu.aspa-* 'swift-horsed' = Skt. *āśvàśva-;* GAv. *ciprā.avah-* beside YAv. *cipravah-* 'manifestly aiding' Ys. 34.4, Ny. 3.10; Av. *ȟⱼviwi.iⱼu-* 'having darting arrows'. See §§ 51, 52 above.

Note. In the Gāthās, as is shown by the metre, all contractions in compounds are to be resolved. See § 51 Note 2.

§ 863.   Examples of consonant Sandhi in compounds are common. The following examples illustrate the inter-change of voiced and voiceless § 74. Observe orig. *s*.

Av. *duˢkᵊrᵊta-* 'ill-done' = Skt. *duṣkṛtá-;* Av. *duścipra-* 'of evil seed'; Av. *duẕuhta-* 'ill-spoken' = Skt. *duruktá-;* Av. *duẕdaēna-* 'of evil conscience'; Av. *vaⱨhazdāh-* 'giving what is best'.

b. Treatment of the prior Member.

§ 864.   Owing to the tendency in Av. to write all words separately the connection between the parts of the noun-compound is much looser than in Skt.; hence the frequent variations in the form of the prior member. Observe particularly that the first member often assumes the form identical with its nominative singular. The principal points may be presented in detail.

§ 865. Final -a of the stem may remain unchanged before consonants, but more often it appears as -ō like the nominative. Occasionally, though more rarely, it is lengthened. Examples are:

Av. *hazaura.gaoša-*, *hazaurō.gaoša-*, *hazaurā.gaoša-* 'thousand-eared' Yt. 17.16, Yt. 10.91, Yt. 10.141 etc. So *hā-*, *hvā-* 'self' in composition, *hādāta-* 'self-governed', *hvāvastra-* 'self-clothed'.

Note. Observe that *a* when preceded by *y* may give *ya, yō, yā*, but sporadic traces of reduction (§ 67) are found, e. g. Av. *naįrε.manah-* (*naįrya + mº*) 'manly-minded' Ys. 9.11, beside *haįþyā.dāta-* Yt. 11.3, *haįþyā.varεz-*. Similarly traces of *u* for *va, vā* are found in Av. *varεdusma-* 'soft-earth' (*varεdva-*).

§ 866. Original *ā* of feminine stems may remain unchanged, but sometimes, like *a*, it becomes -ō. Examples are:

Av. *daēnā.vazah-* nomen propr., *daēnō.disa-* m. 'teacher of the law' (*daēnā-*), *urvarō.baēžaza-* adj. 'having the balm of plants' (*urvarā-*).

Note. Original *mā* (prohibitive) appears as *mā-* in composition in YAv. *makasvīš mastrī* 'no dwarf, no woman' et al. Yt. 5.92; GAv. *mavaēþa-* 'not failing' Ys. 41.1.

§ 867. Final *i, ī, u, (ū)* of a stem remain as a rule unchanged in the prior member of a compound, though *ī* usually appears for *i*. Examples are:

Av. *zaįri.gaona-* 'yellow-colored' (*zaįri-*), *mušti.masah-* 'large as the fist' (*mušti-*), *nāįri.cinah-* 'seeking a wife' (*nāįrī-*). — Av. *āsu.-kaįrya-* 'quickly working', *voᵘru.gaoyaoįti-* 'having wide pastures'.

Note 1. The *u*-stems occasionally show -*uš*, like the nominative singular: e. g. Av. *bāzuš.aojah-* 'strong-armed' (observe -*š*), *nasuš.ava.bərəta-* 'corpse-defiled'. Somewhat different is the -*š* in Av. *ānuš.hac-* 'accompanying' (Skt. *ánuṣāc-*), Av. *pasuš.haᵘrva-* 'cattle-protecting', see above § 754, 2. Observe also YAv. *nasuspacya-* 'corpse-burning' (with *s* before *p*, § 754).

Note 2. Av. *gāu-, gao-* 'cow' appears in composition as *gao-, gava-, gavō-* (cf. Whitney, *Skt. Gram.* § 361 f): e. g. Av. *gaoyaoįti-* 'cow-pasture' = Skt. *gávyūti-*; Av. *gavašiti-* 'abode of cows', Av. *gavō.stāna-* 'cow-stall' = Skt. *gōsthāna-*.

§ 868. Simple stems ending in *p* show forms identical with the nominative singular. Examples are:

Av. *afścipra-* 'containing the seed of waters' *(ap-)*, *awŭdāta-* 'contained in the waters', *kərəfšhvar-* 'corpse-eating' *(kəhrp-)*.

§ 869. The *aṇt*-stems as a rule show the weak form *-aṭ* as final of a prior member. Sometimes, however, they show *-ō*, *-as*, like nominative, § 295. Examples are:

Av. *raŭvaṭ.aspa-* 'having splendid horses', *varədaṭ.gaēþa-* 'increasing the world'. — Av. *barō.zaoþra-* (observe *-ō*), beside *baraṭ.zaoþra-* (observe *-aṭ*) 'bearing the libation' Yt. 10.30, Yt. 10.126; *raŭvas.-* *cipra-* 'of splendid family' (but cf. also § 151).

Note. Observe the form *th* instead of *ṭ* in Av. *zarathuŝtra-* 'Zoroaster', *hamaspaþmaēdaya-* name of a season.

§ 870. The *an*-stems show *a* in composition as in Sanskrit (cf. Whitney, *Skt. Gram.* § 1315 a), or they appear as *-ō*. Examples are:

Av. *aṣavajan-* 'slaying the righteous' *(aṣavan-)*, *nqma.azbāiti-* 'invocation by name', *rāma.ṣayana-* 'having an abode of repose' *(rāman-)*. — Beside Av. *rāmō.ṣiti-* 'abode of repose' *(rāman-)*, *zrvō.-* *dāta-* 'created in eternity' *(zrvan-)*.

§ 871. The *ar*-stems naturally have anaptyctic *(ə)* § 72, and form respectively *arə*, *ərə*. As examples may be noted:

Av. *ayarə.bara-* 'day's journey', *hvarə.barəzah-* 'height of the sun'; — *nərə.barəzah-* 'height of a man'. Observe commonly *ātarə.-* *pāta-*, *ātarə.savah-*, *ātarə-* etc. Yt. 13.102, but *ātravaḫṣa-* name of a priest Vsp. 3.6 etc.

§ 872. The *ah*-stems may appear in their original form *-as* under certain circumstances (§ 110), but otherwise they become *-ō* as usual (§ 120). Examples are:

Av. *təmascipra-* 'containing the seed of darkness', *manaspaoirya-* 'having the mind pre-eminent'. — Av. *ayō.ḫaoda-* 'having a helmet of iron' *(ayah-)*, *savō.gaēþa-* 'useful to the world', *hrarənō.dāh-* 'glory-giving'.

Note 1. Observe *z* (§ 170) in Av. *vaŭhazdāh-* 'giving what is better' Ys. 65.12. Remark also the weak form of *-vah* in Av. *yaẑtuẑ.gao-* nomen propr. Yt. 13.123, *viduẑ.yasna-* 'knowing the Yasna'.

Note 2. Observe the peculiarity *(-ah* retained) in *miþahvacā* 'false-speaking' *(miþah- + və)* Ys. 31.12.

c. Treatment of the final Member.

§ 873. The final member of a compound in Av. as in Skt. (cf. Whitney, *Skt. Gram.* § 1315) often undergoes changes in its original inflection; these will be noticed in the following in detail.

§ 874. There is a special tendency for the final member of a compound to assume the *a*-inflection; a compound is often thus transferred from the consonant to the vowel declension (cf Whitney, *Skt. Gram.* § 1316 c). Examples are:

Av. *hvarᵊ.darᵊsa-* (Skt. *svardʃ̄-*) 'sunlike', beside *parō.darᵊs-*, *parō.darᵊsa-;* Av. *ātᵊrᵊ.vaḫʃa-* title of a priest, beside *ātᵊrᵊ.vaḫʃ-* (cons.).

§ 875. An *an*-stem in the final member often undergoes transformation, as in Skt. (cf. Whitney, *Skt. Gram.* § 1315). As examples may be taken:

Av. *capru.caʃma-* (observe -*a*) 'four-eyed', beside *baēvarᵊ.caʃmana-* (observe -*ana*) 'thousand-eyed', from *caʃman-*.

§ 876. The final member sometimes undergoes abbreviation, owing to an original change of accent in assuming the weak form, or to other causes (cf. Whitney, *Skt. Gram.* § 1315). As examples:

Av. *upasma-* 'upon earth' *(zᵊm-),* *frabda-* 'fore part of the foot' *(pada-),* *fraʃʃu-* 'abundance of cattle' *(pasu-).* Likewise others.

d. Case-form appears in prior Member.

§ 877. In Av., as in Skt. (cf. Whitney, *Skt. Gram.* § 1250), a case-form is sometimes found in the prior member of a compound. Examples are:

a. Accusative (especially before radical finals). Av. *ahūm.-mᵊrᵊṇc-* 'destroying the soul', *aʃᵊmaoja-* 'confounding righteousness' (*aʃᵊm maoja,* *m + m = m,* § 186), *ahūmbiʃ-* 'healing the soul', *daēum.jan-* 'daeva-smiting'. — b. Dative. Av. *yavaē-jī-* 'living for ever'. — c. Genitive. Av. *zᵊmasciþra-* 'having the seed of earth'. — d. Locative. Av. *duraēdars-* 'seeing at a distance', *raþaēʃtū-*, *raþaēʃtar-* 'warrior standing in a chariot' *(raþc-),* *maidyōi.paitiʃtāna-* 'to the middle of the breast'.

Classes of Compounds.
(Cf. Whitney, *Skt. Gram.* § 1246 seq.)

§ 878. Modelled after the Sanskrit Grammar the compounds in Avesta may conveniently be divided into the following classes:—

SYNOPSIS OF COMPOUNDS

- i. Copulative.
- ii. Determinative
  - a. Dependent.
  - b. Descriptive.
- iii. Secondary Adjective Compounds
  - a. Possessive.
  - b. With governed
- iv. Other Compound Forms.   Final.

These different classes may be taken up in detail in comparison with the corresponding Sanskrit divisions.

i. Copulative Compounds.

(Cf. Whitney, *Skt. Gram.* §§ 1252, 1255.)

§ 879. Copulative Compounds (Skt. Dvandva). Two co-ordinate terms which would form a pair connected by 'both—and' may dispense with the conjunction and unite into a compound. The Av. Dvandva-Compounds differ from the Skt. in this that in Av. each member assumes the dual form and is separately declined. Examples of Copulative or Dvandva-Compounds are:

> Av. *ḟasu vīra* 'cattle and men' Ys. 9.4 etc.; *pasubya vīraẻibya* 'by cattle and men' Vd. 6.32 etc.; *pasvā vīrayā* 'of both cattle and men' Vsp. 7.3 etc.; *āpa urvaᶦrɛ, āpɛ urvaᶦrɛ* 'water and trees' Ys. 9.4, Gah 4.5; *pāyū þwōrᵊštāra* 'the keeper and the judge' Ys. 57.2.

> Note. A rather late instance may be cited in which several successive members, though ordinarily found only in the singular, unite as a series each in the plural and form an aggregative compound: Vsp. 10.1 *āyɛsɛ yɛšti arᵊzahibyō savahibyō fradaḟšubyō vīdaḓaḟšubyō voᵘru.barᵊštibyō voᵘru.jarᵊštibyō ahɛca karšvanš yaṭ hʋaniraþahɛ.*

ii. Determinative Compounds.

(Cf. Whitney, *Skt. Gram.* § 1262 seq.)

§ 880. Determinative Compounds are divided into two classes, (a) Dependent Compounds, (b) Descriptive Compounds. In regard to signification, the Determinative may have either a substantival or an adjectival value.

a. Dependent Compounds.

(Cf. Whitney, *Skt. Gram.* § 1264 seq.)

§ 881. Dependent Compounds (Skt. Tatpuruṣa) are those in which the former member stands in relation to the latter member as though it were governed by the latter. The force of the prior member is that of an oblique case (acc., instr. gen. etc.) depending upon the latter; and actual case-forms in such instances do sometimes occur, see § 877 above. The compound has noun or adjectival value according to its final member.

    1. Noun value (Whitney, § 1264): Accusative relation. Av. *miþrō.druj-* m. 'one that breaks his pledge'. — Gen. relation. Av. *vīspaiti-* m. 'lord of the clan'. — Loc. relation. Av. *raþaēštā-* m. 'warrior standing in a chariot' (*raþe* = actual loc., cf. § 877).

    2. Adjective value (Whitney, § 1265): Acc. relation. Av. *kamərədō.jan-* 'smiting the head'. — Dat. relation. Av. *dāmidāta-* 'created for all creatures'. — Instr. relation. Av. *ahuradāta-* 'made by Ahura'. — Abl. relation. Av. *qzō.būj-* 'freeing from distress'. — Loc. relation. Av. *zəmarəgūz-* 'hiding in the earth'.

b. Descriptive Compounds.
(Cf. Whitney, *Skt. Gram.* § 1279 seq.)

§ 882. Descriptive Compounds (Skt. Karmadhārya) are those in which the former member stands not in a case-relation but in attributive relation to the second and adds some qualification to it. The value of the compound itself is substantival or adjectival according to its final member.

    1. Noun value (Whitney, § 1280 b, d): Av. *darəjō.ŋiti-* f. 'a long residence', *pərənō.māṅha-* n. 'full-moon';—Av. *uštradaēnu-* f. 'she-camel', cf. Whitney, *Skt. Gram.* § 1280 d.

    2. Adjective value (Whitney, § 1282): Av. *vīspō.bāmya-* 'all-brilliant', *uparō.kaɨrya-* 'making higher, raising up'. With advbl. prefixes (*a-, an-, hu-, duš-, arš-* etc.), Av. *hukərəta-* 'well-made', Av. *aršuḫda-* 'right-spoken'. Likewise some others.

iii. Secondary Adjective Compounds.
(Cf. Whitney, *Skt. Gram.* § 1292 seq.)

§ 883. The secondary adjective compounds are of two kinds, (a) Possessive, (b) those with governed final member.

a. Possessive Compounds.
(Cf. Whitney, *Skt. Gram.* § 1293 seq.)

§ 884. P o s s e s s i v e C o m p o u n d s (Skt. Bahuvrīhi) are composite a d j e c t i v e s formed from a corresponding Determinative compound (§ 880) merely by adding to the latter the idea of 'having' or 'possessing' that which the determinative itself denotes.

§ 885. The S k t. shows a d i f f e r e n c e o f a c c e n t between a Determinative and its corresponding Possessive; in Av., as there is no written accent, the distinction cannot be drawn in that manner.

§ 886. The second member of the Possessive is generally a substantive; the first member may be a substantive, adjective, pronoun, numeral, participle or indeclinable. The force of the compound always remains adjectival.

P o s s e s s i v e A d j e c t i v e s. — Noun initial. Av. *afšcipra-* 'having the seed of waters'. — Adj. initial. Av. *darəjō.lāzu-* 'having long arms, longimanus'.—Pron. initial. Av. *hvāvastra-* 'having own clothing', *ya.šyaopna-* 'having what actions' Ys. 31.16. — Num. initial. Av. *hazavra.gaoša-* 'having a thousand ears' (cf. Whitney, § 1300). —Ptcpl. initial. Av. *uzgərəptō.drafša-* 'with uplifted banners'. — Indecl. initial (Whitney, § 1304). Av. *ahvafna-* 'not-sleeping', *aiwyāma-* 'having excessive might' (Whitney, § 1305).

b. Adjective Compounds with governed final Member.
(Cf. Whitney, *Skt. Gram.* § 1309 seq.)

§ 887. These adjectives are exactly the reverse of Dependent compounds; they are attributives in which the first member practically g o v e r n s the second member. The second member is always a noun and stands in case-relation to the first. The compound itself has an adjectival value.

This group shows two subdivisions, (1) Participial, (2) Prepositional, according as the p r i o r m e m b e r is a participle or a preposition. Details follow.

1. Participial Adjective Compounds.
(Cf. Whitney, *Skt. Gram.* § 1309.)

§ 888. These compounds are old in Av. as they are in Sanskrit. The prior member is a present participle which in meaning governs the second part. The whole is an adjective. Examples are:

Av. *vanaṭ.pṛ̆jana-* adj. 'winning battles', *varᵉdaṭ.gaᵉpa-* 'increasing the world', *vīkᵉrᵉf.uᵉīlāna-* 'cutting off life'. Likewise in nomina propria *haᵉcaṭ.aspa-* 'Haecataspa'.

2. Prepositional Adjective Compounds.
(Cf. Whitney, *Skt. Gram.* § 1310.)

§ 889. These are combinations in which the first member is a pre-position (adverb) that governs the second member in meaning. The whole is equivalent to an adjective. Examples are:

Av. *āh̆jn̆u-* 'reaching to the knee', cf. Skt. *abhijn̆ú-* (Whitney, § 1310a); Av. *aᵢwi.daḫyu-* 'around the country', *aṇtarᵉ.daḫyu-* 'within the country' (cf. Skt. *antarhastá-*), Av. *uzdaḫyu-* 'out of the country'; Av. *upasma-* 'upon the earth' (*zᵊm-* § 152); Av. *parō.asna-* 'beyond the present' (i. e. *parō* + *azan-*) § 153, cf. Skt. *parókṣa-*; Av. *tarō.yāra-* 'beyond a year', cf. Skt. *tiróahnya-*.

iv. Other Compound Forms.

§ 890. Beside the above regular compounds, in Av. as in Skt., there are also some other composite forms that require notice.

a. Numeral Compounds.
(Cf. Whitney, *Skt. Gram.* § 1312.)

§ 891. Numeral Compounds (Skt. Dvigu) are a species of determinative that have a numeral as prior member, and which are commonly, though not always, used as a singular collective noun in the neuter gender. Examples are:

Av. *þrigāya-* n. 'space of three steps', *þripada-* n. 'three feet, a yard', *nava.karᵉja-* n. 'the nine furrows', *nava.ḫ̆japara-* n. 'space of nine nights'. — Av. *paṇca.yaḫ̆īn̆ī* (fem. acc. pl.) 'five twigs'. — Av. *haptōᵢriŋga* (masc. plur.) 'the Great Bear'.

b. Adverbial Compounds.
(Cf. Whitney, *Skt. Gram.* § 1313.)

§ 892. Adverbial Compounds (Skt. Avyayībhāva) are composites made by the union of a preposition or a particle as prior member and a noun as final member, combined to form an indeclinable noun or rather neuter accusative used adverbially, cf. § 934. The class is quotable in an instance or two: Av. *āþritīm* 'up to three times', cf. Skt. *ādvādaśám;* Av. *paᵢtyāpᵊm* 'against the stream, contrary' (§ 934) Ys. 65.6, Vd. 6.40 = Skt.

pratīpám (cf. Lanman, *Skt. Reader* p. 195); Av. *frā.ãpəm, nyãpəm, upa.-ãpəm* 'from out, down, to the water' Vd. 21.2.

c. Loose Compound Combinations.
(Cf. Whitney, *Skt. Gram.* § 1315.)

§ 893. One or two other points in regard to compounds and their formation may be noticed here.

1. The nomen propr. *nairyō.savha-* m. 'Nairyosangha' sometimes has its component elements separately declined, e. g. *nairyehe savhahe* Yt. 13.85, Vsp. 11.16, beside *nairyō.savhahe* Ny. 5.6. Similarly, the derivative *yavaēca.tāite* beside *yavaētāitaēca* 'for ever' Ys. 62.6, Yt. 13.50, cf. § 842. So in verbal derivatives, *zⁿrazdā-, zⁿrasca dāt*, etc.

2. Observe later such agglomerations, especially from initial words of chapters (cf. Te Deum), as Av. *kamnamaēzqm hāitīm* 'the whither-to-turn Chapter' *(kãm nəmōi zqm)* Ys. 46 end; *taṭ.þwā.pərəsa-* 'beginning with the words This-I-ask-Thee'. Likewise in nomina propria, resembling the Puritanical names, e. g. Av. *ajəm.yewhe.raocå nqma* 'Bright-in-Righteousness by name' Yt. 13.120, et al.

§ 894. Long compounds are not common in Avesta; as examples merely may be quoted, Av. *frādaṭ.vīspqm.-hujyāiti-* 'advancing all good life', *nairyqm.hqm.varʲtivaṇt-* 'having manly courage', *poᵘru.sarʲdō.vīrō.vaþwa* 'having a crowd of many kinds of male offspring' Vsp. 1.5.

Sandhi with Enclitics.
(Cf. Whitney, *Skt. Gram.* § 109 seq.)

§ 895. The principles of euphonic combination may be regarded as twofold: (1) as applied in the building up of a word from its elements; (2) in the union of words in a sentence. The former may be called Internal Combination or Word-Sandhi; the latter, though practically wanting in Av., is called External Combination or Sentence-Sandhi.

§ 896. The laws for the internal combination of formative elements and endings have been treated above under Phonology.

§ 897. Sentence-Sandhi, or the external combination
of words in a sentence, is w a n t i n g in the Avesta (§ 4)
except in the case of enclitics and in compounds, and
there only conditionally. The words otherwise are written separately, each followed by a point. Thus, GAv.
yaþā ahū Ys. 27.13; GAv. *yāscā ūïtī* Ys. 39.3; YAv. *nī
aməm* Ys. 9.17; YAv. *aïpi imąın* Ys. 57.33, and countless others.

Note 1. In Geldner's *Metrik* pp. 54—57, numerous instances are
collected where external sandhi is apparently to be accepted, but they are
uncertain, and in the edition of the Avesta texts Geldner has rightly followed the MSS.

Note 2. Observe the MS. reading GAv. *zīṭ* 'for indeed' (but in
metre properly *zī iṭ*) Ys. 45.8. Conversely GAv. *yɔpāiš* (so also according
to metre, but better MS. authority for *yapā āiš*, Geldner) Ys. 33.1.

Combination with Enclitics and Proclitics.

§ 898. Instances of Sandhi are common in the case
of enclitics like *tū, hē, ciṭ, ca* which form a unit with the
preceding word and are often written together with it; but
even here the manuscripts often preserve the usual law of
keeping each word separate and unchanged. As examples:

YAv. *païri.ṣē* 'round him' (combined like Skt. *hí
ṣaḥ* Whitney, *Skt. Gram.* § 188) Ys. 9.28, beside *nī
hīm* (uncombined) Yt. 13.100. Again YAv. *skəndəm
ṣē manō kərɔnūïḍi* 'make his brain cracked' Ys. 9.28;
GAv. *kas.tē* 'who to thee' Ys. 29.7; GAv. *kasnā* (cf.
Germ. 'man') Ys. 44.4. So GAv. *saškɔn-cā* (observe *n̆*)
Ys. 53.1 beside *uzuḥṣyąn-ca* (observe *n*) Yt. 13.78.—
Similarly with Sandhi after the manner of enclitics
and proclitics, GAv. *huzəntuš⁰ spəntō* Ys. 43.3; YAv.
havayāͦs⁰ tanvō 'of his own self'; GAv. *vasas⁰ ḫša-
þrahyā* Ys. 43.8; YAv. *yas⁰ taḥmō* 'I who am strong'
Yt. 19.87; YAv. *uͥtyaojanō* 'thus speaking', beside
uͥti aojanō.

Note 1. In the MSS., enclitics and proclitics are frequently written together as a single word, e. g. GAv. *kānɩɔnā* for *kā.mɔ.nā* Ys. 50.1; *tāþwā* for *tā.þwā* Ys. 31.13; *tɔŋgā* for *tɔŋg.ā* Ys. 46.13; *nāⁱrīvā* for *nāⁱrī.vā* Ys. 41.2. Likewise YAv. *ātat* and *ā.tat* Vd. 5.2, and many others.

Note 2. Observe that *-ca* 'que' is always written together with the preceding word; notice the difference of treatment of vowels and consonants before it. See *(-āca, -āca, -ica, -asca, -āsca, -ɔsca)* §§ 19, 26 Note, 120, 124, 129.

§ 899. Special attention may be drawn to the treatment of words before an enclitic beginning with *t*. In several instances, especially in the Gāthās, a word before a *t*-enclitic takes a sort of compromise form made by a mixture of the usual pause form and the grammatical Sandhi-form. Thus are to be explained:

GAv. *vɔstā* (compromise between *vas.tā* and *vɔ tā*, hence *ɔ, s*) Ys. 46.17; GAv. *yɔŋgstɔ* (mixture of *yɔŋg tɔ* and *yɔs.tɔ*). Contrast . GAv. *ākɔs-tɔŋg* (= *ɔās + t*) Ys. 50.2, with Av. *gaɩþɔs-ca* (*ɔɔs + c*). But GAv. *dɔs-tɔ* Ys. 28.7, cf. § 124 above.

Note. Observe likewise YAv. *kasɔ.þwqnɩ*, *yasɔ.þwā*, a compromise between *kɔ þwqm* and *kastvqnɩ* etc. § 78 above.

§ 900. The laws of euphonic combination in Noun-Compounds and also in Verbal-Composition have been treated above §§ 753, 861 seq.; they require no further remark here.

(The Sketch of the Syntax and Metre follows in Part II.)

Indexes

to

Part I.

Order of Letters.

Vowels. Av. *a, ai, au, aə, ao — ā, āi, āu — i, ī — u, ū — ə, ə̄ — e, ē — o, ō — æ — q.*

Consonants. *k, x̌, g, j — c, j — t, þ, d, ḍ, t̤ — p, f, b, w — v, ɣ, n, ŋ, m — y (i̭), r, v (v̭) — s, š, ṣ, ž, z, ž — h, h̤, hᵛ.*

I. AVESTA-INDEX

(Grammatical Elements).

The references throughout are to the sections (§§).

Abbreviations are extensively used; but it is believed they will be readily recognized. For example, 'cpd.' is compound, 'cpsn.' composition; 'dcln.' means declension; 'endg.' ending; 'pronc.' pronunciation; 'primy.', 'scdry.' stand for primary, secondary; 'pdgm.' is paradigm; etc.

The Indexes are comparatively full, but if an element is not found under one of its letters look for it under one of its other letters, or under the appropriate head in the other Indexes. Remember that long and short vowels sometimes interchange in Avesta.

Av. ⸴ i.

i, pronc. 6; = Skt. ɪ 15; = Skt. ī
21; long in vicinity of v 23;
lengthened before final m 23;
strengthened to aĕ 60; strengthened in caus. and scdry. deriv.
685, 825 b; stands for Av. ⸴
(-ən, -əm) after palatal consonants 30; for orig. ya 63;
interchanges with ī in opt. 552.

i, epenthetic 70; prothetic 71.

i-, pronominal stem, dcln. 397.

i-, ī-stems, dcln. 251 seq.

√i- 'to go', use in periphr. phrases
724.

i- primy. 771; scdry. 834; (final) in
cpds. 867.

-ika, scdry. 839.

-ita, pass. ptcpl. 712; primy. 786 N.

-iti, suffix 789.

in-stems, dcln. forms 316; -in for
-ən, -yən 491-92.

-in, primy. 774; scdry. 835.

-ina, primy. 775; scdry. 836.

-iŋt, primy. 766.

-iŋti, for -əŋti 491.

-ima, pronom. stem 422 seq.

iy (orig.) = Av. y (i̯) 68.

iv (Av.) = orig. yv 62.

iš-stems, dcln. 358.

iš-Aorist 664.

-iš, primy. 776; -iši scdry. 777.

-išta, superl. adj. formation 365, 813.

Av. ⸴ ī.

ī, pronc. 6; = Skt. ī 15; = Skt. ɪ
20; in fem. formation 362;
primy. 779; scdry. 837; (final)
in cpds. 867.

īm 'this', pronoun nom. sg. fem. 422.

-īš, -ūš, as general plur. case 231.

Av. ⸴ u.

u, pronc. 6; = Skt. u 15; = Skt. ū
21; lengthened before epenthetic i 20; lengthened in acc. sg.
before final m 23; strengthened
to ao 60; strengthened in caus.
685; stands for orig. va 63;
for Av. v, w (= orig. bh) 62 N. 3;
stands for ⸴ 193 N. 2.

u, epenthetic 70; prothetic 71; anaptyctic 72.

u-, ū-stems, dcln. 262 seq.

u- (eighth) class of verbs 470; pdgm.
576-582.

-u, primy. 780; scdry. 838; (final)
in cpds. 867.

-un-, for -van- in verbs 493.

-una, primy. 802-3.

-um, acc. sg. of va-stem 63 N.

-uy = orig. vy 62 N. 3.

-ura, suffix 760; primy. 816.

ᵘrv = Skt. vr (vl) 191.

uv (orig.) = Av. v (u̯) 68.

uš-stems, dcln. 358.

-uš, wk. form 349-50, 822; see vah.

-uš, like nom. in cpds. 867 N.

-uš, primy. 783.

-uši, fem. to -vah-, see 362.

Av. ⸴ ū.

ū, pronc. 6; = Skt. ū 15; = Skt. ŭ
20; for ŭ after y 52 c.

ū-, u-stems, dcln. 262 seq.

-ū, primy. 784.

-ūš, as general plur. case 231.

Av. ⸴ ə.

ə, pronc. 6; = Skt. a before m, n, v
28-9; interchange with a in MSS.
29 N.; becomes i after palatals
30; stands sporadically for u, i

ƀt, in YAv. 90.
ƀd 77 N. 3.
-ƀdr- = orig. ktr 79.
ƀš = Skt. kš 158 N.
√ƀši-, aor. 649.
√ƀšnu-, aor. 664.

Av. ℓ g.

g, pronc. 8; = Skt. g, gh 82-3.
√gam-, jam-, aor. 642-7.
√garw-, conjugation forms 584.
-gᵊd- 89.
gv (GAv.) = YAv. v 187 (1).

Av. ℓ, ǰ.

ǰ, pronc. 9; = Skt. g, gh 83.
ǰš, in GAv. 89.
ǰšar-, intensive 705-6.

Av. ℙ c.

c, pronc. 8; general character 76;
    interchange of c/k 76 N.
-ca 'que', treatment of vowel and
    cons. before it 26 N., 124 N.
c/j, interchange in MSS. 193 N. 2.
√cag-, pdgm. perf. 622.
ci-, interrog. pron. 407.
√ci- 'to atone', conjugation forms
    551.
√ciš-, pdgm. 555.
cy (old) = Av. šy (š) 162.

Av. ℓ j.

j, pronc. 8; general character 88;
    = Skt. j, h 88; = Skt. g 88 N. 2;
    = Skt. gh 88 N. 3; interchange
    of j/z, j/c in MSS. 193 N. 2.
√jam-, gam-, aor. 642-7.

Av. ℙ t.

t, pronc. 8; general character 76;
    = Skt. t 78; loss of t 187 (6);

orig. t becomes Av. s 151; as-
    sumption of t after short root
    in deriv. 745 N. 1, 820; treat-
    ment of enclitics before t 899.
ta-, pronom. stem, dcln. 409.
-ta, ending pass. ptcpl. 681, 710;
    primy. 786; scdry. 840; be-
    comes -da 786 N. 3.
√tan-, conj. forms 579-80.
tar-stems, dcln. 321.
-tar, primy. 787.
-tara, compar. adj. 363 seq., 841.
-tah, suffix 760.
-tât, scdry. 842.
-ti, primy. 788; scdry. 843.
-tu, primy. 790.
-təm, 3 du. 454.
-təma, superl. adj. 363 seq.
-tše, -tayaěca, infin. 720.
-tō (beside -ƀō), ending du. 448 N.,
    451.
ty, for -ƀy- 79 N.
tr (Av.) = orig. tr 79 N.
-tra, -trā, primy. 791.
-ƀrī, fem. to -tar 362.
tv (Av.) = Skt. tv 94.
-tva, -ƀwa, in gerundive 716; primy.
    792.
ts (orig.) = Av. s 143.

Av. ♭ ƀ.

ƀ, pronc. 9; general character 77;
    = Skt. th, t 77; = Skt. s 77
    N. 2; stands for Av. d 86; inter-
    change of ƀ/d in MSS. 193 N. 2;
    stands for t in cpsn. 869 N.
-ƀa, primy. 793; scdry. 844.
-ƀi, -ƀu, primy. 794.
-ƀō (beside -tō), ending du. 448 N.,
    451.
ƀw = Skt. tv 94.

*vh, *iyh*, interchange in MSS. 118 N.;
= orig. *sy* 134, 135.
vhv (Av.) = orig. *sv* 130.

Av. ١, ئے *n, n̄.*

n, n̄, pronc. 10; general character
102-3.
n̄gr (GAv.) = orig. *-sr-* 139 N.
n̄gh = orig. *-ns-* 128.
-na-, weak form in verbs 590.
-na, ending pass. ptcpl. 681, 713,
764; primy. 802; scdry. 848.
-nah, primy. 804.
nā- (ninth) class of verbs 470, 583-92.
-ni, primy. 805.
nu- (fifth) class of verbs 470, 566-74.
-nu, primy. 806.
ns (orig.) = Av. *-vh-* 125.
√*nqs-, nas-,* aor. 658, 663.

Av. ٤ *m.*

m, pronc. 10; general character 105;
= Skt. *sm* 140; instead of *n*
in voc. sg. 193; interchange of
final *m/n* in MSS. 193 N.; ending of acc. sg. 222.
-ma, primy. 808; scdry. 849.
-maine, infin. 720.
*man-*stems, dcln. 300.
√*man-,* aor. 656.
-man, primy. 809; scdry. *(-man,*
-mana, -mna) 850.
-mant, scdry. 851.
√*mar-,* mid.-pass. 680.
√*mark- (mэrэnc-),* conjugation forms
555-63.
√*mard-,* conjugation forms 564.
mā (= mǝā), neg. in cpds. 866 N.
-mi, primy. 810.
mэrэnc-, see √*mark-.*
mōrэnd-, see √*mard-* 564.

√*mrā-,* opp. Skt. √*brū-* 105 N. 1;
pres. pdgm. 517 seq.; aor. 3 sg.
668.
-mna (-māna) = Skt. *-māna* 18 N. 2;
primy. 811.

Av. ٣٠ (²²) *y (i̯).*

y (i̯), pronc. 11; for *i* by resolution
51; in reductions 61; vocalized
to *i* 62; written by abbreviation for *iy* 68, 92 N. 1; *y* initial
91; *i̯* initial 91 N.; *i̯* internal
91; = Skt. *y* 92; = Skt. *v* (in
Av. *uye*) 92 N. 2, 190; *y* lost
after *s* 187 (3).
ya (orig.), becomes Av. *-i- (-ī-)* 63;
becomes Av. *-e* (final) 67, 222
(instr.); is formative element in
pass. 676-7.
ya-, rel. pron. dcln. 399 seq.
ya- (fourth) class of verbs 470, 480-507.
-ya, in gerundive and gerund 716,
718; primy. 812; scdry. *(aya)*
852; final in cpds. 865.
yah, compar. adj. dcln. 345-6, 365,
813.
-yā, primy. fem. 812.
ye, for *-ya-* in verbs 492.
-yehī, fem. compar. to *-yah* 363.
-yu, primy. 814.
yv (orig.) = Av. *-iv-* 62.

Av. ١ *r.*

r, pronc. 11; *r*-vowel 60; = Skt.
r (l) 100; = orig. *sr* 138; trans-
position 191.
*r-*stems, dcln. 333 seq.
-ra, primy. 815; scdry. 853.
√*ras-,* intens. forms 705 N.
-ri, primy. 817.
-ru, primy. 818.

√*zd-*, caus. 685 N. 2.
zd = Skt. *dh* 89, 171.
zn (orig.) = Av. *su* 153.
zb = Skt. *hv* 99.
zm (orig.) = Av. *sm* 152.

Av. ω *ž*.

ž, pronc. 9; = Skt. *j, h* 88 N. 1, 177,
178; in combination *jž, wž, žn*
89, 164 N. 2; = *ž*-voiced 179;
= Skt. *kš* 181; = Skt. *ḍ, ḍh*
182-3.

Av. ϖ, ℧, ⊢ *h, ḥ, ḥ.*

h, ḥ, pronc. 12; general remark 184;
= orig. *s* 110; = orig. *-sy-* 137;
h (= s) dropped before *m*
187 (4).

h- *(s)* stems, dcln. 338 seq.
h- *(s)* aorist, pdgm. 653 seq.
ha- *(sa)* aorist, forms 663.
-ha- *(-ṿha-),* in desiderative 699.
√*harž-,* fut. 672-3.
hiš-aorist, formation 665.
√.*hu-* 'press', pres. forms 567, 588,
591.
-he = Skt. *-sya,* ending gen. sg. 222.
hm, as ligature 3; = orig. *-sm-* 141;
element in pronom. dcln. 379-81.
hy, ḥy = orig. *sy* 131-3.
-hyā, -hyācā, in gen. sg. 222.
hr, for *-r-* 100 N. 1.
ḥv, hv, as ligature 3; pronc. 12;
= orig. *sv* 130.
-hva, -žva, ending loc. pl. 224, 736;
ending 2 sg. imperat. 456.

II. AVESTA-INDEX
(Word-List).

Av. ᴬᵁ a.

a^{i}ƀi- f. 794.
a^{i}wi-ɟac- 745.
a^{i}ɣhe 136.
a^{i}pya loc. sg. 281.
a^{i}wyō dat. pl. 286 N.
a^{i}ryaman- dcln. 300.
aēta- pron. stem, dcln. 417 seq.
aēni dcln. 422 seq.
aēva- dcln. 369.
aēɟa as nom. sg. m. 411, 418.
aēɟa- (aēta-) dcln. 417 seq.
ao̯i 62 N. 3.
aoim 369.
aoḫta 90.
aog^{e}dā 90.
aojᶻā 527.
aoja^{i}te 526.
aojana-, aojəmna- 528.
aojō, aojᴁ nom. sg. 341.
aojᴁs-ca pl. 343.
aka- 'bad' 365.
acišta- 365.
apa^{u}run- 313 N. 1.
advᴁ nom. sg. 315.
adwan- 820.
aɟka- (adka-) 81 N. 1.
apərəse 484 N.
afštacinō 774.

aᵥuhe dat. sg. 265.
ana- pron. stem 426.
aṇtarə.naēmāɟ 731 (4), 737.
aya- instr. 429.
arᵊduš- dcln. 360, form 783.
arš- in cpds. 882.
ava- pronom. stem 432.
avaṇt- dcln. 441.
avavaṇt- dcln. 442.
as, ās 'was' 453, 532.
asti- subst. 794.
astvaṇt- dcln. 291.
asrvātəm 638.
aɟaonī- dcln. 257, fem. 362.
aɟaonīš neut. pl. 315.
aɟavan- dcln. 313, comparative 365 N. 3.
aɟahe 67.
aɟāun- str. form 313, 315, 62 N. 1.
aɟāunqm 62 N. 1.
aɟāum voc. sg. 313.
aškarə 639.
aɟyah-, aɟah- 347, 365.
atāρā 486.
azəm dcln. 386.
azdbīš general pl. case 229.
ahe 137.

ahu nom. sg. 275.
ahmāka- 839.
ahmākəm 440 N. 3.
ahmya loc. sg. 736.
ahyā reflex. 436 N. 5.

Av. ᴬᵁ ā.

āaɟ 53, 731 (4).
ā^{i}ɖi aor. pass. 668.
āḫtū^{i}rīm 375.
āḫɟnūš 77 N. 1, 889.
āɟ, āaɟ advbl. 731 (4).
ātar-, ātr-, āθr- dcln. 331.
āθravan- dcln. 313 N.
āɟbitīm 375.
āp-, ap- dcln. 286.
ābərəɟ- nom. sg. 281, formation 745 N. 1.
āfəṇte 578.
ānuš.hac- 754 (2).
ārōi pf. 612.
ās 'was' 453, 532.
āsišta- 365.
āskə^{i}ti- 789.

Av.) u.

uḫta- 711 (1).
upasma- 876, 889.
uƀōibya 68 N. 1.
ᵘrūraost 607.
ᵘrūrudɟa 651 N. 2.

nqsaṭ, redupl. aor. 651 N.

nmānaya, loc. sg. 239.

Av. ϐ m.

ma-, mavaṇṭ-, pronom. 435, dcln. 438.

maᵢnya, opt. 504.

maᵢnyu-, dcln. 262.

magavan-, magāun- 313 N. 1.

madᵊma 63 N. 3.

mamnuš 350.

mas-, masyah- 365.

masyⱭ, °aṇhō, sg. pl. 346.

maz-, compar. 365.

mazaṇṭ-, dcln. 298.

mazᵊnā, instr. 305.

mazdāh-, form 89, dcln. 356.

mazyah- 365.

mahrka- 100 N. 1, 785.

mā-cᵢš 408 N.

mātᵊrqš-cā 49, 327.

māvōya 386.

mipahvacⱭ 872 N. 2.

minaš 557.

mimarᵊḫšavuha 701.

mᵊrᵊngᵊduyᵊ 556.

mᵊrqjyaṭ 560.

niraoi, 3 sg. aor. pass. 668.

miravī, 1 sg. pret. 519.

miravāᵢre 452, 486, 521.

mūh-, mⱭṇhō, dcln. 355.

Av. ℞ (ʸʸ) y (i).

ya-, rel. dcln. 399.

yaᵉja (ᵢaᵉja) 593 (4).

yaogᵊṭ 637.

yaoš, yaoᵻ 750 N.

yavaᵉtāᵢte 842, 893.

yasna-, dcln. 236 seq.

yāᵢᵻ as general pl. 384.

yāhi, loc. sg. 353.

yᵢaṭ 403.

yuni, voc. sg. 314 N. 1.

yuvan, yvan-, dcln. 314 N. 1.

yū-, dcln. 276.

yūšmākᵊni 440 N. 3.

yeṇhe, form 136, 399, m. for f. 383 N.

yeyq (ᵢeᵢq) 593 (4), 619.

yesnyata, instr. advl. 731.

Av. ℩ r.

raᵉ-, rāi-, dcln. 277.

raost, 2 sg. 518.

rapaᵉšᵢā-, °ar, dcln. 249, 330, form 877, 881.

rarᵊš-, intens. 705 N.

raᵻnvō, gen. instr. 265.

razura· 816.

rⱭṇhaṇhōi 661.

Av. ᑫ (ᵥ) v (ᵤ).

vaᵢnīṭ 637.

vaᵉda, pdgm. 621.

vaᵉni 386.

vaocātarᵊ 613.

vaozirᵊni 607, 616, 652 N. 2.

vak/c-, dcln. 285.

vaḫᵢyeᵢte 672.

vacastaᵉtivaṭ, advl. 730.

vacah-, dcln. 339.

vaṇhu-, compar. 365.

vaṇuhī-, fem. 362.

vaṇhō, vahyō 347.

varᵊš 637.

vastra-, dcln. 237.

vāunuš 350.

vācī, 3 sg. aor. pass. 668.

vātōyōtū 39 N.

vārᵊþrajni- 825 c.

viṇdita 560, 565.

viþuš-, wk. stem 349-50.

viþiᵻi, loc. sg. 359.

vīdōyūm 63 N. 2.

vīdqni, imperative 456, 627 N., 640.

vīdōiþre, infin. 787 N. 3.

vᵢᵈvah-, dcln. 349-50.

vivᵊnghatū 701.

vīs-, dcln. 279.

vīsaᵢti, num. 374.

vīspa-, dcln. 443.

vīspᵊni 20.

vīspāiš 229.

vᵊrᵊþrajan-, dcln. 317, compar. 365 N. 3.

vᵊrᵊþravan-, comparat. 365 N. 3.

vᵊrᵊnvaᵢtᵊ, du. 451, 568.

vᵊrᵊzyatqm 485.

vᵊ 'we' 389.

vᵊ 'you' 393.

vohu-, compar. 365.

vōijnāuyō 62 N. 3, 247.

vⱭ 393.

Av. ᑯ s.

saᵉna- 187 (3).

sata 374.

sanaṭ 591.

sar-, dcln. 335.

saškᵊni 607.

sāhīṭ 527, 637.

sūn- see span- 314 N.

sōire 452, 526.

star-, dcln. 329.

stⱭ, stō 531.

III. GENERAL INDEX.

ADDITIONS AND CORRECTIONS.

a. Corrections.

A few obvious misprints are passed over without notice.

page vii (line 17) —for practise read practice.

   „   1 (foot-note) — „ *antar°* read *aŋtar°*.

   „   3 (§ 6 l. 14) — „ fawing read fawning.

   „   6 (§ 19 l. 9) — „ *apāhtaraṭ* read *apāhtaraṭ*.

   „   8 (§ 28 l. 1) — „ *e* read *ə*.

   „   9 (§ 29 l. 6) — „ *evisti* read *ᴢvisti*.

   „ 59 (§ 192 N.) — „ 'thou didst promise' read 'he promised'.

  „ 117 (foot-note) — omit gen. sg. *tahe* and strike out
                                foot-note.

  „ 125 (§ 440 l. 16) — for *yavākú* read *yuvākú*.

  „ 137 (§ 466 l. 13) — strike out Note 2.

  „ 148 (§ 505 l. 3) — for *vāᵘr°* read *vāur°*.

  „ 151 (§ 516 l. 12) — „ *váṣ-ti* read *váṣ-ṭi*.

  „ 164 (§ 576 l. 1) — „ eigth read eighth.

  „ 179 (§ 637 l. 5) — „ *cor°ṭ* read *cōr°ṭ*.

  „ 191 (§ 694 l. 4) — „ Ys. read Yt.

b. Additions.

page, 5 (§ 17 l. 5) — add: Av. *vāyu-* 'wind' = Skt. *vāyu-*.

  „ 10 (§ 32 l. 10) — „ GAv. *ṭąm* 'her' Ys. 53.4 = Skt. *tām*.

  „ 15 (§ 51 l. 16) — „ Note 4. In the Gāthās, as is shown by
                                  the metre, all contractions are to be re-
                                  solved.

  „ 29 (§ 77 l. 9) — „ Av. *vahšapa-* 'growth' = Skt. *vakṣ-*
                                  átha-.

  „ 38 (§ 95 l. 4) — „ Av. *zafar-*, *zafan-*, cf. √*zᴣmb-*.

  „ 42 (§ 109 l. 9) — „ Av. *raocas.pairišta-*.

  „ 53 (§ 162 l. 10) — „ So Av. *mᴣrąžyāṭ* from *marᴣ̨c-*

page 57 (§ 183 l. 4) —add: So also Av. *zōiždižta-, zōižnu-,* cf. Skt. *hiḍ-, hēḍ-;* Av. *vōiždayaṇt-, vōiždaṭ,* cf. Skt. *viḍ.*

„ 58 (§ 187 l. 4) — „ So also in Av. *yazâi* Yt. 10.14 = *yaza(h)i.*

„ 59 (§ 193 l. 14) — „ Orig. *pm* becomes Av. *hm,* cf. GAv. *hahmī (haf-šī),* YAv. *vah-mâi* (√ *vap-*)—Geldner.

„ 59 (§ 193) — „ Note 3. Av. *u, a* occasionally = Skt. *a* (derived from nasal sonants), e. g. Av. *vātō.žūta-* 'wind-riven' (cf. Skt. *kṣa-ta-*), Av. *vayō.tūïte* 'storm-bound' (√ *tan-*) — Paul Horn.

„ 75 (§ 254 abl.) — „ Observe abl. YAv. *ažtažd-a* 'in concord' *(ažti-)* Vd. 3.1.

„ 84 (§ 286 l. 2) — „ Dat. *āpe, ZPhl. Gloss.* p. 86.

„ 95 (§ 331 l. 4) — „ *āprāṭ* (a-dcln.) Afr. 4.5.

„ 103 (§ 362 l. 10) — „ *maēša-* (m.) 'sheep, ram', *maēšī-* (f.) 'ewe'; *hšaþra-* (m.) 'lord, king', *hšaþrī-* (f.) 'mistress'.

„ 184 (§ 660 l. 1) — „ YAv. *vaṇhaṇt-* aor. act. ptcpl. with fut. meaning Yt. 13.155. See Justi s. v. √ *van-.*